THE RETURN OF THE DEFICIT

BELGIAN INSTITUTE OF PUBLIC FINANCE

History of Belgian Public Finance

Volume VII

THE RETURN OF THE DEFICIT

PUBLIC FINANCE IN BELGIUM OVER 2000-2010

Edited by
Etienne de Callataÿ
and
Françoise Thys-Clément

LEUVEN UNIVERSITY PRESS

© 2012 by Leuven University Press / Presses Universitaires de Louvain / Universitaire Pers Leuven. Minderbroedersstraat 4, B-3000 Leuven (Belgium).

All rights reserved. Except in those cases expressly determined by law, no part of this publication may be multiplied, saved in an automated datafile or made public in any way whatsoever without the express prior written consent of the publishers.

ISBN 978 90 5867 923 9
D / 2012 / 1869 / 62
NUR: 784

Lay-out: Jurgen Leemans

Table of contents

Foreword   7
Herman Van Rompuy

Introduction   11
BELGIUM ON THE EVE OF THE GREAT SOVEREIGN
DEBT CRISIS
Etienne de Callataÿ

1. The European context   25
EVOLVING GOVERNANCE IN THE EU:
FROM THE SGP TO HELL AND BACK?
Guy Quaden, Jan Smets, and Geert Langenus

2. Overview   51
MAIN DEVELOPMENTS IN PUBLIC FINANCE
Maud Nautet and Luc Van Meensel

3. The fiscal stance   65
THE RETURN OF THE PUBLIC BUDGET DEFICIT
Reginald Savage

4. Tax revenue and tax policy   95
A DECADE OF TAX CUTS
André Decoster, Marcel Gerard, and Christian Valenduc

5. Approaches to primary expenditure   121

5.1 THE STRUCTURE OF EXPENDITURE OF THE REGIONS
AND COMMUNITIES: A COMPARISON 2002-2011   122
Valérie Schmitz, Bastien Scorneau, and Robert Deschamps

5.2 TRENDS IN PUBLIC EMPLOYMENT IN BELGIUM   134
   Stefan Van Parys and Luc Van Meensel

5.3 THE PRACTICE OF PERFORMANCE CONTRACTING
   BY BELGIAN GOVERNMENTS: RE-CONSIDERING THE
   CONTROL OF AUTONOMOUS AGENCIES   146
   Koen Verhoest

5.4 MEASURING AND MANAGING PUBLIC PERFORMANCE   161
   Jean Hindriks

6. Social Security   173
   THE ACTIVE WELFARE STATE: A STYLISED RETROSPECTIVE
   Frank Vandenbroucke, with Kim Lievens

7. Indebtedness   215
   INTEREST PAYMENT AND PUBLIC DEBT
   Natacha Gilson and Jean Deboutte

8. Fiscal federalism   241
   THE TRANSITION TO A NEW MODEL OF FISCAL RELATIONS
   Koen Algoed and Frédérique Denil

Conclusion   291
   Françoise Thys-Clément

ANNEX 1: PRESENTATION OF THE BELGIAN
INSTITUTE OF PUBLIC FINANCE   297
   Aloïs Van de Voorde

ANNEX 2: STATISTICAL OVERVIEW   303
   Maud Nautet and Luc Van Meensel

ANNEX 3: LIST OF CONTRIBUTORS   327

Foreword

In the 1990s, Belgium's public finances were dominated by rigorous consolidation which reduced the budget deficits of all government entities from more than 8% of GDP in 1992 to virtual balance in 2000. The primary surplus actually exceeded 6% of GDP throughout the 1998-2001 period. This was necessary so that, in the ensuing 15 years or so, the public debt could be reduced to the 60% target under the European Stability and Growth Pact. It must be said that the pressure to join the euro – resulting from the Maastricht Treaty – was a powerful argument for persevering.

In the first decade of the present century, this strategy was abandoned to some extent. While the budget was roughly balanced until 2007, the surplus on the balance of primary transactions (excluding interest payments on the public debt) shrank to 3.8% of GDP. The overall balance was maintained only by taking advantage of the declining interest rate for that purpose, instead of using these 'windfall' profits – applicable throughout the euro area – to achieve an even bigger reduction in the public debt ratio, which in fact dropped to 84% in 2007.

The 2008 financial crisis negated many of the efforts made in preceding years. Our primary balance dropped to -2% of GDP in 2009, putting us back more than twenty-five years.

In the EU, it was agreed that the economy would not be allowed to slide deeper into recession. Hence the argument that we should not just allow the automatic stabilisers to operate on the budgets, but should actually pursue a real recovery policy. When I was appointed Prime Minister at the end of December 2008, I proposed taking no additional measures to stimulate the economy beyond those already decided by the previous government (+/- 0.5% of GDP). And that is what happened. I also proposed starting to bring down the deficit gradually as soon as economic growth became positive again, at a pace tailored to the strength of the growth. When drawing up the budget for 2010-2011 (we produced a budget covering two years) we were already able to start cutting the deficit. The year 2010 – for which I, as Prime Minister, had drawn up the budget – ended with a deficit of 3.8% of GDP (compared to 5.6%. in 2009), which was good, certainly in comparison with neighbouring countries. In 2011, the year without a federal government, the deficit was maintained at roughly the 2010 level (3.7%). The primary balance also improved in 2010, from -2.0% to -0.4%. Once we had a federal government again we could work to achieve the 3% deficit target for 2012 with a view to leaving the Excessive Deficit Procedure. For 2015 we must aim at a balanced budget for all government entities together, which implies an effort of 1% of GDP per annum. The difficult 2015 budget will be drawn up after the June 2014 elections.

All in all, the situation today cannot be compared with that of 1981 or 1993. In the latter year, for instance, the difference between our debt and the European average was close to 70% of GDP; in 2012 Belgian government debt would only be 9% of GDP higher than the average for the euro area!

In general, Belgium has pursued a cautious fiscal policy since the financial crisis, even though this crisis had a serious impact on us in view of our 'overbanked' character: banks too big for such a small country. That caution was necessary because we had learnt some hard lessons in the 1980s and 1990s. 'Never again', said all the traditional parties.

We could have done even better if we had made wiser use of the interest rate bonus – provided by the strong euro with low interest rates from 2000 to 2007 – in order to reduce the national debt. We could also have done better in apportioning the burden between the federal government and the federated entities, and thus would have been expected Entity II to contribute more towards the consolidation. We did the opposite. A third mistake was the failure to reform social security. The 2005 Generation Pact was too timid, but fortunately we had the pension reforms of 2012. The growth in health care spending also persisted at too high a level after the rigours of the 1990s. Overall, however, up to the end of the decade, Belgium proved reasonably resilient compared to other countries, but our system is too dependent on economic growth. Without an annual 2% increase in real GDP, our social system is in trouble. That structural reinforcement of our growth potential is absolutely vital, though the same applies throughout the EU.

The new macroeconomic surveillance instruments available principally to the European Commission will be used to force our economy to become more competitive. In that sense, economic growth should ensure sustainable public finances. However, a growth policy requires just as much courage as a consolidation policy. For example, labour and product market reforms are impossible without taking action against vested interests. A growth policy based on stimulating demand is no longer an option. On the contrary, in the midst of further fiscal 'consolidation', we have to set priorities and safeguard expenditure that promotes growth, namely in the fields of education, research and development, green infrastructure, etc., accounting for at least 10% of GDP. As a result, we have to cut socially sensitive expenditure and/or increase taxes. Both are equally unpopular.

After 2015, population ageing will become increasingly significant and the maintenance of a balanced budget will require an effort every year because the budget has to cope with the costs of that ageing. The Fiscal Compact in the Treaty on Stability, Coordination and Governance in the EMU which has just been concluded obliges us to enshrine a structural balanced budget rule in the Constitution or in equivalent legislation.

Government is a difficult task, and will remain difficult at every level of administration.

Herman Van Rompuy
President of the European Council

Introduction

BELGIUM ON THE EVE OF THE GREAT SOVEREIGN DEBT CRISIS

Etienne de Callataÿ [1]

> *I would prefer not to*
> HERMAN MELVILLE, 1853

The decade from 2000 to 2010 in Belgium is characterised by a sharp deterioration in the most popular performance indicator in the field of public finance, i.e. the overall fiscal balance, which went from balance to a 4% deficit. But there is no such thing as a key performance indicator (KPI) when it comes to assessing fiscal policy. The quality of the latter, in particular in terms of efficiency, fairness and sustainability, cannot be summarised by a single figure leading to a thumbs up / thumbs down type of conclusion.

The ultimate objective of the collection of essays presented in this book is not to provide a final, authoritative assessment of the policy choices made by those who have been in charge of our collective purse over the first decade of the millennium. Its purpose is to gather *à chaud* a first set of contributions providing a detailed factual overview of the major developments over the recent past in the field of public finance in Belgium coupled with an in-depth analysis carried out by the best experts in the various sub-domains, whether academics or civil servants. The caveats

---

1. Etienne de Callataÿ is chief economist at Bank Degroof, senior fellow at the Itinera Institute, and guest lecturer at the University of Namur and at the Catholic University of Louvain (UCL). He is grateful to Françoise Thys-Clément for her comments.

of such an exercise are well known, including the personal bias of the contributors, the limited distance view, and the lack of exhaustiveness.

1. FISCAL DETERIORATION

From the outset, the choice of the general title for this collection of essays – that does not bind the contributors – deserves some explanation. While nuance is always required for an academic work, every book needs a title, preferably short and fair and eye-catching all at once. The decision to go for "The return of the deficit" for a book devoted to public finance in Belgium from 2000 to 2010 was driven by two considerations. First, it appears indeed that the aforementioned deterioration in the fiscal balance has been a key evolution over the decade under review. The deterioration is even more pronounced when one leaves aside interest payments that benefited from a sharp decline in interest rates and from the so-called reverse snowball effect resulting from the fiscal consolidation recorded between 1993 and 1999. Indeed, the primary balance went from a surplus of 6.5% in 2000 to a deficit of 0.4% ten years later, and the structural primary balance exhibits the same pattern. Secondly, as this book is the seventh in the collection of publications edited every ten years under the auspices of the Belgian Institute of Public Finance and dealing with the recent history of public finance in Belgium, the general title also echoes that chosen in 2002 for the previous edition, which covered the years 1990-2000. Indeed, the title then was "*The end of the budgetary deficit*".[2] The end appears to have been short-lived!

2. THE *VANISHING DEBT* HASN'T VANISHED

The sharp improvement in public finance underlying the choice of the title ten years ago was not restricted to Belgium. The end of the budgetary deficit was a reality, or at least in sight, in many developed countries. In the European Monetary Union, countries had committed themselves, through sound fiscal balances, to lowering their debt-to-GDP ratio at a

---

2. de Callataÿ, 2002a.

sustained pace. In the US, public projections made in 2000 announced that the US would have a zero debt-to-GDP ratio by the year 2012 – which, seen in 2012, serves as a gentle reminder about how volatile long-term fiscal projections and about how costly any departure from modesty and prudence may be.

The fiscal consolidation was so firmly established that well-known economists published papers about the consequences of the so-called vanishing public debt. To mention just one of them, Vincent Reinhart, together with Brian Sack, in 2000 authored a paper under the explicit title of "The Economic Consequences of Disappearing Government Debt". It talks about the US, in a situation quite different from that of a small open economy like Belgium having lost exchange rate and monetary autonomy, but nevertheless it is illustrative. By the way, it may bring some mental relief to remember that the then expected debt disappearance was raising concerns, in particular about how the central bank and, more broadly, financial markets would operate without the open market instrument and the benchmark provided by public debt. At least today we are saved those concerns!

3. THE LACK OF REFORMS AS A CONSTANT

Is the seemingly radical deterioration in the fiscal outlook over the recent past such a surprise? Based on the aforementioned much flawed US projections, it is without any doubt a surprise but at the same time warnings had been issued in due times, including in Belgium. The theme of the introductory chapter of the 1990-2000 edition of our collection about the history of public finance in Belgium, published in 2002, was "Fiscal consolidation without reform".[3]

It is well known that reforms are hard to swallow for voters and therefore difficult for politicians to get passed. That is so because reforms go against the interest of *insiders* and because short-sightedness increases the discount rate against reforms exhibiting a J curve profile, meaning that they are

---

3. de Callataÿ, 2002b.

painful before bearing fruit. In order to make structural reforms more acceptable to the electorate, fiscal sweeteners may be required, preferably in the form of temporary expansionary measures to offset the initial recessionary impact of some reforms. In that case, fiscal deterioration may be seen as the price to pay for hard-to-get-through reforms and, beyond that, for the fostering of the potential output growth rate which in the long run will lead to stronger public finance. Next to the sweeteners for painful reforms, there is a second sort of positive fiscal deterioration, i.e. that coming from reforms requiring time to pay them off. For instance a given tax shift from labour tax towards consumption tax may lead to a revenue loss in the short run but to a revenue increase in the long run. More broadly, no country should be blamed for a less favourable fiscal balance when it is the price that has to be paid in order to get sound reforms passed. However, at first sight, the fiscal deterioration over the years 2000-2010 cannot in the main be blamed on structural reforms having had a negative short-term impact. In the same vein, part of the fiscal tightening of the 90s was not sustainable and called for some relaxation, in particular in the field of health care outlay, but again only a fraction of the deterioration may be explained by such a budgetary ebb and flow phenomenon.

A catchy, but simplistic, way of characterising the fiscal policy of 2000-2010 is to state that the "fiscal consolidation without reform" of the nineties mutated into a "fiscal deterioration without reform". The following chapters will help tine-tune the assessment, taking into consideration in particular what has been achieved and the nature of the political and economic circumstances.

4. FINANCIAL VS. FISCAL CRISIS

The financial crisis that emerged in the summer of 2007 and became obvious in 2008 before turning into a full blown economic recession is most often put forward as the core explanation for the currently dire fiscal position of many industrial countries. It fits well with the apparent surprise of the deterioration in public finance. However, there is no ground for such a surprise and the deterioration comes largely from a relaxation of fiscal discipline in the years before the outburst of the financial crisis despite a rather supportive economic climate. On that score, Belgium is no exception, as is illustrated by the evolution of the primary surplus between 2000 and 2007 as a percentage of GDP, i.e. a decline by 2.7 per cent. The structural primary surplus deteriorated by the same amount.

The financial crisis has impacted on public finance through numerous channels: impact of the automatic stabilisers, i.e. loss of tax income and increase in social expenditure as a result of the economic recession, discretionary measures to support the activity, recapitalisation of financial intermediaries, financing of the deposit insurance scheme, funding of rescue mechanisms. As a result, the debt-to-GDP ratio which had declined to 84% in 2007 ended at 96% in 2010 and the fiscal balance went from equilibrium to a 3.8% deficit over the same period. Based on those two indicators, the fiscal deterioration is solely attributable to the financial crisis.

A proper assessment of how much of the current fiscal misery is due to the financial crisis requires an intergenerational perspective taking into account trend output, foreseeable ageing costs and the desirable room for absorbing shocks. It has also to rely on a model about how structural reforms in due time such as the scrapping of the tax deductibility of interest charges, a tax shift out of labour income, Pigovian taxes on negative externalities or a review of the incentives provided by social provisions would have mitigated or offset the impact of the financial crisis. It goes beyond the scope of this introductory chapter but it seems misleading to state that save for the financial crisis public finance would have improved over the last decade. By the way, the financial crisis is the other side of the coin of the ever increasing financial leverage bubble that artificially boosted economic activity and, as a result, the fiscal outcome prior to the crisis. The financial sector cannot be blamed for the post-2007 budgetary deterioration without getting the credit (!) for having embellished the fiscal position before it.

As a reminder, analysis of the interaction between public finance and the financial crisis should also cover the opposite causal relationship, i. e. the role of fiscal policy and of the budgetary stance in the swelling of the debt bubble and in other factors, including those relating to tax distortions. Of course, at times when bankers again deserve to be nicknamed *banksters*, it should not be appropriate to put the full blame for the financial crisis on public finance *sensu lato*.

5. BELGIUM'S OUT-PERFORMANCE

The fiscal slippage in Belgium prior to the financial crisis could have been more pronounced given (i) the internal institutional pressures, that called for extra transfers to the Communities without a matching devolution of responsibilities; (ii) the high tax rates on labour income and on corporations, that called for cuts in a world of mobility and tax competition; (iii) the large size of the primary surplus at the outset of the decade – 6.5% of GDP – allowing the relaxation of the fiscal stance without endangering the trend decline of the debt-to-GDP ratio; and (iv) the convergence of the debt-to-GDP ratio over the same period between Belgium and the Euro area average. During 2000-2007, that went down from 108% to 84% in Belgium and from 69% to 66% in the Euro area. It means the halving of the debt-to-GDP gap over 7 years, from 39 percentage point to 18! The evolution of the fiscal balance gives the same, half full, half empty glass message: its stabilization over 2000-2007 is disappointing with regard to declining interest payments and to future additional ageing costs, but satisfactory with regard to the gap versus the Euro area average. While Belgium managed over the years to maintain the balanced budget achieved in 2000, the Euro area, starting from an identical balanced position in 2000, recorded continuous deficits over the following years.

The out-performance of Belgium over the last decade in terms of debt-to-GDP evolution and of fiscal balance does not mean that public finances – that used, together with the labour market, to be the other weak spot of the Belgian economy – became a problem of the past. The high debt-to-GDP level raises concerns, together with the higher than average extra burden imposed, ceteris paribus, by population ageing. Certainly, the high public indebtedness is offset by the large net savings position of the private sector having led to the building up of a significant external surplus position vis-à-vis the rest of the world, but those private savings are not captive, which differs from the Japanese situation. In addition, the risk of a political and institutional crisis preventing the authorities from taking urgent measures cannot be ruled out. It means that due to this institutional fragility the structural position has to be better in Belgium than on average abroad.

6. FISCAL MEDIUM IS MESSAGE

Communication has also played an important role in the fiscal evolution. In the nineties, the consolidation had been "sold" to the population as required for Belgium to be one of the founding members of the common currency. Countries willing to be in the first batch of EMU members had to subject themselves to the Caudine forks of the Maastricht treaty. Once this had been achieved, the drive for further fiscal consolidation vanished. It would have been much better to present the fiscal consolidation to the population as a requirement of inter-generational fairness, but this was more difficult to convey to public opinion and did not have the binding character of a precise deadline imposed by external parties.

In addition, fiscal discipline suffered from the choice of the overall fiscal deficit as the reference indicator when evaluating the soundness of public finance. Thanks to the decline in interest rates, the negative snowball effect and the supportive economic environment, the fiscal deterioration prior to the financial crisis remained hidden from most of the population. On the contrary, the balanced budget achieved over the years 2000-2007 and the declining debt-to-GDP ratio conveyed a message of improving public finance, while the underlying position was deteriorating. For the sake of simplicity, the pedagogical mission of political representatives and/or the media having been given up, the wrong motivation and the wrong indicator were chosen and this contributed significantly to the loss of support for effective fiscal discipline.

The way the electorate assesses the quality of the national policy stance does not provide the right incentives for politicians, in particular in times of shrinking interest payments. Then the government may enjoy the political benefits of an expansionary policy and at the same time of a seemingly prudent fiscal policy. That such a course may be neither sustainable, being exposed to a cyclical downturn or to financial tensions, nor fair, given the high indebtedness ratio and the high – and higher than in the Euro area on average – cost of ageing, was not perceived by the local population. In the end, the view of fiscal qualitative out-performance in Belgium prevailed.

7. NO EXTERNAL PRESSURE? NO EFFORT !

The fiscal challenges facing industrial countries are clearly identified, including the financing of social security within a changing demographic pattern, the broad-based fostering of the human capital, tax and regulatory competition on mobile factors, the large inequalities, within and across countries, and climate change. If calls for reforms and for lower debt ratios may flow from dogmatism or from some vested interest, they may also be based on concerns for intra- and inter-generational fairness. However it appears that there is no widespread internal support for such policy changes, either in Belgium or in most developed countries. Political candidates anticipate that calls for fiscal prudence and for detailed budgetary reform do not pay off and that fiscal slippages, especially if they are not too visible, are not punished.

What may overcome the resistance to change? It may be a traumatic experience, such as the one Germany has undergone following reunification. For the most successful economy in the post World War II era to become the "sick child" of the continent has been a serious shock and led to a dramatic change in the fiscal stance that enjoyed large popular support spanning the traditional political dividing lines. The perception that to rely on European solidarity was no option also played a role in the policy changeover.

Barring such events, changes can only come from external pressure, as illustrated by the recent history of Belgian public finance. The consolidation effort of the eighties is directly related to the requirements of the then prevailing exchange rate arrangements, as illustrated by the measures announced at the time of the February 1982 devaluation. In the nineties, the second wave of consolidation came as a pre-requisite to

Euro area membership. From 2000 until 2007, the absence of effective external pressure led not only to the renunciation of additional measures but also to a gradual decline in the fiscal primary surplus despite vocal commitments to generate surpluses in order to pre-finance – part of – the ageing cost. As a matter of fact, the policy loosening in Belgium was not restricted to the budgetary side, as shown by the evolution of indicators such as wage costs, unit labour costs, export market shares and current balance in Belgium vs. neighbouring countries. Very recently, it has again been under external pressure, being that of sovereign bonds markets together with supra-national authorities, so that a new consolidation effort has been announced.

8. THE EURO LEGACY

The 2000-2010 period has been the decade of the rapid ascent of a new currency, the euro, combined with a stalemate in European integration. Before the introduction of the euro, the European house was like a cabin, with walls to protect against the wind but no roof to protect against the rain. The cabin was not very solid and there was no agreement about how to consolidate it, and even about the need to make it more robust. The only agreement was about making it bigger, not out of generalised enthusiasm but because nobody dared to turn down requests to enlarge it. The brilliant idea of the spiritual fathers of the euro was that the currency union would allow the killing of two birds with one stone, i. e. to get a roof and to make the consolidation of existing walls a necessity.

The euro introduction was a gamble. There is no problem as such with political gambles. Politicians that are often blamed for demagogy, for following the crowds, should not be blamed when they are ahead of their time. It is possible that the current crisis within the euro area will be seen by historians as having paved the way for a positive change, and it is therefore too early to offer any form of assessment, but, as of now, the gamble seems to have been lost. Indeed, and again at this juncture, the current benefits of the currency union are outweighed by the difficulties associated with it. It provided some impetus to trade and to growth but it allowed an increase in macroeconomic imbalances and, as a result, led to a major confidence crisis.

Among the imbalances fuelled by the European single currency, there are the growing divergences of unit labour costs, the deterioration in current accounts balances due to the loss of competitiveness and to the rapid decline in interest rates, and the relaxation of budgetary discipline. There are several channels of transmission between the single currency and fiscal leniency. They include the decline in interest rates, providing an incentive for debt financing while allowing the underlying deterioration in the fiscal position to be hidden, and some moral hazard if authorities did reckon on debt mutualisation.

The weak nature of the fiscal standards within the Euro area over the years 2000-2010 is illustrated by various features. Firstly, the fiscal criteria for gaining membership were not what they were supposed to be, as the former Belgian Minister of Finance acknowledged that it was well known that Greece was cheating with official data. Secondly, those criteria – which later turned out to be insufficient to guarantee the sustainability of public finance – were relaxed in 2003 to please Germany and France. Thirdly, the commitments in terms of future fiscal consolidation taken by the national governments within the framework of the Convergence Plans submitted to the European authorities were reneged on through a generalised procrastination in reaching budgetary targets. Finally, the fiscal criteria were too narrow-minded, and as a result "stupid" as they were candidly characterised by Romano Prodi, suffering from the major flaws of budgetary accounting.

9. LIVING APART TOGETHER

While welfare-destroying in the short run, any crisis has the virtue of pinpointing the failures of the current arrangements and of calling for action. Regarding the current fiscal crisis, next to the aforementioned failures, numerous actions have already been taken.

At the national level, austerity packages have been adopted in many countries, encompassing wage and employment cuts, the tightening of social security programmes, in terms of eligibility and/or individual amounts, the reduction of current and capital expenditure, and tax increases, most often on consumption to start with. At the European level, significant fiscal reforms have been announced, including the "European Semester", the "six-pack", the "fiscal compact" including a golden rule, etc.

More European integration has to come. Countries are reluctant to give up sovereignty, even where emergency assistance has been called for, and it is important to keep a feeling of national empowerment, but the integration is unlikely to be restricted to the determination of a maximum deficit level or of a debt-to-GDP ceiling. Recent history, in Spain as in Ireland, has sadly shown that fulfilling such criteria does not protect against fiscal slippages generating negative externalities for other member countries. In addition, penalties in the event of non-compliance may not be effective and quantitative rules may lead to harmful policy choices.

The national institutional set-up is another challenge for European fiscal policy. The decade from 2000 to 2010 witnessed a further devolution of power towards sub-national authorities, in Belgium and abroad. At the same time only federal authorities are accountable as regards the European commitments and the mutualisation of risks across Europe is between supra-national and national institutions, not the regional ones. The seemingly ideal double-move model of devolution towards both the European level and sub-national authorities, at the expense of the federal level, does not fit with the reality of today where the accountability of central governments has increased.

The loss of the exchange rate adjustment tool involved by the single currency calls for alternative adjustment mechanisms. Solidarity across countries with centralised peer control is likely to play a crucial role. As a matter of fact, it is the broader notion of solidarity at large that will be central, as it also encompasses three other key issues. Firstly, it concerns inter-generational fairness, the key consideration in terms of debt sustainability analysis. Most people do enjoy higher living standards than their parents, but this may no longer be the case for the future generations. A decline in trend output growth that may come from the demographic evolution, and the expected financial de-leveraging and fiscal consolidation processes, is likely to exacerbate sensitivity towards this issue. Secondly, fiscal consolidation will test social cohesion. Even if the evolution of the equity markets in 2000-2010 has eroded the assets of the wealthy, the last decade is largely seen as having led to growing income inequalities across households. Thirdly, the resolution of a debt crisis ultimately raises the issue of who will foot the bill. Of course, "growing out of debt" is the most attractive strategy, as growth means effortless consolidation, but growth-enhancing reforms, while available, take time to be implemented and face the fierce opposition of "insiders". As a result, the solution to the debt crisis lies largely in a burden-sharing arrangement, whatever the practicalities, being debt restructuring, a bail-in of creditors of financial institutions, the recapitalisation of banks by domestic or foreign authorities, diluting existing shareholders, or the public take-over of large liabilities.

10. THE CONSOLIDATION ROAD AHEAD

Just as a rear view mirror allows one to drive better, economic history allows for better policy action. In order to make the link between analysis of the recent past and recommendations for the future even more obvious, ten years ago, in the introductory chapter to the previous edition of the history of Belgian public finance, we offered an overview of what had not yet been done in terms of fiscal reforms. It is unfortunate that most of those suggestions, while deemed to rely on a broad analytical consensus, are still awaiting implementation. It does not mean that the exercise was useless, but reminds us that ideas take time to become realities. By the way, the ongoing crisis may shorten the time lag between academic proposals and political decisions.

That an in-depth analysis of the recent history of public finance in Belgium is motivated by the desire to lead, through better understanding, to better policy recommendations can be illustrated by comments about the fiscal consolidation theme that is likely to dominate the current

Introduction 23

decade. These comments are stimulated by the contributions gathered herein, but do not commit their authors.

1. On top of current market pressure for fiscal consolidation and of European commitments, intergenerational considerations invite further fiscal restraint for the years to come.

2. The fiscal consolidation process will have to be carried forward within a medium- to long-term framework geared towards sustainable economic growth, macroeconomic balances, social cohesion, and making the polluters, whether environmental or financial, pay.

3. The quality of the adjustment matters more than its speed. The focus on short-term narrow indicators, in particular the fiscal balance position to be reached by the end of the calendar year, is misleading. The quality of fiscal policy, even if difficult to establish, definitely matters more than any numerical target that does not say much, particularly in terms of sustainability.

4. To some extent it is possible to combine growth enhancement and fiscal restraint, beyond the positive, Ricardian-like, confidence effects, for instance through the postponement of the retirement age, the differentiation of social security contributions on the basis of the unemployment rate of former employees, a tax shift from labour income tax to consumption tax, or the strengthening of the incentives provided by the unemployment benefits scheme. If there is a political trade-off between more short-term austerity measures and more structural reforms, the preference has to be for the latter.

5. Measures showing that the lessons from the crisis are well learned matter in order to prevent a repetition and to foster confidence. These encompass various sorts of tax distortions, including in favour of debt and of alternative remuneration.

6. The stabilisation function of public finance should be reaffirmed through automatic stabilisers. Structural fiscal balances, as measured by independent authorities, should be preferred, as performance

indicators, to the expense of nominal fiscal balance. Of course, the weight given by financial markets to nominal balances cannot be ignored by countries facing potential financing difficulties. There, it makes sense to design contingency plans in the event of further deterioration in the economic and fiscal situation. While automatic stabilisers do have a role to play, caution is warranted with respect to discretionary measures due to their various caveats, including time lags, the risk of decisions being driven by corporatism and beggar-my-neighbour considerations, and the lack of international coordination.

7. Reliance on fiscal rules, and in particular on any variant of the golden rule, should be tempered due to their quantitative nature and due to enforcement problems. Furthermore, it may be desirable to allow a country with a large structural external surplus to follow a more expansionary fiscal course.

8. The balance between solidarity and responsibility will be central. Fiscal federalism, from supranational authorities to sub-national ones, will have to be revisited with an eye to accountability. Policy makers have to face the right incentives also as regards the electorate. A proper assessment by the voters requires the computation of the right indicators by independent bodies and their widespread use in the media.

With such a storyboard, there is a chance that the next edition of the series of books about the recent history of public finance in Belgium will look quite different from this one.

REFERENCES

1. Vincent Reinhart and Brian Sack, "The Economic Consequences of Disappearing Government Debt," Brookings Papers on Economic Activity (2000), 163-220.
2. Etienne de Callataÿ, ed., La fin du déficit public. Analyse de l'évolution récente des finances publiques belges (Louvain-la-Neuve: De Boeck-Université, 2002a)
3. Etienne de Callataÿ, "L'assainissement sans réforme. Introduction à l'histoire récente des finances publiques belges", in La fin du déficit public. Analyse de l'évolution récente des finances publiques belges, ed. Etienne de Callataÿ (Louvain-la-Neuve : De Boeck-Université, 2002b), 17-24.

1.
The European Context

EVOLVING GOVERNANCE IN THE EU: FROM THE SGP TO HELL AND BACK?[1]

Guy Quaden, Jan Smets, and Geert Langenus[2]

On 1 January 1999, at the start of the so-called Stage Three of the Economic and Monetary Union, eleven EU Member States took the historic step of introducing a new common currency. The creation of the euro was as much a political decision as an economic one: the adoption of a common currency was considered to be a logical and necessary step in the gradual process towards greater European integration. Meanwhile, the euro has firmly established itself on the world stage, the European Central Bank has successfully kept euro area inflation rates low in accordance with its mandate, and six additional Member States – three of which were until relatively recently part of countries that were located behind the 'Iron Curtain' – have joined the monetary union.

From a purely economic point of view the move to a single currency and a unified monetary policy for the euro area countries was not entirely uncontroversial. First, it is widely recognised that the euro area countries to some extent fell short of the theoretical benchmarks for an optimum currency area. The relatively low degree of labour mobility between countries and the lack of an important cyclical fiscal transfer

---

1. This article reflects the views of the authors and not necessarily those of the National Bank of Belgium. We would like to thank, without implicating them, Jef Boeckx, Hugues Famerée, Hans Geeroms and Luc Van Meensel for helpful comments and discussions.
2. Guy Quaden is Honorary Governor of the National Bank of Belgium, Jan Smets is Board Member of the National Bank of Belgium. Geert Langenus is member of the Research Department of the National Bank of Belgium.

system were thought to be significant weaknesses as this reduced the area's capacity to deal with asymmetric shocks and developments. In such an environment, the flexibility of prices and labour markets becomes all the more important (Ilzkovitz et al, 2007). Secondly, and more generally, doubts were raised regarding the longevity of currency unions between different countries where only monetary policy is fully centralised. It was feared that, given the heterogeneity of the participating countries in particular, political conflicts could arise over the economic policies that ought to be implemented. Around the turn of the century, at least some observers were convinced that the euro was an institutional adventure, boosted by the historic momentum, which was doomed to fail because of the lack of political union.

At the same time, there was some moderate optimism in the early years of the euro that participating economies would converge further and that the criteria for optimum currency areas were to some extent endogenous: euroland may not have been an optimum currency area at the start but could become one over time (e.g. De Grauwe and Mongelli, 2005). In addition, a common currency could in itself foster greater political integration. This was clearly the intention when the euro was introduced. However, the common currency sailed into heavy seas when the sovereign debt crisis hit Europe towards the end of the decade. Policy-makers have recently resorted to highly exceptional measures to keep the ship afloat.

A key success factor for cross-border monetary unions is the absence of externalities, i.e. the union's capacity to avoid policies – and, in particular, irresponsible ones – in one participating country spilling over to other participating countries or to the common monetary policy. In this connection, an independent central bank and the ban on taking on debts issued by other Member States (the so-called 'no-bail-out' clause), both guaranteed in the Treaty on the Functioning of the European Union, and cornerstones of the EMU architecture, are of the utmost importance. However, it was clear from the outset that, in the longer term, the smooth functioning of the euro area would crucially depend on the degree of economic convergence between the participating countries and success in consolidating public finances. Diverging economic trends across participating countries may complicate the identification of the appropriate monetary policy stance, while sizeable fiscal imbalances may ultimately undermine the credibility of the commitment to low inflation and raise inflation expectations.

In this article we review the developments in the governance framework of the European Monetary Union. We argue that the euro area's recent problems are to a large extent rooted in both flaws in the initial design of this framework and inadequate implementation of existing rules. The failure to contain the externalities coming from unsustainable fiscal and macroeconomic policies, in particular, has seriously threatened the stability of the euro area. As we will focus on governance and institutional developments, we do not constrain ourselves to the 2000-2010 period but also briefly comment on the changes in the EU governance framework in the wake of the sovereign debt crisis even though most of them were decided in 2011 and 2012.

The remainder of this article is organised as follows. In section 1 we analyse the implementation of the fiscal rules. Section 2 changes the focus to macroeconomic trends and looks at the development of large imbalances that preceded the sovereign debt crisis. The third section then zooms in on the ongoing efforts to strengthen EU economic governance. Finally, in the concluding remarks we draw some lessons from the mixed track record of EU governance during the first decade of the euro.

1. 'FISCAL FATIGUE' AND THE EROSION OF EU FISCAL RULES

1.1 The Stability and Growth Pact

The Maastricht Treaty on European Union already imposed some degree of fiscal discipline on the prospective members of the monetary union through the so-called Excessive Deficit Procedure. This defines specific ceilings (of 3% and 60% of GDP respectively) for the deficit and the debt ratio. However, these ceilings were not framed as 'hard' fiscal rules. In certain exceptional circumstances a deficit exceeding 3% of GDP was not considered as 'excessive' if the deviation was limited and temporary, while the debt criterion was deemed to be satisfied even if the debt ratio substantially exceeded 60% of GDP on the condition that the ratio was sufficiently diminishing and approaching this reference value at a satisfactory pace. In actual practice, that clause was never made operational and the Excessive Deficit Procedure basically focused only on government deficit levels, even for countries that entered the euro area with very high debt levels.

The Excessive Deficit Procedure included in the Maastricht Treaty was not only one of the convergence criteria that prospective members of the monetary union had to comply with but amounted to permanent constraints on the deficit and – in principle – debt levels of the euro area countries. Failure to comply with these rules would result in corrective action (including financial sanctions). However, even before the actual introduction of the euro, it was felt that these fiscal rules provided insufficient guarantees for budget discipline in the monetary union. One of the concerns related to the reconciliation of the operation of the automatic stabilisers with a fixed deficit limit: if the deficit were to stay below 3% of GDP in bad times, the budget targets in a neutral cyclical environment or in good times should be significantly more ambitious than this nominal limit.

Protracted political negotiations to sharpen the budgetary rules finally led to an agreement at the European Council in Dublin in December 1996 on a 'Stability and Growth Pact', which was adopted in 1997. The Pact reaffirms the conviction that sound public finances are a precondition for stable economic growth in the monetary union. It comprises a number of preventive and corrective procedures aimed at ensuring fiscal discipline in the EU Member States.

The preventive part primarily consists of a rule for the deficit corrected for the business cycle: the budgetary deficit was to be 'close to balance or in surplus' over the medium term. This came to be interpreted as a ceiling for cyclically-adjusted deficits of 0.5% of GDP and should guarantee that, for normal business cycles, the nominal deficit stays below 3% of GDP during economic downturns. In addition, detailed medium-term programmes (stability programmes for the countries that have adopted the euro, convergence programmes for the other EU Member States), which are updated annually, should specify how this medium-term target will be achieved. Finally, the European Commission should continuously monitor public finance developments in the EU Member States and propose to the Council that it should give an 'early warning' to Member States where the risk of an excessive deficit exists.

The corrective part is based upon the Excessive Deficit Procedure and confirms the deficit ceiling of 3% of GDP, as well as the sanctions for non-compliance. The circumstances under which a deficit above 3% of GDP is not considered to be excessive are clarified in particular as regards the 'exceptional' nature of the deviation. This should stem from either an unusual event outside the control of the Member State (e.g. a natural disaster) or a severe economic downturn.[3] Once an excessive deficit is identified, the Pact imposes a clear timeline with well-defined procedural steps for its prompt correction – in principle not later than one year after its identification – and for sanctions to kick in if this does not happen. The financial sanctions defined in the Pact in principle apply only to euro area countries but other, not necessarily less dissuasive measures, such as limiting the access to Cohesion Fund resources, can be taken against other Member States.

Unlike the deficit limit, the aforementioned debt criterion was not made more operational in the Pact. It was even explicitly indicated that financial sanctions could be applied only in the event of non-compliance with the deficit criterion, which seems to suggest that – at that time – policy-makers were not primarily concerned with debt developments (Cabral, 2001).

While the EU fiscal framework was based upon (more or less) clear rules, the assessment of compliance with those rules left a lot of room for discretion. Any procedural step – from the identification of an excessive deficit to the decision that a Member State has not taken effective action in response to Ecofin Council recommendations and the actual

---

3. This was defined as a fall of real GDP by at least 2% even though the Member State could argue that a less severe contraction was also 'exceptional' (and, hence, justified a deficit exceeding 3% of GDP) taking into account the 'abruptness of the downturn and the accumulated loss of output relative to past trends'. However, there was an agreement not to use such arguments if real GDP did not post a decline by at least 0.75%.

imposition of financial sanctions – required the explicit adoption, by a qualified majority in the Ecofin Council, of a recommendation by the European Commission. As no specific guidelines restricted the Council's discretion in this respect, the implementation of the fiscal rules was particularly vulnerable to political pressures. A coalition of a small number of important Member States could essentially block corrective steps proposed by the Commission.

1.2   Fiscal developments after euro adoption

As the rules of the Stability and Growth Pact came into effect from 1999, EU Member States had the obligation to further reduce remaining structural deficits with a view to converging to a budgetary position that was close to balance or in surplus. In reality, fiscal policy was loosened in most EU Member States, immediately after the decision on the first wave of euro adopters was taken. In many cases, the fiscal efforts made to comply with the Maastricht convergence criteria were largely or completely offset, as witnessed by the changes in the cyclically-adjusted primary balances: only Portugal, Spain and Denmark (slightly) increased their cyclically-adjusted primary balances in the first six years of the euro area. The 'fiscal fatigue' observed after the adoption of the euro implied that progress towards sound budgetary positions was very uneven. In the first six years of the euro area cyclically-adjusted deficits widened in more than half of the (then) 15 Member States and actually increased to more than 3% of GDP in the largest EU economies (Germany, France, the United Kingdom and Italy), as well as in Greece and Portugal. As a result, the average public debt ratio declined only slightly in these 15 Member States and stayed above the 60% reference value.

Belgium was no exception to the general trend. While the country's admission in the euro area was based upon the understanding – if not the actual commitment – that Belgium would maintain its primary surplus over the medium term[4] at a high level of some 6% of GDP or more with a view to speeding up the decline in the government debt ratio, the

---

4. This objective effectively pertained to the cyclically-adjusted primary surplus.

The European Context   31

structural primary surplus was in fact gradually reduced and even turned into a significant deficit in 2009. This substantial fiscal loosening was due to both cuts in particularly personal income taxes and social contributions and an expenditure growth that far outpaced that in trend GDP (National Bank of Belgium, 2009).

Graph 1: 'Fiscal fatigue' in the early years of the euro (percentages of GDP)

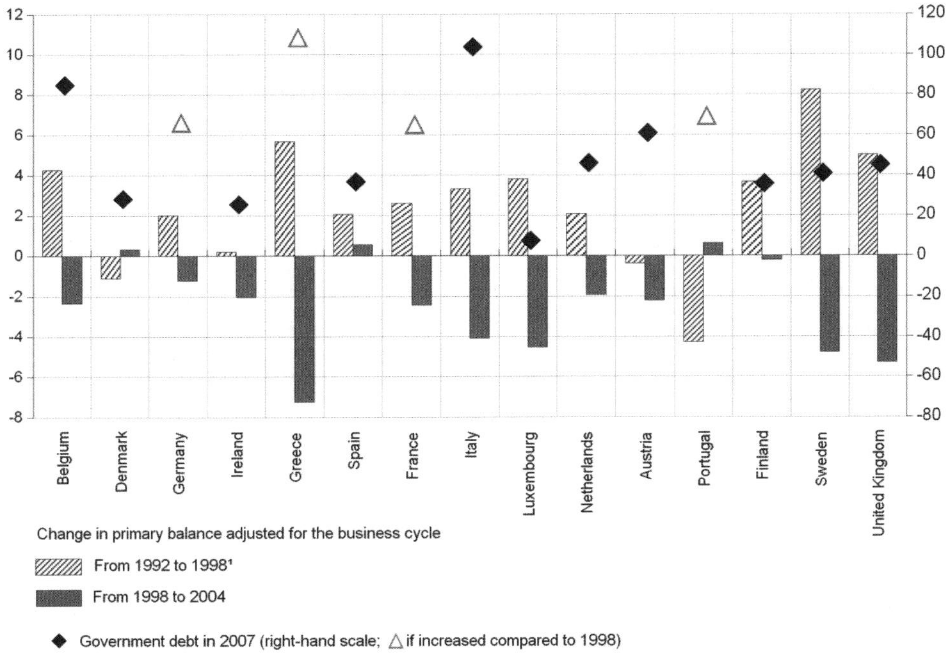

Change in primary balance adjusted for the business cycle
- From 1992 to 1998¹
- From 1998 to 2004
- ◆ Government debt in 2007 (right-hand scale; △ if increased compared to 1998)

Source: EC.
¹ From 1993 to 1998 for Sweden and from 1995 to 1998 for Spain.

This general loss of fiscal discipline should be seen against the backdrop of the increasing desire to relax the budgetary stance after several years of 'belt-tightening' in the run-up to the introduction of the euro and to use budgetary tools to enhance growth and employment. However, it was facilitated by a number of elements. First, effective fiscal monitoring was to some extent impeded by the unreliability of fiscal indicators. A number of EU countries clearly misrepresented deficit and debt data in their public finance statistics, with Greece being the most notorious repeat offender. In addition, undue optimism regarding trend economic growth clouded the analysis of the fiscal policy stance at the turn of the century. In this connection, real-time estimates of cyclically-adjusted budget balances, that are – and should be – affected by projections of future economic developments substantially underestimated the true size of the structural fiscal deficits due to trend revision effects (Langenus, 2005).

Second, there was an obvious hiatus in the fiscal governance framework: in the preventive part of the Pact, no precise limit was set on the length of the transition period towards a budgetary position that was close to balance or in surplus. In addition, the Pact lacked coercive instruments – other than peer pressure – to make countries comply with the preventive rules. Hence, these rules remained largely ineffective.

Third, policy-makers may have had reasonable doubts regarding the institutions' and, in particular, the Council's willingness actually to implement the fiscal rules and impose sanctions. If anything, these doubts were only fuelled by the lack of a forceful reaction to the first wave of excessive deficits in the euro area.

1.3   Erosion of the fiscal rules

Economic growth in the EU slowed down significantly after the turn of the century, from an average annual rate of some 3.3% in the 1998-2000 period to only 1.5% in the three following years, and countries quickly paid the price for their lack of compliance with the Pact's preventive rules as regards the reduction of remaining structural deficits. As early as 2001, nominal deficits started to exceed the 3% of GDP limit again in certain countries. The institutional response was rather tepid. The Excessive Deficit Procedure was initiated, but the rules were gradually bent in the direction of maximum leniency and the implementation never came close to actual financial sanctions.

In the end it was the increasing disagreement, in the autumn of 2003, between the European Commission and the Council over the procedures to be taken against France and Germany that delivered the fatal blow to the original Stability and Growth Pact. The bone of contention was the November 2003 Commission recommendation to give notice to France and Germany after establishing that both countries had failed to take effective action in response to Council recommendations to put an end to the excessive deficit. Even though the recommendations were quite reconciliatory[5], they were flatly rejected by the Council. The European Commission brought the case before the European Court of Justice but the Court's July 2004 ruling essentially confirmed the Council's right to reject Commission recommendations.[6]

Ultimately, the Pact was reformed in 2005. As regards the preventive rules, the uniform 'close-to-balance-or-in-surplus' requirement was replaced by country-specific medium-term objectives (MTOs), which could be determined by the Member States themselves within certain limits. These MTOs were to provide adequate safety margins with respect to the 3% of GDP deficit limit (taking into account past output volatility) and ensure rapid progress towards fiscal sustainability, as well as allow for sufficient budgetary room for manoeuvre (in particular for investment needs). In practice, the MTOs range from minor deficits[7] to small surpluses (as in the case of Belgium which targets a 0.5% of GDP surplus, taking into account the high debt ratio and important ageing-related spending increases in the following decades). In addition, the focus shifted from merely cyclically-adjusted to structural budget balances as both the MTO and the required convergence towards it were measured in structural terms, i.e. excluding the cyclical component but, in principle, also temporary measures and factors. A 'benchmark' adjustment speed towards the MTO – an annual reduction of the structural deficit by 0.5% of GDP – was defined (thereby confirming an earlier Eurogroup agreement) but no sanctions were introduced to actually enforce convergence to sound budgetary positions.

5. Far from proposing financial sanctions, the recommendations called only for larger fiscal efforts and imposed increased reporting requirements. In addition, the deadline for correcting the excessive deficit was pushed back to 2005, even though the procedures were initiated on the basis of excessive deficits existing since 2002.
6. However, the actual Council conclusions of November 2003 were annulled on technical grounds (including not respecting the Commission's right of initiative when formulating new recommendations to Member States in an Excessive Deficit Procedure).
7. For euro area countries and Member States participating in ERM II, the MTO cannot be lower than a 1% of GDP deficit.

While certain changes to the preventive rules were welcome, the disciplining nature of the corrective procedures was further weakened in the 2005 reform. First, the definition of 'exceptional circumstances' under which a deficit exceeding 3% of GDP is not considered as excessive was widened considerably.[8] Second, the procedure for the correction of excessive deficits was lengthened significantly (e.g. by the possibility of defining longer deadlines, extending deadlines and even repeating procedural steps); the general principle that this should be done at the latest one year after its identification was maintained only on paper.

All in all, the reform only institutionalised the lenient approach to fiscal governance witnessed previously. More specifically, it moved the EU fiscal governance further away from a strictly rules-based framework and significantly widened the discretionary powers and the scope for interpretation of the European Commission and the Council. While the 2005 reform was presented by policy-makers (including the European Commission) as making the Pact more flexible and intelligent, European central banks were typically much more sceptical and pointed to the risks of fiscal imbalances for price stability (Clarke, 2005). At the time, Mervyn King, the Governor of the Bank of England, was one of the more vocal critics: "[t]he finance ministers have driven a coach and horses through the stability and growth pact… Whatever word you use to describe these changes to the pact, it isn't discipline".[9]

After the 2005 reform of the Pact, public debt ratios and nominal deficits initially declined, but this was mainly due to buoyant economic growth in 2006 and 2007. However, under the new rules progress towards sound budget positions remained very slow. As a result European countries entered the Great Recession with relatively weak fiscal fundamentals. The cyclically-adjusted deficit of both the EU and the euro area did not fall significantly below 2% of GDP and shot up again in 2008.

---

8. Any negative growth and, possibly, a long period of low positive growth that is below the potential rate could constitute an exception while the analysis of the excessive nature of the deficit is also to take account of a wide range of 'other relevant factors'.
9. Parliamentary hearing, 24 March 2005.

2. THE BUILD-UP OF IMBALANCES AND THE SOVEREIGN DEBT CRISIS

2.1 'Soft' surveillance and diverging macroeconomic trends

In contrast to the fiscal governance framework, a much 'softer' coordination approach was chosen for broader economic policies. Countries entered the euro area with very different economic fundamentals and, unlike fiscal developments, macroeconomic policies in euro area countries were not constrained by specific area-wide rules. While stated common objectives often implied specific reform agendas, EU coordination devices fell short of actually imposing these reforms.

The very ambitious Lisbon strategy is a case in point. It was set out by the European Council in March 2000 and aimed at promoting productivity, innovation and competitiveness, as well as modernising the European social model, boosting employment and combating social exclusion, with a view to turning the EU into 'the most competitive and dynamic knowledge-based economy in the world capable of sustainable economic growth with more and better jobs and greater social cohesion'. The Lisbon strategy was anchored to the traditional EU coordination mechanisms defined in the Treaty – the Broad Economic Policy Guidelines and the Employment Guidelines – that were complemented with a new intergovernmental Open Method of Coordination, in particular as regards social policies. However, these coordination devices were of the 'soft law' type. While they provided benchmarks and promoted best practices via detailed information exchange and peer pressure, there was no actual legal obligation to modify national policies. Member States remained competent for taking the appropriate measures to attune these policies to area-wide objectives.

In such a setting progress in the area of structural reforms crucially depends on national ownership of the EU policy agenda. However, Ioannou et al (2008) argue that there may be strong resistance to structural reforms at the national level due to political economy considerations, information asymmetries and the impact of pressure groups. In the end, while some progress was made in specific areas, the quantitative targets of the Lisbon strategy were generally not met and existing weaknesses were not addressed.

The observed inertia in the further adjustment of the euro area economies to the requirements of a monetary union through structural reforms provided an ideal breeding ground for structural macroeconomic imbalances. In this connection, the different trends in competitiveness and domestic demand between euro area countries are perhaps the most telling and important.

Graph 2: Balance of payments and developments in unit labour costs and domestic demand

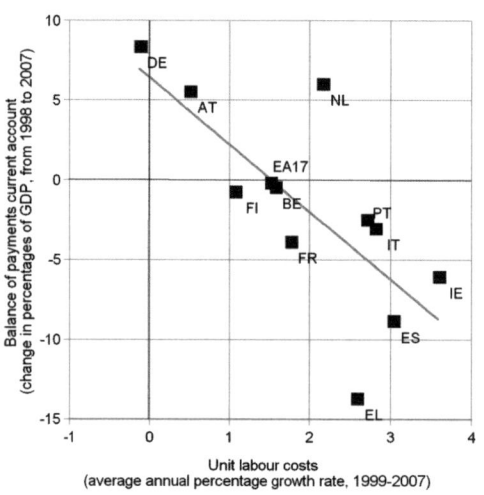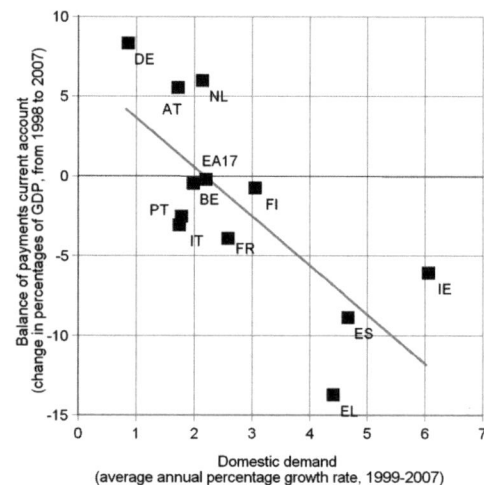

Source: EC.

In certain countries both labour costs and domestic demand rose sharply after the introduction of the euro. This was particularly the case for Greece, Ireland and Spain, while unit labour costs also increased more than on average in the euro area, in Portugal and Italy. Buoyant domestic demand was typically accompanied by strong growth of credit to households and burgeoning real estate markets. Growth in domestic demand and labour costs was much more moderate in other euro area countries including, in particular, Germany and Austria, where economic growth relied to a greater extent on net exports.

The European Context

These diverging macroeconomic trends were reflected in the balance of payments. The current account balance improved by more than 8% of GDP in Germany and by some 5% to 6% of GDP in Austria and the Netherlands from 1998 to 2007. In the same period it worsened by more than 6% of GDP in Ireland, by some 9% of GDP in Spain and even by close to 14% of GDP in Greece. Obviously, this had a significant impact on the international asset positions of the respective countries. By 2007, net external debts in Spain and Portugal amounted to around 80% of GDP and more than 90% of GDP, respectively, while Greek net external debt even significantly exceeded GDP.

In Belgium growth in labour costs and domestic demand remained close to the euro area averages. The significant current account surplus declined only marginally in the pre-crisis period and, in particular due to private-sector saving, the Belgian international net asset position was among the highest in the euro area in 2007.

Graph 3: Net international asset positions prior to the Great Recession (percentages of GDP, end of 2007)

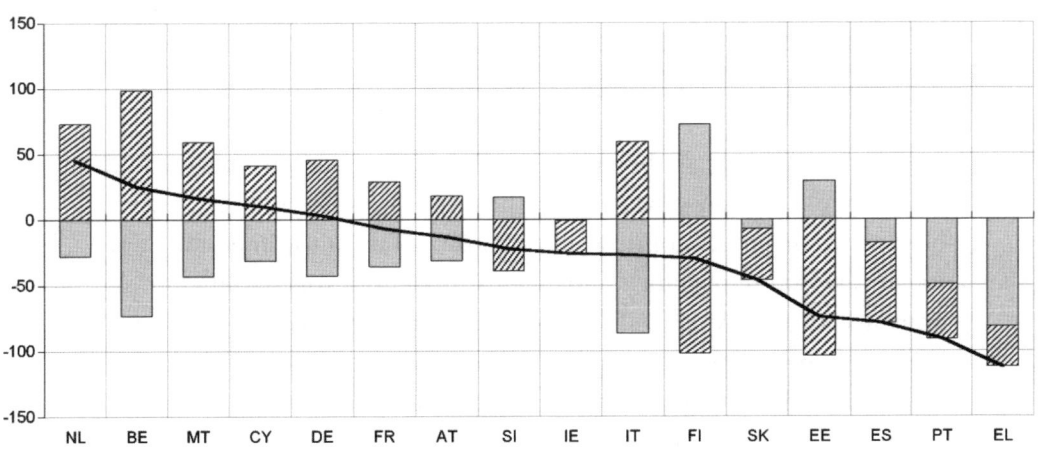

Source: EC.
[1] As Luxembourg is a clear outlier with a net international asset position of more than 312% of GDP in 2007, it is not included in the graph.

While financial flows between countries of a currency union such as those witnessed after the introduction of the euro are not necessarily a problem in itself, their persistence can be a cause for concern. This may indicate that the adjustment mechanisms in the form of price and wage flexibility are not functioning properly. In addition, it complicates the definition of the appropriate 'one-size-fits-all' monetary policy stance. In this connection, policy analysis based upon standard Taylor rules, for instance, tends to suggest that common ECB monetary policy has been quite closely attuned to the needs of Germany and other 'northern' countries, but was insufficiently constraining in the 1999-2007 period for countries such as Greece, Spain, Portugal and Ireland (e.g. Nechio, 2011), where the common monetary policy was accompanied by different national macroeconomic or macroprudential policy choices: in particular, the excessive credit expansion was insufficiently restrained by national authorities. Finally, and in retrospect most importantly, persistent one-way financial flows make debtor countries more vulnerable to changes in financial conditions and expose them, in particular, to risks of 'sudden stops' in international financing.

2.2 Financial market pressures: too late and with contagion effects

Some observers initially believed that financial market pressures would make up for the inadequate enforcement of fiscal rules and the absence of effective macroeconomic policy coordination. At the end of the day markets would rein in unsustainable fiscal and macroeconomic developments. In reality, spreads on government bonds strongly declined in the run-up to the introduction of the euro and remained negligible throughout the whole period up to 2007. Very different policies did not translate into significant differences in risk premia and government funding costs: financial markets brushed aside all financial risks from unsustainable policies (or had doubts about the credibility of the 'no-bail-out' clause of the Treaty).

Graph 4:(Belated) Financial market pressures (spreads on 10-year government bonds compared to the German Bund, daily data, basis points)

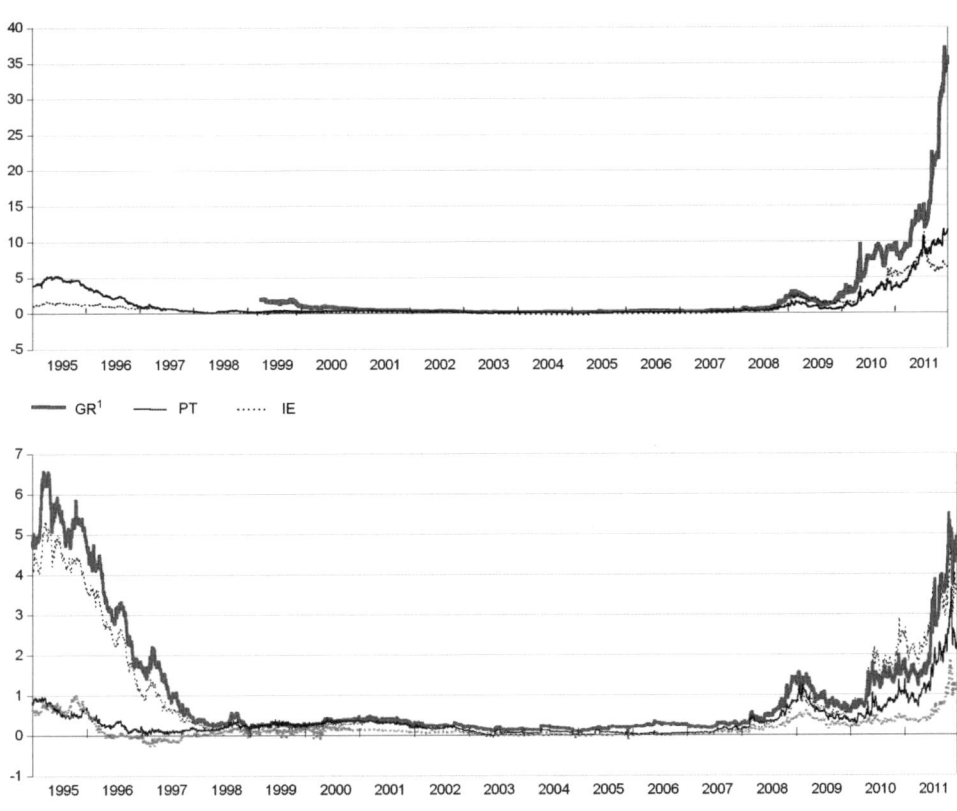

Source: Thomson Reuters Datastream.
[1] Data for Greece are only available from the second quarter of 1999 onwards.

However, the financial crisis gave rise to a renewed sharper risk assessment of both private and public indebtedness and, finally, turned into a sovereign debt crisis. Against the background of the financial crisis in the last years of the decade, the general repricing of sovereign risks quickly caused government bond yields in euro area countries to diverge strongly. While the return on German government bonds, which were considered as a safe haven, fell, funding costs for certain other governments sharply increased. For Greece, Ireland and Portugal, both spreads and yields rose even above the levels seen in the early 1990s (when they were also reflecting exchange rate risks). In the end, official funding in the context of international financial assistance programmes became the only viable option for meeting financing requirements.

Apart from the fact that market forces did not exert a disciplining influence in a more gradual and timely manner, the sovereign debt crisis has also rekindled interest in the basic reason for effective rules in a monetary union, i.e. the avoidance of externalities across participating countries. While, by and large, borrowing costs generally appear to have risen more for countries that have followed more expansive policies and/or relied to a greater extent on external financing, co-movements in sovereign bond markets raise the question whether a higher spread in one euro area country can spill over to other euro area countries. A number of recent studies including Favero and Missale (2012) and Boeckx and Dewachter (2012) find evidence of such 'contagion' effects. The presence of these externalities in government bond yield dynamics is crucially important for the EMU architecture as they suggest that market reactions, in addition to not being a viable alternative for effective rules, actually make such rules all the more necessary for the smooth functioning of monetary union.

2.3 A fiscal landslide from 2008 onwards

In the 2008-2010 period European public finances worsened substantially. The average euro area and EU government deficit widened to more than 6% of GDP – i.e. twice the reference level for excessive deficits – in 2010 while, in the space of three years, public debt ratios ratcheted up by close to 20 percentage points on average. Several factors contributed to this fiscal slippage, unseen since the introduction of the euro.

First, government budgets and debt ratios obviously suffered the impact of the very important recession that followed from the banking and financial crisis and, on average, shaved more than 4% off European GDPs in 2009. On the basis of the cyclical adjustment method that is used by the European Commission for the implementation of the EU fiscal rules, nearly half of the increase in euro area and EU deficits would be due to a worsening of the cyclical component. It should be stressed that in a number of countries

Graph 5: Deficit and debt developments in the 2008-2010 period (percentages of GDP)

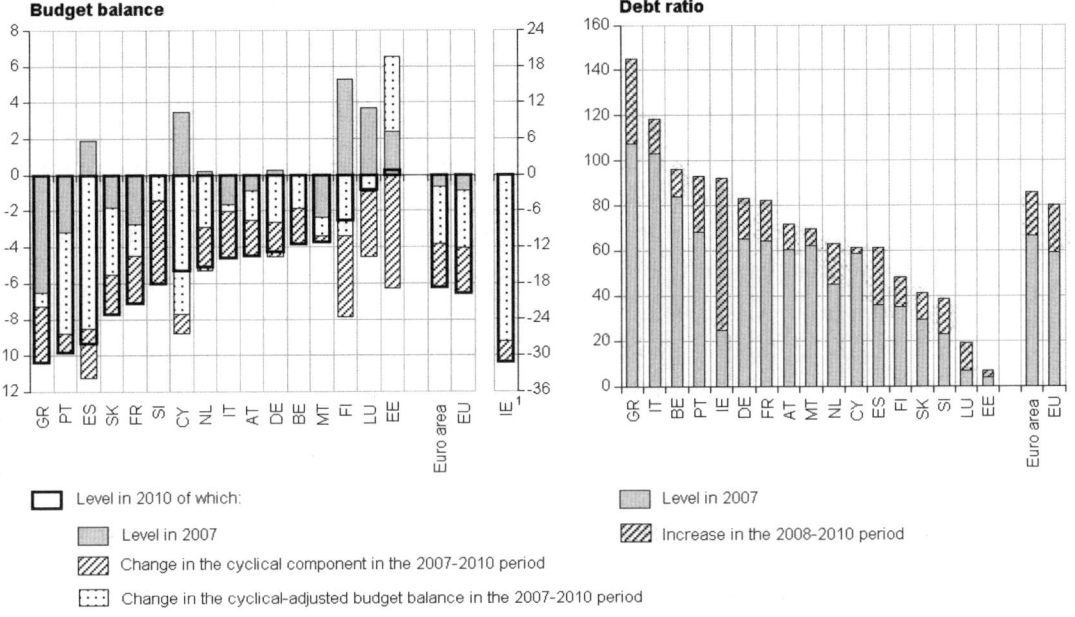

Source: EC.
[1] Right-hand scale.

(including those where government revenue relies to a relatively larger extent on real estate transactions) actual cyclicality in government budgets is significantly more important than is suggested by the elasticities used in cyclical adjustment methods (Morris et al, 2009). The budgetary impact of asset price cycles, in particular, is not picked up by the conventional cyclical adjustment approaches (Morris and Schuknecht, 2007). Other than the aforementioned trend revision effect, this is another reason why cyclically-adjusted budget balances should be interpreted with caution and, in some cases, may provide a false sense of security.

Second, in addition to the automatic cyclical impact, governments actively pursued countercyclical policies, largely in the context of the European Economic Recovery Plan (EERP). This was a common framework, designed by the European Commission, to boost demand with a budgetary stimulus of 1.5% of GDP. Similar stimulus programmes were implemented in other large economies, including the US and China. This fiscal reaction may have prevented the recession from turning into a depression similar to the one in the 1930s. While there is some evidence that certain measures have indeed limited the fall in real GDP in a number of countries (e.g. Hamburg et al., 2010), they have also further worsened government finances: cyclically-adjusted deficits widened by more than 3% of GDP in both the EU and the euro area.[10]

Finally, many governments took sizeable measures to support ailing financial institutions in the context of the financial crisis. Apart from very important capital transfers in Ireland in 2010, the direct impact of these support measures on government budgets was on average quite limited. Financial sector support mostly amounted to the transfer of (often impaired) assets to government balance sheets. This increased euro area government debt ratios by more than 5% of GDP. In addition, governments also provided massive guarantees of various sorts to financial institutions. According to harmonised Eurostat data these contingent liabilities amounted to some 6.5% of the euro area GDP at the end of 2010 but were larger for certain individual countries. In Belgium outstanding contingent liabilities due to financial sector support were as high as 16% of GDP, a figure that had risen to close to 20% of GDP by the end of 2011, taking into account new guarantees given, in particular to Dexia, in that year.

3. GENERAL OVERHAUL OF THE EU GOVERNANCE FRAMEWORK

3.1 Exceptional measures in exceptional times

The aforementioned liquidity problems for some euro area countries faced with skyrocketing funding costs forced EU policy-makers rapidly to elaborate a crisis response strategy in the course of 2010. In part due to the speed of the events this was initially characterised by an ad hoc approach. The first financial assistance scheme, for Greece in May 2010, took the form of a set of three-year bilateral loans from the other euro area countries amounting to some 80 bn EUR, in addition to a 30 bn

---

10. The extraordinary magnitude of the financial sector support in Ireland in 2010 affected the euro area and EU aggregates: it accounted for around 0.3% of the (nominal and cyclically-adjusted) change in the euro area government deficit from 2007 to 2010.

EUR intervention by the IMF. Then a temporary financial assistance mechanism was created through the European Financial Stability Facility (which issues its own loans guaranteed by euro area countries, initially for a maximum amount of 440 bn EUR) and, to a much lesser extent, the European Financial Stabilisation Mechanism (which is financed by loans issued by the European Commission up to 60 bn EUR). Both Ireland (November 2010) and Portugal (May 2011) received financial assistance from these funds, for seven and three years respectively. In March 2012, a second financial assistance programme for Greece, this time including private-sector involvement, was also approved. All of these financial assistance programmes are conditional on the debtor countries implementing in-depth macroeconomic reforms and fiscal consolidation. Finally, agreement was reached in July 2011 on a permanent crisis resolution mechanism, the European Stability Mechanism (ESM), which would replace the temporary facilities. Initially, it was planned that the ESM would be operational from July 2013 onwards, but this was later brought forward to July 2012 and the effectiveness of the resolution mechanism was enhanced (including by increasing the EFSF/ESM maximum loan capacity). Most recently, an agreement in principle was reached in June 2012 to make available a 100 bn euro EFSF/ESM credit line to recapitalise certain Spanish financial institutions.

At the same time several 'non-standard' measures were also taken by the monetary authorities. These measures included more ample liquidity provision in various ways, a programme to buy systemically important covered bonds, the relaxation of collateral requirements and even outright sovereign bond purchases on secondary markets that were deemed to be 'dysfunctional' in the context of the Securities Markets Programme. Most recently, in December 2011 and February 2012, the ECB conducted two three-year refinancing operations to provide liquidity to financial institutions for a longer period with the aim of avoiding a disorderly deleveraging of banks' balance sheets.

It seems fair to say that, until relatively recently, the financial assistance schemes for euro area countries were unthinkable. Providing financial assistance to other euro area countries to avert default would also seem to be at odds with the spirit of the 'no-bail-out' provision in art. 125 of the

Treaty on the Functioning of the European Union. Therefore, it is crucially important and well understood that such measures should remain exceptional and serve only to provide the necessary breathing space to carry out fiscal and macroeconomic adjustments that have not been prompted in a more gradual manner by market forces. The conditionality of these financial assistance schemes is key: the economic adjustment targeted in the programmes should reduce imbalances, raise potential growth and restore the capacity of debtor countries to repay loans. The implementation of these adjustment programmes is to be monitored closely and programmes should be modified if initial choices do not lead to the desired outcome.

The logic behind the non-standard monetary policy measures is very different. While some of them may also reduce the financial pressure on heavily indebted governments – either directly in the case of the Securities Market Programme or indirectly through so-called carry-trade with financial institutions using ample liquidity in part to buy government bonds –, this is not their purpose. All these measures are generally aimed at removing impediments to the effective transmission of monetary policy and, hence, supporting bank funding and maintaining the regular flow of bank credit to the private sector. Clearly, there is a degree of judgement involved in the assessment of the effectiveness of monetary transmission and, in particular, the 'dysfunctional' nature of certain sovereign bond markets. Such judgment inevitably comes with risks (Trichet, 2010). Regular evaluation of the impact of these measures is therefore necessary. The Eurosystem should, in particular, be mindful of the risk that economic agents may come to depend on these exceptional measures.

3.2 The new regulatory framework

Apart from the crisis resolution measures, EU policy-makers have taken significant steps to strengthen the governance framework. Since March 2010, when a specific taskforce chaired by the President of the European Council, Herman Van Rompuy, was commissioned to present proposals to strengthen EU fiscal rules and economic governance, a broad range of new rules and surveillance instruments has been agreed upon or is in the

Table 1: Overview of the new EU governance framework

	SIX PACK	TSCG[1]	TWO PACK
What?	5 EU Regulations and 1 EU Directive	International treaty	2 EU Regulations
Who?	EU-27 (with some distinction made between euro area and other countries)	EU-25 (excl. UK and CZ)	euro area countries
Starting date	13 December 2011	upon ratification by at least 12 euro area countries	target date: summer 2012 (after the 'trialogue')
Contents	- broader and enhanced fiscal policy surveillance (incl. operational debt criterion and expenditure rule) - wider macroeconomic surveillance (incl. corrective procedures) - new decision-making procedures - minimum requirements for national budget frameworks	- limits on structural deficits, preferably laid down in the constitution - obligation for euro area countries to accept EDP recommendations from the EC in principle[2] - role for the European Court of Justice - greater macroeconomic coordination	- further-reaching fiscal policy surveillance and coordination in the euro area - independent national institutions oversee compliance with fiscal rules - precise schedule for annual budgets and prior examination by the EC - stronger surveillance regime for countries with 'financial problems' (automatic upon receipt of the assistance)

[1] Treaty on Stability, Coordination and Governance in the EU. The fiscal matters covered in this Treaty are often referred to as the 'Fiscal Compact'.

[2] The euro area countries commit themselves to always accepting an EC recommendation as regards the existence of an excessive deficit unless there is a qualified majority against this recommendation (reverse qualified majority rule).

process of being introduced. The new rules regarding fiscal and macroeconomic surveillance that are included in the five EU Regulations that, together with the Directive on the requirements for budgetary frameworks of the Member States, are commonly known as the 'Six Pack', entered into force as early as in December 2011. In March 2012, 25 EU Member States signed the Treaty on Stability, Coordination and Governance in the EU which includes the so-called 'fiscal compact' that further enhances fiscal governance. Finally, two additional EU Regulations, the so-called Two Pack, that were proposed by the European Commission in November 2011 and would further strengthen fiscal policy surveillance for euro area countries were still under discussion at the time of writing. Rather then describing all these new rules in detail, we review the main trends in the new regulatory framework in this section.

First, the 'soft' coordination approach for macroeconomic policies is clearly abandoned and the EU regulatory framework is broadened to macroeconomic developments. As for the fiscal rules, the macroeconomic surveillance framework includes both preventive and corrective procedures. The former are anchored to a scoreboard of a broad range of ten economic indicators (such as the current account balance, unit labour costs, the international net asset position and private-sector credit growth), an alert mechanism based upon threshold values[11] for each indicator that may point to internal or external imbalances, as well as expert judgement in the form of reports and in-depth reviews by the European Commission. The corrective Excessive Imbalance Procedure is activated when an excessive imbalance is deemed to exist. It requires the Member State concerned to design and implement a corrective action plan and, in the case of non-compliance by euro area countries, includes financial sanctions that range from an interest-bearing deposit to a fine of 0.1% of GDP.

Second, the fiscal rules are extended. As regards the preventive procedures of the Stability and Growth Pact, the assessment of the progress towards

---

11. For certain indicators symmetric threshold values are defined, implying that, in principle, very high or very low levels could require corrective action. However, it should be stressed that the nature of this assessment is rather limited and e.g. the European Parliament advocated a more symmetric approach.

the medium-term objective will now also be based upon compliance with a new expenditure rule that is anchored to prudent estimates of trend economic growth. With respect to the corrective procedures, the debt rule of the Excessive Deficit Procedure is made more operational by defining a benchmark annual reduction, for debt ratios exceeding 60%, of $1/20^{th}$ of the difference from this reference value.

Third, more attention is paid to the national 'ownership' of EU fiscal rules and procedures. The latter should be fully reflected in the national legislative framework. To this end, minimum standards are defined, in the aforementioned Directive but also in the fiscal compact and the Two Pack, for several key aspects of national budget frameworks. These range from numerical fiscal rules (including a restriction on the structural deficit that, in accordance with the fiscal compact, should preferably be included in the Constitution) to medium-term budget planning and unbiased macroeconomic and budgetary projections, as well as independent fiscal councils, as referred to in the Two Pack.

Fourth, a number of procedural changes aim at a more effective enforcement of the rules. Via a new reverse qualified majority voting procedure, for instance, it would become more difficult for the Council to reject European Commission proposals to impose financial sanctions in the framework of both the Excessive Deficit and the Excessive Imbalance Procedure. In addition, a sanction is now also in place for non-compliance with the preventive rules of the Stability and Growth Pact. However, these procedural changes do not amount to far greater automaticity but modify the balance between the Council and the European Commission with respect to decision-making responsibilities.

Finally, several measures aim at improving the reliability and usefulness of government finance statistics. In this connection, Eurostat's powers to verify the quality of statistical data were extended considerably in July 2010, and now include the ability to conduct actual audit missions to Member States. Moreover, the Six Pack makes it possible for the Council, acting on a recommendation by the European Commission, to impose a fine of up to 0.2% of GDP when a Member State misrepresents deficit and debt data, either intentionally or by serious negligence.

CONCLUSION

The sovereign debt crisis has shaken the foundations of the Economic and Monetary Union in Europe and continues to threaten its stability. Looking back on the first decade of the euro area, as we do in this article, one inevitably comes to the conclusion that, while it was triggered by the preceding financial crisis and the Great Recession, it is deeply rooted in governance failures. Sound fiscal rules to reduce budgetary imbalances that existed at the start of the euro area were not adequately enforced, and neither the soft EU coordination approach nor market forces fostered the required macroeconomic convergence.

Unlike the 2005 reform of the Stability and Growth Pact, the recent and continuing modifications to the EU governance framework clearly constitute a step in the right direction. However, these reforms generally amount to an extension of the rules-based framework, rather than greater automaticity in the implementation of these rules or stronger institutional integration, even though certain elements in the two-pack[12], in particular, can be interpreted as embryonic features of the latter model. This approach has certain drawbacks. Greater complexity of the rules may make them more difficult to implement. More importantly, in the absence of more automatic procedures, effective enforcement remains vulnerable to political pressures.

Time will tell whether the early years of the euro have truly been formative and the character of the monetary union has been strengthened by hardship. In our view, four issues will be key to more effective governance. First, community institutions should apply the new rules in a rigorous manner and treat all countries equally. Second, any governance framework needs reliable real-time indicators to be effective. Determined efforts should be made to verify the quality of statistical data and close statistical surveillance should extend to implicit liabilities

---

12. At the time of writing the two draft Regulations included, for instance, an ex ante assessment of euro area countries' annual budgets by the European Commission, as well as the provision that this institution shall provide 'technical assistance' to euro area countries which experience serious difficulties with respect to their financial stability and fail to implement a macroeconomic adjustment programme correctly.

of governments and quasi-fiscal activities. In addition, more analytical work is needed to improve the assessment of structural budget balances. Third, responsible fiscal policies should be viewed as a matter of common interest. In this connection, countries should converge to their MTOs and carefully assess whether they truly correspond to sound budgetary positions, in particular in an environment where ageing-related spending increases slowly start to materialise. Finally, it is clear that imbalances outside the purely fiscal sphere may be equally damaging to the smooth functioning of monetary union. The euro will not be out of the woods as long as systemic risks coming from the financial sector are not contained and macroeconomic trends continue to diverge strongly. As regards the first issue, a well-functioning EMU clearly implies stronger banking supervision and resolution mechanisms at the European level. With respect to the latter issue, deeper structural reforms, addressing weaknesses in the labour and product markets and competitiveness problems, are still required in most euro area countries. More generally, fiscal consolidation needs to be supported by a clear and comprehensive growth agenda: in this connection the objective of enhancing potential growth should, for instance, also be reflected in the specific composition of government budgets.

Finally, one may recall the initial intention when the euro was introduced: greater monetary integration should at some point be followed by greater political integration in order to strengthen the foundations of the common currency and guarantee its stability. The common European destiny of all members is best reflected by further integration based on both the individual responsibility of participating countries and solidarity between them.

LIST OF REFERENCES

1. Jef Boeckx, and Hans Dewachter, "Contagion in Euro Area Sovereign Bond Markets", Bank- en Financiewezen, No. 4 (2012).
2. António J. Cabral, "Main Aspects of the Working of the SGP" in *The Stability and Growth Pact – The Architecture of Fiscal Policy in EMU*, edited by Anne Brunila, Marco Buti and Daniele Franco (2001).
3. William Clarke, "The pact's last stand", Central Banking, Volume XV, No. 4 (May 2005).
4. Paul De Grauwe and Francesco Paulo Mongelli, "Endogeneities of Optimum Currency Areas: what brings countries sharing a single currency closer together?", ECB Working Paper, No. 468 (April 2005).
5. Carlo A. Favero and Alessandro Missale, "Sovereign spreads in the euro area: which prospects for a Eurobond?", Economic Policy, No. 70 (April 2012).
6. Britta Hamburg, Sandro Momigliano, Bernhard Manzke and Stefano Siviero, "The reaction of fiscal policy to the crisis in Italy and Germany: are they really polar cases in the European context?" in *Fiscal Policy: Lessons from the Crisis* (papers presented at the Banca d'Italia workshop held in Perugia, 25-27 March 2010).
7. Fabienne Ilzkovitz, Adriaan Dierx, Viktoria Kovacs and Nuno Sousa, "Steps towards a deeper economic integration: the Internal Market in the 21st century – A contribution to the Single Market Review", European Economy, Economic Papers, European Commission (January 2007).
8. Demosthenes Ioannou, Marien Ferdinandusse, Marco Lo Duca and Wouter Coussens, "Benchmarking the Lisbon Strategy", ECB Occasional Paper, No. 85 (June 2008).
9. Geert Langenus, "The Stability and Growth Pact: an eventful history", Economic Review (National Bank of Belgium, June 2005).
10. Richard Morris, Francisco de Castro Fernández, Steven Jonk, Jana Kremer, Suzanne Linehan, Maria Rosaria Marino, Christophe Schalck and Olegs Tkacevs: "Explaining government revenue windfalls and shortfalls: an analysis for selected EU countries", ECB Working Paper, No. 1114 (November 2009).
11. Richard Morris and Ludger Schuknecht, "Structural balances and revenue windfalls: the role of asset prices revisited", ECB Working Paper, No. 737 (March 2007).
12. Fernanda Nechio, "Monetary policy when one size does not fit all", Economic Letter, Federal Reserve Bank of San Francisco (June 2011).
13. National Bank of Belgium, Report 2008 (2009).
14. Jean-Claude Trichet, "Reflections on the nature of monetary policy non-standard measures and finance theory", opening address at the ECB Central Banking Conference, Frankfurt (18 November 2010).

2. Overview

MAIN DEVELOPMENTS IN PUBLIC FINANCE

Maud Nautet and Luc Van Meensel [1]

INTRODUCTION

The purpose of this chapter is to give a brief overview of the main developments in Belgian public finances during the 2000-2010 period. It does not aim to provide detailed explanations on the subject, but to establish a general context. It is based on the statistics presented in the annex, up to date at the end of June 2012. The other chapters in this publication will go into more detail on the key facts concerning public finances during the period analysed.

The first section focuses on the budget balance and the public debt. The second describes the main changes concerning public revenues. Next come some comments on primary expenditure. The fourth section offers a very succinct account of debt management. The last section briefly describes the developments relating to the budget balances of each sub-sector for the period analysed. Finally, a set of conclusions is drawn.

---

1. Maud Nautet is a member of the Public Finance Division of the Research Department at the National Bank of Belgium. Luc Van Meensel is Head of the Public Finance Division of the Research Department at the National Bank of Belgium.

I. GENERAL GOVERNMENT BUDGET BALANCE AND DEBT

1.1 Overall balance

In 2000, the general government budget was in balance for the first time in decades, and the primary balance exhibited a large surplus of 6.5 % of GDP. That situation suggested an extremely promising outlook for public finances in the future. The April 2000 report by the Federal Planning Bureau embodies this optimism, projecting a budget surplus that would expand in future years[2]. With no change of policy, the institute then estimated the surplus at 2.4 % of GDP for 2005. In this context, the federal government of the day made plans to reduce the tax burden on labour, to provide for additional expenditure on some items, to refinance the Communities and to gradually build up budget surpluses. Those surpluses were to be set aside in the Ageing Fund and would cater for the expected rise in expenditure on pensions due to the population ageing which would have an impact primarily from 2010 onwards.

This balanced budget was the outcome of many years of fiscal rigour, divided into two phases. The first phase started with the 'economic recovery policy', implemented from 1982 onwards. At that time, an austerity policy had become indispensable on account of the ballooning deficit during the 1970s. In 1981, the budget deficit even reached a peak at 15.5 % of GDP according to the actual public finance statistics. During the 1990s, in the run-up to monetary union, a second consolidation phase was implemented in order to satisfy the Maastricht criteria. Due to the substantial budgetary efforts made, Belgium was among the first wave of countries to adopt the euro.

From 2000 to the outbreak of the financial and economic crisis that dominated the end of the 2000-2010 decade, the budget remained in balance

---

2. Federal Planning Bureau (2000), Economic outlook 2000-2005, April.

Chart 1: Total revenue, total expenditure and budget balance of general government (% of GDP)

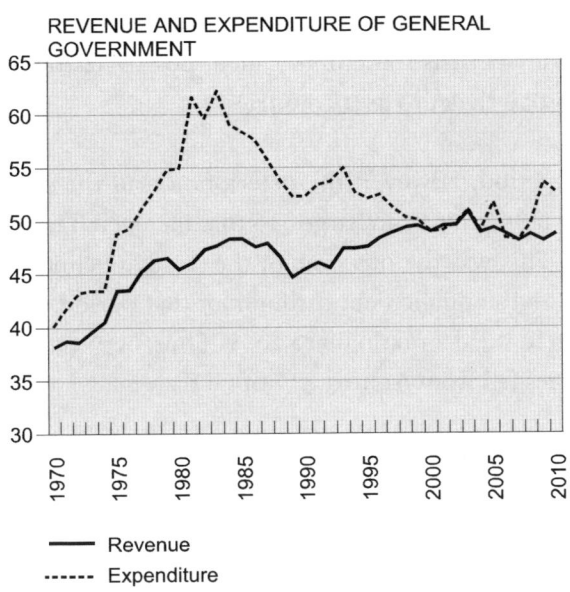

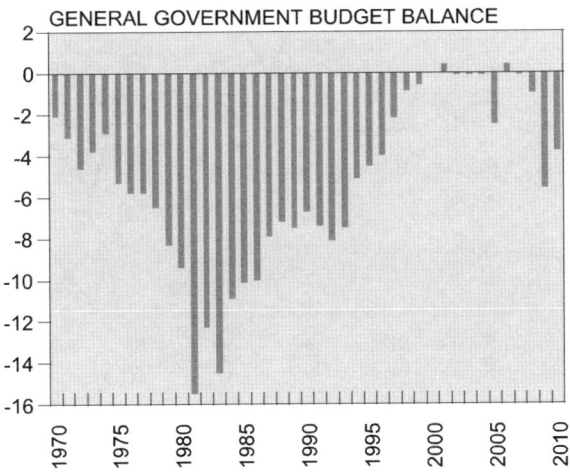

Source: NAI.

overall[3]. However, the primary balance, which had recorded a sizeable surplus in the initial years of the decade, declined steadily over the years, reflecting an easing of fiscal policy after the start of monetary union. That trend was not confined to Belgium; relaxation of budget discipline connected with what is sometimes called 'post-Maastricht fatigue' was seen in almost all the euro area countries.

During this period, however, the deterioration in the primary balance was offset by falling interest charges, so that the overall fiscal balance was maintained. This was the outcome of the steady decline in the implicit interest rate on the public debt throughout that period, combined with the reduction in the debt ratio up to 2008. Thus, between 2000 and 2010, interest charges fell from 6.6 to 3.4 % of GDP.

Chart 2: General government budget balances
(% of GDP)

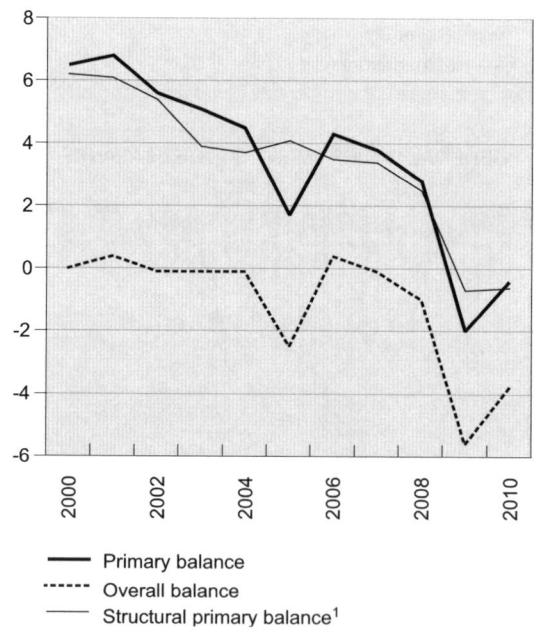

— Primary balance
----- Overall balance
— Structural primary balance[1]

Source: NAI.
1   According to the ESCB methodology.

---

3. Note that in 2005 an exceptional item caused a serious deterioration in the Belgian overall balance: the reorganisation of the SNCB group and the assumption of a large part of its debt by the Railway Infrastructure Fund led to a large transfer of capital from the general government sector to the non-financial corporations sector.

Overview

The financial crisis and subsequent severe recession in 2008-2009 seriously derailed the government accounts. While the overall budget had in practice been in balance throughout the years from 2000 to 2007, in a favourable economic context, it deteriorated sharply in the following years. In 2009, Belgian public finances recorded a deficit of 5.6 % of GDP, or almost double the threshold beyond which a country is in an excessive public deficit situation according to the current European fiscal rules. The borrowing requirement then reached a level not seen since the early 1990s. In 2010, the budgetary balance improved, but still showed a substantial deficit. Indeed, Belgium ended the decade with a deficit of 3.8 % of GDP.

The sharp deterioration in budget outcomes from 2008 onwards happened throughout the euro area. The general government budget balance in the euro area deteriorated from a deficit of 0.7 % of GDP in 2007 to deficits of respectively 6.4 and 6.2 % of GDP in 2009 and 2010.

Chart 3: Consolidated gross debt and overall balance of general government (% of GDP)

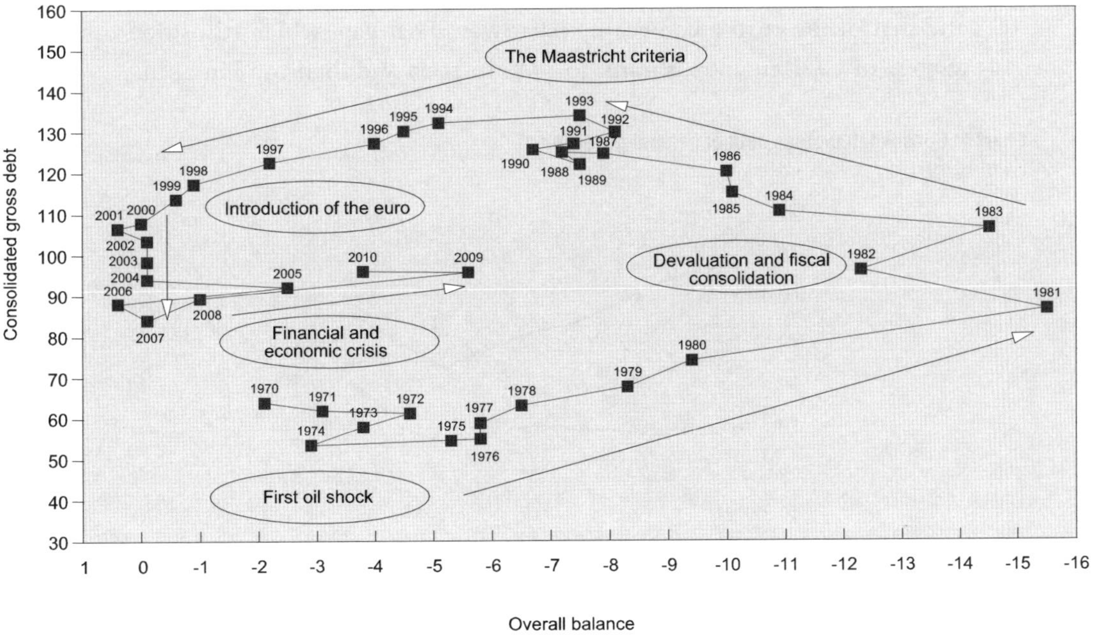

Sources: EC, NAI, NBB.

1.2 General government debt

The change in the general government debt ratio reflects to a large extent the general government budget balances. Thanks to the austerity policy initiated in 1982, the Belgian budget deficit began to recede. At first, that was not enough to halt the snowball effect on the public debt. Thus, the overall debt of general government continued to rise until 1993, when it peaked at 133.9 % of GDP. Thereafter, the debt declined steadily to reach 84 % of GDP in 2007. However, that was still a very long way from the European target debt ratio of 60 % of GDP. It was also well above the euro area average.

The reduction in the Belgian debt ratio ended with the eruption of the financial and economic crisis at the end of the decade. In 2008, the debt had risen owing to public intervention in a number of financial institutions. In 2009, when the deficit had increased and GDP had fallen, the surge was amplified. At the end of 2010, the public debt thus reached 95.9 % of GDP.

However, the expansion of Belgian debt was more moderate than the rise seen in the euro area, so that the gap between the Belgian debt ratio and that of the euro area became narrower. That gap, which still stood at 39 % of GDP in 2000, shrank to 18 % in 2007 and then 10 % in 2010.

Chart 4: Consolidated gross debt of general government
(% of GDP)

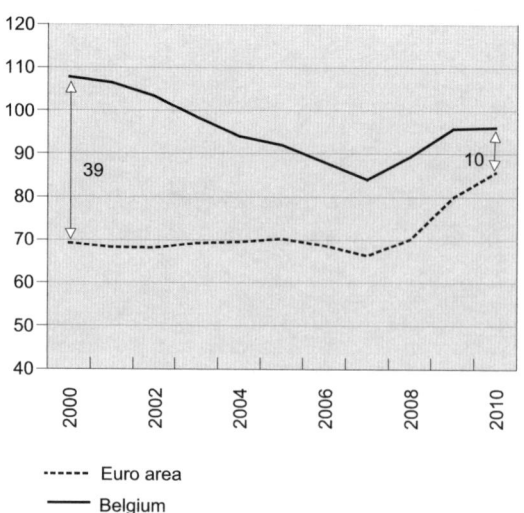

Sources: EC, NAI, NBB.

2. REVENUE

Between 2000 and 2010 there was a very slight fall in public revenues expressed as a percentage of GDP. However, this virtually stable position contrasts with the upward trend seen from the early 1970s: over the 1970-2000 period public revenues increased from 38.1 % of GDP to 49.0 %. They subsided thereafter to 48.8 % of GDP in 2010.

In the early 2000s, various measures were taken to reduce the tax burden on labour in Belgium, which is very high compared to the European average. To that end, personal income tax was reformed and social security contributions were reduced. The aim of these reforms was to boost employment, particularly for certain categories of workers such as the low paid, the young, and older workers. These measures were phased in and their effects were felt over several years. Corporate income tax was also reformed with the lowering of the statutory tax rate, the broadening of the tax base and the introduction of the risk capital allowance.

Chart 5: Total revenue and fiscal and parafiscal revenue
(% of GDP)

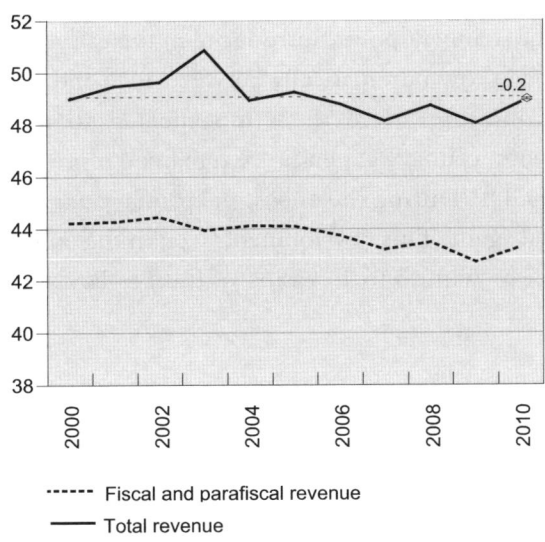

Source: NAI.

At the same time, during the 2000-2010 period, the government took measures to generate additional revenues. It raised certain consumption taxes, such as the tax on tobacco and mineral oils, and other levies on several occasions. The government also tried to step up the battle against tax evasion and improve the collection of revenue.

The government also benefited from one-off measures, as in 2003, when the federal government received a capital transfer from Belgacom on its taking over the company's pension obligations. From 2009, non-fiscal and non-parafiscal revenues were swollen by payments from financial institutions which had received State support during the crisis.

In international terms, from 2000 to 2010 Belgian public revenues as a percentage of GDP remained well above the euro area average, owing to the high ratio of taxes and parafiscal levies in Belgium, especially those on labour income.

3. PRIMARY EXPENDITURE

In 2000, primary expenditure amounted to 42.5 % of GDP. That was achieved by the stringent policy introduced in the early 1980s as primary expenditure had grown dramatically between 1970 and 1980. Draconian consolidation measures were then implemented to reduce its level. During the 1990s, primary expenditure remained more or less stable as a percentage of GDP. During the 2000s, the primary expenditure growth rate accelerated again. This development, seen in the euro area as well as in Belgium, bears witness to an easing of fiscal policy at the start of the decade.

Chart 6: Primary expenditure
(% of GDP)

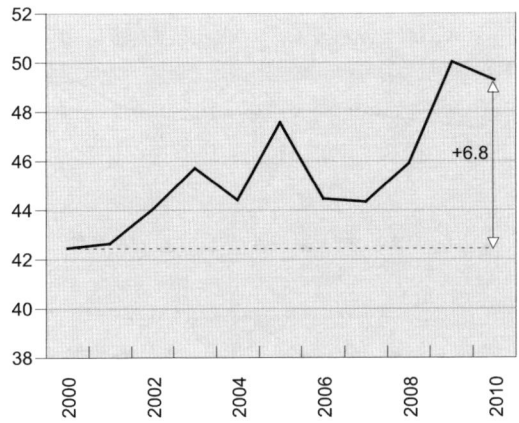

Source: NAI.

From 2008, the financial and economic crisis triggered a dramatic increase in Belgium's spending ratio. While primary expenditure as a percentage of GDP had risen fairly slowly from 2000 to 2007, it then increased sharply. Also in most other euro area countries, the financial and economic crisis led to a sharp increase in the spending ratio. The crisis drove up expenditure on unemployment benefit, while the contraction of GDP automatically increased the variables expressed as percentages of GDP.

At the end of the decade in 2010, the ratio of primary expenditure to GDP had consequently risen to 49.3 % of GDP, a good 6.8 per cent higher than in 2000. It thus reached its highest level since the early 1980s. In the decade from 2000 to 2010, virtually all expenditure categories outpaced the growth of economic activity.

Chart 7: Primary expenditure by category
(% of GDP)

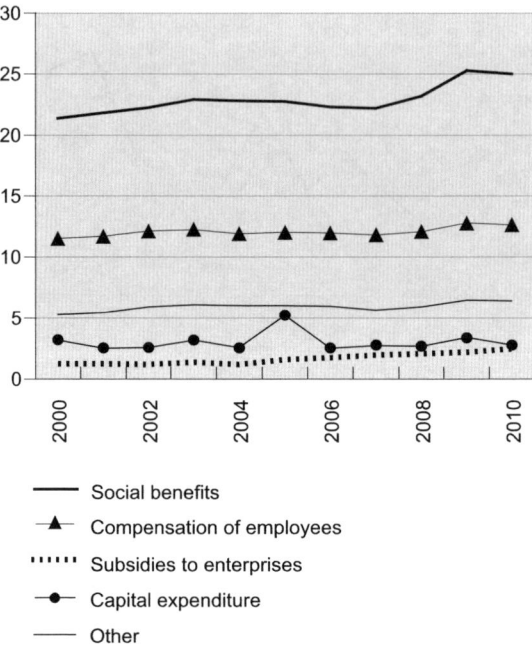

Source: NAI.

Expenditure on welfare benefits, representing around half of primary expenditure, was a key factor in the expansion of primary expenditure between 2000 and 2010. It contributed 3.7 per cent of GDP to the increase in expenditure. Health care spending recorded a very steep rise, growing by 3.6 % in real terms annually. But pensions, which felt the first impact of population ageing at the end of the decade, also increased significantly. Among the other social benefits, there was also a large increase in invalidity benefits.

The remuneration of general government sector personnel, which accounts for a quarter of primary expenditure, also made a major contribution to the growth of that expenditure. Indeed, this expenditure item increased by 1.1 per cent of GDP between 2000 and 2010. This rise is due partly to the expansion of public sector employment. During the 2000-2010 period, the number of public sector jobs increased by more than 13 %, significantly outpacing the 9 % growth in total national employment.

The last quarter of primary expenditure, consisting of intermediate consumption expenditure, capital expenditure, subsidies paid to enterprises, transfers to the rest of the world and other transfers, and miscellaneous current taxes, contributed 2 per cent of GDP to the increase in expenditure. This was to a large extent due to subsidies paid to enterprises. Their growth was due partly to the reductions in withholding tax on earned incomes – which are recorded as subsidies to enterprises in accordance with the ESA95 – and partly to the increasing success of the service voucher system introduced in 2003. The rise in other current transfers to non-profit-making institutions, the European Union and the rest of the world also contributed to the rise in primary expenditure expressed as a percentage of GDP.

The whole of the increase in the spending ratio during the 2000-2010 period originates from current spending, as capital expenditure was down slightly. In this respect, it should be noted that investment expenditure is greatly influenced by the impact of the local government election cycle: it tends to increase before elections and diminish thereafter. Hence, investment expenditure reached a relatively high level at the start of the decade, as local elections took place in 2000. However, it is quite remarkable that the expansionary fiscal policy that characterises the 2000-2010 decade did not relate to investment expenditure, although this expenditure item is considered as productive and beneficial for supporting economic growth.

4. DEBT MANAGEMENT

Since the introduction of the euro Belgian debt has become increasingly internationalised. However, there has been a slight reversal in that trend since 2008, as the crisis led foreign investors to be a little more wary of Belgian public debt.

Chart 8: Consolidated gross debt by holder
(percentages of the consolidated gross debt)

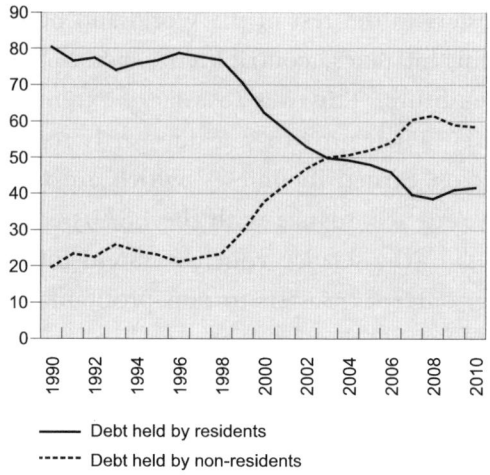

Sources: NAI, NBB.

Regarding the breakdown of the debt between short-term and long-term, there has been a decline in the proportion of short-term debt since the early 1990s. Thus, in 1990, 30 % of debt consisted of short-term debt, compared to 10 % in 2005. However, at the time of the 2008 financial crisis, the government made greater use of short-term borrowing to cater for unexpected, substantial liquidity needs. The share of short-term debt then increased to 18 % before stabilising at 15 % in 2009 and 2010.

5. BUDGET BALANCE OF THE SUBSECTORS

During the 2000-2010 period, the accounts of the general government subsectors showed a divergent picture.

The deterioration in the Belgian government budget balance at the end of the decade is attributable mainly to the federal government. The federal government deficit increased from 0.4 % of GDP in 2000 to 3 % of GDP in 2010. A principal reason is the strong growth of transfers of tax revenues from the federal government to the other subsectors during the period, increasing by 2.6 per cent of GDP between 2000 and 2010.

Chart 9: Budget balance of the general government subsectors
(% of GDP)

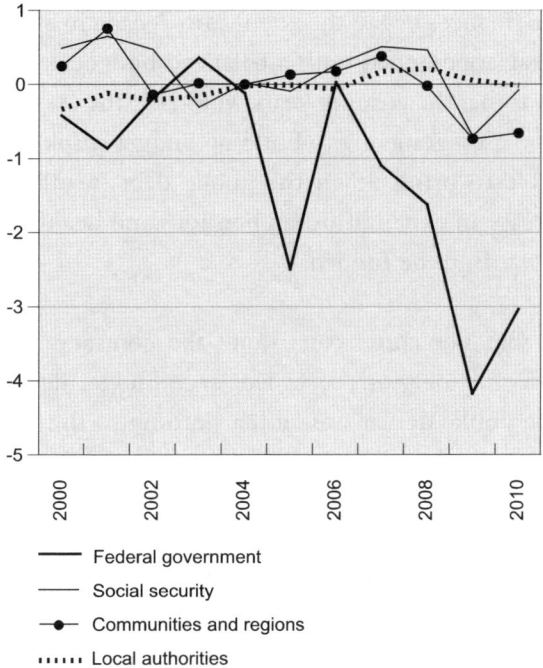

Source: NAI.

Those transfers went mainly to the social security sector, which was therefore able to maintain a balanced budget, despite the growth in expenditure on health care, pensions and other welfare benefits, and spending on the service voucher system and the activation programmes.

The Communities and Regions registered a small budget surplus in 2000, but ended the decade with a deficit of 0.7 % of GDP.

Finally, the local authority balance in the 2000-2010 period was converted from a small deficit to budget equilibrium.

CONCLUSION

Belgian public finances began the 2000-2010 decade in a very good position, as the year 2000 ended with a balanced budget. Furthermore, the expectation was that the ensuing years would see the creation of margins which could be used gradually to build up budget surpluses. This would make it possible to bring down the public debt steadily and it would allow the increase in expenditure on pensions and health care, expected from 2010 onwards, to be funded.

This scenario did not come true: quite the contrary. In the last two years of the decade Belgium recorded large budget deficits, putting it in an excessive public deficit situation according to the European rules. Moreover, the gradual decline in the debt ratio came to an abrupt halt in 2008, and the ratio increased sharply at the end of the decade.

Two factors lie behind these adverse developments. First, Belgian public finances – like those of almost all other European countries – were hard hit by the financial and economic crisis that dominated the end of the decade. Secondly, the high primary surplus recorded at the start of the decade declined steadily, and had disappeared completely by the end of the decade, as a result of an expansionary fiscal policy. In almost every year, the primary expenditure of general government grew faster than GDP. As a result, the ratio of government expenditure to GDP rose to a historically high level at the end of the decade.

The adverse position of Belgium's public finances at the end of the 2000-2010 decade of course forms the starting point for the new decade. The challenges for this new decade are therefore immense. It is again necessary to eliminate the budget deficit and safeguard the long-term sustainability of public finances, taking into account the impact of population ageing in the coming years. The attainment of these goals will require a substantial consolidation effort, as well as measures to promote the growth of economic activity.

3.
The Fiscal Stance
THE RETURN OF THE PUBLIC BUDGET DEFICIT

Reginald Savage [1]

EXECUTIVE SUMMARY

The 2000-2010 decade got off to a most auspicious start from a budgetary point of view. The Belgian public budget deficit had almost disappeared at the end of the 90s and the economic outlook was optimistic for the coming years, based on the expected dynamics of the "new economy" technological paradigm. In that context, the medium-term projections by the Federal Planning Bureau (FPB) in 1999 and 2000, under unchanged policy assumptions, forecast the gradual emergence of substantive fiscal surpluses and, as a result, significant fiscal margins for expansionary policies.

At the beginning of the decade, the fiscal policy framework was thus adopted on a dual basis: a) a policy of long-term sustainability geared towards the pre-funding of the future costs of ageing through the accumulation of budget surpluses in an 'Ageing Fund'; b) a medium-term expansionary orientation mainly targeted to support employment and reduce the tax burden, this within margins consistent with the sustainability policy.

---

1. Reginald Savage is General Advisor at the Federal Public Service (FPS) Finance (Research Department) and Professor at the UCL. He is member of the Secretariat of the High Council of Finance.

The slowdown in economic activity at the beginning of the 2000s following the collapse of the dot-com bubble and the 11/9 attacks seriously damaged the economic outlook. The cumulated loss of growth in 2001-2003, combined with the expansionary structural measures decided by the new federal government in its overoptimistic view, undermined the growing budget surplus targets. Deficits were prevented through recourse to one-shot measures (especially in 2003-2004).

During the following term of office (2004-2007), the economic recovery and the continuing reduction in interest charges were not sufficient to offset the further deterioration of the structural primary balance. It was essentially from that period onwards that the structural budgetary slippage occurred: budgetary margins for expansionary policies disappeared, as shown by the sustainability gap indicator calculated by the FPB. Still, the expansionary fiscal and budgetary stance was maintained and even reinforced at the federal level (incl. social security), with a pro-cyclical bias in a favourable macroeconomic context.

The financial crisis in 2008 spread rapidly to the real economy (with a very severe recession in 2009) and, later, turned into a European sovereign debt crisis. This, combined with a further expansionary budgetary stance, in this case anti-cyclical, resulted in the resurgence of substantial deficits. These are considered largely structural in nature, especially since the crisis led to a sharp downward revision of potential output estimates, even retroactively for 2002-2007.

Over the whole decade, the primary balance deteriorated by about 7% of GDP, of which 6% in structural terms (i.e. without the cyclical component or one-shot measures), more than offset the increase in the structural primary balance (3.5% of GDP) that was achieved in the previous decade that prepared Belgium for accession to the single currency area.

The structural deterioration of 6% of GDP corresponds roughly to the discretionary fiscal stimuli brought to the economy in the 2000s. These stimuli originated from both structural cuts in taxation and a growth rate of primary expenditure exceeding the pre-crisis estimated potential growth rate of the economy. Based on the methodology presented in Savage (2011) considering the evolution of tax revenue that would have been achieved under unchanged legislation, about three quarters of these stimuli are located on the revenue side (including fiscal expenditure imputed as wage subsidies in the national accounts).

Finally, decomposition per sub-sector of general government shows that a more than proportional part of the discretionary stimuli emanates from Entity I (the federal level inclusive social security). This can be put in perspective in view of the fact that, during the previous budgetary consolidation stage (1992-1998), the restrictive effort had been fully carried out at Entity I level. With the benefit of hindsight, one can also suggest that the 2002 structural refinancing of the Communities worsened the coming vertical fiscal imbalance between the federal and sub-federal levels, already identified by the High Council of Finance (HCF) in its July 2004 Report.

As regards the ambitions of conducting a policy of long-term sustainability through pre-funding of the future costs of ageing, the failure is obvious. Cumulative downward growth revisions are one part of the story, as are the political difficulties in downsizing accordingly the persistent expansionary fiscal stance over the whole period (and even more to reverse it in good times). So, this story is one of missed opportunities to combine short to medium-term political priorities and a vision on long-term sustainability.

Rewriting a new sustainability strategy is a challenge for the years to come, in a context of future languorous potential economic growth prospects, and with the background of the reform of Belgian fiscal federalism initiated after the 2010 elections. This strategy will also have to take into account the contingent debt, which arose in the post-2008 crisis and corresponded to the State guarantees for financial institutions and States in difficulty, that adds to the effective debt and to the implicit debt related to ageing in terms of sustainability risks.

TABLE OF CONTENTS

In this paper, we shall describe and analyse:
1. The implementation and failure of the long-term sustainability policy
2. The contextual macro background and budgetary evolutions per sub-periods
3. Belgian cyclically corrected budgetary developments in a European perspective
4. In more details, globally and per Entity, the budgetary and fiscal policy

I. IMPLEMENTATION AND FAILURE OF A POLICY OF SUSTAINABILITY [2]

The coalition that came out of the elections of 1999 produced a real innovation in the history of Belgian public finances: the implementation of a policy of sustainability that was founded on a quantified long-term vision. Previously, the conduct of the budgetary policy, notably during the episodes of budgetary consolidation of the 80's and 90's, was not based systematically on long-term projections, and therefore did not refer explicitly to the notion of sustainability.

It was only at the end of the 80's that the FPB drew up the first long-term projection for Belgium with the aim of preparing for the pension reform of 1990, and then for that of 1996. The Working Group on Ageing Populations and Sustainability was created in 1999 to produce such projections at the European level on the basis of common assumptions for all the countries. These institutions highlight the budgetary challenge that population ageing will present, of which the first effects are expected for the decade beginning in 2010. In parallel, the European budgetary surveillance framework implemented at the end of the 90's as part of the introduction of the single currency provides that the stability programmes must demonstrate a sustainable long-term budgetary trajectory.

---

2. This Section was written by Michel SAINTRAIN and Vincent FROGNEUX. They both work at the Federal Planning Bureau.

Graph 1: Normative Trajectories for Budgetary Balances – % of GDP

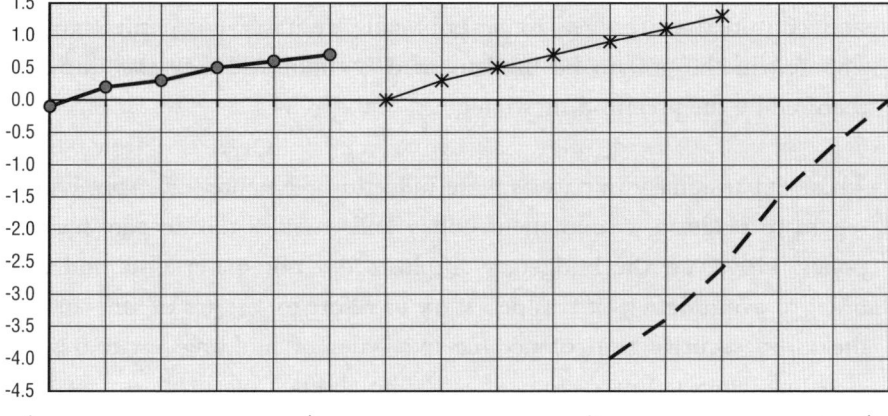

⎯⎯⎯ Stability programme 2001-2005
⎯∗⎯ Stability progamme 2006-2007 and Law on Ageing Fund
⎯ ⎯ Stability programme 2009-2013

Source: Stability Programmes and Law of 2005 on the Ageing Fund

The policy of sustainability implemented in Belgium rested on the idea of the pre-funding of the future costs of ageing by setting aside the contemporaneous budgetary margins freed up by declining interest charges. Indeed, at the beginning of the 2000s, a rapid fall in the debt ratio and in interest charges was forecast for the years to come: the budgetary consolidation of the 90's and the favourable prospects for economic growth and interest rates were to bring about a 'reverse snowball effect'. The government decided to save part of these margins so that the public finances became sufficiently solid not to be endangered by the emergence of ageing costs in the following decade. This strategy was concretised in the creation of the Ageing Fund in 2001, which was intended to receive and capitalize the budgetary surpluses necessary for the success of the pre-funding strategy (Graph 1). The relevant law provided that the Fund could contribute to the financing of pensions from the 2010s on in as much as the debt ratio is below 60% of GDP.

The budgetary and macroeconomic projections from the beginning of the 2000s indicated that not only would these budgetary surpluses arise without any adjustment effort, but that the margins for manoeuvre were such that they would, moreover, allow short- and medium-term expansionary initiatives (judged to be politically desirable given the rigour imposed in the 90s) to be implemented without affecting the surplus required by the pre-funding strategy.

These expansionary initiatives were indeed implemented, notably with regard to taxation, employment policy and, later in the decade, social policy. However, the budgetary surpluses did not materialise, and in order to avoid deficits it was necessary to resort to a series of 'one-shot' measures (securitisation of tax receipts, sales of buildings, withdrawals from pension funds, and others). The absence of surpluses can be explained by the slowdown in economic activity at the beginning of the decade and by the scale, greater than initially envisaged, of the various initiatives implemented.

At the end of 2005, the law on the Ageing Fund was revised to, i.a., stipulate the normative numerical path of the budgetary surpluses until 2012. This recourse to legislation to make the targets more binding did not lead to better adherence to them: as early as in 2007, the update of the stability programme indicated a new postponement of the surplus targets.

The financial crisis hit in 2008 and spread rapidly to the real economy. This led to a deepening of deficits, as much due to the effect of the automatic stabilisers as to the countercyclical policy that was implemented. The European Commission proposed to the Member States that they agree on a set of coordinated measures, targeted to maximise the stabilisation effects of the limited resources. These measures were to be temporary in order to avoid the structural deterioration of budgets. Nevertheless, in Belgium a large part of the recovery plan was to consist of labour-cost reduction measures (in the form of exemptions from the retained tax on wages) that are difficult to reverse.

The resurgence of strong deficits interrupted the fall in the debt ratio and re-started a 'snowball effect'. Furthermore, it is through borrowing that public funds were raised for the recapitalisation and acquisitions of Belgian financial institutions shaken by the crisis, and for the financing

The Fiscal Stance   71

of EU Member States in difficulty. Finally, the State has been brought in as guarantor of certain debts of financial institutions and of borrowing by the European Financial Stability Facility, to increase its guarantee of private deposits and to extend it to life insurance policies. The contingent debt that corresponds to these guarantees has come to be added, in terms of sustainability risk, to the effective debt and to the implicit debt related to ageing.

Graph 2: Budgetary Balances in Structural Terms for the Period 2000-2008 – % of GDP

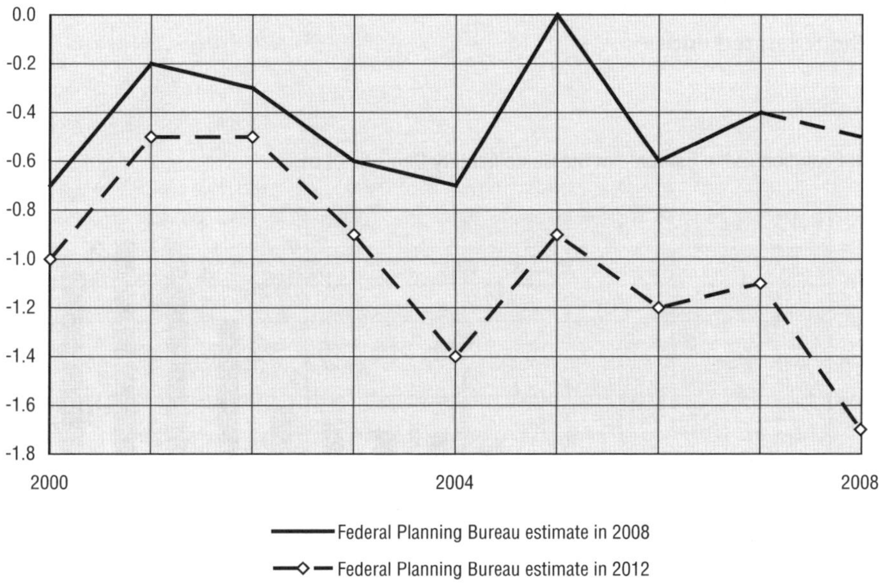

———— Federal Planning Bureau estimate in 2008
—◇— Federal Planning Bureau estimate in 2012

Source: Federal Planning Bureau (FPB) calculations

The impact of the crisis on the capital stock and on structural unemployment has led economists to revise down their view of the economy's growth potential, not only for the post-crisis decade but also for the pre-crisis decade. This revision has negatively affected the outlook for the evolution of the budgetary balance, as well as the assessment of the structural position of the budgetary balances of the recent past. While before the crisis the budgetary balances for the 2000-2008 period expressed in structural terms (i.e. without the cyclical component or one-shot measures) appeared to be slightly negative and relatively stable, they are now seen as more clearly in deficit and as having a deteriorating trend (Graph 2).

The period of crisis beginning in 2008 was therefore the final nail in the coffin of the policy of sustainability put in place at the beginning of the 2000s. While it was founded on the idea that budgetary surpluses were going to be achieved without effort, structural readjustment efforts of several per cent of GDP are now necessary to re-balance the general government budget. While the fruits of debt reduction at the federal level should have pre-funded the cost of ageing, this federal level is now in a position such that the HCF (according to its report of September 2009) no longer believes it can rebalance its budget in the medium term, unless (according to its report of March 2012) there is a transfer of some costs to the federated entities.

Graph 3: Evolution of the Estimate of the Sustainability Gap – % of GDP

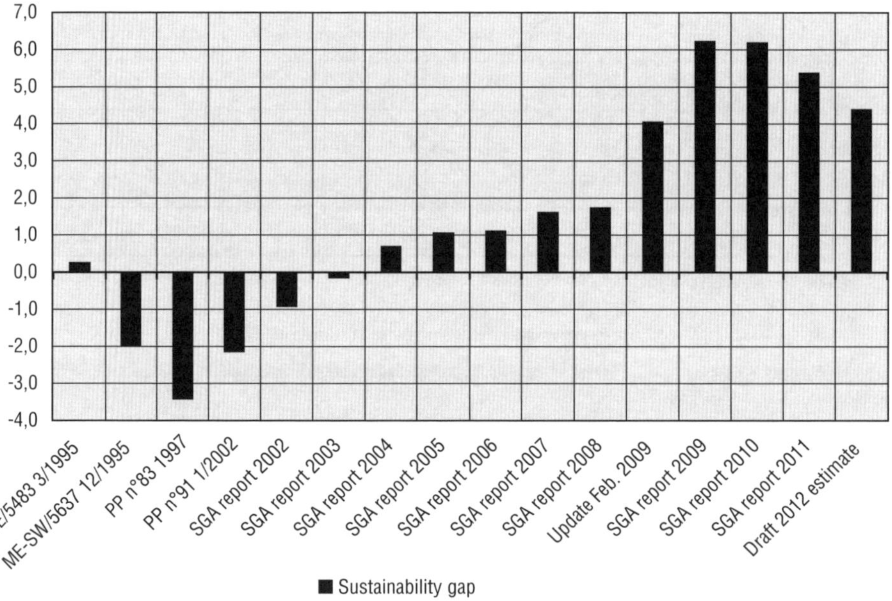

Source: FPB calculations (SGA: Study Group on Ageing)

The transformation of the financial and economic crisis into a crisis of sovereign debts puts the policy of sustainability squarely back to the fore of concerns, to the detriment of the policy of stabilisation. In 2010 and 2011, the European budgetary surveillance framework was significantly strengthened in order, in particular, to assure the credibility of the budgetary consolidation plans of States in excessive deficit. In Belgium, budgetary policy adopted a restrictive bias as from 2010. The federal government that finally came out of the 2010 elections strongly reinforced this restrictive stance for 2012 despite the languor in economic activity. As an effortless full pre-funding of the costs of ageing is no longer possible, the government has put into place structural reforms that aim to reduce the costs of ageing and increase the potential of the economy.

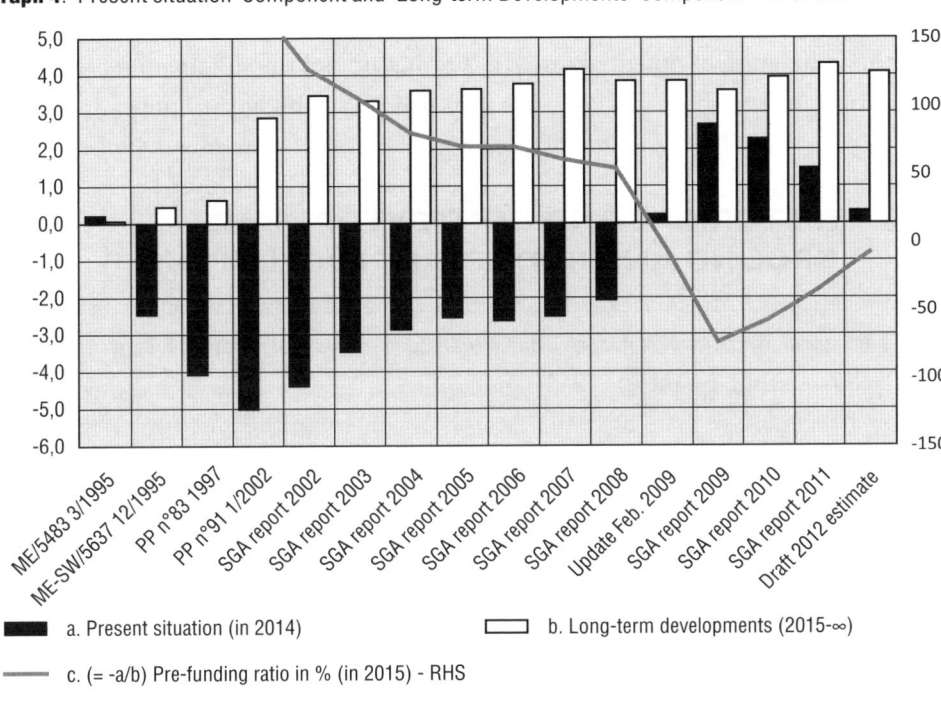

Graph 4: 'Present situation' Component and 'Long-term Developments' Component – % of GDP

a. Present situation (in 2014)
b. Long-term developments (2015-∞)
c. (= -a/b) Pre-funding ratio in % (in 2015) - RHS

Source: FPB calculations (SGA: Study Group on Ageing)

Graph 3 shows how the assessment of sustainability in the different vintages of projections carried out by the FPB has evolved from the end of the 90s to today. It is measured by the gap between the primary structural surplus assuming constant policy, and the primary surplus required by the inter-temporal budget constraint. This sustainability gap can be broken down into two parts (Graph 4): the contribution of the 'current situation' with respect to debt and the primary balance, and the contribution of the 'long-term developments' (implicit debt charge linked to ageing). The risks implied by the contingent debt are not taken into account in this approach.

At the end of the 90s, the sustainability gap was negative, reflecting the margins for manoeuvre. The 2002 projections revised the ageing cost strongly upwards (hence the 'long-term developments' component of the sustainability gap). Thereafter, this 'long-term development' component remained fairly stable. In contrast, the 'present situation' worsened in the successive projections made from 2002 to 2009 because of, first, the progressive inclusion of expansionary budgetary measures and, later, the weakening of potential growth. From 2010 on, the sustainability gap shrinks due to the restrictive turn imposed on the budgetary policy.

2. HISTORICAL AND CONTEXTUAL BACKGROUND AND BUDGETARY EVOLUTIONS [3]

The past decade has been characterised by several major factors for Belgian public finances:

1. two severe financial crises, among which the second was systemic by nature, and turned into an exceptionally deep recession (2009) and subsequently into a European sovereign debt crisis

2. an important intermediary State reform at the beginning of the decade (2001-2002) that led to the significant internal redistribution of budget margins and constraints between the levels of government

3. various convergent policies aiming at reducing compulsory contributions (reform of personal income tax, decrease in the employer's social security contributions, introduction of the 'notional interest' system at the corporate level, etc.)

---

3. This Section, like the next ones, was written by Reginald. SAVAGE.

The Fiscal Stance

2.1 Introduction

Belgium ended the 90s in a structurally much sounder budgetary position and with the near-disappearance of the budget deficit ([4]). This guaranteed Belgium its access to full Euro participation and made it possible to look to the future with much greater optimism than before.

For the chronological analysis, a distinction will be made in this Section between three sub-periods, among which the first two correspond to complete federal terms of office:
1. 1999-2003 (4 years)
2. 2003-2007 (4 years)
3. 2007-2010 (3 years)

Table 1: Macro-budgetary Context and Indicators

MACROECONOMIC CONTEXT AND PARAMETERS YEARLY AVERAGES (EXCEPT (3) OUTPUT-GAP)		1999-03 A	2003-07 B	2007-10 C	1999-10 D	1989-99 E	DIFFERENCE F = D - E
Real GDP growth	(1)	1.6%	2.6%	0.1%	1.6%	2.2%	-0.6%
Trend Growth	(2)	2.1%	1.7%	1.5%	1.8%	2.3%	-0.5%
Output-Gap (Cumulat. Evolut.)	(3)	-1.7%	3.6%	-4.1%	-2.1%	-0.9%	-1.3%
Real growth Gap	(4)=(1-2)	-0.4%	0.9%	-1.4%	-0.2%	-0.1%	-0.1%
GDP deflator (pY)	(5)	2.0%	2.3%	1.6%	2.0%	2.0%	0.0%
Weighted PE deflator	(6)	2.0%	1.9%	2.2%	2.0%	2.1%	-0.1%
Relative Price "Pr"	(7)=(5-6)	0.0%	-0.4%	0.6%	0.0%	0.1%	-0.1%
Joint Indicator (Gap + Pr)	(8)=(4-7)	-0.4%	1.3%	-2.0%	-0.2%	-0.2%	0.0%
Nominal GDP growth "n"	(9)	3.7%	5.0%	1.7%	3.6%	4.2%	-0.6%
Nominal implicit Interest rate "i"	(10)	5.7%	4.7%	4.1%	4.9%	7.6%	-2.7%
Corrected difference "i-n"	(11)=(10-9)	2.0%	-0.3%	2.4%	1.3%	3.3%	-2.0%
Real Interest rate (/ pY)	(12)	3.7%	2.3%	2.5%	2.9%	5.5%	-2.7%
% GDP - YEARLY AVERAGES		**1999-03**	**2003-07**	**2007-10**	**1999-10**	**1989-99**	**DIFFERENCE**
Net financing balance (NFB)	(13)	0.0%	-0.8%	-3.7%	-1.3%	-5.0%	3.7%
Interest payments (EDP)	(14)	6.0%	4.2%	3.6%	4.7%	9.4%	-4.8%
Actual primary balance (PB)	(15)=(14-13)	6.0%	3.4%	-0.1%	3.4%	4.5%	-1.1%
Required primary bal. (RPB)	(16)	2.1%	-0.3%	2.1%	1.3%	4.2%	-2.9%
Differ. = Endog. Debt-Reduct.	(17)=(16-15)	-3.9%	-3.7%	2.2%	-2.1%	-0.3%	-1.9%
Total Debt-ratio evolution	(18)=(17+19)	-3.8%	-3.6%	4.2%	-1.5%	-0.8%	-0.7%
Stock and Flow Adjustment	(19)	0.1%	0.1%	2.0%	0.6%	-0.5%	1.1%

Yearly Real Growth Rates of Corrected Primary Expenditure (PE) (°)

---

4. This explains the title of the previous vintage (Part VI) of the decennial history of Belgian public finance (1990-2000) « La fin du déficit budgétaire », ed E. de Callataÿ, De Boeck, 2002.

First, we will describe the macro-budgetary outlook as then estimated at the beginning of each of those three sub-periods; this will be done on the basis of the medium-term macroeconomic outlook of the FPB (in 1999-2000, 2003-2004 and 2007) and of the official Belgian Stability Programmes. After that, we will analyse how the actual Belgian budgetary developments can be evaluated in the light of the effective macroeconomic, financial and cyclical developments.

2.2 The 1999-2003 Period

At the turn of the last two decades (1990s and 2000s), the budgetary outlook seemed to be particularly promising. The earlier decade ended with a deficit lower than 1% of GDP, and the multi-annual outlook of the FPB, in spring 1999 as well as 2000, was characterised by expectations that, *under unchanged policy*, budgetary positions would be rapidly brought back into balance, and that substantial budget surpluses (from 1.7% to 1.9% of GDP) would follow in 2004 and even more in 2005. The central issue of the allocation of expected "budgetary margins" appeared in this context. In spring 1999, those margins were estimated by the FPB at no less than 1.7% of GDP by 2004. This analysis was confirmed the following year (Economic Outlook 2000-2005 of the FPB), with budgetary margins under unchanged policy then estimated at 2.2% of GDP by 2005.

The new federal government therefore built its policy agenda for the 2000-2003 term of office in that context of extremely favourable and promising macro-budgetary expectations. This agenda included at the same time:

1. a balanced budget target and then a limited budget surplus target (after 2002), later designed to feed a new Ageing Fund set up by the Ageing Law.

2. a programme aimed at decreasing the fiscal and para-fiscal 'tax burden' (abolition of the supplementary crisis contribution and reform of personal income tax, employer's social contributions reductions, etc.),

3. strengthening of the active policy as regards employment, the fight against poverty, mobility and investment in human capital, and

4. the structural refunding of federated entities (essentially the Communities), via notably a longer-term linking of their VAT revenue to real economic growth, that did not exist at that time. In the Stability Programme of the end of 2000 (2001-2005 period), that budgetary surplus target for the Global Government was brought down to 0.7% of GDP for 2005.

The budgetary situation at the end of the 2000-2003 term of office can be shortly assessed. In practice, 2003 ended admittedly with a very limited deficit (0.1% of GDP according to the EDP definition), but this deficit was greatly reduced and masked by favourable net one-offs and exceptional operations (exclusive reversible tax incidences) up to 1.3% of GDP. Even exclusive wage subsidies, the structural real growth (^{5}) of primary expenditure over the 1999-2003 term of office appeared to be significantly higher (2.6% a year) than the government's ex ante estimates (1.5%). It was thus 1% higher a year on average than the effective real growth in GDP (1.6%), while at the same time this last appeared to be on average much lower than initially foreseen (2.5%). So, instead of declining by 1.4% of GDP, the (adjusted) ratio of primary expenditure increased by 1.6% of GDP – an accumulated difference of 3.0% of GDP. On the contrary, the ratio of public revenue (exclusive non-fiscal one-shots) decreased to a lesser extent than expected (-0.7% of GDP instead of −1.2%) because mainly of unforeseen favourable structural developments on the revenue side, essentially in 2000-2001. And at the same time the burden of interest charges fell slightly more than expected (-1.6% of GDP instead of −1.2% of GDP as estimated). Exclusive of non-fiscal one-shots, the actual primary balance recorded a deterioration amounting to 2.4% of GDP instead of an anticipated improvement of 0.2% of GDP.

Finally, this first period turned out to be *not* very favourable on average from a macroeconomic point of view, despite the cyclical peak of 2000. Over these four years, the measured output gap recorded a cumulative

---

5. Adjusted for the one-shot operations (OS), for the local authorities' investment cycle and for the cyclical unemployment.

deterioration of up to 1.7% (more than 0.4% a year). In terms of the average annual differential of 2% between the average implicit interest rate on the debt and the nominal GDP growth, the macro-financial conditions were not particularly favourable. However, the effective average primary balance (PB) remained on a high level at no less than 6.0% of GDP and was very clearly much higher than the required debt-stabilising minimum (2.1% GDP). The difference between those two figures led to a further average endogenous decrease in the debt ratio by 3.9% of GDP a year. Operations "exclusive NBR" ([6]) played a minor role, up to 0.1% of GDP a year only.

2.3 The 2003-2007 Period

At the end of 2003, the economic outlook for the new parliamentary term ([7]) became at last rather more favourable. The expected real growth in the 2004-2007 Stability Programme of the end of 2003 amounted to 2.3% a year on average for the next four years. The official budget target however remained to keep an unchanged budgetary global balance in 2004-2005 and "to reach [a surplus of] 0.3% of GDP in 2007 with growth at the trend rate" (Stability Program, op. cit. p. 9). Despite better growth perspectives, sustainability (surpluses) objectives were thus significantly revised downwards by the new federal government compared to the recommendations of the HCF (July 2003 Report) in favour of a surplus target of 0.7% of GDP for the year 2007.

In this second period (2003-2007), the macroeconomic conditions turned out to be much more favourable than in the first period. Starting from a cyclical low point in 2003, this period was characterised by three years of sustained and above-trend GDP growth out of four (2005 was the exception) and a high annual average of 2.6%, above an expected average real GDP growth of 2.3%. The output gap, as measured ex post, therefore recorded a strong improvement (+3.6% of GDP over four cumulative years), with, as a consequence, high cyclical budgetary gains. On top of this, there were also favourable developments as regards relative prices

---

6. Such as shareholdings or other credit granting, net of sales of financial assets (privatisation proceeds, etc.).
7. See Belgian Stability Programme (2004-2007) of November 2003, Table 1, p. 5.

(an annual decline of 0.4%) resulting in an increase in the total positive non-discretionary budgetary incidences (up to +0.7% of GDP a year in average ([8])). Despite that very promising effective cyclical and macro-financial context, the average actual primary surplus on the other hand *decreased* very significantly (by 2.6% of GDP on average or almost 45% in relative terms). But on the other hand, thanks to the favourable evolutions of the "i-n" differential or interest-growth dynamics (see Table 1) and the subsequent reduction in the *required* primary balance, the endogenous debt reduction could remain sustained and almost unchanged in % of GDP in comparison to the previous (first) period.

As far as realisations are concerned, it can be claimed however that the fixed budgetary targets were not really reached in a structural or sustainable way. In spite of stronger than expected economic growth, 2007 at its cyclical peak ended finally with a deficit of 0.3% of GDP instead of the expected 0.3% surplus, already downgraded with respect to previous official or recommended targets. The *structural* budgetary primary slippage observed during the 2004-2007 term of office in comparison to the targets can be estimated at at least 1.0% of GDP.

2.4 The 2007-2010 Period

2008 marked the start of a period characterised by internal political instability and a major international financial crisis; this completely reversed forecasters' expectations. In Belgium's Stability Programme (2008-2011) of 2008, the government reaffirmed its commitment, as laid down in the government agreement of March 2008, to "achieving structural surplusses for the whole public administration from 2009 onwards. Those [surpluses] should reach at least 1% of GDP by the end of the current legislature, i.e. in 2011", so that "fiscal policy will be back on the original path set out in the amended law on the Ageing Fund". The macroeconomic scenario was still based on an expected average real growth of almost 2% in 2008-2010 (3 years). In this context, the budget target fixed for 2010 aimed at reaching a significant surplus amounting to 0.7% of GDP.

---

8. Taking into consideration the total cyclical incidences (output gap) and 'relative prices' effects. See Section IV for more details.

At the same time, real growth collapsed (to hardly 0.1% on average) as a consequence of violent shocks resulting from the financial crisis of 2008-2010, the poor growth performance in 2008, the major recession in 2009 and the rather mild recovery of 2010. Meanwhile, the actual budgetary shortfall for 2010 in comparison with the initial target was colossal and amounted to no less than 4.8% of GDP. Admittedly, the cumulative three-year effective growth loss for the whole 2008-2010 period in comparison to the 'initial expectations (2008)' amounted to no less than 5.9%, which implied a huge negative cyclical impact (budgetary loss) estimated at 3.2% of GDP. On that basis, there still remained a 'structural' deterioration estimated at 1.5-1.6% of GDP, which was more important than the impact of the one-off measures and of the reversible budget stimulus of 0.5% of GDP, such as recommended by the European institutions in order to dam the sharp recession of 2009.

Finally, despite a further significant decrease in the implicit interest rate on the debt, falling to a low of 4.1% on average, there was a complete negative reversal of the conditions relating to the (reverse) 'snowball effect'. The 'i-n' differential again became clearly positive (unfavourable); this led to a rise in the required primary surplus just when the (average) actual primary balance became negative again for the first time in a long period (from the mid-1980s). The « endogenous » debt ratio increased again strongly (+7.5% of GDP in hardly 3 years), while there were, on top of this, expensive financial operations (exclusive NBR), costing 6% of GDP, and relating to the rescue and recapitalisation of the financial sector. In total, the debt ratio (Maastricht definition) increased by 13.5% of GDP in 3 years; this neutralised the major part of the decrease recorded in 2003-2007.

3. BELGIAN CYCLICALLY CORRECTED BUDGET DEVELOPMENTS IN COMPARISON TO THOSE IN THE EURO AREA (EA)

The next graph tries to compare developments recorded in 1989-2010 as regards cyclically adjusted primary balances ([9]). Those are based on the common and standardized European methodology (AMECO database).

Graph 5: Cyclically Adjusted Primary Balances Compared, Based on Potential GDP

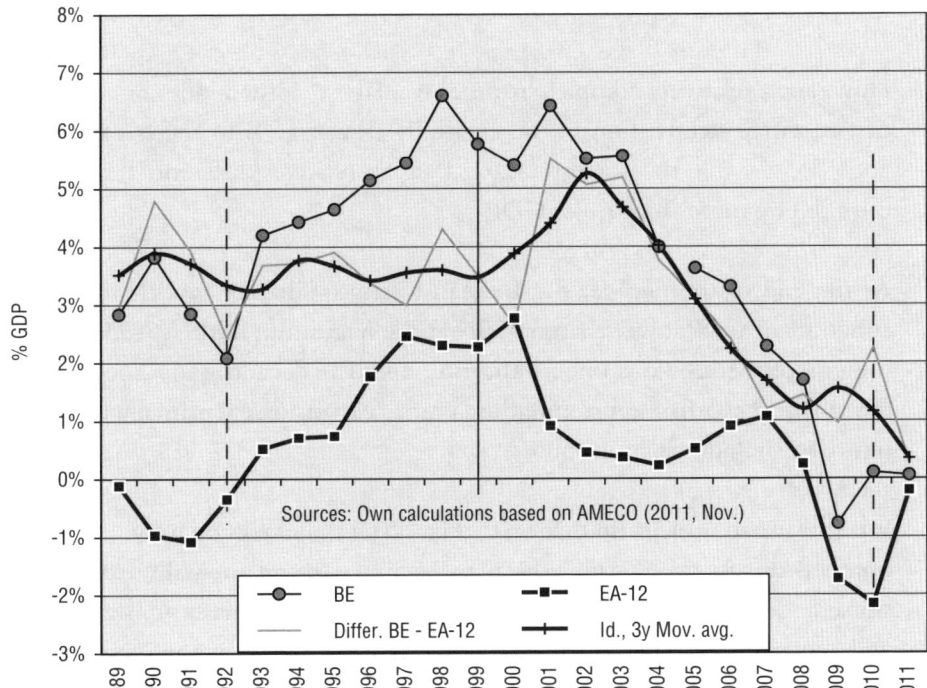

Until the turn of both the last decades, the budgetary *trend developments* in Belgium had not fundamentally differed from those in the Euro area (EA). Conversely, at the beginning of the following decade (2001-2003), an identifiable difference appeared, especially in 2001, with a marked deterioration in the EA-12 ([10]) balance, with no comparable developments in Belgium.

---

9. But not adjusted for one-shot incidences, except for the exceptional assumption of the SNCB/NMBS debt in Belgium in 2005.
10. Including Belgium

However, the figures for 2003 (and therefore also for the centred moving averages from 2001-2003 to 2003-2005) were certainly partially skewed by the exceptional increased favourable one-shot operations in Belgium in 2003 ([11]).

In total, over the period 1999-2001 or 1999-2002, the difference with respect to the evolution of the cyclically adjusted balance between Belgium and the average in the EA-12 was close to and even exceeded 2% of GDP. In macroeconomic terms, budgetary or fiscal policy was in that period seemingly less expansionary in Belgium than in the EA.

However, a relatively complete reversal was later recorded: one can identify a relative stabilisation of the cyclically adjusted PB in the EA until 2006-2007, while the corresponding Belgian relative (differential) indicator fell by more than 4% of GDP.

At the end of the decade, the Belgian relative indicator was therefore about 2% of GDP lower than initially at the beginning of the decade (or the end of the previous one), indicating over the decade (1999-2000) as a whole and as a first approximation a more expansionary primary fiscal stance in Belgium than in the EA.

It is striking to notice also that on that basis the Belgian budgetary developments during the decade appear to have been fundamentally expansionary – and thus pro-cyclical – during the cyclical upturns (1999-2000, 2004-2007), while the global stance in the EA-12 was on the contrary rather slightly anti-cyclical (restrictive in the context of a cyclical recovery). As a result, Belgian developments were actually rather atypical in the European context.

At the end of the period, that is to say in 2008-2009, Belgian developments converged again towards the average in the EA (very expansionary policy in 2009) and then recorded a further deviation during the next two years (less restrictive in the cyclical recovery of 2010-2011).

---

11. Especially the integration of the Belgacom Pension Fund in (capital) non-fiscal revenue and conversely one-shot expenditure (pre-financing) in favour of the SNCB/NMBS, up to a total net amount of 4 billion euro or 1.4% of GDP.

Unfortunately, the indicator used here remains quite rough and is based on a simplified standardised and common methodology. This methodology certainly facilitates an easy international comparison but takes into account neither numerous national particularities nor the consequences of specific non-discretionary and non-cyclical (endogenous) incidences also having an impact on actual budgetary outcomes.

The next section is based on an alternative indicator of the structural (primary) balance for Belgium to that of the European Commission. In addition to a traditional adjustment for cyclical incidences ([12]), several other adjustments have been applied to prevent non-discretionary but non-cyclical (endogenous) structural incidences from being erroneously misinterpreted as corresponding to *discretionary and voluntary fiscal and budgetary policy impulses*.

4. DETAILED ANALYSIS OF THE NON-DISCRETIONARY INCIDENCES AND THE DISCRETIONARY STIMULI

4.1 Methodological Introduction

As has already been mentioned ([13]), the cyclically adjusted budget balance as measured by the European Commission is often implicitly interpreted as a precise and reliable indicator of the *discretionary* budgetary or fiscal stance. This is a conceptual shortcut, and potentially empirically flawed, especially in a short term perspective. The traditional cyclically adjusted budget indicators do *not* indeed integrate a certain number of other endogenous adjustments for non-cyclical and non-discretionary incidences, which are either one-off ([14]) or, on the contrary, very broadly not automatically reversible and, as a result, of a structural nature. Among these last there are notably a) the so-called 'relative prices' effects (see

---

12. Based on trend growth and not on potential growth.
13. R. SAVAGE (2012, 2), « Soldes structurels primaires et impulsions discrétionnaires de politique budgétaire et fiscale en Belgique en 1990-2010 : une analyse quantitative au niveau global et par grandes Entités », BDMF, to be published end 2012.
14. Still called 'one-shot' measures

above) as regards primary expenditure (PE), b) 'structural' or 'composition' effects as regards public revenue ([15, 16]), c) other structural incidences — for instance socio-demographic — as regards PE, d) the local authorities' (politico-electoral) investment cycle, etc. Only the quantified integration of those other non-discretionary incidences can make it possible to assess and quantify the actual broad budgetary or fiscal discretionary *stance* — restrictive or on the contrary expansionary — correctly, and, more particularly, to make a specific and measurable distinction between the respective revenue and primary expenditure components of that discretionary effort or orientation.

For illustrative purposes, the next Graph (6) compares the two indicators for Belgium (one from AMECO and one resulting from research at the RDD of the Belgian FPS Finance), with some comments.

- in the short and medium term, significant differences appear between the two indicators, notably in 1992-97, 1997-2001 (2001), then in 2003-2009 (especially 2003-2004 and 2009);
- on the contrary, in the longer term — and notably over both successive decades — those differences almost neutralise each other and the two indicators converge;
- over the 1999-2010 period, the two indicators result in a convergent strong structural deterioration (5.7% of GDP according to AMECO and 5.9% of GDP according to the our indicator). In the previous decade, the difference was slightly higher (0.5% of GDP in 10 years, and a great deal more — nearly 2.0% of GDP — in the 1990-1997 period).

There is an important conclusion to be drawn from this comparison: taking into consideration non-discretionary and non-cyclical budget incidences facilitates a more accurate analysis of the discretionary episodes — and of their contents — in a short or medium term perspective

---

15. … linked to fluctuations of the growth components and, in particular, to the growth differentials (and the revenue intensity) of the various tax bases and of their relative weighting, linked to very different partial elasticity dynamics.
16. See notably R. SAVAGE (2011) – See bibliography.

Graph 6: Compared Primary Balance (PB) Structural Indicators

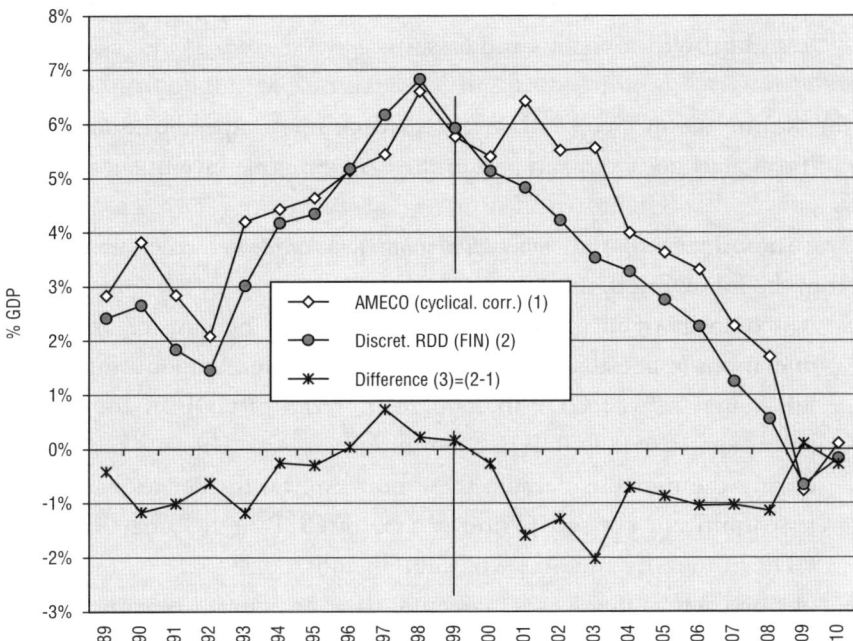

4.2 Retrospective Empirical Analysis

A correct and time-consistent assessment of this discretionary path logically requires a 'neutral' or unchanging non-discretionary and reference budgetary primary path in the long term, simultaneously and separately taking into account both the revenue and the expenditure sides.

The methodological aspects of that discussion are developed in a working paper to be published end of 2012 ([17]). The following figures are based on that methodology. The *'other non discretionary incidences'* (exclusive cyclical or 'pure' business cycle) have been grouped here in two main items:

3a) all non-cyclical incidences which are irreversible in principle, that is to say the endogenous 'structure effects' on the revenue side and the non-discretionary incidences as regards PE ('relative prices'

---

17. R. SAVAGE (2012, 2).

effects and other structural incidences, among which are principally socio-demographic incidences and the impact of post-crisis trend growth revisions and losses)

3b) the one-shot (OS) operations (as regards primary expenditure and non-fiscal revenue) and the impact of the LA's reversible investment cycle.

The importance of the *non-cyclical budgetary incidences* emerges clearly from the following figure:
- it is quite marked in the past decade, notably because of one-shot operations (especially in 2003), with a global impact amounting to no less than +2.1% of GDP in 1999-2003, −1.2% of GDP in 2003-2007 and at last −0.6% of GDP in 2007-2010;
- during the previous decade, these non-cyclical incidences had been less significant per sub-period (+0.5% of GDP in 1989-92, -0.3% of GDP in 1992-95 and −0.4% of GDP in 1995-99);
- during each of the decades covered, these incidences remained limited with a cumulated sub-total of −0.2% of GDP only for the first decade, of +0.3% of GDP for the second decade, and therefore an almost neutral long-term total.

As far as discretionary impulses are concerned, the expansive stance (exclusive non-fiscal one-shots) also appeared to be very clear in 1999-2003 and in 2003-2007 (2.2% of GDP identically for both 4-years periods) as in 2007-2010 (1.5% of GDP in 3 years). Over the whole decade, the discretionary budgetary and fiscal stimulus was quite massive: 6.1% of GDP considering the limited restrictive discretionary reversal of 2010, and even 6.5% of GDP in 1999-2009. This stands in sharp contrast to the restrictive stance or effort in the previous decade (+3.4% of GDP) and in particular in the 1992-99 period (+4.5% of GDP and even +5.3% of GDP in 1992-98).

The quantification of various identifiable non-cyclical and non-structural incidences regarding revenue and primary expenditure makes it possible to identify and measure the composition of the total discretionary stimuli, as well along a 'primary expenditure / revenue' dividing line as for each of the two large Entities ([18]) respectively.

---

18. As a reminder, Entity I groups together the Federal State (FS) and the Social Security (SS), and Entity II groups together the federated entities (Communities and Regions (C&R)) and the local authorities (LA).

Graph 7: Developments in Primary Balances and Cumulated Determinants, % of GDP

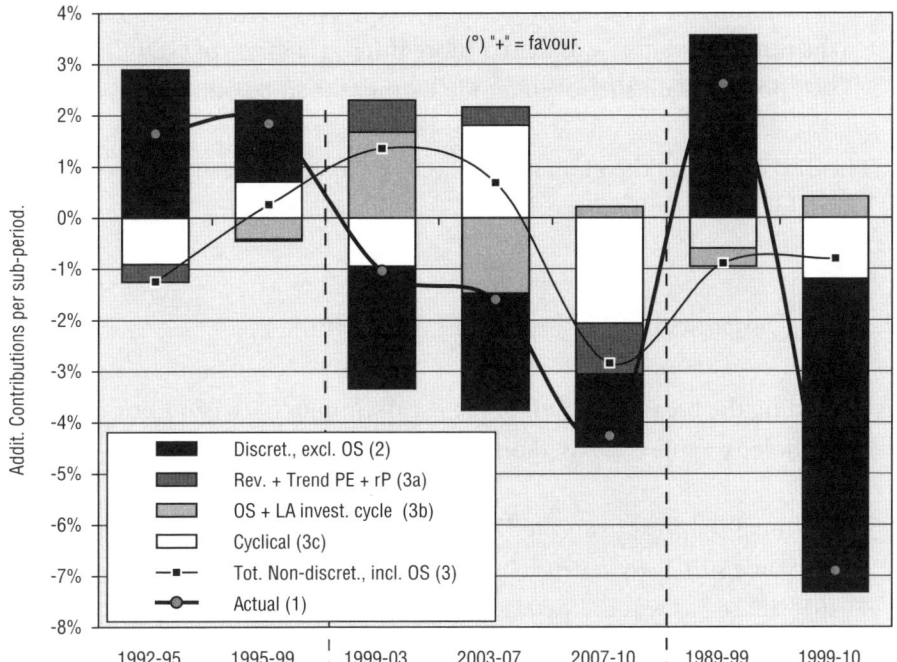

The following Table 2 and the associated graphs illustrate the results of the estimates.

- over the whole period covered (1999-2010) and for all government levels together, the global expansionary impulse (that is to say a little more than 6.0% of GDP) is located for more than ¾ (4.7% of GDP) on the public revenue side ([19]), while the discretionary growth of real primary expenditure above its neutral reference trajectory ([20]) represents an impulse of 1.4% of GDP only in 11 years (less than the remaining quarter);
- for comparison purposes, during the last clearly restrictive period (1992-98), the already mentioned net restrictive *effort* of 5.3% of GDP (also Global Government) was located up to 70% on the revenue side

---

19. Including all deductions in social security contributions (including those recorded, in ESA95, as primary expenditure under the category of wage subsidies) and including payroll tax reductions (personal income tax) in favour of some employers (for night shifts, team work, academic researchers, etc.), which are also recorded, in ESA95, as employment subsidies (expenditure).
20. The neutral 'trend' is estimated at 2.25% a year on average for the whole decade, corresponding to the evolution of revenue under the unchanged legislation hypothesis.

(3.7% of GDP) and the remaining 30% (1.6% of GDP) on the primary expenditure side. During the whole of the previous decade (1989-99), the restrictive effort was a little more limited, at 3.4% of GDP ([21]), and was polarized on the revenue side by more than 80%.

The distribution of the global discretionary stance between the two large Entities is also worth noting.

4.3   Discretionary Analysis by Large Entities

Regarding the breaking down of the fiscal stimulus between Entities, the methodology applied is based on the principles that:

1. the fiscal transfers from the FG, via the Special Financing Law (SFL), are *non discretionary* (even when funding mechanisms are changed by special acts, as was the case as from 2002) and

2. the 'neutral' reference growth rates of both large Entities' primary expenditure are supposed to be the same for the "non-ageing" primary expenditure.

– Over the whole 1999-2010 period, Entity I was more than proportionally ([22]) responsible for the expansionary global fiscal stance (4.8% of GDP out of 6.1% of GDP in total, that is to say nearly 80% of that total). But symmetrically, over the previous 1991-1999 period ([23]), Entity I was in charge of more than the full ([24]) discretionary consolidation effort to ensure the admission of Belgium to the Euro. The new

---

21. Resulting notably from the expansionary stance in 1989-92 (-1.2% of GDP, essentially as regards primary expenditure) and in 1999 (election year after the admission to the Euro...).
22. According to the HCF definition of final primary expenditure (exclusive intra-public budget transfers), Entity I represented on average almost 65% of the expenditure, in comparison to 35% for the consolidated Entity II (exclusive public pensions actually borne by the FS).
23. At least the first two years of the previous decade (that is to say the years 1990-91) must not be integrated in the sample period, because, in the context of the 1989 State Reform, transfers of competences only occurred progressively for a part and were spread over 3 years (1989-91). The comparison would therefore have been distorted until at least 1991.
24. That is to say 4.5% of GDP for a total of somewhat more than 4.0% of GDP, the net stance for Entity II being on the contrary globally expansionary (up to 0.5% of GDP, especially as regards primary expenditure with +1.0% of GDP).

The Fiscal Stance

Graph 8: Developments 1999-2010 of Primary Balances per Entity and Determinants

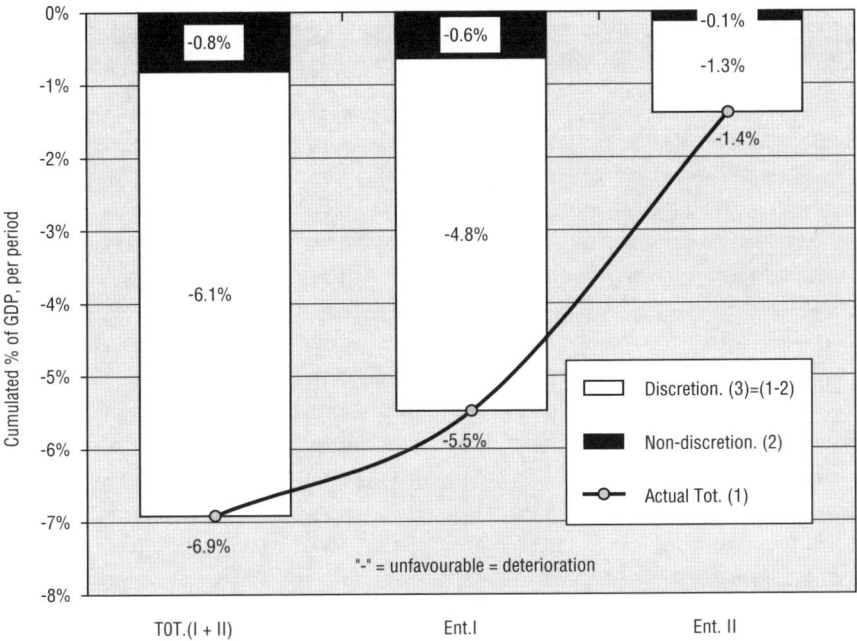

Graph 9: Discretionary Primary (Cumulated) Impulsions, and Composition

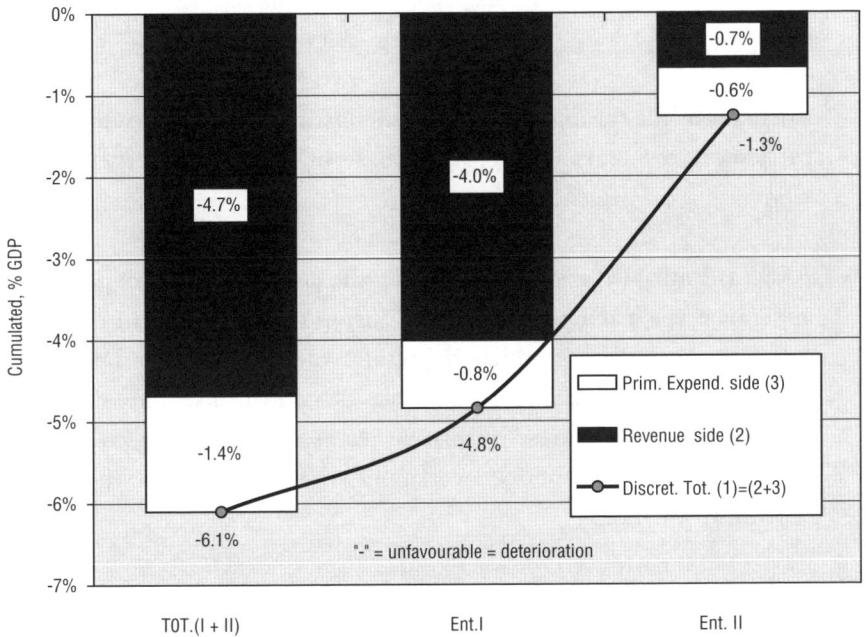

Table 2: Evolutions of the Effective Primary Balances per Sub-period, and Determinants

% ACTUAL GDP, PER SUB-PERIOD	1999-03	2003-07	2007-10	1999-10	1989-99	1992-98	1998-01	2001-08	2008-10
Actual Primary Balance (PB)	-1.0%	-1.6%	-4.3%	**-6.9%**	2.6%	3.7%	0.5%	-4.3%	-3.3%
Non-discretionary PB.	1.4%	0.7%	-2.9%	**-0.8%**	-0.9%	-1.7%	2.5%	0.0%	-2.5%
+ Cyclical impacts (PE)	-0.9%	1.8%	-2.1%	**-1.2%**	-0.6%	-0.8%	0.7%	0.6%	-1.9%
+ Other, non-discretion., of which:	2.3%	-1.1%	-0.8%	**0.4%**	-0.3%	-0.9%	1.7%	-0.6%	-0.6%
: Revenue composition effects	0.7%	0.3%	1.0%	**2.0%**	0.8%	-0.5%	1.8%	0.7%	0.1%
: Non-fiscal One-shots (revenues)	1.9%	-1.9%	0.0%	**0.1%**	0.0%	-0.1%	0.1%	-0.1%	0.0%
: Non-cycl., Primary expenditure (PE)	-0.3%	0.5%	-1.9%	**-1.7%**	-1.2%	-0.4%	-0.2%	-1.2%	-0.7%
* Deviation from trend growth	0.0%	-0.7%	-1.2%	**-1.9%**	-0.4%	-0.2%	-0.1%	-1.0%	-0.9%
* Other, miscellaneous	-0.3%	1.1%	-0.6%	**0.2%**	-0.8%	-0.2%	-0.2%	-0.2%	0.1%
+ One-shots (OS)	-0.4%	0.5%	0.1%	**0.2%**	-0.2%	-0.3%	0.2%	0.0%	0.0%
+ Relative prices	0.0%	0.7%	-0.8%	**-0.1%**	-0.4%	0.1%	-0.5%	-0.1%	0.1%
+ Other (LA's invest. cycle)	0.1%	0.0%	0.0%	**0.1%**	-0.1%	0.0%	0.0%	-0.1%	0.0%
pm. Tot. Non-fiscal One-shots	1.6%	-1.4%	0.2%	**0.3%**	-0.2%	-0.3%	0.3%	-0.1%	0.0%
Global discretion., excl. One-Shots	-2.4%	-2.3%	-1.4%	**-6.1%**	3.5%	5.4%	-2.0%	-4.3%	-0.7%
+ Revenue (excl. Non-fisc. One-shots)	-1.6%	-1.9%	-1.1%	**-4.7%**	2.7%	3.7%	-2.1%	-2.8%	-0.5%
+ PE (excl. One-shots)	-0.8%	-0.3%	-0.3%	**-1.4%**	0.8%	1.7%	0.1%	-1.4%	-0.3%
Global discret., excl. One-Shots, det.									
* Entity I (PB)	-1.7%	-2.1%	-1.0%	**-4.8%**	4.8%	5.3%	-1.8%	-3.2%	-0.7%
+ Revenue	-1.5%	-1.7%	-0.8%	**-4.0%**	2.3%	3.3%	-1.9%	-2.2%	-0.6%
+ Final Primary Expenditure (PE)	-0.3%	-0.3%	-0.2%	**-0.8%**	2.5%	2.0%	0.2%	-1.0%	-0.1%
* Entity II -Final	-0.7%	-0.2%	-0.4%	**-1.3%**	-1.3%	0.0%	-0.2%	-1.1%	-0.1%
+ Revenue	-0.2%	-0.2%	-0.3%	**-0.7%**	0.5%	0.4%	-0.1%	-0.6%	0.1%
+ Final Primary Expenditure (PE)	-0.5%	0.0%	-0.1%	**-0.6%**	-1.7%	-0.4%	-0.1%	-0.5%	-0.2%

calculations for the 1991-1999 period confirm the analysis which was carried out ten years ago ([25]) on the basis of a very similar methodology.

— As far as Entity I is concerned, during the last decade, the expansionary stance was particularly marked during the second term of office (2003-2007), with a cumulated impulse of 2.1% of GDP over four years. On the contrary, as far as Entity II is concerned, the expansive stimulus was the clearest in relative terms in the 1999-2003 period ([26]), that is during the period overlapping the refinancing of the C&R starting from 2002.

---

25. See R. SAVAGE (2002), op. cit.
26. This is -0.7% of GDP in 2003-2007, in comparison to only -0.2% and -0.4% of GDP respectively for each of the other two sub-periods.

- With regard to Entity I, more than 80% (4.0% of GDP out of a total of 4.8 % of GDP) of the expansionary discretionary stimulus concerned public revenue (imputed wage subsidies included) and the remaining 0.8% of GDP was located on the final primary expenditure side (exclusive wage subsidies). As far as Entity II is concerned, its expansionary stimulus of 1.3% of GDP in eleven years is to be found for a little more than 50% of the sub-total (0.7% of GDP) in its own (final) revenue ([27]) and the remainder in its final primary expenditure.

4.4 Real Primary Expenditure Growth, and Revenue (ex ante and ex post) Elasticity's

The following table gives a comparative summary of the compared real growth of (final) primary expenditure at the global consolidated Government level and of both large Entities, according to the adjusted HCF definition ([28]).

Table 3: Compared Real Growth Rates of Final Primary Expenditure

	1990-00	2000-10	2000-05	2005-10	1999-03	2003-07	2007-10
Tot. Final corr. Prim. expendit. (PE),	2.3%	2.6%	2.7%	2.4%	2.6%	2.3%	2.8%
* Social benefits (ageing PE)	2.3%	2.8%	2.8%	2.7%	2.8%	2.4%	3.2%
* PE excl. Social benefits	2.2%	2.4%	2.7%	2.1%	2.4%	2.1%	2.2%
pm. Idem, incl. Wage subsidies	2.3%	2.9%	2.8%	2.9%	2.7%	2.6%	3.2%
pm. Impact of Wage subsidies	0.0%	0.3%	0.1%	0.5%	0.1%	0.3%	0.5%
Final PE of Entity I, cyclic. corrected	1.6%	2.6%	2.6%	2.6%	2.4%	2.3%	3.0%
* Correct. Social benefits (ageing PE)	2.0%	2.7%	2.6%	2.7%	2.5%	2.4%	3.2%
* Final PE excl. Social benefits	0.0%	2.2%	2.5%	2.0%	2.1%	2.2%	2.3%
Entity II, corr. for the LA's invest. cycle	2.9%	2.6%	3.0%	2.3%	3.0%	2.1%	2.4%
* Social benefits (ageing PE)	4.7%	4.2%	5.3%	3.0%	7.7%	2.7%	3.5%
* Corr. final PE excl. Social benefits	2.7%	2.4%	2.7%	2.2%	2.5%	2.1%	2.2%

(°) HCF definition, excl. wage subsidies, corrected for cyclical unemployment, LA's invest. cycle, One-shots and perimeter

27. The major discretionary deductions were implemented in the Flemish Region, with the complete abolition of the radio and television licence fee, a significant reduction in registration duties and the introduction – even if it was temporary – of the 'Jobkorting'.
28. Exclusive of the reductions in fiscal and para-fiscal revenue or charges which are recorded, in ESA95 accounts as primary expenditure (wage or employment subsidies) and not as revenue reductions or losses. Those PE are also defined in structural terms, that is to say cyclically adjusted, exclusive of LA's investment cycle, exclusive of one-shot measures and at constant perimeter.

Between the last decade (2000-2010) and the previous one (1990-2000), the acceleration (+0.3% a year) in the average annual growth of final primary expenditure was not very marked at the global or aggregated level (Global Government). However, this hid one of the divergent developments between the two large Entities: a very clear acceleration for Entity I (as regards social benefits and even more with respect to the other PE, exclusive ageing) and a limited deceleration for Entity II.

Moreover, those global figures over ten years also hid two very different budgetary or fiscal 'regimes' within each decade: 1) a clearly restrictive budgetary stance in 1992-99 or 1992-98, preceded by a shorter expansive stage in 1989-1992, while 2) the second decade, starting with a rather neutral regime (1999-2001), was on the contrary characterised by a very expansionary discretionary stance from 2002-2003 onwards.

This distinction between two clearly different budgetary regimes was particularly sharp at Entity I level, globally and at each level of both major categories of primary expenditure. There was no such break in Entity II, for which there is evidence that a slightly but lasting expansive regime was in place in PE over both decades.

The budgetary regime of the last decade was therefore globally expansionary, and the break with the previous decade (the 90s) is particularly marked and spectacular in Entity I in which this regime had been on the contrary very austere during that period (Global Plan of 1993, etc.). Globally, in % of GDP, the expansive discretionary stimulus, measured at the PE level (and at constant prices), remained relatively limited and under control (1.5% of GDP in ten years) in comparison to a much more marked visible non-discretionary or endogenous increase in the non-adjusted value ratio of PE (+5.4% of GDP). Most of that rise at the end of the decade can be linked to negative cyclical impacts and to the very recent ex post downwards revision of the estimated potential growth of the past decade.

As far as public revenue, and in particular compulsory levies, is concerned, it can be very misleading to judge the figures at their face value. Exclusive one-shot measures and corrected for the reduced fiscal and social charges recorded by Eurostat as expenditure relating to operating subsidies, the ratio decreased by 2.7% of GDP in ten years. However, a detailed analysis of the ex ante path of those revenues *under unchanged legislation* showed that, in the absence of cumulative discretionary stimuli over the post-1999 period, their 'ex ante' ratio should logically have increased – ceteris paribus – by 2.0% of GDP ([29]).

The ex-post elasticity of the effective (fiscal and para-fiscal) revenue in comparison to the nominal GDP was lower than 1.0 and did not even reach 0.85, while the ex-ante elasticity (before discretionary measures) can be estimated at 1.075, which is clearly – even if slightly – higher than unity: this results from composition or 'structure' effects on the revenue side, with the slight ex ante progressiveness of the whole tax-levying system at the beginning of the period.

BIBLIOGRAPHIC INFORMATION

Federaal Planbureau (FPB), Economische vooruitzichten 2000-2004 (May 1999) and 2001-2005 (May 2000).

Belgian Stability Programme 2004-2007, November 2003.

HCF (Section 'Public Sector borrowing requirements'), Annual Reports (July 2000 to 2004, July 2007, June 2008, March 2009).

F. DENIL & R. SAVAGE, « Crise économique et finances publiques belges: implications et réponses de politique budgétaire », CIFOP, 2011.

H. BOGAERT, « Le retour de l'effet boule de neige », FPB, Document 10/HJB/bd/2824, 2010.

M. SAINTRAIN, « Stratégie de soutenabilité budgétaire : évalation critique et options envisageables », Note FPB (09)/ADDG/MS/6895/ms/9881, June 2009.

M. SAINTRAIN and S. WEEMAES, « Begrotingsoverschotten opbouwen om de vergrijzing in België aan te pakken: realiteit en verkenningen – Accumuler des surplus budgétaires pour faire face au vieillissement démographique en Belgique: réalités et perspectives », FPB, Working Paper 5-08, February 2008.

R. SAVAGE, « La politique budgétaire », in *La fin du déficit budgétaire – Analyse de l'évolution récente des finances publiques belges (1990-2000)*, ed. E. de Callataÿ, De Boeck, 2002.

R. SAVAGE, « 40 ans de politique fiscale et parafiscale en Belgique (1970-2010) – Effets de composition et Impulsions discrétionaires en Recettes publiques :

---

29. Without taking into consideration the fiscal cost of restoring full indexation of the parameters relating to the PIT-system after 1999.

Une synthèse théorique et appliquée », Documentatieblad – Bulletin de Documentation du SPF Finances (BDMF), 4th trimester, 2011, n°4.

R. SAVAGE, « Politique budgétaire et fiscale discrétionnaire globale et par grandes Entités: Le cas belge 1990-2010 », BDMF, forthcoming, end 2012.

NOTATIONS

BDMF	Documentatieblad – Bulletin de documentation du SPF Finances
C&R	Communities and Regions
GDP	Gross Domestic Product
EA	Euro Area
EDP	Excessive Deficit Procedure
EU	European Union
FPB	Federal Planning Bureau
FPS	Federal Public Service
FS	Federal State (or Government)
GG	General Government
HCF	High Council of Finance
LA	Local Authorities
NBR	Net Borrowing Requirement
NFB	Net Financing Balance
OS	One Shots
PA	Public Administrations
PB	Primary Balance
PE	Primary Expenditure
RDD	Research and Documentation Department
rP	Relative prices
RPB	Required Primary Balance

4.
Tax Revenue and Tax Policy
A DECADE OF TAX CUTS

André Decoster, Marcel Gerard, and Christian Valenduc [1]

During the nineties, the tax policy stance was clearly subordinated to the fiscal consolidation strategy of the federal government. "Maastricht" and "3%" were the key word and figure that dominated the decennia (Decoster, Gérard and Valenduc, 2001). On the revenue side, two main reforms contributed to fiscal consolidation: the automatic indexation of personal income tax was suspended, apart for the zero rate bands and the related family tax credits, and a crisis surcharge was introduced for personal income taxes (PIT in the rest of this chapter) and corporate income taxes (CIT in the rest of this chapter). On the CIT side, the nineties appears to be, ex post, a decennium of base broadening and the gap between nominal and effective taxation was substantially reduced (Valenduc, 1999). Finally, on the PIT side, no new tax expenditures were introduced and the tax incentives for long-term savings were made less generous by replacing allowances evaluated at the marginal tax rate by a tax credit that ranged from 30 to 40%.

The fiscal environment changed radically at the turn of the century. The words "room for manoeuvre" came back into the glossary of tax policy

---

1. André Decoster is Professor at the Catholic University of Leuven (KU Leuven) and Deputy Director of the Belgian Institute of Public Finance. Marcel Gérard is Professor at the Catholic University of Louvain (UCL). Christian Valenduc is General Advisor at the Belgian Ministry of Finance, guest lecturer at the University of Namur and at the Catholic University of Louvain (UCL), and Director of the Belgian Institute of Public Finance.

makers and the "tax to GDP ratio" (²) exhibited a downward trend that contrasted with the outcome of the contribution of tax policy to fiscal consolidation that prevailed during the nineties.

Figure 1: Taxes and social security contributions, % GDP

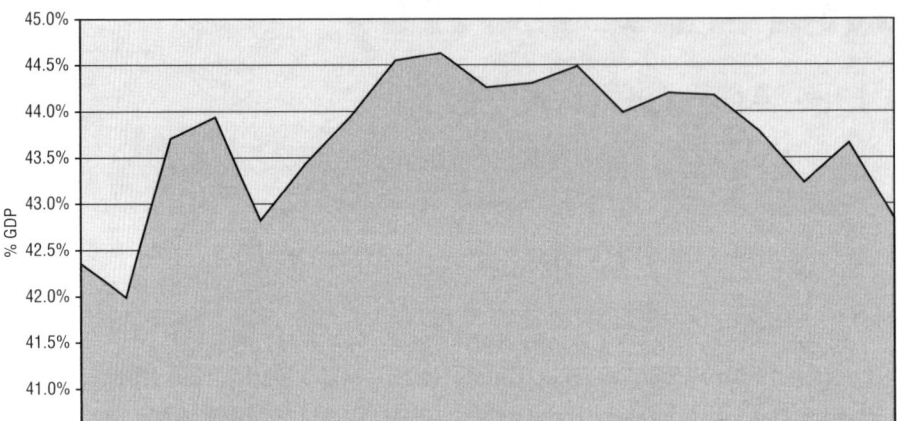

Source: National Accounts Institute – own calculations

The coalition agreement of the "rainbow" government (a coalition of liberals, socialists and green) that arose after the 1999 election included PIT tax reform of which the main objectives were to reduce the taxation of earned income and to have full tax neutrality between singles and spouses. The tax cut was significant (€ 3.3 billion). In addition, new tax expenditures were introduced, the cost of which increased over the decennium.

On the CIT side, the "rainbow" government opted for a "broad based low rate" tax reform that aimed to be revenue neutral. The next government made a more fundamental reform in introducing the allowance for corporate equity as a substitute for the coordination centre regime that had to be abolished in accordance with the implementation of the EU code of conduct on business taxation. That reform was also intended to be revenue neutral but, as will be documented later in this chapter, there are strong presumptions that that was in fact not the case and that the reform had a significant negative impact on CIT tax revenue.

2. Sum of taxes and social security contributions revenue, expressed as % GDP.

Finally, on the social contributions side, reductions in the employer's contributions contributed to the reduction of the tax wedge on labour, and targeted measures were also introduced to raise the employment rate of the long-term unemployed. In addition, wage subsidies were introduced through the tax system to ease the labour cost of researchers, time and shift workers, and overtime work.

Section 1 of this chapter describes how the tax policy conducted during the last decade affected the taxation of labour, capital and consumption. Section 2 discusses the effects of the main reforms that have been introduced. In Section 3, we turn to the "silent" part of the tax policy conducted during the nineties: reforms that have not been carried out, and that could have contributed in a positive way to the main problems of the Belgian tax system: the absence of neutrality in the taxation of savings and the lack of a green tax reform that could address the climate change issue as well as the high taxation of labour.

1. TAXATION OF LABOUR, CAPITAL AND CONSUMPTION

When discussing the tax policy stance, the main question is not necessarily "How much do we raise?" but "How do we raise a given amount of taxes (and social security contributions) in the most efficient and equitable way?". The first question is a debate on the size of the government, which is not the focus of this chapter.

The second question is the heart of tax policy and may be dealt with from various perspectives, including that of the tax mix: does revenue collection rely more on income or on consumption? And what about the taxation of labour and capital?

The "implicit tax rates" methodology (ITR in the rest of this chapter) enables us to answer that question. Implicit tax rates are macroeconomic indicators of the tax burden on labour, capital and consumption obtained by dividing the total revenue of some specific taxes by their total (macroeconomic) tax base (European Commission

2012, Valenduc 2011). They are complementary to but different from "effective tax rates". The latter are calculated at the microeconomic level of the taxpayer. As such these indicators come closer to the formal expression of the "tax wedge" as they capture the differences between prices on the demand side and on the supply side of the market. Yet, linked to the situation of one specific taxpayer (e.g. a single wage earner at the average wage), they tell only part of the story of the effects of tax reforms. Moreover, effective tax rates indicate the ex ante change in incentives for economic agents, brought about by the change in the tax system, whereas implicit tax rates are ex post indicators, revealing what effectively was the result of the reform in terms of revenue collection.

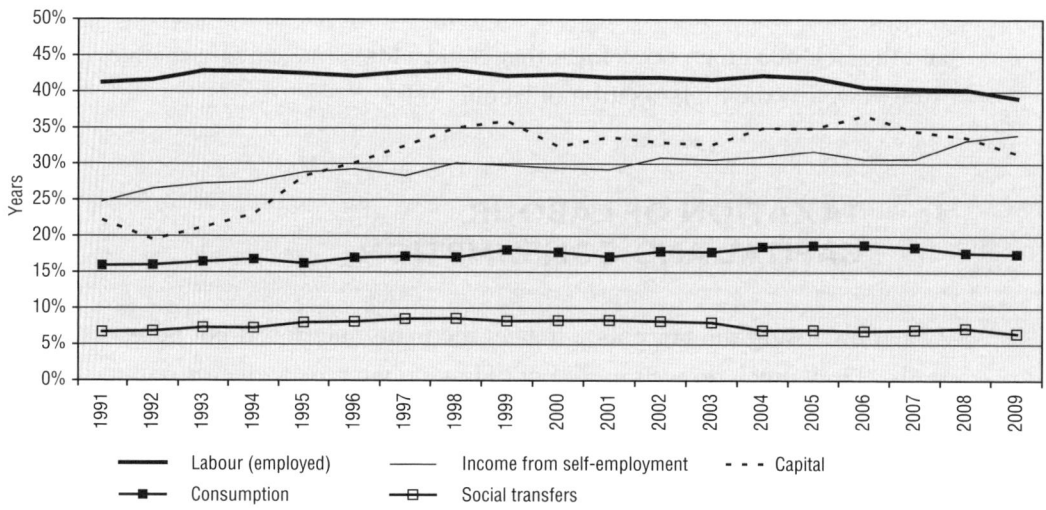

Figure 2: Implicit tax rates

Source: Valenduc (2011)

Figure 2 illustrates the trends in implicit tax rates over the past two decennia. At the macroeconomic level, the reduction in the taxation of labour appears to be small, but significant. As this is the main tax base, lowering the ITR by one per cent comes at a substantial revenue cost for the budget. Moreover, as we will discuss below, the ex post situation should be compared with the "no-policy change" scenario which normally leads to an increase in the ITR. The taxation of capital peaked in 2006 and then decreased, when the Allowance for Corporate Equity was introduced. The taxation of consumption increased slightly during the first part of the decennium but then decreased. The taxation of social transfer is still low and has been further reduced by the PIT tax reform of the middle of the decade. An in-depth analysis of these trends was conducted in Valenduc (2011), and we summarize here the main results of his analysis.

1.1 Taxation of labour

As indicated at the beginning of this chapter, the 1999 coalition agreement included a PIT tax reform. The previous government had already re-established the full and automatic indexation of the brackets and nominal thresholds in personal income tax. The main goal of the reform of the 1999 coalition was a reduction in the taxation of earned income. The reform came into force in 2002-04. But, as a significant part of these policy changes was not implemented in the withholding taxes on wages, part of the effect was delayed, through the PIT assessment process, until 2006. Prior to this reform, the government had already abolished the crisis surcharge. The removal of this additional tax was phased out over five years, starting in 1999 with low income earners.

Reductions in the employer's social security contributions were increased and contributed to the decreasing trend in the tax wedge. At the end of the period, wage subsidies were gradually introduced through the tax system [3]. At first they were targeted to researchers, and gradually extended from a very narrow range of beneficiaries [4] to any researcher with a PhD or a master's degree in science hired by a private company located in the country. The rate of the subsidy has gradually increased and now amounts to 75% of the withholding tax. Obviously, it is a federal tax incentive to stimulate R&D. Later, similar schemes were introduced for overtime and

---

3. The process is the following: the scheme reduces the amount of the withholding tax the employer has to pay to the tax administration, without a corresponding reduction in the PIT liability of the worker. It amounts to a wage subsidy and is also considered as such in the national accounts. In some sense the subsidies resemble a "negative payroll tax". In the calculation of the implicit tax rate on labour, we subtract these subsidies from the numerator. We consider them as a negative component of the tax wedge, since they are expressed as a percentage of the wage or of the withholding tax. The European Commission (2012) does not take these wage subsidies into account when computing the implicit tax rate on labour.
4. Researchers hired by universities and/or researchers hired by the private sector and involved in partnerships with universities.

night and shift workers. The first might be justified on efficiency grounds because it lowers the tax on a relatively elastic sector of labour supply and demand. However, the rationale for the scheme supporting night and shift workers is less clear ([5]). Finally, at the end of the period, a standard rebate was introduced for the whole of the private sector, as a component of two last general wage agreements concluded by the social partners.

Table 1: ITR on labour (employed) and the no-policy change scenario

	ITR ON LABOUR (EMPLOYED)		UNDER UNCHANGED TAX POLICY	
	GLOBAL	OF WHICH PIT	GLOBAL	OF WHICH PIT
2000	42.4%	17.9%	44.2%	17.7%
2001	42.0%	17.7%	44.6%	18.2%
2002	42.0%	17.5%	44.9%	18.3%
2003	41.7%	17.3%	44.9%	18.3%
2004	42.3%	17.8%	45.4%	18.5%
2005	42.0%	17.9%	45.5%	18.7%
2006	40.6%	17.1%	45.4%	19.1%
2007	40.4%	16.9%	45.7%	19.4%
2008	40.3%	17.2%	45.6%	19.9%
2009	39.1%	16.2%	44.8%	19.4%

Source: Valenduc (2011)

Table 1 compares the actual evolution of the ITR on labour with the counterfactual baseline scenario of no-policy change ([6]). On this baseline, the ITR on labour would have increased slightly from 44.2% to 44.8%, due to the progressivity of income tax ([7]). The discretionary change appears to be significant. Comparing the actual ITR at the end of the period (39.1) with that of the counterfactual (44.8), the ITR on labour was 5.7 per cent below the baseline at the end of the period, whereas it was just 1.8 per cent below at the beginning of the period. The PIT component contributes 3.2 per cent, which is quite significant.

5. The scheme was conceived as a response to competitive pressure in the car industry. As any sector targeting is forbidden by the EU State Aid Rules, the scheme was from the beginning extended to the whole of the private sector.
6. The "unchanged tax policy scenario" includes the automatic indexation of PIT.
7. Reductions in employers' social security contributions have also made these payments slightly progressive, contributing to the increasing trend in the unchanged tax policy scenario.

Tax Revenue and Tax Policy

Figure 3 compares the trend of the implicit tax rate on labour with the trend of the effective tax rate (ETR) on the average wage. The ETR is taken from the OECD annual publication *Taxing Wages* (OECD, 2012 for the last edition). It computes the tax wedge for a single worker earning the average wage in the private sector. The tax wedge only includes the nominal PIT and social security contributions rate, local taxes at the average rate and standard tax allowances and standard reductions in social security contributions ([8]).

Figure 3: Implicit (macro) and effective (micro) tax rates on labour

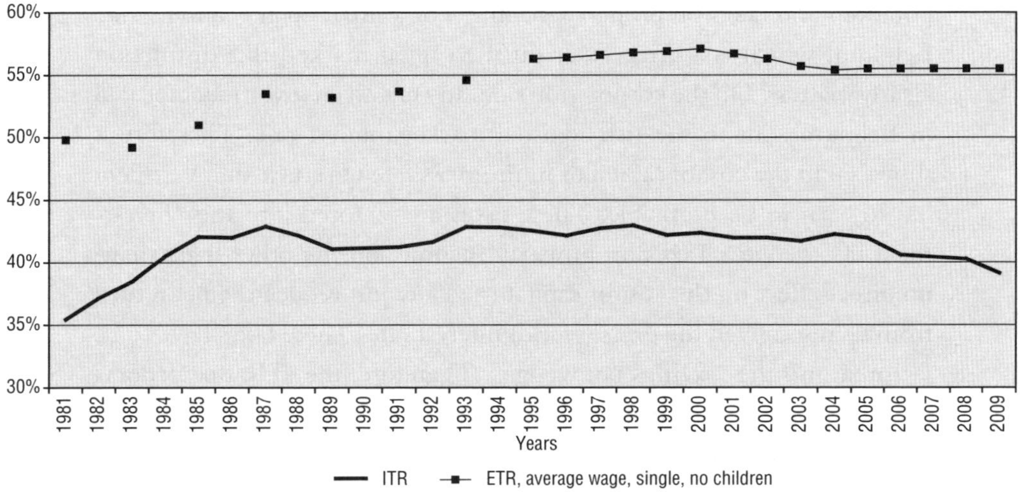

Source: Valenduc (2011)

The decline in the ETR is clearly less pronounced than the decline in the implicit tax rate. The main reason for this is that most of the reductions in social security contributions, introduced during the last decade, have been targeted at low wage earners and hence have no or very little effect on the tax wedge of the average wage. Also the wider use of tax expenditures, which contributes to the decreasing trend in the ITR, does not show up in the effective tax rates of the OECD.

---

8. In the case of Belgium, "standard tax allowances" just includes the standard deduction for professional expenses and the zero rate band on the tax side. On the "social security contributions" side, the standard reductions (low wages) are taken into account, but reductions targeted according to specific characteristics of the employee are not (for example in the case of hiring long-term unemployed).

1.2 Capital

The decrease in the implicit tax rate on capital is the second main event of the past decennium. The ITR on capital groups a large number of quite different taxes. They differ not only in terms of their tax base (profits of corporations, income from savings) but also by type (income taxes, transaction taxes). The economic incidence of these various taxes may well be different.

Figure 4 disentangles the ITR on capital by distinguishing taxes on corporations and taxes on property income. For a small open economy like Belgium, which is a price-taker on the capital market, this distinction clearly matters. On the corporation side, any tax on an investment located in Belgium adds to the risk adjusted market interest rate. Therefore it shows up in the cost of capital or in the gross rate of return an investment has to earn to be profitable. These taxes are factored into the "investment tax wedge". Taxes on property income, on the other hand, have no direct effect on the cost of capital ([9]). They just reduce the net return from savings, given the gross (world) interest rate. These taxes have to be factored into the "savings tax wedge". Therefore, the ITR on corporations may be considered as the macroeconomic proxy of the investment tax wedge, while the ITR on property income may be considered as the macroeconomic proxy of the "savings tax wedge."

The ITR on corporations showed a clearly increasing trend in the nineties. The tax policy stance of that period has been widely documented in previous publications (Decoster, Gerard and Valenduc, 2001; Valenduc, 1999; Valenduc 2004a). The nineties appear to have been a period of "gradual tax reform" resulting in base broadening after an initial cut in the nominal CIT rate of 4 per cent. By narrowing the gap between the nominal and the implicit (effective) tax rates, this reform improved the neutrality of CIT. During the last decade, the ITR on corporations clearly picked up in 2006 and decreased significantly at the end of the decennium, when the allowance for corporate equity (the "Notional

---

9. The financing of SMEs may differ from the small open economy model, as most of them do not have access to the world capital market. For these enterprises, personal taxes paid by the shareholders may have an effect on the cost of capital.

Tax Revenue and Tax Policy

interest deduction") was introduced. On the other hand, the ITR on property income showed no clear trend over the last decade and fluctuated at around 20%.

Figure 4: ITR on capital: corporations and property income of households

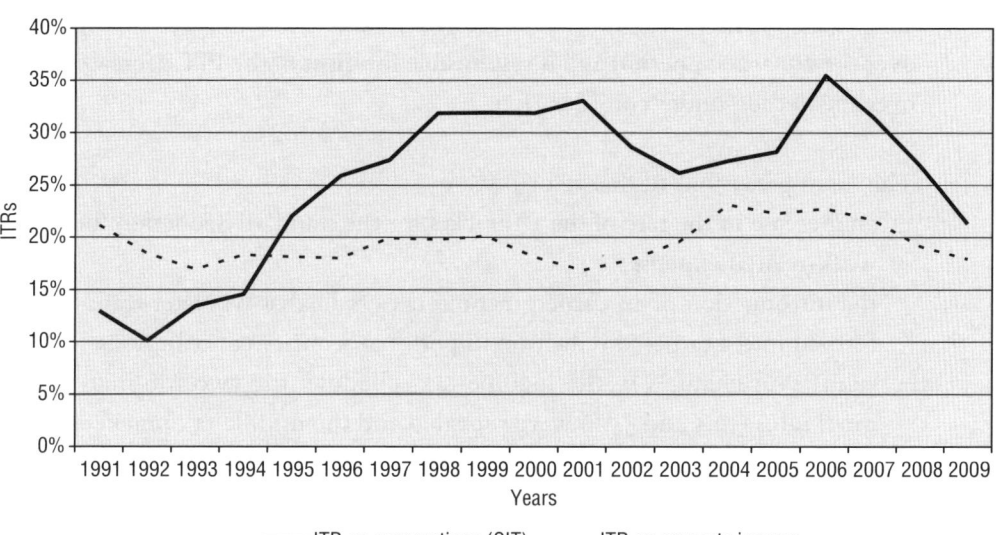

Source: VALENDUC (2011)

1.3 Consumption

The "silence" from the consumption tax side contrasts with the considerable political activity on the income tax side (personal and corporate income taxes). No major changes were made in VAT, apart from an extension of the reduced rate for the renovation of 15-year-old dwellings to 5-year-old ones. Excise duties on energy were monitored by means of a "cliquet" system which converted decreases in pre-tax prices partly into excise duties. Sometimes, a reverse "cliquet" was also introduced, but in a less systematic way. The net effect was an increase in excise duties in nominal terms. But these schemes failed to maintain the real value of excise duties over the period, as pointed out by Valenduc (2011).

2. THE MAIN TAX REFORMS OF THE LAST DECADE

2.1 The PIT reform

The PIT reform (The "Reynders reform") came into force gradually over the 2002-2004 period and is responsible for most of the PIT decrease over the decade under consideration.

The main provisions of that reform were:
- an increase in the rate of the 1st bracket for the standard deduction for work-related expenses;
- the introduction of an earned income tax credit that was later transformed into a targeted reduction in personal security contributions;
- significant changes in the income tax schedule: the two top marginal rates (52.5 and 55%) were repealed and the middle tax brackets were widened;
- an upward alignment of the zero-rate band for spouses and singles;
- full neutrality between singles and spouses. This includes the separate taxation of un-earned income. It also includes a significant change in the income testing of the tax credits for social transfers: the reform changes the system from income testing at the level of the household to that at the level of the individual.

Ex ante evaluations of the reforms were carried out by Cantillon et.al. (2000) and by Valenduc (2002). Both concluded that the reform was broadly neutral as far as income redistribution was concerned. According to Valenduc (2002), this resulted from a combination of an increase in the progressivity of the personal income tax and a reduction in the average tax rate ([10]).

---

10. This is best seen from the Kakwani decomposition of the redistributive effect of a tax $RE = tP/(1-t)$, with RE = redistribution, P = progressivity, defined as the difference between the GINI indices of taxes and pre-tax incomes, t = average tax rate. Cf. KAKWANI (1977).

Valenduc (2002) also investigated the effect of the reform on effective tax rates on labour and on "participation rates" ([11]). Unsurprisingly, he found a decrease — albeit rather limited — on the ETR on labour. On the "participation decision" side, he concluded that the "making work pay" effect was widely dispersed and not targeted to the cases in which the unemployment trap was the most acute. This was due to the policy choice to have a "simple" earned income tax credit, designed for individual rather than household income testing. Moreover, since the Earning Income Tax Credit (EITC in the rest of the paper) was tested only on earned income, and not on hours worked, it introduced a part-time premium.

As indicated above, the EITC for wage earners was later transformed into a targeted reduction in personal security contributions. The new scheme was also based on hours worked. This removed the part-time premium and therefore significantly changed the profile of the beneficiaries.

The labour supply side effect of this EITC has been investigated by Orsini (2006) and documented in Conseil supérieur des Finances (2007). Orsini's evaluation is also an ex ante one. The expected supply side effects differ widely according to gender. For female workers, most of the effect is on the participation side and it arises from the earned income tax credit and the increase in the zero rate band for married women. The phasing-out of the EITC may have an adverse effect on hours worked and the repealing of the two top marginal income tax rates will have roughly no effect. For male workers, there is a positive effect at the intensive margin as well which is mainly triggered by the widening of the tax brackets in the middle of the income tax schedule. The repealing of the two top marginal rates does not seem to have a great (expected) effect.

---

11. "Participation rates" capture the effect of the tax and benefit system on the participation decision (return to work). It is defined as the ratio of the difference in tax (and employee's social security contributions) to the difference in gross income, when comparing in and out of work cases for a typical worker. The numerator also includes changes in benefits, due to the switch from not working to working.

2.2 Tax expenditure in personal income tax: away from neutrality?

The growing use of tax expenditures during the last decade stands in sharp contrast to the tax policy conducted during the nineties: the trade-off between neutrality and incentives has been reversed. The revenue forgone from tax expenditures increased from 12.4% in 2000 to 18.0% in 2009 (Figure 5).

Figure 5: Revenue forgone from tax expenditures, PIT

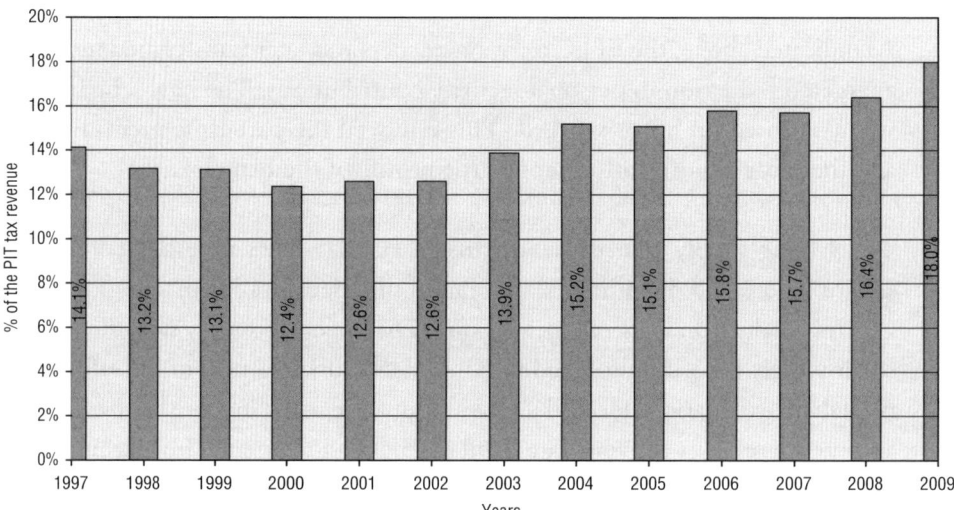

Source: Tax expenditures Reports – Own calculations

Of the new tax expenditures which have been introduced the main one is the tax credit for energy saving schemes. It has been expanded gradually with a steadily increasing revenue cost as a consequence. As noted by Conseil supérieur des Finances (2009) and Baveye and Valenduc (2011), the case for these environmental tax rebates is rather weak. From a welfare point of view, a green tax the revenue of which would be recycled in the form of a labour tax cut would clearly have been better.

The tax regime for housing was made more favourable in 2005. The previous tax regime, which allowed the deduction of mortgage repayments against earned income and the deduction of mortgage interest against imputed income, was changed into a new tax allowance which allows mortgage repayments and interests to be set against earned income. Moreover, refinancing mortgages also qualified for the new regimes, which resulted in a windfall gain. There is a well-known presumption that tax incentives for housing capitalise into prices due to (at least short term) inelastic supply. Valenduc and Van Reybrouck (2012) confirm that this seems to have been the case with the new tax regime for housing.

The ceiling for deductible pension savings was increased, child care deductibility was expanded for children from 3 to 12 years old, and other tax expenditures – the policy rationale for which was quite weak – have been introduced. ([12])

2.3 Personal income tax, progressivity and redistribution

On the efficiency side of the coin, the combination of an extension of the reductions in social security contributions for low wage earners with the "Reynders tax reform", has been successful in reducing the taxation of labour. And ex ante simulations also indicated that the "Reynders tax reform" was roughly neutral on the distributional front. But the use of tax expenditures has been expanded, and it is well known that the bulk of tax expenditures benefits middle and high income earners (Conseil supérieur des Finances, 2002 ([13]); Valenduc, 2004). Therefore, the combination of these two effects renders the evolution of the overall redistributive power of the PIT system during the last decade opaque, the more so because the underlying distribution of taxable income itself has also changed during the decade. Therefore we now complement the ex ante analysis, described in Section 2.1, with a description of the actual evolution of the redistributive effect of the PIT.

Figure 6 displays the GINI indices of taxable income and income after PIT. Inequality in taxable income increased, and redistribution (the bars in Figure 6) clearly decreased. This seems to contradict the result of the ex ante simulation of PIT reform as in Valenduc (2002). Note first that

---

12. For example the tax credit for the costs of improving the security of dwellings against burglary and fire.
13. Also available in Dutch (Hoge Raad van Financiën (2002))

the increase in pre-tax inequality is not specific to Belgium. It appears to be a common trend in most OECD countries (OECD, 2009). However, there is a specific Belgian component in this trend. The PIT reform has made some tax credits refundable. Therefore, the tax administration decided that low income earners should go through the assessment process even if they were not liable to pay income tax. As a consequence, a significant number of low income earners, previously not included in the statistics (which rely on the PIT assessment), do now enter the administrative statistics. Hence, a significant part of the increase in the pre- and post-tax inequality, and therefore also of the decrease in redistribution, can be attributed to this "administrative change".

Figure 7 disentangles the index of redistributive effect of a tax system using the well-known Kakwani decomposition ([14]) into the change in the average tax rate and the disproportionality of the tax liabilities (defined here as progressivity).

Mainly during the first half of the decade, the Reynders reform and the wider use of tax expenditures triggered a downward trend in the average tax rate. Progressivity (defined as the difference between the concentration index of PIT liability and the Gini index of the pre-tax income distribution) increased slightly over the period. This is surprising. The ex ante simulations predicted that the Reynders reform would increase progressivity, due to the introduction of the EITC. As indicated above, the EITC was transformed into a targeted reduction in employee's social security contributions in 2004 and was thus removed to outside the "progressivity of income tax", as captured in Figure 7. Others things being equal, the legislative change should have resulted in a decrease in progressivity. The administrative change just described also pushes the progressivity index upward, due to the inclusion of low income earners with a zero (or even negative) PIT liability.

The specific effect of the administrative change in the PIT assessment process on inequality and redistribution has never been assessed. The

---

14. See footnote 9, page 7.

Tax Revenue and Tax Policy

direction in which they affect inequality and redistributive effect is clear. But, unfortunately, the magnitude of this effect is unknown.

Figure 6: Inequality and redistribution

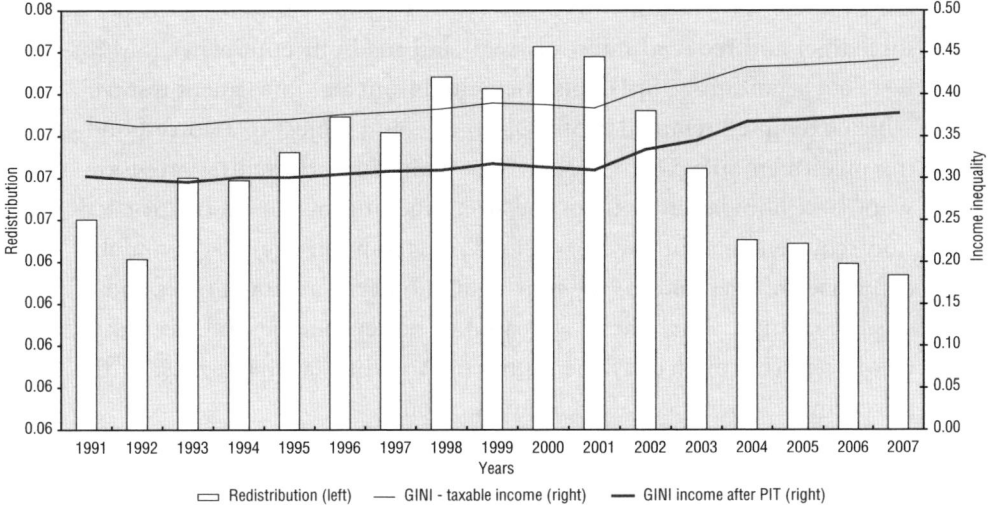

Figure 7: PIT: progressivity and redistribution

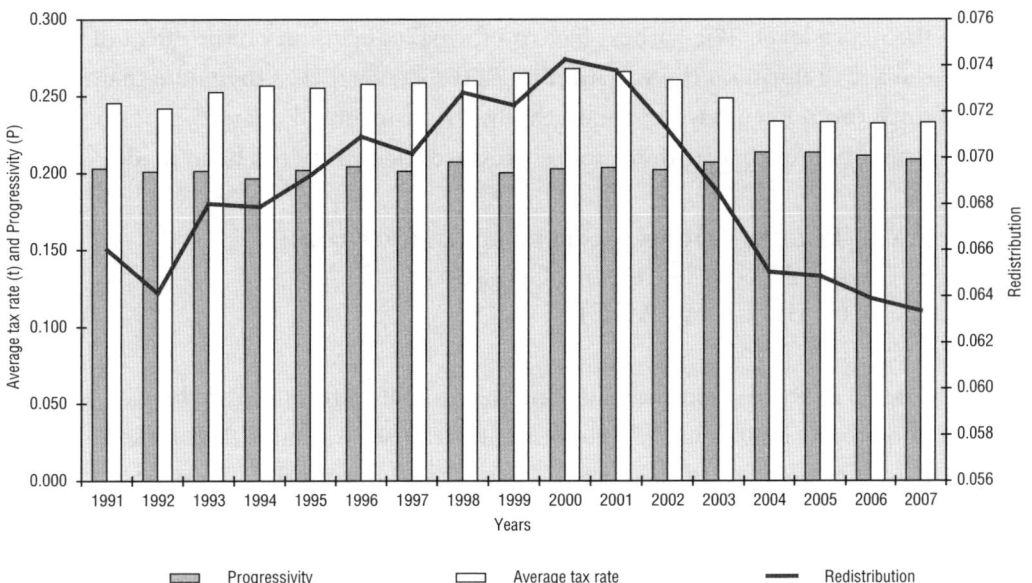

2.4 Corporate income tax reforms

2.4.1 THE 2003 REFORM

The first main reform of Corporate Income Tax took place in 2003. It was a typical example of a "broad base, low rate" tax reform. The nominal CIT rate was cut from 39 to 33% (40.17 to 33.99% including the crisis surcharge) and reduced rates for small and medium enterprises (SMEs) were cut accordingly. SMEs also benefited from an "investment reserve" which exempted retained profits up to a ceiling subject to a corresponding investment in a 3-year period. The main base broadening provisions were (a) a liquidation tax, (b) the strengthening of the upstream taxation requirements for the "participation exemption", (c) less favourable depreciation rules and (d) the non-deductibility of regional taxes and of specific charges. The reform appeared to be revenue neutral, according to the report provided by the Court of Auditors "at the request of the government" (See Cour des Comptes, 2006).

A "broad base, low rate" reform is intended to make the tax system more neutral by reducing the dispersion in effective tax rates at the micro level. Using micro data, Halleux and Valenduc (2007) conducted a study on the dispersion in effective tax rates. The disregarded charges ([15]) appears to be the main determinant of the dispersion in ETRs at the micro level. The authors have no formal conclusion on the effect of the 2003 reform on the variation in ETRs. Nevertheless they note that, since the reform has expanded the list of disregarded charges, it is far from obvious that further progress towards neutrality has been made.

2.4.2 THE "NOTIONAL INTEREST DEDUCTION": AN ALLOWANCE FOR CORPORATE EQUITY IN BELGIUM (ACE)

The CIT reform, concluded during the nineties, left unaltered the well-known preferential tax regime of the coordination centres. But most of the other preferential tax regimes, introduced during the two previous

---

15. « Disregarded charges » refers to charges that are not deductible from a tax point of view, while being considered as deductible expenses from an accounting viewpoint. This is the case, for example, with a fixed percentage of car and restaurant expenses.

decades, were abolished or started to be phased out. The same holds for the 2003 reform: the base broadening provisions did not hit the coordination centre regime. That regime was clearly under pressure from the EU and OECD codes of conduct ([16]) and from the European Commission, under the "State aid rules" examination procedure.

The coordination centre regime was listed as harmful by the EU and OECD codes of conduct and declared incompatible with EU law. The main reason was that it was assimilated to ring-fencing ([17]). Therefore, and instead of simply removing the debated system, Belgian authorities followed their Irish counterparts and decided to introduce a new tax regime. This regime was accessible to any, since the Belgian authorities decided to introduce a deduction for risk capital or notional interest: a presumptive – or notional – interest rate on a firm's own funds became deductible against the corporate income tax base. For that aim, the own funds are computed net of participations and investments in foreign branches in order to avoid cascade deductions. The reform included a series of base broadening provisions that aimed to make it revenue neutral ([18]).

This important reform deserves a series of comments. First, it has the encouraging property of removing discrimination in the tax system between financing by own funds and by debt, provided that the gross return equals the long-term interest rate. This kind of tax policy has featured in the economic literature for many years, under the name of Allowance for Corporate Equity (ACE) (see Boadway and Bruce, 1984; Gammie, 1991; IFS, 1991). Note that a similar measure had been introduced previously in Croatia (Keen and King, 2002) – but was then removed. In Brazil it was adopted at more or less the same time as in Belgium (Klemm, 2007).

Of course, the two gross rates of return are not identical. The rate of interest on corporate debt is determined by the market and eventually corrected

---

16. See OECD (1998). The European Council agreed on the principles of the EU code of conduct for business taxation on the 1st December 1997.
17. "Ring fencing" means that the regime is accessible only to firms with a non-domestic involvement. This was obviously not the case with the coordination centre regime, but the EU Council assimilated the regime to a ring-fenced one, due to the fact that it was mostly used by non-residents.
18. The investment allowance was repealed, apart from RD and green investments. A tax credit for new share issues was also repealed and the exemption of capital gains was made on a net basis instead of a gross basis.

for firm-specific risks. The notional interest rate is based on past rates on 10 year maturity government bonds. The latter rate is usually below the former. Moreover an upper limit of 6 per cent was imposed. This limit was decreased to 3 per cent in 2012. The reform appears to be very close to the pure version of the allowance for equity (Gérard 2006a,b).

The memorandum put to the Parliament stresses the neutrality property of the reform because it enables corporate income tax to overcome the well-known debt equity bias. It ends by indicating that the reform also provides an alternative for financial companies using the coordination centre regime. Most would argue – rightly – that of the two motivations the second was the more important and the neutrality properties are more a consequence of the reform than its main policy motivation.

How is it that an allowance for corporate equity can be an alternative for the coordination centre (CC) regime? Most of the CC activities related to the intra-group banking and financing of investment. The basic scheme was the following: instead of direct financing of the subsidiary by the parent, the financial flow was routed through a CC to which the parent provided equity, used by the CC to provide debt to the affiliates of the group. The interest due was deductible "at source" (in the hands of the indebted affiliated company), tax exempt at the level of the CC, and the dividends attributed by the CC were not subject to tax either at the CC level, or at the parent level ([19]). Valenduc (2004b) computed the effects on METR and AETR on the intra-group financing of investment. METRs appear to be strongly negative and AETR was substantially lowered. As a result, the CCs were highly capitalised. That is why an allowance for corporate equity provided an alternative, subject to the conditions that (a) it should apply to the existing stock of capital and (b) the use of the triangle schemes just described should not be disallowed.

The Belgian government decided to make the ACE accessible to the existing stock of capital, which resulted in a windfall gain for the existing shareholders, but it was considered to be "the price to pay" for keeping the CCs located in Belgium. On the other hand, when the Italian government

---

19. The same held when the profits were retained by the coordination centre.

recently decided to introduce an allowance for corporate equity, the choice was made not to extend the benefit to the existing stock of capital.

Empirical evidence provides mixed and disputed results. The reform was intended to be revenue neutral, but this has been intensively discussed. A report by the central bank at the request of the federal government (Burggraeve e.a, 2008) argued for a low budgetary cost. The report however failed to include the budgetary costs of the "triangular schemes" and attributed any inward Foreign Direct Investment (FDI) to the reform instead of considering the difference between inward FDI and a benchmark scenario. According to Valenduc (2009), the budgetary cost may be higher than initially indicated and higher than the evaluation by the central bank.

The ITR on corporations exhibits a clear downward trend in Figure 4 after the introduction of the ACE. Valenduc (2011) performs an in-depth examination to explain that trend. He concludes that (a) the 2006 peak is due to a timing effect (a change in the timing of CIT assessments that boosted CIT revenue in 2006) combined with the compensatory provisions of the reform; (b) starting from 2006, there is a clear decline in the effective tax rate of corporations, defined as the ratio of CIT to the "benchmark tax base" ([20]); and (c) there has been a widening of the tax base. Surprisingly, the widening of the tax base comes from an increase in gross profitability, and not from an increase in the size of the corporate sector. The increase in gross profitability seems quite strange: it does not fit with what one would expect from a reform which lowers the corporate income tax in a small open economy. Valenduc (2011) makes the point that the triangular structures that have been put in place by financial companies (reviving from the coordination centre regime) just have this type of effect.

Princen (2012) conducted a difference-in-difference investigation to look at the effects of the ACE on the balance sheets of non-financial companies. She concluded that the reform had been successful in correcting the

---

20. What the tax base should be with no tax expenditures and full deduction of any charges.

debt-equity ratio towards more equity, but that there was no effect on tangible and intangible investment on the left hand side of the balance sheet.

The ACE reform raises a set of other issues. Firstly, the reform in some sense isolates Belgium among EU Member States at a time when the European authorities, together with Member States' administrations, are preparing a directive on tax base consolidation at the EU level with a single method for computing that base. This does not preclude the fact that such a measure could be an interesting avenue for the future of corporate taxation in Europe – see Bond (2000) and Sorensen (2007). Secondly, the measure makes the Belgian tax system less transparent by creating a large gap between the statutory and the effective corporate income tax rates. Finally, with respect to the "rate cut, base broadening" recommendation of economic theory, the ACE partially goes in the wrong direction – see Radulescu and Stimmelmayer (2007).

2.4.3 THE PATENT BOX

Since the 2008 tax year, Belgium has joined the – as yet – very small club of countries offering a patent box, by which is meant a partial deduction of patents income against the corporate tax base. In Belgium the deduction amounts to 80 per cent and the tax rate is thus 6.8 per cent. Other members of the club now include The Netherlands (10 per cent tax rate decided in 2007), Luxembourg (5.9 per cent decided in 2008) and The United Kingdom with its 10 per cent, effective rate in 2013 (see Griffith et alii 2011).

In Belgium, this deduction applies to income from patents, totally or partially developed, or improved in research centres located in the Belgian territory. Those incomes consist of income obtained from third parties as well as of income that the company would have received from third parties instead of itself exploiting the patent. As a consequence the tax on patent income went down from a statutory rate of 33.99 per cent to an effective value of 6.80 per cent, providing Belgium with a new discrepancy between the easily observable statutory rate and the economically crucial effective rate, but also with a very reduced rate on highly mobile intangible assets. Combined with the ACE deduction, the patent box may result in exempting from CIT a rate of return up to 5 times the interest rates on 10-year governmental bonds.

This new instrument of tax policy may be expected to be of great importance in the new competition for ideas and development and the location of intellectual property, especially when those intangibles are the primary resource of the country. In some sense it completes the set of instruments that Belgium has put in place to boost research activity in its territory, especially the "wage subsidy" for research staff members.

2.5 Taxation of savings income

The year 2000 was marked by an agreement between the EU Member States on the taxation of savings income. The system, decided in the Portuguese city of Feira, was turned into a Directive in June 2003 – see European Commission (2003) – and has applied since 1 July 2005.

The Directive recognises that "residents of Member States are currently often able to avoid any form of taxation in their Member State of residence on interest they receive in another member state" and that "this situation is creating distortions in the capital movements between member states, which are incompatible with the internal market", before adding that "the ultimate aim of this Directive is to enable savings income in the form of interest payments made in one member state to beneficial owners who are individuals resident in another member state to be made subject to effective taxation in accordance with the laws of the latter member state".

The mechanism thus deals with payments of capital income made by paying agents of the European Union, mostly banks, to EU citizens who are not residents of the member state in which the payment takes place. The information on the transactions is transmitted by the paying agents to the local tax administration and by the latter to the tax administrations of the countries of residence of the beneficial owners. This exchange of information is systematic and automatic; in that respect the EU system differs from that of the OECD which is based on exchange of information upon request. However the EU system applies only to interest income and claims dominated by interest income. Its extension to other forms of capital income like dividends and insurance products is under discussion.

Nevertheless, three countries obtained the right not to take part in the exchange of information as long as a similar agreement was not found with competing countries located outside the European Union. Instead of exchanging information, those three countries, Austria, Belgium and Luxembourg, committed to levying a withholding tax on interest payments and to transferring 75 per cent of the revenue collected to the country of residence of the beneficiary, but without revealing her identity. The rate of that withholding tax was initially fixed at 15 per cent. It was progressively increased to the current rate of 35 per cent. In 2009, Belgium decided to leave this group of countries. It joined the former one to participate in the exchange of information.

As mentioned above, "the ultimate aim of this Directive is to enable savings income … to be made subject to effective taxation in accordance with the laws of the latter member state". This is to be interpreted as the willingness to allow a member state to tax interest paid at home and abroad equally, provided it is in the territory of the European Union and whatever the tax system may be. Indeed, in organising individualised exchange of information the EU makes possible the application of tax systems based on individualised taxation like the Global Income Tax and the Danish version of the Dual Income Tax. The operation of tax systems where capital income is subject to a flat tax as in Belgium over the decade examined and in the other Dual Income Tax Nordic countries, or still in The Netherlands, is a fortiori facilitated.

During the same decade the United States signed an agreement with most banks across the world making them Qualified Intermediaries of the US Inland Revenue Service and allowing the US administration to supervise the commitment of those banks without regard for the local authorities. That agreement includes the commitment to provide the US administration with the taxpayer identification of US beneficiaries of income from US sources paid by the bank and it was complemented by a revision of the Belgium-US Tax Treaty.

As of April 2009, Belgium radically changed its position on exchange of information, having been included in the "grey list" issued by the G20. The position of the G20 was motivated by the fact that bank secrecy was invoked by Belgium to oppose to exchange of information requests from its treaty partners. The reservation that Belgium placed on article 26 of the OECD model convention – the provision that organises the exchange of information between treaty partners – was withdrawn and the Belgian government engaged extensively in signing agreements allowing the exchange of information with treaty partners.

From an economic point of view, all these changes have resulted in making the taxation of savings residence-based, rather than source-based.

3. WHAT HAS NOT BEEN DONE

Significant tax reforms were conducted during the nineties. However, a lot remains to be done.

On the PIT side, the "Reynders reform" did not include any base broadening provision and the tax credit for social transfers was expanded. In this sense, this reform appears to be a missed opportunity. It should have been possible to reduce the taxation of earned income by cutting tax expenditures. But the government chose to take a route in the opposite direction, increasing the number of tax expenditures and extending the coverage of some of them. By the end of the decade, the tax system had clearly moved further away from neutrality.

On the CIT side, the introduction of the ACE is notable progress towards neutrality. However, the reform clearly suffers from the lack of anti-abuse rules which should act against triangle structures that result in double dip deductions, or deductions with no corresponding taxation. This undermines the sustainability of the reform and progress towards neutrality.

Taxation of savings is still far from being uniform: effective tax rates differ widely across assets (Valenduc, 2003; OECD 2009b). Interests from savings accounts are still tax free, which enables the banking sector to keep the regulated interest rate low. It is a typical example of a tax exemption that benefits not the saver, but the banker. The Belgian tax system still lacks a generic rule that taxes capital gains, and prevents loopholes created by financial products which aim to avoid the final withholding tax on savings.

Finally, the first decade of the century appears to be the "missed decade" on green tax reform. There is clearly potential for reform which could internalise the external cost of CO_2 emissions, including those relating to transport, into prices. Moreover, this should facilitate a further lowering of labour taxation. The 2009 report of the "Conseil supérieur des Finances" clearly indicates the potential for such a reform and make suggestions for overcoming the distributive and competitive obstacles. No support came from policy makers, while the most damaging environmentally harmful subsidy in the tax system – the company car regime – was still alive at the end of the decade.

REFERENCES

BAVEYE, J., VALENDUC, C. (2011), *Are "environmental" tax incentives efficient ?* Ministère des Finances, Bulletin de documentation, No 2, pp. 139-166.

BOADWAY, R. and BRUCE, N. (1984), '*A General Proposition on the Design of a Neutral Business Tax*', Journal of Public Economics, 24, 231–39.

BOND, S.R. (2000), '*Leveling Up or Leveling Down? Some Reflections on the ACE and CBIT Proposals, and the Future of the Corporate Tax Base*" in S. Cnossen, ed., *Taxing Capital Income in the European Union*, Oxford University Press, Oxford.

BURGGRAVE, K, JEANFILS, Ph., VAN CAUTER, K., VAN MEENSEL, L. (2008), *Macroeconomic and fiscal impact of the risk capital allowance*, Economic Review, No 3, pp.

CANTILLON, B., KERSTENS, B., VERBIST, G. (2000), *De verdelingseffecten van het ontwerp van fiscale hervorming: microsimulatie resultaten*, CSB-Berichten, Centrum voor sociaal beleid, UFSIA, Antwerpen.

CONSEIL SUPÉRIEUR DES FINANCES (2002), *Avis sur les déductions à l'impôt des personnes physiques*, Ministère des Finances, Bruxelles.

http://www.docufin.be/websedsdd/intersalgfr/hrfcsf/adviezen/PDF/avis_ipp2002.pdf

CONSEIL SUPÉRIEUR DES FINANCES (2007), *Taxation du travail, compétitivité et emploi*, Ministère des Finances, Bruxelles.

http://www.docufin.be/websedsdd/intersalgfr/hrfcsf/adviezen/PDF/CSF_fisc_travail_2007.pdf

CONSEIL SUPÉRIEUR DES FINANCES (2009), *La politique fiscale et l'environnement,* Ministère des Finances, Bruxelles.

http://www.docufin.be/websedsdd/intersalgfr/hrfcsf/adviezen/PDF/CSF_fisc_environnement_2009.pdf

COUR DES COMPTES (2006), *Réforme de l'impôt des sociétés : évaluation de la neutralité budgétaire.*

DECOSTER, A., GÉRARD, M. and VALENDUC, C. (2001), *Recettes publiques et politique fiscale,* dans DE CALLATAY E., Editeur, *La fin du déficit budgétaire,* DE BOECK, Bruxelles, pp. 107-134.

EUROPEAN COMMISSION (2003), "Council Directive 2003/48/EC of 3 June 2003on taxation of savings income in the form of interest payments", Official Journal of the European Union, L 157/38 (26.6.2003).

EUROPEAN COMMISSION (2012), *Taxation trends in the European Union,* Eurostat, Brussels.

GAMMIE, M. (1991) *Corporate Tax Harmonization: An 'ACE' proposal,* 31 European Taxation 8 (1991), pp. 238-242.

GERARD, M. (2006a), '*A Closer Look at Belgium's Notional Interest Deduction*', Tax Notes International, February 6, 449–53.

GERARD, M. (2006b), *Belgium moves to Dual Allowance for Corporate Equity,* European Taxation, 4 (April), pp. 156-162.

HALLEUX, E. and VALENDUC, C. (2007), *Effective tax rate and the size of the company in Belgium: an empirical investigation on micro-data,* Ministère des Finances, Bulletin de documentation, No 2, pp. 217-254.

http://www.docufin.be/websedsdd/intersalgfr/thema/publicaties/documenta/2007/BdocB_2007_Q2e_Halleux_Valenduc.pdf

INSTITUTE FOR FISCAL STUDIES, CAPITAL TAXES GROUP, 1991, *Equity for Companies: a corporation tax for the 1990s,* Commentary 26, Institute for Fiscal Studies, London.

KEEN, M. and KING, J. (2002), *The Croatian Profit Tax: An ACE in Practice',* Fiscal Studies 23(3), 401–18.

KLEMM, A. (2007), *Allowances for Corporate Equity in Practice,* CESifo Economic Studies, 53, 229-262.

OECD (1998), OECD Paris.

OECD (2009a), *Growing unequal;* OECD, Paris.

OECD (2009b), *OECD Economic Surveys: Belgium,* OECD Paris.

OECD (2012), *Taxing wages,* OECD, Paris.

PRINCEN, S. (2012), *Taxes do affect corporate financing decisions: the case of the Belgian ACE,* CESIfo wp 3713

RADULESCU, D. and STIMMELMAYER, M. (2007), *ACE vs CBIT ? Which is Better for Investment and Welfare ?,* CESifo Economic Studies, 53 (2), pp. 294-328.

SORENSEN, P.B. (2007), "*Can Capital Income Taxes Survive? And Should They?*",CESifo Economic Studies 53(2):172-228.

VALENDUC, C. (1999), *La réforme de l'impôt des sociétés,* Ministère des Finances, Bulletin de Documentation, No 5, pp. 147-208.

VALENDUC, C. (2002), *La réforme de l'impôt des personnes physiques : ses effets sur l'imposition des salaires, l'incitation à l'emploi et sur la distribution des revenus,* Ministère des Finances, Bulletin de documentation, No 3, pp. 145-206

VALENDUC, C.(2003), *Effective taxation of household savings in Belgium,* Paper presented at the 59th congress of the International Institute for public finance "Public Finance and Financial markets" Praha, 25-28 august 2003

VALENDUC, C. (2004a), *Corporate income tax and the taxation of income from capital: some evidence from the past reforms and the present debate on corporate income tax in Belgium,* European Commission, TAXUD, Working paper N°6

VALENDUC, C. (2004b), *Les dépenses fiscales,* Reflets et perspectives de la vie économique, No1, pp. 87-104.

VALENDUC, C. (2009), *Les intérêts notionnels : une réforme fondamentale et controversée,* Courrier hebdomadaire du CRISP, No 2018.

VALENDUC, C. (2011), *Imposition des revenus du travail, du capital et de la consommation: évolutions récentes,* Ministère des Finances, Bulletin de documentation, No 3, pp. 15-61.

VALENDUC, C., VAN REYBROUCK, G. (2012), *Taxation of Housing in Belgium: facts and reforms,* European Commission, forthcoming.

5. Approaches to Primary Expenditures

In this chapter different authors shed light on a particular aspect of government expenditure or public governance in general. In one way or another, they all address the theme of government efficiency. The contribution by Valérie Schmitz, Bastien Scorneau and Robert Deschamps focuses on the spending differences between regions. Why does a higher share of the budget not always imply a better output? Stefan Van Parys and Luc Van Meensel describe the evolution of employment in the public sector in both a narrow and a broad sense. The Belgian story is also compared with those of other European countries. A reduction in government employment is one of the possible ways of achieving budget cuts and increasing government efficiency. The two remaining contributions do not make use of an economically analytical approach to the same extent, but are certainly no less interesting for that. Koen Verhoest, after a brief theoretical introduction, discusses the evolution of performance contracting as an instrument of control used by the different Belgian governments during recent decades. To what extent and under what conditions can performance contracting be used to achieve a more efficient government? Finally, Jean Hindriks's contribution makes one think about the concept of government efficiency, how to measure it and what tools exist to improve it.

5.1. THE STRUCTURE OF EXPENDITURE OF THE REGIONS AND COMMUNITIES: A COMPARISON 2002-2011

Valérie Schmitz, Bastien Scorneau, and Robert Deschamps [1]

1.1 Introduction

In the process of the federalization of Belgium, Regions and Communities have seen a major expansion of their competences and responsibilities. Within this broader autonomy, Regions and Communities may allocate their budgets as they think best, which can possibly lead to large discrepancies between them. Because budgets are the visible expression of political choices, differences in their allocation also pinpoint diverging political priorities.

The aim of this paper is to compare the budgetary expenditures of the Regions and Communities for the territories of Wallonia, Brussels and Flanders in the period from 2002 to2011 and to highlight the implicit priorities of those governments. Those priorities are to be analysed in terms of their impact on the economy, employment and sustainable development. The purpose of our contribution, however, is not to study the expenditures' efficiency, but to quantify them in terms of budget shares.

Budgetary expenditures are classified into five categories: regional, social and cultural, education, debt and administration expenditures. Budgetary expenditures for each territory have to be carefully defined; regarding the Walloon territory, they come from the budgets of the Walloon Region and of the French and German Communities. For the territory of Brussels, they come from the budgets of the Brussels-Capital Region, of the French, Flemish and Common Community Commissions, and also from the French and Flemish Communities' budgets. Budgetary expenditures for the Flemish territory come from the Flemish Community's

---

1. Valérie Schmitz and Bastien Scorneau are researchers at CERPE, Faculty of Economics, University of Namur. Robert Deschamps is professor at CERPE, Faculty of Economics, University of Namur.

budget. Corrections have to be made for each territory's expenditures in order to neutralize transfers between entities.

1.2 Methodology[2]

1.2.1 PERIOD

We studied the evolution of the structure of expenditures for the 2002-2011 period, 2002 being the first year after the Lambermont reform (2001). This reform of the Belgian federal system was the last one before the reform the current government will have to implement.

For each of these 10 years we have published comparisons from a territorial and from a linguistic point of view. For the Brussels-Capital Region, however, our analysis starts only in 2005.

1.2.2 REGIONAL TERRITORIES & ADJUSTMENTS

Budgetary expenditures for the Walloon territory or "Wallonia" ("Walloon expenditures") consist of the expenditures out of the Walloon Region's budget (except for transfers to the German Community), of the German Community's budget and of a share (defined below) of the French Community's budget (except the transfers to the Walloon Region and the French Community Commission of Brussels).

Budgetary expenditures for the territory of Brussels cover the expenditures from the Brussels-Capital Region's budget (except for transfers to the French, Flemish and Common Community Commissions, as well as transfers to the debt management Fund) of the French, Flemish and Common Community Commissions, and of shares (defined below) of the French and of the Flemish Communities.

---

2. For full details about applied methodology see the series of research papers about this comparison exercise (CERPE-University of Namur, "Comparaisons interrégionale et intercommunautaire des budgets de dépenses des Entités fédérées", 2002-2011, available online at http://www.fundp.ac.be/eco/economie/cerpe).

Budgetary expenditures for the Flemish territory or "Flanders" ("Flemish expenditures") consist of the expenditures of the Flemish Community, except for transfers to the Flemish Community Commission and a share (defined below) of the Flemish community's expenditures.

The corrections for the French and the Flemish Communities' budgets aim to distinguish, on the one hand, budgetary expenditures respectively dedicated to Wallonia and Flanders and, on the other hand, budgetary expenditures dedicated to the French- and Flemish-speaking populations in Brussels.

The shares of the French and the Flemish Communities attributed respectively to Wallonia and Flanders are equivalent to the proportions of the Walloon population in the French Community (80.8% in 2002, 79.5% in 2011) and to the proportion of the population of Flanders in the Flemish Community (96.8% in 2002, 96.6% in 2011). The remaining shares are attributed to Brussels. The population of each Community in Brussels is computed using the 80-20 key (80% of the Brussels population is French-speaking, 20% is Flemish-speaking).

The outgoings of the Flemish Community and Flemish Region are presented in the same budget, making it difficult to distinguish between them. When a distinction is possible, Regional expenditures remain unchanged and Community expenditures are adjusted as described above. The nature of various other expenditures, however, cannot easily be identified, as they seem to belong to both the Community and the Region (this is particularly true for central administration or operating expenditures). Those expenditures may also be related to the Flemish population of Brussels, so we first calculate a "mixed key" to distinguish expenditures of the Flemish territory from those of the Flemish population in Brussels. This key is equal to the average between the Flemish Community's expenditures key (96.6% in 2011) and the implicit Flemish Region's expenditures (100%). We then split the remaining expenditures between the Flemish Region and Community using the average proportions of the Region's and Community's expenditures in the Flemish budget.

1.2.3 CATEGORIES OF EXPENDITURES

We distinguish between five categories of expenditures, determined on the basis of the Entities' competences:
- Regional expenditures, which represent competences that are exerted by the Regions. They include expenditures relating to the economy, employment and professional training, natural resources and the environment, local administration, territorial planning and housing policy, equipment and transport.
- Social and cultural expenditures relate to competences concerning health and social action, culture, sport and tourism.
- Education and research expenditures concern competences relating to fundamental and secondary education, higher education and universities, scientific research and other spending on education and research.
- Debt expenses (interest payments).
- Administration expenses: this category covers expenditures such as allocations to parliaments and governments, ministers' offices and secretariats. They also comprise short-term provisions used if the macroeconomic environment deteriorates or if expenditures are higher than expected.

Each category contains several sub-categories. Each sub-category is built mostly by aggregating budgets' "activity programmes"[3] (the second lowest level in budgets). Sometimes, however, we had to distinguish between "budget articles", the most disaggregated level in the budgets. For more information on the classification we refer the reader to the collections of publications by the CERPE on this comparison exercise.

1.2.4 METHOD OF COMPARISON

We compared the budget shares of the three regions (territories) for each expenditure category. The comparison is built on a "comparison ratio" for each expenditure category, which is the share of the expenditures category in the Walloon (Brussels) budget divided by the share of the same category in the Flemish budget. A ratio greater than 1 indicates that

---

3. We use initial budgets, and we focus on non-differentiated appropriations and payment appropriations.

Wallonia (Brussels) spends a higher share of its budget than Flanders. A ratio equal to 1 means that Wallonia (Brussels) spends exactly the same proportion as Flanders, while a ratio smaller than 1 implies that Wallonia (Brussels) spends a smaller share of its budget than Flanders.

Those ratios have been computed by the CERPE for each year from 2002 to 2011 for Wallonia, which makes it possible to analyse the evolution of the categories of expenditures we have determined. However, the comparison for Brussels has been available only since 2005.

1.3 Core Analysis

1.3.1 First point: static analysis

The results for 2011 are presented in Tables 1 and 2. The average ratios for the 2002-2011 period (2005-2011 for Brussels) are presented in the last column. The results for the years 2002-2010 (2005-2010for Brussels) are not presented here but can be found in the research papers indicated above.

Overall, the comparisons between Wallonia and Flanders and between Brussels and Flanders offer clear similarities. All five categories of expenditures follow the same pattern when compared in terms of budget shares to Flanders; for regional expenditures, comparison ratios in 2011 are greater than 1 in Wallonia (1.03) and in Brussels (1.11). This means that, compared to Flanders in 2011, the budget share for regional expenditures is higher in Wallonia, and even higher in Brussels. Average comparison coefficients for the period are also greater than 1 in both regions (1.14 for Wallonia, 1.21 for Brussels). On the other hand, budget shares for social-cultural and education spending are higher in Flanders than in Wallonia and in Brussels, in 2011 and on average for the period.

Debt expenses and administration spending account for a higher budget share in Wallonia and in Brussels than in Flanders. Higher budget shares for debt expenses are the result of greater public deficits in Wallonia and in Brussels leading to a higher indebtedness level. Higher budget shares

Table 1: Comparison of the budgets of Wallonia and Flanders (on a territorial basis)

2011	EXPEND. ON THE FLEMISH TERRITORY	EXPEND. ON THE WALLOON TERRITORY	COMPAR. RATIO (2011)	COMPAR. RATIO (2002)	COMPAR. RATIO (AVG. 2002-2011)
I. Regional expenditures	**8,408,918**	**5,207,955**	**1.03**	**1.16**	**1.14**
A. Economy	1,321,987	976,269	1.23	1.63	1.55
Foreign relations	91,020	100,231	1.83	1.7	1.73
Economic policy and economic expansion	601,303	391,753	1.08	1.55	1.82
Agriculture	119,617	133,416	1.85	2.73	2.53
Energy, technology	78,792	125,965	2.65	1.31	3.03
Research funded by the Region	431,255	224,904	0.87	-	0.72
B. Employment policy and professional training	1,309,943	1,150,359	1.46	1.51	1.57
Employment	1,100,396	854,694	1.29	1.47	1.46
Professional training	209,547	295,665	2.34	1.67	2.10
C. Natural resources and environment	505,459	211,565	0.69	0.67	0.71
D. Local administrations	2,389,092	1,411,206	0.98	1.11	1.06
Municipalities	2,258,097	1,181,153	0.87	1.08	0.90
Provinces	89,312	142,873	2.65	2.58	2.68
Other	41,683	87,180	3.47	0.87	14.54
E. Spatial planning and housing	624,570	397,892	1.06	0.7	1.03
F. Equipment and transport	2,257,867	1,060,663	0.78	1.2	0.98
II. Cultural and social expenditures	**4,089,995**	**1,992,763**	**0.81**	**0.69**	**0.74**
A. Health and social work	3,106,002	1,394,049	0.74	0.64	0.70
B. Culture	801,404	452,169	0.94	0.78	0.82
C. Sport et tourism	182,589	146,545	1.33	1.09	1.10
III. Education expenditures	**10,029,096**	**5,580,175**	**0.92**	**0.88**	**0.92**
A. Fundamental and secondary	6,532,271	3,888,600	0.99	0.93	0.97
B. Higher education and university	1,474,506	871,939	0.98	0.83	0.91
C. Scientific research	302,138	106,305	0.58	0.71	0.61
D. Other	1,720,182	713,330	0.69	0.73	0.75
IV. Debt expenditures	**233,349**	**418,844**	**2.98**	**2.18**	**3.37**
V. Administration expenditures	**1,089,262**	**1,176,360**	**1.79**	**1.33**	**1.16**
A. Councils, parliaments, govern. and ministerial offices	116,358	128,509	1.83	1.62	1.93
Councils/parliament allocations	85,316	71,086	1.38	-	1.46
Governments/minist. offices allocations	31,043	57,423	3.07	-	2.92
B. General secretariats	967,663	1,028,310	1.76	1.28	1.16
C. Reserve funds	5,241	19,541	6.19	-	1.73
TOTAL EXPENDITURES	**23,850,620***	**14,376,096**	**1.00**	**1.00**	**1.00**

* Except "Jobkorting" (75 million EUR)
** Comparison ratio = share of expenditures in the Walloon budget / share of expenditures in the Flemish budget
Source: CERPE-University of Namur (2002-2011)

Table 2: Comparison of the budgets of Brussels and Flanders (on a territorial basis)

2011	EXPEND. ON THE FLEMISH TERRITORY	EXPEND. ON THE BRUSSELS TERRITORY	COMPAR. RATIO (2011)	COMPAR. RATIO (2005)	COMPAR. RATIO (AVG. 2005-2011)
I. Regional expenditures	**8,408,918**	**2,249,078**	**1.11**	**1.27**	**1.21**
A. Economy	1,321,987	216,163	0.68	0.63	0.74
Foreign relations	91,020	25,698	1.17	1.21	1.22
Economic policy and economic expansion	601,303	68,225	0.47	0.61	0.78
Agriculture	119,617	760	0.03	0.02	0.02
Energy, technology	78,792	79,297	4.17	5.7	6.19
Research funded by the Region	431,255	42,183	0.41	0.34	0.37
B. Employment policy and professional training	1,309,943	322,168	1.02	1.3	1.07
Employment	1,100,396	274,077	1.03	1.35	1.09
Professional training	209,547	48,091	0.95	1.11	0.97
C. Natural resources and environment	505,459	224,964**	1.84	2.1	1.98
D. Local administrations	2,389,092	456,370	0.79	0.66	0.79
Municipalities	2,258,097	456,008	0.84	0.56	0.70
Provinces	89,312	362	0.02	0	0.01
Other	41,683	0	0	2.36	1.84
E. Spatial planning and housing	624,570	256,089	1.7	1.79	1.82
F. Equipment and transport	2,257,867	773,324	1.42	2.26	1.74
II. Cultural and social expenditures	**4,089,995**	**756,901**	**0.77**	**0.73**	**0.75**
A. Health and social work	3,106,002	545,343	0.73	0.69	0.72
B. Culture	801,404	179,991	0.93	0.86	0.87
C. Sport et tourism	182,589	31,567	0.72	0.78	0.74
III. Education expenditures	**10,029,096**	**1,846,082**	**0.76**	**0.75**	**0.77**
A. Fundamental and secondary	6,532,271	1,248,583	0.79	0.75	0.77
B. Higher education and university	1,474,506	276,100	0.78	0.68	0.74
C. Scientific research	302,138	38,046	0.52	0.51	0.51
D. Other	1,720,182	283,354	0.68	0.88	0.82
IV. Debt expenditures	**233,349**	**384,686**	**6.83**	**4.91**	**12.19**
V. Administration expenditures	**1,089,262**	**517,522**	**1.97**	**1.18**	**1.34**
A. Councils, parliaments, govern. and ministerial offices	116,358	83,850	2.99	4.22	4.06
Councils/parliament allocations	85,316	54,050	2.63	2.44	2.61
Governments/minist. offices allocations	31,043	29,800	3.98	7.62	6.93
B. General secretariats	967,663	433,546***	1.86	0.96	1.19
C. Reserve funds	5,241	127	0.1	-	0.16
TOTAL EXPENDITURES	**23,850,620***	**5,754,269**	**1.00**	**1.00**	**1.00**

** Including dotation to the regional agency for cleansing "Bruxelles-Propreté" (118.9 million EUR). In other regions, this competence is attributed to local administrations.
*** Including dotation to the fire brigade and emergency medical service "SIAMU" (82.2 million EUR). In other regions, this competence is attributed to local administrations.
Source: CERPE-University of Namur (2005-2011)

for administration spending are partly the result of more complex institutional frameworks.

Despite the similarities between those two comparisons, one must be careful in their interpretation with regard to the specific status of Brussels-Capital, a Region with a smaller territory and a higher population density than Wallonia and Flanders. Budget shares in Brussels thus sometimes reflect these characteristics, which imply different policy choices from in the other two Regions. Another feature of this comparison however needs to be stressed: among regional expenditures, the budget share for expenditures dedicated to research was significantly smaller in Brussels than in Flanders in 2011 and on average over the period (with an average comparison ration of 0.41). It was smaller than in Wallonia (with an average comparison ratio of 0.87). The same pattern applies for expenditures relating to scientific research, with budget shares smaller on average over the period in Brussels (comparison coefficient equals 0.51) and in Wallonia(comparison coefficient equals 0.61) than in Flanders.

Some differences between Wallonia and Flanders should be further noted among regional expenditures; the budget share of expenditures relating to energy and technology policies is higher in Wallonia than in Flanders (2.65 in 2011, 3.03 on average over the period) due to the "Plan Marshall 2. Vert". On the other hand, expenditures relating to natural resources and the environment represent a higher share of the Flemish budget(avg. 0.71).

1.3.2 SECOND POINT: DYNAMIC ANALYSIS

In 2002, budget shares for all categories of expenditures were quite different in Wallonia and in Flanders. With the exception of debt expenditures and administration spending, it nevertheless seems that these differences have diminished during the period. This does not automatically mean that Walloon spending behaviour converges towards the Flemish. Indeed, convergence in terms of budget shares can be explained either by an adjustment of both Entities or of one Entity alone.

When budget shares are studied separately for Wallonia and Flanders, trends show that the share of regional expenditures remained quite stable in Wallonia between 2002 and 2011 while it increased in Flanders. Within this category of expenditures, this pattern is less true for the share of expenditures for equipment and transport, which decreased in the Walloon budget (from around 10% in 2002 to 8% in 2011), while it increased in the Flemish budget (from 8% in 2002 to 10% in 2011).

The evolution of the budget shares for social and cultural expenditures in Wallonia and in Flanders is also quite different. While this share steadily increases over the whole period in Wallonia (from 11% in 2002 to 14% 2011), it displays an irregular trend in Flanders with ups and downs (between 16% and 18%). This results in a comparison ratio increasing over the period (from 0.69 in 2002 to 0.81 in 2011). Within this category, it is worth noting that the budget share for expenditures relating to culture increased regularly in Wallonia (from 2.8% of the budget in 2002 to 3.1% in 2011) while it decreased in Flanders (from 3.9% in 2003 to 3.4% in 2011).

Graph 1: Evolution of budget shares of Wallonia relatively to Flanders for regional, social-cultural and education expenditures.

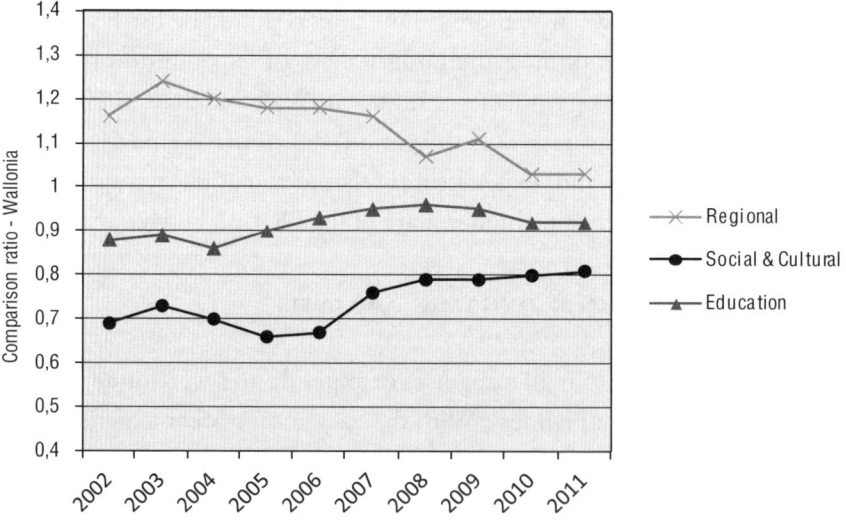

Sources: CERPE-University of Namur (2002-2011)

The budget shares for education expenditures in Wallonia and Flanders evolved in a similar way over the whole period, which explains the stability of the comparison ratio over the period. Within this category of expenditures, however, comparison ratios evolve in opposite directions concerning scientific research (it decreased from 0.71 in 2002 to 0.58 in 2011) and higher education and universities (it increased from 0.83 to 0.98). Indeed, while the Walloon budget share for scientific research stayed low over the period (around 0.72% on average), it increased in Flanders (from 0.98% in 2002 to 1.27% in 2011). Regarding higher education, the share of the Walloon budget remained constant over the period (around 6%) but it slightly decreased in Flanders (from 7.33% in 2002 to 6.18% in 2011).

The evolution of budget shares for debt expenditures and administration spending is less clear. Although budget shares for debt expenditures are always higher in Wallonia (but vary greatly every year), that is not the case for budget shares for administration spending, sometimes also higher in Flanders.

Graph 2: Evolution of budget shares of Brussels relatively to Flanders for regional, social-cultural and education expenditures.

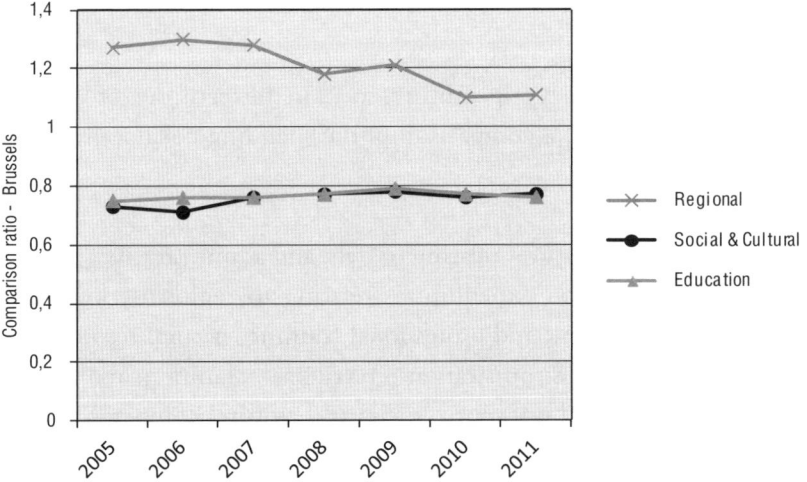

Sources: CERPE-University of Namur (2005-2011)

The convergence observed in the analysis of the comparison ratios for Wallonia and Flanders can be found for Brussels in the case of regional expenditures. For Wallonia, this seems to be mainly the result of an increasing budget share for regional expenditures in Flanders (from 29%

in 2005 to 35% in 2011), while this share remains more stable in the Brussels budget (from 37% to 39% between 2005 and 2011).

The comparison ratios for the remaining expenditures presented on the graph (social-cultural and education expenditures) show that the differences in budget shares between Brussels and Flanders remain remarkably constant over the period. This constancy is due to the similar evolution of respective budget shares from 2005 to 2011. Let us however mention that, as for Wallonia, the comparison ratio for scientific research in Brussels remained quite similar over the period (from 0.51 in 2005 to 0.52 in 2011), though smaller on average than in Wallonia.

Finally, budget shares for debt expenditures remained higher in Brussels than in Flanders over the period, as well as budget shares for administrative expenditures.

1.4 Conclusion

By sorting out budgetary expenditures spent in the territories of Wallonia, Brussels and Flanders, a comparison of the spending behaviours of each region can be made.

Leaving aside expenditures relating to debt and administrative spending, our analysis focuses on expenditures relating to regional competences (economy, employment and professional training, natural resources and environment, local administrations, territorial planning and housing policy, equipment and transport), social and cultural competences, education and scientific research.

Differences between regions in terms of budget shares for those categories may be interpreted as the result of implicit political choices. They should be analysed in the light of objectives such as employment promotion or support of the economic activity. Factors that are known to contribute to these objectives, such as public investment in private enterprises, in human capital, in R&D and scientific research, should then get all the attention.

The main results show, firstly, that budget shares for regional expenditures are higher in Wallonia and in Brussels than in Flanders. This difference tends however to decrease, as this share of the Flemish budget has increased over the 2002-2011 period, while shares in the Walloon and Brussels budgets have remained stable.

Secondly, budget shares for social and cultural expenditures are smaller in Wallonia and in Brussels than in Flanders. The difference between Wallonia and Flanders however seems to decrease over the years, due to a growing budget share in Wallonia. The budget shares in Flanders and Brussels remain stable.

Finally, the evolutions of budget shares for education spending in the three regions are remarkably similar, though the share is smaller in Wallonia than in Flanders, and even smaller in Brussels. Furthermore, within this category of expenditures, budget shares for scientific research in Brussels and in Wallonia are very much smaller than in Flanders. Research funded by the Regions also accounts for smaller budget shares in Brussels and in Wallonia than in Flanders.

Our analysis assesses political priorities only in terms of budget shares and does not provide any information concerning spending efficiency. This raises questions which should be analysed further. For instance, with a roughly equivalent budget share for education, the Flemish Community performs better in international comparisons (PISA studies[4]) than the French Community. Wallonia dedicates a higher budget share to professional training than Flanders, but the proportion of poorly qualified unemployed workers remains higher.

1.5 References

CERPE-University of Namur, "Comparaisons interrégionale et intercommunautaire des budgets de dépenses des Entités fédérées", *Cahiers de recherche du CERPE – Série politique économique*, Faculté des Sciences économiques sociales et de gestion FUNDP, 2002-2011.

---

4. OECD, "Education at a Glance 2011", OECD indicators, 2011

Hermans, Schmitz, Scorneau, de Streel, Deschamps, "Comparaisons interrégionale et intercommunautaire des budgets de dépenses 2011 des Entités fédérées", *Cahiers de recherche du CERPE – Série politique économique*, n°60 2011/09, Faculté des Sciences économiques sociales et de gestion FUNDP, 2011

OECD, "Education at a Glance 2011", OECD indicators, 2011

5.2. TRENDS IN PUBLIC EMPLOYMENT IN BELGIUM

Stefan Van Parys and Luc Van Meensel [5,6]

Introduction

This chapter analyses the main trends in public employment in Belgium between 2000 and 2010, based on the most coherent possible set of public employment statistics. The first section surveys the characteristics and developments in employment in Belgium's general government sector. The second section highlights public employment in a broad sense, while in the third section an international comparison is made. Finally, some conclusions are drawn.

2.1 Employment in the government sector in Belgium

According to the national accounts data compiled in accordance with the ESA 1995 rules, just over 840,000 people were employed in the general government sector in 2010.

The federal government and social security jointly account for only one fifth of employment in the general government sector. The federal government employs only 16.4% of general government sector workers, of whom almost one third are military personnel and the remainder work

---

5. Stefan Van Parys is a member of the Public Finance Division at the Research Department at the National Bank of Belgium. Luc Van Meensel is Head of the Public Finance Division at the Research Department at the National Bank of Belgium.
6. The authors would like to express their gratitude to Thomas Stragier for supplying the data used in this study.

mainly in administration.[7] Social security employs 3.6% of workers in the general government sector.[8]

Chart 1: Employment within general government by sub-sector and by branch of industry (thousands of persons, 2010)[(1)]

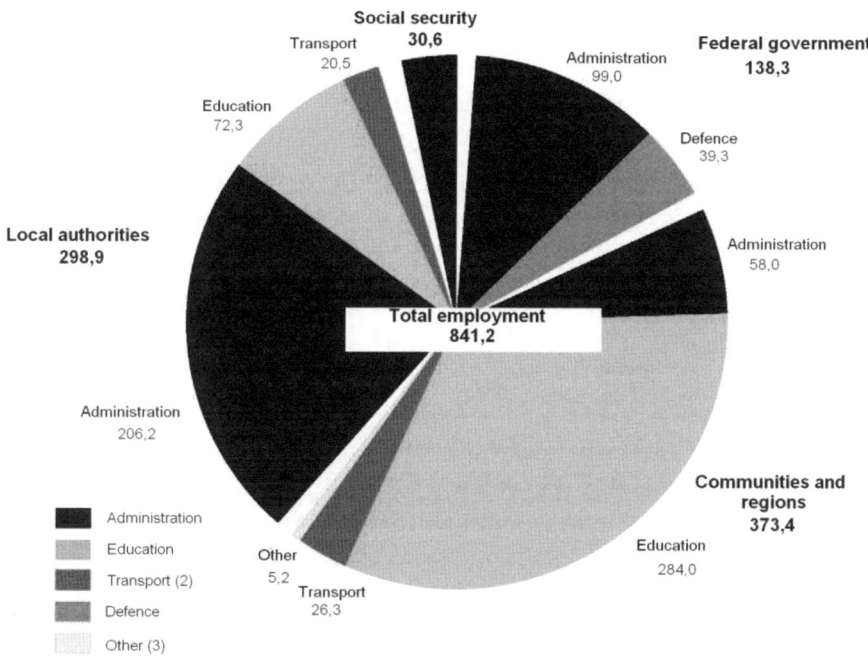

Sources: NAI, NBB.
(1) Table 17 in the annex shows the employment figures between 2000 and 2010.
(2) Regional public transport companies and ancillary services for transport.
(3) Mainly public broadcasting companies.

The communities and regions represent the lion's share of employment in the general government sector, accounting for 44.4%. This high percentage is attributable to education, since employment in schools run by the communities and subsidised privately run schools, which are included in this sub-sector, makes up 33.8% of total employment within the general government sector. Administration and transport and related services also have a large number of personnel in service, amounting to

---

7. The branch 'administration' encompasses not only personnel with administrative tasks but also *inter alia* magistrates, prison officers, federal police officers, etc.
8. Half of the employment in this sub-sector consists of health fund personnel who are deployed on compulsory insurance with respect to health care.

6.9 and 3.1% respectively of employment in the sector. The transport sector mainly concerns the staff of MIVB, De Lijn and TEC, which – in contrast to the Belgian National Railway Company group – are regarded as non-market producers since their own revenues do not cover half of their costs. The other categories – mainly the public broadcasting companies – represent 0.6% of general government employment.

Local authorities employ just over one third of the workers in the general government sector. Schools run by municipalities and provinces account for 8.6% of employment within the general government sector. Overall, therefore, education represents no less than two fifths of that employment. Moreover, almost a quarter of the personnel in the general government sector work in the branch of administration within the sub-sector of local authorities.[9]

Chart 2: General government sector employment in Belgium (thousands of persons)

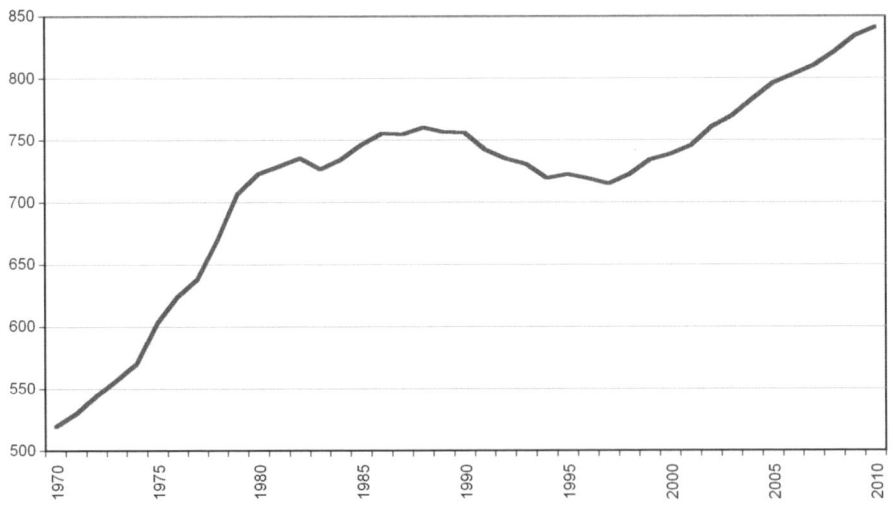

Sources: NAI, OECD, NBB.

In Belgium, employment in the public sector has clearly been on the rise since 1970. There have been three phases within this trend, which coincide with the main swings in fiscal policy. Between 1970 and 1982,

9. This activity covers a large number of functions, ranging from local police tasks to social services *inter alia* set up by the CPAS/OCMWs, and including the municipal and provincial administrations.

more than 200,000 government jobs were created. At that time, civil servants and teachers were recruited in large numbers in order to counteract the private sector job losses caused by the economic crisis and the structural loss of competitiveness. In those days, the fiscal policy stance was expansionary.

Chart 3: Employment in general government by branch of activity (percentage changes between 2000 and 2010[1])

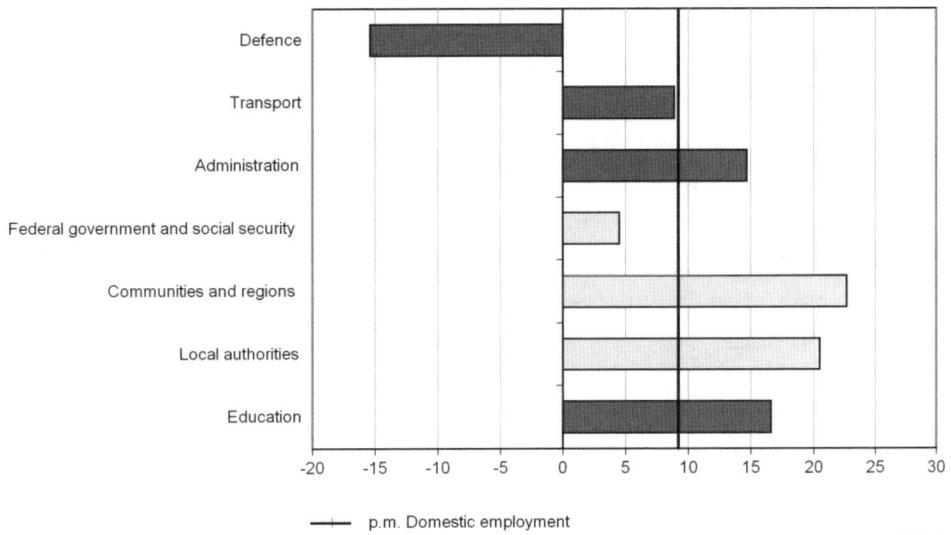

Sources: NAI, NBB.
(1) Not including the public broadcasting companies, Aquafin and neutralising the impact of the transfer, in 2002, of 8,500 former gendarmes from the federal government to the local authorities.

From 1982 onwards, putting the public finances in order became the priority for successive governments. This restrictive fiscal policy stance was tightened up still further during the 1990s, when Belgium tried to comply with the convergence criteria for joining the euro area from the outset. In that context, the number of workers employed in the general government sector initially stabilised, after which it declined. It reached a low point in 1997, which was also a result of the abolition of compulsory military service which took effect in 1994. Over a time span of a few years, therefore, about 30,000 people doing military service disappeared from the general government employment statistics. Finally, between 1997 and 2010, the volume of general government employment rose by 126,100 jobs. During this period, the fiscal policy stance reverted to expansionary, so that the primary surplus of general government in Belgium decreased over the years.

Focusing on the 2000-2010 decade, an increase in the number of jobs in the general government sector of 13.8%, or around 102,300 posts, was notable. It was a bigger rise than that for total domestic employment, which amounted to 9.2%. Breaking employment down into the various branches of activity in the general government sector and its sub-sectors, a sharper picture of the development of employment becomes apparent.

Between 2000 and 2010, general government sector employment in the administration branch increased by 14.7%. The communities and regions and local authorities in particular are responsible for this sharp increase. While the rise in employment in the administration branch remained limited to 4.5% within the federal government and social security, it rose by 22.7% and 20.5% respectively within the communities and regions and local authorities.

In the education branch, employment also experienced strong growth of 16.6%.

In the transport-related branches, comprising mainly the regional public transport companies and other supporting transport services, employment grew by 8.9%, slightly less than the growth rate of total domestic employment.

Within the general government sector, defence was the only branch of activity to record a fall in employment after 2000. The number of army personnel decreased sharply, by 7,150 or 15.4%.

2.2 Public employment in the broad sense

The definition of employment in the general government sector according to the national accounts does not include either workers in the public enterprises that are market producers or those in subsidised employment.

Taking these people also into account, the number of public employees would be well over 1.5 million.

Table 1: Employment in the general government sector and other public or subsidised jobs (thousands of persons, unless otherwise stated)

	NUMBER OF PERSONS IN 2000	NUMBER OF PERSONS IN 2010	CHANGE SINCE 2000	CHANGE SINCE 2010 (IN %)
General government sector	739	841	+102.3[1]	+13.8[1]
Public enterprises of which	131.5	120.8	-10.7	-8.2
Market-oriented intermunicipal associations[2]	18.3	21.0	+2.7	+14.8
Non-financial public enterprises of which	110.4	97.5	-12.9	-11.7
Belgacom	20.0	16.2	-3.8	-19.1
The Post Office	44.6	33.1	-11.5	-25.7
Belgian National Railway Company group	41.9	38.4	-3.5	-8.5
NBB	2.8	2.3	-0.5	-19.2
Subsidised jobs of which	331.4	560.0	+228.6	+69.0
Social Services	154.7	233.5	+78.8	+51.0
Health Care	176.7	223.1	+46.4	+26.2
Service voucher system	-	103.4	+103.4	-
Total in the broad sense	1 201.9	1 522.0	+320.2	+26.6
p.m. Total domestic employment	4 114.1	4 491.3	+377.2	+9.2

Sources: NAI, NBB.
(1) The increase would be limited to 97,700 persons (or 13.2%) if no account is taken of the public broadcasting companies, which have only come under the general government sector since 2002, and Aquafin, which ceased to be part of this sector in 2005.
(2) Inclusive of certain autonomous municipal undertakings, such as the ports of Antwerp and Ghent. Retirement homes and hospitals are included in social services and health care respectively.

The public enterprises accounted for a total of about 120,000 jobs in 2010. These are mostly to be found in the non-financial public enterprises, which have approximately 97,500 people in service, and specifically in the Belgian National Railway Company group, the Post Office and Belgacom. In 2010, some 21,000 people were employed by market-oriented intermunicipal associations active mainly in electricity, gas and water supply, in ancillary activities for the transport industry and in waste collection and waste management.

There is no statistical definition of subsidised employment. It is approximated here on the basis of the jobs that result from the service voucher system and from those in the health care and social services branches. In this respect, the categories under consideration also include non-subsidised jobs. This approach is not exhaustive. For instance, no account is taken of various subsidised activities such as those of a large number of autonomously run associations that work in the social, sporting and cultural spheres. In 2010, 223,000 jobs were recorded in health care, including hospitals, and 234,000 in social services, including retirement homes. The service voucher system, introduced in 2003, which is also very substantially subsidised, was a great success and accounted for more than 100,000 jobs in 2010.

In total, employment within general government and subsidised employment in the broad sense expanded by almost 27% between 2000 and 2010. Its growth outpaced that of the general government sector and that of domestic employment as a whole, which rose by 13.8% and 9.2% respectively. During this period, almost 85% of the increase in domestic employment was attributable to public employment in the broad sense. The dynamism of subsidised and public employment is mainly due to the rapid expansion of the service voucher system, as well as to the substantial increase in employment in social services and health care. Employment in the public enterprises, on the other hand, has fallen.

2.3 Public employment in the European context

Apart from the analysis of public employment by branches of activity and sub-sectors within Belgium, it is also interesting to compare public employment in Belgium with that in other European countries.

International comparisons of general government employment are particularly thorny, as the ESA 95 methodology may result in there being significant differences between countries in what is included in this sector. These differences are due to organisational structures in the fields of health care, education, transport, broadcasting, the environment, etc. To avoid the problem of the differing boundaries of the general government sector between one country and another, international comparisons sometimes focus on employment in a number of branches of activity in which the general government sector has a strong presence, such as administration and education. In this section, the situation in Belgium is compared with that in the euro area.[10]

Chart 4: European comparison of public employment
(employment per 100 inhabitants; 2010 unless otherwise stated)

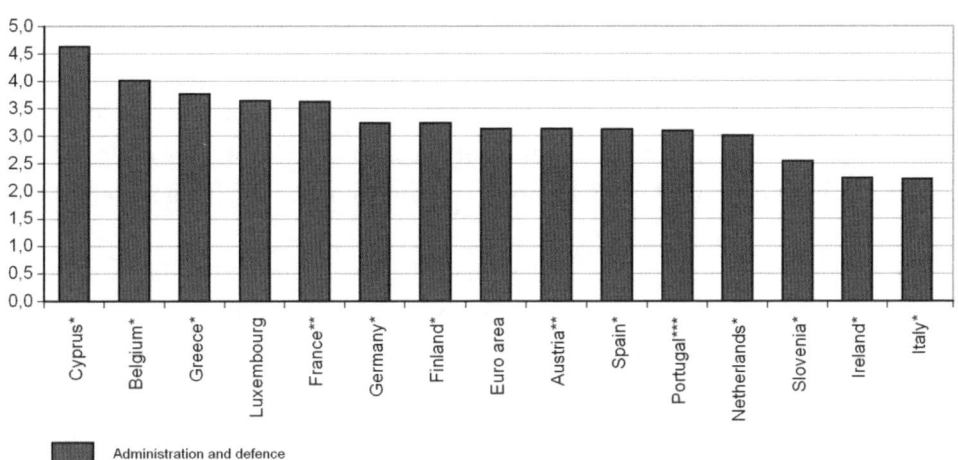

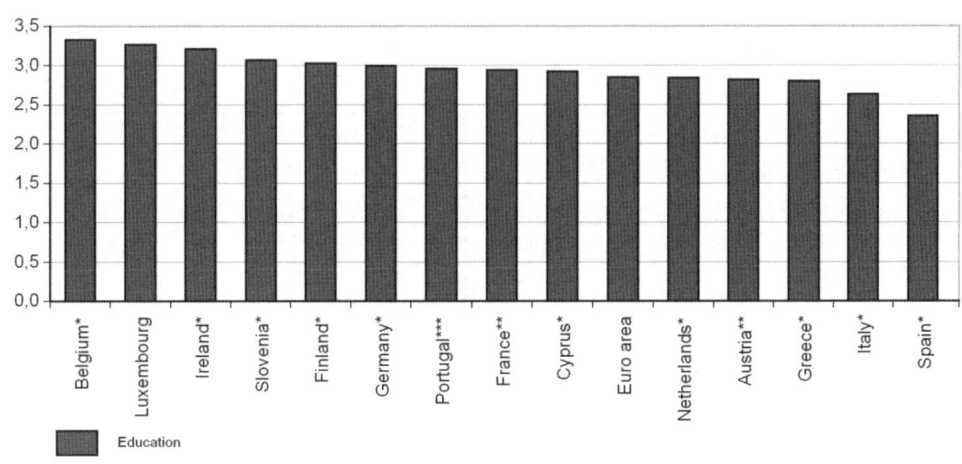

Sources: EC, OECD, NBB.
* 2009
** 2008
*** 2007

10. More specifically, this involves 14 member countries of the euro area, owing to incomplete data in the case of Malta, Slovenia and Estonia.

With regard to employment in the branch of administration per inhabitant, Belgium is surpassed only by Cyprus. In Belgium, almost one person more per 100 inhabitants works in this sector than on average in the euro area. The international comparison of employment in this sector is nevertheless distorted to a considerable degree. In Belgium, the NAI classifies many different activities as coming within the branch of administration – *inter alia* social services excluding retirement homes at the local level – whereas that is not the practice in most other countries.

In the education sector, Belgium has more teachers per inhabitant than any other country in the euro area. The international comparison of employment in this branch of activity is also not free of bias, since there are also private jobs in education. In Belgium, that mainly concerns driving schools.

Focusing on the changes – rather than the level – in employment per sector within each country limits the problem of the differences in the sector boundaries in comparing between countries. It allows one to look not only at the branches of administration and education but also the government-related branch of health care and social services, of which the sector definition differs even more sharply across the countries.

Chart 5: Changes in employment per inhabitant in government-related branches of activity (percentage changes between 2000 and 2010)

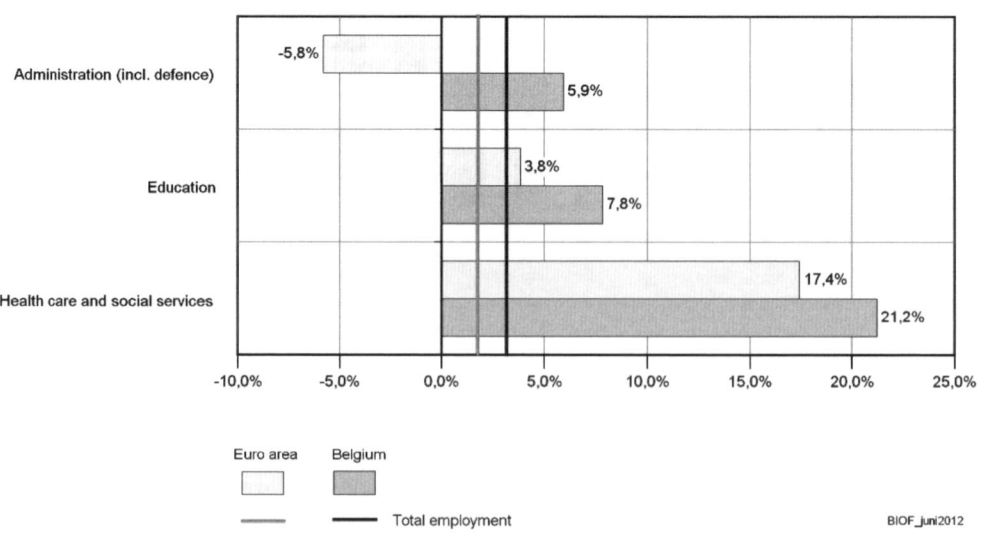

Sources: EC, NBB.

The reference point for the changes in employment per inhabitant in the different branches of activity can be taken as the growth rate in employment per inhabitant for the overall economy between 2000 and 2010 in Belgium and in the euro area, which is 3.1% and 1.7% respectively. In the administration and education sectors, and also health care and social services, the growth in employment in Belgium exceeds that of employment in all the other branches of activity put together. In comparison with the euro area too, employment is growing more rapidly in each of the government-related branches of activity. In the administration sector (including national defence), employment per inhabitant fell on average by 5.8% in the euro area, primarily due to the impact of sharp falls in Italy and Germany and to a lesser extent in the Netherlands. Belgium, on the other hand, experienced an increase which was higher than that for overall employment, in spite of the reduction in the number of defence jobs. As far as the education sector is concerned, employment in Belgium rose 4.7 percent faster than total employment per inhabitant, compared with 2.1 percent faster in the euro area as a whole. The rise in employment over the 2000-2010 period was, finally, most pronounced in the health care and social services sector. In Belgium, employment per inhabitant in this sector increased by 21.2%, higher than the average increase of 17.4% in the euro area.

Finally, we also look at the trend – between 2000 and 2009 – in the share of salaries of employees in the government-related branches of activity within the overall economy.[11] This allows the relative economic scope of these branches to be evaluated. Moreover, this concept dovetails more closely with the concept of full-time equivalents. In any case, the above employment figures take account only of the number of employees, irrespective of whether they work full- or part-time. However, part-time work is common in the government-related sectors.

---

11. Compensation is defined as the remuneration of employees, both in money and in kind, including the social contributions paid by the employer. The results of the analysis are qualitatively the same if 'gross wages and salaries' are used, where the social contributions of the employer are not included. The first concept (compensation) was chosen since there are more and more recent data available.

Chart 6: Share of compensation of employees in the government-related[1] branches of activity within the overall economy (in %)

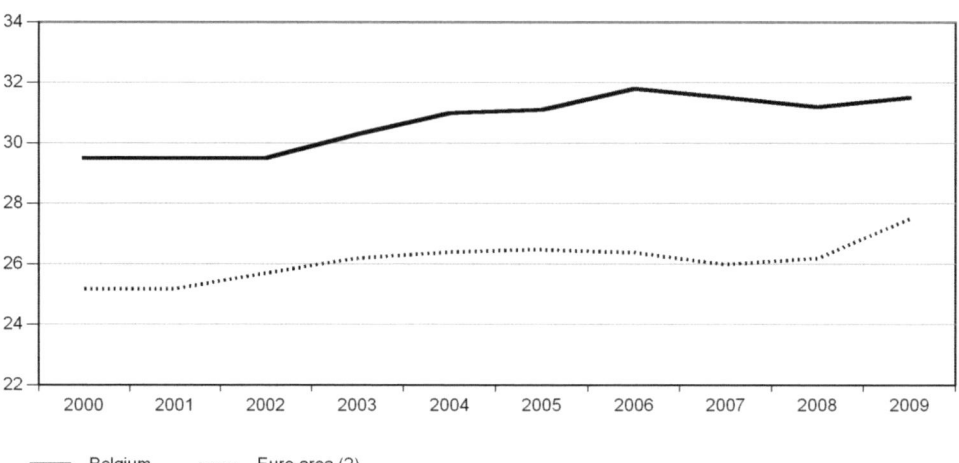

Sources: EC, NBB.
(1) The branches of administration, education and health care and social services.
(2) This involves a selection of 12 euro countries for which data are available over the period 2000-2009, specifically Belgium, Netherlands, Luxembourg, Germany, Spain, Italy, Austria, Finland, Ireland, Greece, Malta and Slovenia. The projected figure is the average of these 12 countries weighted in accordance with the labour costs of the overall economy of these countries.

In Belgium, the share of salaries in the administration, education and health care and social services sectors amounted to 31.5% of salaries in all sectors together in 2009. This is 4 percent more than in a selection of the euro area countries.[12] As far as the trend is concerned, a rise is noticeable both in Belgium and in the euro area. In Belgium, the share of remuneration in government-related sectors increased in comparison to the overall economy by 2 percentage points in the 2000-2009 period. This rise is slightly less pronounced than that in the case of euro area countries, where it amounted to 2.3 percentage points.

The analysis in this section indicates that Belgium has a larger share of government-related employment and pays more remuneration to employees in the overall economy than the euro area. As far as the trend is concerned, the number of employees in these government-related

12. Data on compensation are available for the whole of the 2000-2009 period for only 12 euro area countries. These are Belgium, Netherlands, Luxembourg, Germany, Spain, Italy, Austria, Finland, Ireland, Greece, Malta and Slovenia.

sectors per inhabitant is rising more rapidly in Belgium than in the euro area, but this did not result in a sharper rise in the share of the salaries of employees in these sectors within the overall economy.

Conclusion

The public sector – i.e. general government in the narrow sense – employed about 840,000 people in Belgium in 2010. Almost 80% of these work in the sub-sectors of communities and regions and local authorities. If employment within the public enterprises and the subsidised jobs is also added – i.e. public employment in the broad sense – the number of jobs rises to well over 1.5 million.

Employment in the general government sector in the narrow sense rose sharply in the period from 2000 to 2010, namely by 13.8%. This is considerably higher than the increase in total domestic employment of 9.2% in the same period. In particular, the rise in employment in the sector of administration within the communities and regions (+22.7%) and within local authorities (+20.5%), but also the growth of employment in the education sector (+16.6%), contributed to this.

Over the same period, there was a spectacular rise in the number of subsidised jobs, from 331,000 to 560,000. This stems from the introduction of the service voucher system in 2002 (accounting for 100,000 extra jobs) and the increase in employment in the health care and social services sectors (+38%).

Compared to the other euro area members, Belgium has the highest number of employees per inhabitant in the education sector, and the second highest in the administration sector (including national defence). Moreover, in every government-related branch of activity, Belgium has posted a more rapid rise in the number of jobs per inhabitant since 2000 than on average in the euro area, even if it is looked at in comparison to the growth in total employment. The relatively large scope of employment within general government in Belgium is also apparent from the size of the share of the government-related sectors in the total remuneration of employees. This amounted to 31.5% in Belgium in 2009, compared to 27.5% in the euro area. According to this measure, the difference in comparison to the euro area actually fell slightly.

This analysis shows that both in the national historical context and in the European context, employment within general government is high in Belgium. The possible lowering of government expenditure within the framework of the necessary budgetary consolidation that Belgium is faced with could therefore be accomplished in part by a reduction in the number of personnel in government service.

5.3. THE PRACTICE OF PERFORMANCE CONTRACTING BY BELGIAN GOVERNMENTS: RE-CONSIDERING THE CONTROL OF AUTONOMOUS AGENCIES

Koen Verhoest, Martijn van den Hurk, Steven van Garsse [13]

Introduction: agencification and performance contracting – international phenomena

The creation of 'agencies', public sector organisations which have extended degrees of autonomy and managerial flexibility, is not a new phenomenon. However, since the 1980s the pace and the kind of agencification has changed dramatically in most European countries, and even within the wider set of OECD countries (Pollitt and Talbot 2004; Verhoest et al. 2012). In most countries, a huge increase in semi-autonomous agencies was combined with a shift in the way these agencies were controlled, i.e. from mainly ex ante input-oriented control to ex post result-oriented control by means of performance contracts between government and the agencies.

---

13. Koen Verhoest is assoc. Research Professor at the Research Unit of Public Administration and Management, Department of Political Sciences (University of Antwerp), affiliated to the Public Management Institute (University of Leuven), and expert in agencies, performance contracting, regulation and partnerships. Martijn van den Hurk is PhD candidate at Research Group Public Administration & Management, University of Antwerp. Steven Van Garsse is Professor at University of Antwerp.

In the 1980s a set of new administrative doctrines, nowadays referred to as New Public Management (NPM), emerged in the public sector (Hood 1991). Traditional, centralised and hierarchical public governments were perceived to be unable to adapt to the fast changing environment and to deliver services efficiently and effectively (Walsh 1995). One of the basic ideas of the NPM movement was to focus on the need to stress the primacy of managerial principles over bureaucracy, requiring attention to be paid to decentralization, delegation and deregulation (Verhoest et al. 2007). In particular, the basic trend was to devolve extended managerial autonomy to public service delivery organisations and to focus the control of these organisations on results in an ex post way (OECD 1999; Bouckaert and De Corte et al. 1999; Pollitt and Bouckaert 2004; Windey et al. 2008). Basically, the idea was to 'let managers manage' by granting them degrees of flexibility in managing their organisations, their staff and financial resources, but at the same time 'to make managers manage' by pressurising them by setting clear performance targets and incentives in a performance contract.

The shift from input control to result or output-oriented instruments in order for government to control public service delivery organisations was necessary to meet accountability requirements that followed from the increase in managerial autonomy. However, the introduction of new controlling mechanisms resulted in the juridification and contractualisation of public management relations (Verhoest 2005). The OECD (1999) distinguishes seven broad types of performance contracts: framework agreements; budget contracts and resource agreements; organisational performance agreements; chief executive agreements; funder-provider agreements; intergovernmental performance contracts and partnership agreements; and customer service agreements.

The focus in this chapter is on organisational performance agreements between government and semi-autonomous agencies as a form of performance contracts. Also in Belgium and its regions (Wallonia, Flanders and Brussels) a similar trend towards more managerial autonomy for agencies in exchange for result control through performance contracts was by and large apparent, although the difference in pace and coverage between the different governmental levels was considerable. In this chapter, we first define the concept of performance contracting, highlighting the theoretical advantages and potential disadvantages. We then highlight the use of performance contracts at the different levels of government, and see to what extent this use is linked to the phenomenon of an increasing number of agencies, or their increasing levels of autonomy. We also refer to the experiences different governments have with performance contracting. We do not focus on performance contracts between local authorities and their agencies, although recently initiatives have been taken to generalise these kinds of performance agreements also at the local level (see e.g. in Flanders).

3.1 Performance contracting: what, why and how?

Formally, the performance contract is a mutual agreement between the government or minister on the one hand and the semi-autonomous agency (its senior management or governing board) on the other hand, which outlines the conditions under which the agency exercises its legally mandated tasks during the contract term. This term is normally several years, and increasingly the contract term is aligned with the cabinet period, making performance contracts a useful instrument to translate the policy objectives of the enacting cabinet into organisational objectives for agencies. The performance contract is primarily meant as a steering and controlling device which is geared towards efficient and effective implementation of policies. In essence a "performance contract"-like document stipulates which goals and objectives the contracting organisation ('agent') needs to attain and what (financial and other) resources the contracting government ('principal') provides for these purposes.

Performance contracts require both parties' commitment. The level of the agencies' commitment may vary from strategic objectives to more operational and activity-oriented objectives, which are optimally linked to performance targets to be achieved during the contract period. The performance contract should link the performance objectives of the agency with the wider policy objectives of the government. Furthermore, besides the financial resources granted by the government, the performance contract stipulates to what extent and under what conditions the agency may raise own income. Moreover, such contract normally clearly outlines how the information exchange between agency and government is structured: the translation of the multi-year performance contract into annual business plans, the way and frequency with which the agency reports to the government and with which the government monitors the contracts, as well as the procedure for the annual and final evaluation of the contract. The performance contract may define sanctions (or rewards) for the contracting parties, although this is not necessarily the case. Moreover, the contract should outline procedures for contract renewal, renegotiation, arbitration and dispute settlement. So, essentially, performance contracts are about an exchange of activities and outputs for resources with a result-oriented focus, based on the equality of partners, including a consistent and congruent system of target setting, monitoring, evaluation and feedback (Verhoest 2005). Defining responsibilities and expectations between parties to achieve mutually agreed results is central to this instrument (OECD 1999; Windey et al. 2008).

Using performance contracts to formalise and structure the relationship between government and their semi-autonomous agencies is believed to have some clear advantages (OECD 1999; Verhoest 2005; Verhoest et al. 2012). Performance contracting helps to articulate clearer definitions of objectives and support new management tools as well as monitoring and control methods. It provides a useful tool to guide the behaviour of both ministers and agencies in a more disaggregated, decentralised and devolved context. Second, it reconciles the primacy of politics with the accountability of agency managers. Next, it helps to distinguish responsibilities between the government and its agencies. It is believed that performance contracting stimulates the formulation of clearer internal goals, more cost awareness as well as more result-oriented and customer-oriented service delivery by agencies. The negotiations force both governments and agencies to think in the longer term and guarantee continuity in the provision of the resources. Finally, the use of performance contracts promotes a potentially more intensive collaboration and dialogue between government and its agencies and may help to build up confidence and share information (Verhoest 2005; Windey et al. 2008). However, the extent to which these potential advantages manifest themselves depends on the context and the process of performance contracting and the attitudes of both ministers and agencies. Performance contracting may also result in more negative outcomes, like check-list behaviour from the agency management, inflexibilities and inability to react to new circumstances ('stick to the contract'), political disinterest, or failure to use the contract as a steering instrument (OECD 1999).

3.2 Performance contracting: the Belgian experience

3.2.1 THE TRADITIONAL FORM OF CONTROLLING AGENCIES IN BELGIUM

Traditionally within the Belgian state, the 'Law of 16 March 1954 concerning the control of some institutions with a public function' regulated the control of the parastatal public law agencies. In order to rationalise the control and oversight of the then existing public law agencies (which the parliament described as a 'complete chaos'), this law defined four types of public institutions, each with its own control regime (*Openbare Instellingen* category A, B, C and D), into which most existing public law agencies were categorised. The focus of the 1954 Law was strongly on administrative, financial and budgetary issues, *ex ante* concentrating controlling power in the responsible minister and the ministers of Finance and of the Civil Service (Verhoest et al. 2012). The *ex ante* control regime was very much inspired by the French system of *tutelle* or tutelage, taking three forms, being general tutelage through the so-called *regeringscommissarissen*; specific tutelage and exceptional tutelage (Verhoest et al. 2012). Thus, this control led to overall low levels of managerial autonomy because of its orientation on the legality of decisions and its focus on inputs and procedures. On the other hand, governments and their control agents paid much less attention to the content and strategic orientation of agencies, giving them considerable discretion about these issues. However, the generic Law of 16 March 1954 was never fully and strictly applied (Verhoest 2002).

Since the 1988 state reform, the regional governments have been able to no longer use the 1954 law as the main legal basis for the control of public law agencies, because they received the sovereign competence to define new legal frameworks. Basically, only the Flemish government in

2003 issued a completely new framework law to create agencies of different types (departmental agencies, public law agencies and private law agencies). The other regional governments as well as the federal government chose to retain the 1954 Law as the basic organising framework for agencies under their remit, while supplementing this basic law with additional regulations for newly defined categories of agencies or for new controlling instruments (Verhoest et al. 2012).

From 1991 onwards there were partial efforts to re-orient the ex ante control system towards a more result-oriented ex post system, with multi-year performance agreements, including performance objectives and targets, as a central tool. Over the years, the federal and regional governments have taken initiatives to expand this performance contracting tool to the majority of or even all public law agencies (especially in the case of Wallonia and Flanders), but with varying success.

3.2.2 THE PRACTICE OF PERFORMANCE CONTRACTING AT THE FEDERAL LEVEL

Performance contracting as a control instrument between governments and agencies was introduced for the first time through legislation in Belgium by the 1991 Law concerning the reform of some economic public companies. The Law changed the former category A and B agencies which delivered postal, telecom, railway and airways services into a new kind of hybrid agencies. They were turned into the so-called Autonomous Public Companies in order to prepare them for the future liberalisation of their markets. The 1991 Federal Law was crucial because it introduced new ideas concerning the control of agencies which would become common practice at all other governmental levels in the following decade: substantial managerial autonomy was granted to these Autonomous Public Companies and the possibilities for *ex ante* control by the *regeringscommissarissen* were restricted, although not abolished. In return, the Autonomous Public Companies were required to conclude multi-year performance contracts *(beheerscontracten)* and three-year business plans with the federal government, stipulating their tasks of general interest and financial resources, and setting performance objectives and targets on which they were evaluated (De Broux 2010). Although ultimately only six of the federal agencies under the

1954 law changed to the status of an Autonomous Public Company under the 1991 Law, they were nevertheless the largest public sector organisations in the Belgian landscape.

A second initiative affected the 15 category D institutions under the 1954 law which managed social security benefits. By the Federal Law of 26 July 1996 with respect to the modernisation of social security and the guarantees for viability of legal pension systems, and the related Royal Decree of 3 April 1997 the *ex ante* control by the *regeringscommissarissen* and the managerial autonomy of these agencies were relaxed to some extent on the condition that these agencies concluded a three-year performance contract (called an 'administration contract' or *bestuursovereenkomst*) with the federal government and issued a business plan. The major impetus for this legal change was the need to increase the cost-effectiveness of the social security system in Belgium, and hence the responsibilisation of these agencies. However, the first administration contracts were signed only in 2002. At this moment the implementation of the third generation of administration contracts is ongoing.

Besides these two changes, since the 1990s only a limited number of new departmental and public law agencies have been created, which have not always been controlled by a performance contract. The Copernicus reform programme did however introduce the management plan for top managers within the Federal Governmental Services, to be agreed with the minister. Following this, the government coalition agreement of 18 March 2008 demanded that all Federal Services (=ministries) sign an administration contract with their minister, as a substitute for the management plans; these proved to be less effective instruments in streamlining the work and quality of the Federal Services. In 2009 the first two-year administration contract was signed between the Federal Service for Personnel and Organisation and its minister. The Federal Service for Social Security in 2011 submitted a draft administration contract to its minister.

Experiences with performance contracts at the federal level are improving as the result of a learning process, but they are still rather mixed. With respect to the first generation of administration contracts of the Social Security Institutions, several advantages of the instrument were noted (see e.g. Legrain 2007): the contract enabled the senior management of the institutions to set clear strategies for their organisations and to mobilise their staff more intensively to achieve the contractual objectives. Moreover, the contract increased transparency internally but also towards external stakeholders. It improved the goal-orientedness and quality of service delivery, infused the Social Security Institutions with a reform-minded attitude and facilitated stronger coordination across the institutions by the inclusion of transverse objectives and actions (Legrain 2007). Also, the Federal Service for Social Security equipped itself with good coordination capacities in the form of a dedicated team created specifically to monitor and coordinate the contracts on behalf of the minister (Legrain 2007).

On the other hand, several shortcomings and threats were to be observed. A first set was related to the quality of contractual and monitoring documents that needed further improvement (for one fifth of the objectives in the different contracts there was insufficient information to evaluate them) and the need for stronger systems of internal control and audit in the institutions. But a second and more important set was related to the inability of the Federal Government to act as a dedicated and trustworthy contractual partner, because of the proliferation of and lack of coordination between the number of controlling actors (different ministers, *regeringscommissarissen*, Court of Audit, auditors); the persistent use of *ex ante* control mechanisms which reduces the responsibilisation of senior managers; the lack of monitoring and evaluation capacity; unilateral adjustments to contractual terms which violates the 'equality' of the contracting partners; and a lack of flexibility in adjusting the contracts. Moreover, the sanctioning system was incomplete, with the financial sanctions provided for never materialising (Legrain 2007).

Similar criticisms about the inability of the Federal Government to fulfill its role as contract manager and evaluator were raised by the Court of Audit (Belgian Court of Audit 2005) with respect to this sector, but also with respect to contracts with the Autonomous Public Companies. An audit report on the 2005-2007 management contracts with the Belgian Railway Group (*NMBS-groep*) showed clearly the lack of monitoring and evaluation by the Federal Government, as well as the lack of transparent reporting by the companies involved (Belgian Court of Audit

2008). However, there was a learning process, and nowadays the monitoring and evaluation process, the internal organisation of the Federal Government as contract partner, and the quality of documents in both sectors have clearly improved.

3.2.3 THE PRACTICE OF PERFORMANCE CONTRACTING IN THE FLEMISH GOVERNMENT

Until the early 2000s, the Flemish government followed largely the same route as the federal and Walloon governments, at the same time strengthening the uniform application of the 1954 law and its *ex ante* controls (e.g. financial reporting and personnel statutes) on the one hand and the partial introduction of elements of result control. One of these elements was to enter into performance contracts with about nine of the most salient public law agencies, like the VRT, the Flemish Public Broadcasting Company (from 1991 onwards), De Lijn, the Flemish Bus Company (from 1993 onwards), and the VDAB, the Flemish Public Employment Service (from 1994 onwards). A Court of Audit report was quite critical of the quality of the contracts (in particular the measurability of the performance objectives and targets) and of the way the Flemish government negotiated and monitored these contracts, but it strongly advocated the generalisation of this instrument to all semi-autonomous agencies at the Flemish level as an instrument to improve control over a very diverse agency landscape (Court of Audit 2001).

Inspired by international experiences (mainly from Sweden) and NPM doctrines, the new Liberal-Socialist-Green government decided in 1999 fundamentally to revise the agencification landscape and control arrangements. The *Beter Bestuurlijk Beleid* reforms (BBB) were implemented in 2006 and integrated many of the reform elements which had been partially adopted in the 1990s: the agencification of all policy implementation tasks; the restructuring of existing agencies into four clear types of agencies, based on an explicitly defined set of criteria and a preference for departmental agencies; an (at least formally) radical shift to *ex post* and result-oriented control and a further generalisation of performance contracts; the overall introduction of accrual accounting (which remains unimplemented) and increased budgetary flexibility for departments and agencies, and the marketisation of management support tasks (Verhoest et al. 2010). This resulted in a massive structural reorganisation of the Flemish agency landscape with about 52 departmental and public law agencies being transformed or newly created in 2006–2007, and being hierarchically at the same level as the policy departments. Being very radical in nature, the reform efforts were initially mainly structural, while several of the related management and control instruments did not materialise fully or functioned in a less than optimal way (Verhoest, Vandendriesse & Rommel 2010; Spanhove and Verhoest 2008). The original intention to make a radical shift to ex post result-based control of agencies was scuppered by new regulations which re-installed the *regeringscommissarissen* in their original pre-BBB form as control agents for public law agencies with a governing board. However, hitherto not all such agencies have included these control agents on their boards, as is the case with the Flemish Energy Regulator (VREG).

As has been said, relationships with all departmental agencies (which are still hierarchically subordinated to the minister) and all public law agencies were to be governed by a performance contract *(beheersovereenkomst)*; those with private law agencies by a 'collaborative agreement' *(samenwerkingsovereenkomst)*. About two thirds of the departmental and public law agencies signed performance contracts with the Flemish government for the period 2008-2010, and in 2010 the objectives in the new coalition agreement, as well as in the ministerial policy notes, were translated into organisational objectives in five-year performance contracts (for the 2011-2015 period) for most of the agencies. Moreover, the secretaries-general of the different policy departments also signed a five-year management contract with the Flemish government. The Department of Governmental Affairs provided manuals and templates to support the drafting and negotiation of performance contracts.[14] Moreover, increasingly performance contracts with individual agencies and departments are also used to implement government-wide administrative policies and reforms, by including common horizontal objectives in the individual contracts.

---

14. Flemish Government, *Vision on performance contracting (Visienota Beheersovereenkomsten)*, 22 March 2002. Flemish Government, *Note on Performance contracts in the Flemish Government: Concept, implementation and model (Nota Beheersovereenkomsten in de Vlaamse overheid: Concept, implementatie en model,*.22 July 2005.

The Flemish experiences also clearly show the potential of performance contracting as a control device, and that this potential is not being made enough use of. In a recent series of reports on the quality of reporting documents, the Court of Audit (2011) stated:

> 'Using performance contracts as tools for a remote steering of the agencies is for the time being compromised by the lack of clearly defined objectives, indicators and target values. As a result, the implementation reports are, in general, purely descriptive. Although the preparation of management contracts and implementation reports requires significant efforts from the Flemish authorities, these tools are hardly used for steering, monitoring and justification purposes' (Court of Audit 2011: English abstract).

The Internal Audit Office *(Interne Audit van de Vlaamse administratie – IAVA)* also made similar comments about the quality of the performance contracts (IAVA 2007). Although the contract template was followed by most agencies, the link with the policy objectives of the government, the measurability of performance objectives and the translation of the contractual objectives into targets for organisational subunits and personnel were considered to be suboptimal in many cases (IAVA 2007). In an evaluation report of 2008, Spanhove and Verhoest (2008) asserted that many ministers do not really use the performance contract to steer and monitor their agencies. They put forward three reasons for this: control of agencies by ministers and their political staff took place still predominantly in the traditional way, by means of direct instructions and ad hoc monitoring, to a large extent independently of the contract cycle. Given that the use of performance contracts in the evaluation by senior managers of agencies and departments was unclear, it has been decided that the annual business plan, which is the translation of the performance contract into yearly steps, will be the main basis for accountability by senior managers. Moreover, performance contracts are mainly drafted by the agencies themselves, and because of a lack of expertise on the part of the minister (or the entities which support the minister), no sharp debate or negotiation is possible. Besides, some ministers consider performance contracts too rigid when urgent new policy measures are needed to deal with an unexpected policy problem. However, it is clear that with the new generation of performance contracts which were signed in 2010 there is evidence of experience by both the agencies and departments and ministers, which is reflected in the quality of the contracts, but also monitoring and evaluation.

3.2.4 THE PRACTICE OF PERFORMANCE CONTRACTING IN THE WALLOON GOVERNMENT

Apparently, the Walloon government (used here as an umbrella term for both the government of the French-speaking Community and that of the Walloon Region) was the first to elaborate some kind of performance contract with an agency under its remit. As early as in 1989, the Walloon government concluded such an agreement with FOREM, the Walloon Public Employment Service. By 2004, performance contracts with 12 different agencies existed. In terms of regulatory frameworks, the Walloon government issued new framework regulations on public law agencies. Nevertheless, these new regulations aimed at clarifying and enhancing the uniform enforcement of the 1954 law, and supplementing this law with new control mechanisms, rather than replacing it. Inspired by the 1991 federal Law on Autonomous Public Companies, the Walloon government in 2003 (for agencies under the French-speaking Community)[15] and in 2004 (for agencies under the Walloon Region)[16] issued regulations ordering some of its agencies to conclude performance contracts with standardised elements, including a business plan, a *tableau de bord*, and an annual report on the implementation of the contract. Please note that the 2004 decree distinguished between agencies governed by a performance contract and those governed without a performance contract. For the latter, uniform but less burdensome information obligations were designed (Nihoul & Barcena 2010). Moreover, related decrees issued in 2004 further defined the rights and obligations of the agency CEO, as well as those of the *regeringscommissarissen*, in a charter in order to improve their effectiveness.

---

15. Decree of 9 January 2003 on the transparency, the autonomy and control of public entities which are dependent from the French-speaking Community.
16. Decree of 12 February 2004 on the management contract and on information obligations (the Walloon region).

In 2007, the Walloon government introduced mandate positions for top civil servants in the central administrations, with 'mission letters', operational plans and performance indicators. As at the other governmental levels in Belgium, the enforcement of these regulations proved to be somewhat problematic, resulting in a continuing diversity of autonomy and control arrangements with performance contracts being concluded for most, but not all, public- and private-law agencies, and with diverging quality levels of performance contracts (Nihoul & Barcena 2010;Cipriano and Van Haeperen 2010).

3.3 Performance contracting: effects and remaining challenges

At the time of writing (Spring 2012), performance contracting between government and the agencies under its remit is quite institutionalised and generally accepted as an instrument for control and interaction across the different governmental levels in Belgium. These experiences tell us about the added value of performance contracts, in terms of increased customer orientedness and cost consciousness on the part of the agencies, a stronger long-term orientation and stability in terms of objectives and resources, more transparency and clear accountability lines. International research indeed shows that result control of agencies results in more innovative behaviour and an increased use of modern management tools within the agencies (Verhoest et al. 2007; Verhoest et al. 2010). Performance contracts appear to be excellent instruments for agency managers to focus their staff on the contractual objectives their organisations need to meet. We see increasingly a stronger link between policy objectives as defined by governments and ministers, organisational objectives as defined in performance contracts, and individual objectives as defined in the mandate of the senior management. We also note the expansion of performance contracting beyond autonomous agencies and towards departments.

However, also common to these experiences is the difficulty of drafting high quality contracts with clear objectives and measurable targets, the sheer impossibility for governments and ministers to act as real contract partners and to reduce unilateral, ad hoc instructions, the persistent emphasis on ex ante control instruments (like the *regeringscommissarissen*) and the underdeveloped practices of monitoring, evaluation and sanctioning. Although there is clearly a learning curve, we also need to reconsider some aspects of performance contracts to make them more acceptable and usable for both ministers and agencies. First, performance contracts need to reconcile some degree of stability with the need for political flexibility. Second, they need to be more strongly linked to policy and budget documents. Third, there is a strong need to reconsider the role of *regeringscommissarissen* and other ex ante control instruments. Fourth, performance contracts should be more often accompanied by and used within a strategy to strengthen coordination and collaboration between government organisations.

References

Belgian Court of Audit – *Reports requested by the federal Parliament: Compliance with management contracts and use of public funds by the Belgian national railways holding company, Infrabel and the Belgian national railways* –November 2008

Belgian Court of Audit- *Reports requested by the federal Parliament: Administration contracts with Social Security Institutions: a management tool for Government* – March 2005

Bouckaert, G., Peters, B., Verhoest, K. (2010). *The coordination of public sector organizations: shifting patterns of public management.* London Hampshire: Palgrave Macmillan.

Bouckaert, G., De Corte, J. (1999), *Contractmanagement en management van contracten (Contract management and management of contracts).*Brugge: Die Keure, 211 p.

Cipriano S. and Van Haeperen B. (2010). *Les agences dans le paysage de la fonction publique Wallone.*IWEPS Discussion Papers n° 1003.

Court of Audit 2011. *De rapportering over de uitvoering van de beheersovereenkomst met het Agentschap Wegen en Verkeer (The report on the implementation of the performance contract with the Agency for Roads and Traffic).*Dutch Chamber of 25 May 2010.

Court of Audit . 2001. 'Performance contracts with the Flemish Public Institutions, Annex to the letters N12-1.795.805 B16-B20. 3 July 2001.'

De Broux P.-O. (2010) Introduction à la décentralisation administrative : évolutions théoriques and pratiques politiques. In: Jadoul P., Lombaert B., Tulkens F. (Eds.), *Le Paraétatisme. Nouveaux Regards sur la Décentralisation Fonctionnelle en Belgique et dans les Institutions Européennes.* Bruxelles: La Charte, pp. 3-32.

Bouckaert, G. and J. De Corte. 1999. *Contractmanagement En Management Van Contracten.* Brugge: die Keure.

Hondeghem A., Depré R. (2005) *De Copernicushervorming in perspectief: Veranderingsmanagement in de federale overheid.* Vanden Broele: Brugge.

Hood, C. (1991) 'A Public Management for all Seasons?', *Public Administration*, 69 (1), 3-19.

François, A. (1987). La modernisation de l'administration de l'Etat en Belgique. *Revue Internationale des Sciences Administratives*, 53 (3): 355-399.

IAVA. *Jaarverslag van het auditcomite en het agentschap interne audit van de Vlaamse administratie (Annual Report of the audit committee and the Internal Audit Office of the Flemish Government)* 2007.

Jadoul P., Lombaert B., Tulkens F. (Eds.), *Le Paraétatisme. Nouveaux Regards sur la Décentralisation Fonctionnelle en Belgique et dans les Institutions Européennes* (pp. 307-345). Bruxelles: La Charte.

Legrain A. (2007). Risico's en uitdagingen met betrekking tot het beleid van responsabilisering en contractualisering van de relaties tussen de instellingen en de voogdijoverheid binnen de Belgische sociale zekerheid: kenmerken van de hervorming en afhankelijkheid van de omgeving. *Burger, Bestuur & Beleid. Tijdschrift voor bestuurskunde en bestuursrecht*, 2007, 4 pp. 286-305.

Nihoul M., Barcena F. –X. (2010).La décentralisation fonctionelle en Région wallonne et en Communauté française. In : Jadoul P., Lombaert B., Tulkens F. (Eds.), *Le Paraétatisme. Nouveaux Regards sur la Décentralisation Fonctionnelle en Belgique et dans les Institutions Européennes* (pp. 307-345). Bruxelles: La Charte. pp. 415-468

OECD (Organisation for Economic Cooperation and Development), 1999. *Performance Contracting: Lessons From Performance Contracting Case Studies. A Framework for Public Sector Performance Contracting. OECD-PUMA.* unclassified document.

Pollitt, C. and G. Bouckaert (2004) *Public Management Reform. A Comparative Analysis*, 2nd Edition (Oxford, Oxford University Press).

Pollitt, C. and C. Talbot (eds) (2004) *Unbundled Government. A Critical Analysis of the Global Trend to Agencies, Quangos and Contractualisation* (London, Routledge).

Spanhove, J. and Verhoest, K. (2008). *Deugdelijk Bestuur in de Vlaamse Overheid anno 2008: een kwalitatieve analyse van nieuwe Government Governance mechanismen in BBB (Government Governance in the Flemish Government anno 2008)*, 180 pp. Leuven: SBOV.

Troupin, S., Verhoest, K., Rommel, J. (2010). Décentralisation fonctionnelle? Leçons d'expériences internationales. In: Jadoul P., Lombaert B., Tulkens F. (Eds.), *Le Paraétatisme. Nouveaux Regards sur la Décentralisation Fonctionnelle en Belgique et dans les Institutions Européennes* (pp. 307-345). Bruxelles: . La Charte. Pp.307-346.

Verhoest, K., Van Thiel, S., Bouckaert, G., Laegreid, P., (Eds.) (2012). *Government Agencies: Practices and Lessons from 30 Countries.* Basingstoke: Palgrave Macmillan.

Verhoest, K., Van den Driessche F. Rommel, J. (2010a). Verzelfstandiging in Vlaanderen : theorie en praktijk. In: Jadoul P., Lombaert B., Tulkens F. (Eds.), *Le Paraétatisme. Nouveaux Regards sur la Décentralisation Fonctionnelle en Belgique et dans les Institutions Européennes.* Bruxelles: . La Charte. Pp. 369-414

Verhoest, K., Roness, P., Verschuere, B., Rubecksen, K., MacCarthaigh, M. (2010b). *Autonomy and control of State agencies: comparing states and agencies.* Hampshire: Palgrave Macmillan Ltd.

Verhoest, K., Verschuere, B., Bouckaert, G. (2007). Pressure, legitimacy and innovative behaviour by public organizations. *Governance: an international journal of policy and administration, 20*(3), 469-498.

Verhoest, K. (2005). The impact of contractualisation on control and accountability in government-agency relations: the case of Flanders (Belgium). In: Drewry G. (Eds.), *Contracts, performance measurement and accountability in the public sector* (pp. 135-153). Amsterdam: IOS.

Verhoest, K. (2002) *Resultaatgericht verzelfstandigen. Een analyse vanuit verruimd principaal agent perspectief (Result-driven agencification. An extended Principal-Agent Perspective analysis)* (Leuven, Katholieke Universiteit Leuven, Faculteit Sociale Wetenshappen, PhD-dissertation).

Walsh, K. 1995. *Public Services and Market Mechanisms: Competition, Contracting and the New Public Management.* Basingstoke: Macmillan.

Windey, J., Bouckaert, G., Verhoest, K. (2008). Contracts and Performance: Managing Museums. In: Demarsin B., Schrage E., Tilleman B., Verbeke A. (Eds.), *Art & Law* (pp. 520-555). Oxford/Brussel: . Hart Publishing/ Mercatorfonds/die Keure.

5.4. MEASURING AND MANAGING PUBLIC PERFORMANCE

Jean Hindriks[17]

> *We can no longer afford to sustain the old ways when we know there are new and more efficient ways of getting the job done.*
> (BARACK OBAMA)

4.1 The efficiency priority

It is fair to say that the collapse of the financial markets in 2007/2008 was an epoch-making event. Few industries and sectors remained unscathed by the global economic recession that was triggered by the collapse of the financial markets. Although we have avoided the deep "depression" that

---

17. Jean Hindriks is Professor in the Economics Department, Co-director of the Centre for Operations Research and Econometrics (CORE) at the Université catholique de Louvain, and Senior Fellow at the Itinera Institute.

was widely predicted at the turn of 2009, the recession can still be seen as a massive economic catastrophe, and it is safe to claim that the road to full recovery will be long and treacherous and many more well-known organizations may well die en route. The recovery plan will inevitably involve the government sector, too. With the debt crisis and the rising cost of our pension and health systems due to the aging population, the pressure for spending constraint will become stronger and stronger. Of course Belgium is not the only nation facing spending constraints; the same holds true for public sector funding in just about every other developed nation. Without significant efficiency gains, public sector bodies will simply not be able properly to deliver their services in the next decade although the demand for public services will keep increasing. As a result, the need to become efficient has become perhaps the key performance imperative for public sector bodies.

The next budget round will mean reduced budgets for most government organisations – be it central government departments, agencies, educational institutions, schools, hospitals, police forces, fire and emergency services, justice organisations, local authorities, etc. All those will be forced to cut costs and become leaner and more efficient, which is a trend that is likely to continue for many years until the massive public debts are repaid and public purses look healthier again. But efficiency is not just spending cuts. Rather than cutting spending, we should ask: how can we create the most value with less money? To do so we must first evaluate public activities and then we can prioritise. Prioritise "just to say no" to the lowest-priority and lowest-value activities. This is hard to do, as we have painfully discovered, but structural deficits make it necessary. Each government body can then eliminate several programmes which could not demonstrate strong value and merge others. Making these kinds of tough calls also enables them to put *more* money into activities that deliver the greatest value, which is what matter in the end.

In short, public sector bodies are being asked to become both more effective *and* more efficient (not therefore becoming efficient at the expense of being more effective). Often seen as interchangeable words, we can define efficiency as "doing things right" and effectiveness as "doing the right things". The expectation of public sector leaders is that they deliver "more value for less money".

4.2 What is the contribution of the government sector?

What is the contribution of the government sector to the economy and to social welfare? According to the rules of national income accounting, in the absence of market prices, the contribution of the government sector to GDP is measured by the wages paid out by the government, regardless of how productive or useful government jobs are. Thus, the economic and welfare performance as measured by conventional accounting can differ between two countries with different sized public sectors. The small-government country collects taxes to spend on unemployment benefits, whereas the big-government country gives its unemployed a desk (if recruited in a public job) and counts the public wage (instead of unemployment benefits) as value-added in the government sector and, therefore, a contribution to GDP. So the high share of government employment contributes to the big-government country's low unemployment rate. Moreover, it also contributes greatly to the high per capita GDP figures of that country, for the simple reason that the value-added created by these government jobs is part of GDP, even if it could never have been produced in a market economy. Obviously, apart from the accounting bias implicit in national income accounting, the high share of government in employment may also be helpful for coping with the challenge of globalisation. Indeed, the equilibrium wage of unskilled labour has fallen throughout the western countries due to competition from the low-wage economies, specialisation, outsourcing, and even immigration. Yet western governments are not willing to let actual wages fall for obvious social reasons. If they want to defend the incomes of the unskilled, the best option is to educate the unskilled better, but this will take time and so it cannot offer a short-term solution. In the short term, there are only three options. The first is to defend the wages of the low skilled through minimum-wage laws or by paying wage replacement income. This is the strategy that most EU countries have chosen. It results in mass unemployment that is inefficient and financially unsustainable. The second option is to pay wage subsidies to allow for the wage dispersion necessary for full employment without letting the incomes of the unskilled fall. This is the strategy chosen by the Anglo-Saxon countries with their earned-income tax credit. The third option is the public job solution. Here government demand for labour keeps wages high. This is the Scandinavian strategy, which is often viewed as a second-best solution. Indeed, it is better to let people work in the government sector than have them do nothing, as when paying wage replacement income. Even though GDP is artificially inflated, some useful activities are carried out. Nevertheless, it might be better to let the market decide what kinds of products the low-skilled and less motivated part of the workforce should and could reasonably make, which supports the subsidy solution.

4.3   Measuring non-market output

Gross national product (GDP) is both a measure of the major economic flows and an indicator of the contribution of economic activity to increasing welfare. GDP is widely used by analysts, politicians, the press, the business community and the public at large as a summary, global indicator of economic activity and welfare. In the case of final consumption by households, the justification for the welfare interpretation is that consumers are assumed to purchase an item until its marginal value, measured in terms of money, is equal to the price. If Q denotes the quantity of the product, and P denotes the price per unit, then the value to the consumer of the marginal unit is P, and the total value is found by valuing all units at P, so the contribution to national income is PQ. Goods for which there is a high marginal willingness to pay (high P) receive greater weight in national income than goods for which there is a low marginal willingness to pay (low P). It should be stressed that the resulting measure is not the same as consumer surplus; indeed, we are not taking any account of the fact that the consumer would be willing to pay much more for the first unit of the product. The key element is that the welfare justification lies in measuring the added value to consumers. This value is inferred from the fact that economic agents are undertaking the transactions.

Figure 1: Marginal valuation and total cost

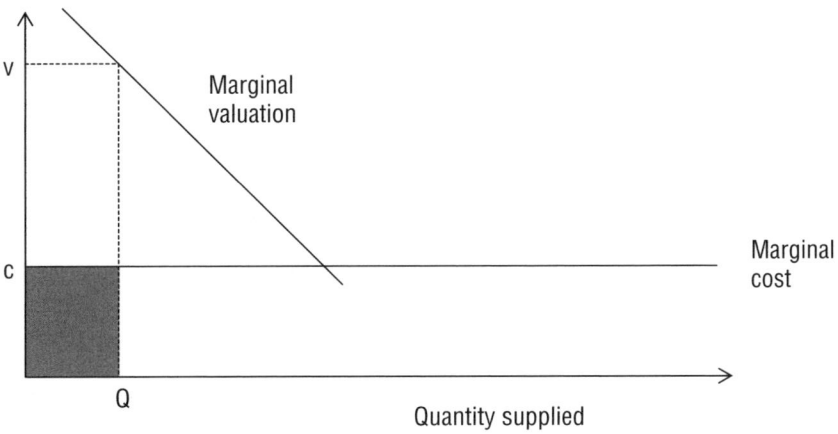

The problem in the case of non-market output is that there is no transaction from which the price or quantity can be observed. There are, in fact, two difficulties. First, there is no revelation of preference by consumers' choice, but, second, neither can the costs of supplying a marginal unit be taken as a measure of the individual or collective benefit. There is no reason to suppose that government output is supplied to the point where the benefit from a marginal unit is equal to the marginal cost of supply. This is illustrated in Figure 1, which shows a declining marginal valuation as more output is supplied, and, to simplify, a constant marginal cost of production. The total cost is found in this case by multiplying the marginal cost by the quantity, giving the shaded area. As we have seen, the convention that (output=input) is no longer one that we can regard as acceptable. So we cannot simply take the shaded area. What we have to attempt therefore is to measure the whole rectangle under the marginal valuation curve, i.e. VQ. Even if we can observe Q, the quantity supplied, we still need to construct, or find ways of inferring, the marginal valuation, V, of that quantity supplied. This is particularly difficult in the case of those services where the nature of the service is not adequately defined, i.e where there are no terms of sale specifying, at least in part, what is constituted by the transaction.

4.4 The input/output/outcome distinction

In order to consider the implementation of this approach with respect to individual services, we turn to the input/activity/output/outcome distinctions made in the Eurostat Handbook. To remind the reader, and taking the health service as an example, we identify the *inputs* as the time of medical and non-medical staff, the drugs, electricity and other inputs purchased, and the capital services from the equipment and buildings used. These resources are used in primary care and hospital *activities*, such as a GP making an examination or the carrying out of a heart operation. These activities are designed to benefit the individual patient. To the extent that they do, the health care provided constitutes the *output* associated with these input activities. Finally there is the health *outcome*, which may depend on a number of factors apart from the output of health care, such as whether or not the person follows up treatment correctly and adopts a good lifestyle. Inputs are not an appropriate measure for reasons already made clear, and, while activities may be the only available indicator and hence have to be used, they, too, are an intermediate variable. The relationship between output and outcome, on the other hand, is less obvious, and encounters the problem of defining the quantity unit for the measurement of output.

4.5 Output indicators

The procedure of defining direct output indicators within a government function should start by seeking to identify the services provided by government to households and firms, and attempts made to find data to reflect these services as comprehensively as possible, with appropriate allowance for quality change. The services should be the starting point, not the available indicators. If, initially, it is necessary to apply an indicator from another service, this should be made clear. A condition for the introduction of a new indicator should be that it adequately covers the full range of services for the functional area. The coverage of indicators within a function should be reassessed on a regular basis.

The procedure of defining output requires first the specification of the scope of the public service. When production is by nature multidimensional and many different stakeholders are involved, the definition of the mission and objectives of the public service is not easy. This is clearly illustrated by the following comment of a public top-manager in the UK: « The leaders of public sector bodies have a great deal of difficulty in knowing what they are there to produce in terms of outcomes and what they need to support that. So their greatest shortcoming is that they lack a real sense of what their business is. It's not like a private company where you are just pitching it at a profit measure which is a nice, simple thing to have as a prime directive. Public sector organizations have so many things that they are seeking to deliver that they end up not knowing what they are supposed to do. How can they set realistic and useful performance objectives and targets and prioritize performance when they are not sure what they are supposed to do in the first place? » (Peter Ryan, manager, « Planning and Performance at Christchurch City Council », cited in Marr and Creelman, *More with Less*, Palgrave Macmillan, 2011)

4.6 Scorecarding

To help define and achieve both their external and internal goals, government bodies can bring these together in one document, using a Balanced Scorecard as its core management framework. A Balanced Scorecard is essentially a strategic management framework that comprises both financial and non-financial performance perspectives. First popularised in the early 1990s by Harvard Business Professor Dr Robert Kaplan and management consultant Dr David Norton, a "classic" Balanced Scorecard comprises learning and growth, and internal process and customer perspectives, in addition to the financial perspective. These perspectives are collocated within a Strategy Map and an accompanying scorecard of indicators, targets and initiatives. It is very clear that government organisations should not see the "classic" scorecard template (imported from private sector) as a straitjacket and should be encouraged to change the standard templates better to reflect their unique strategies. One such evolution is the Value Creation Map that describes the strategic objectives, initiatives and supporting key performance questions and key performance indicators that an organisation must master in order to deliver to its vision or mission. Figure 2 provides a diagrammatical overview of a Balanced Scorecard.

Figure 2: Balanced scorecard

A key reason for the popularity of the Balanced Scorecard is that it enables public sector leaders to contend successfully with a challenge that is normally far tougher for them than their private sector counterparts – prioritising where to spend money (which of course has today taken on a significantly more important focus than was previously the case). Simply put, whereas private organisations can boil everything down to some form of shareholder value focus, for public sector bodies there is a requirement to deliver equal value to a range of stakeholders: for example, funding authorities, consumers and partners. This can confuse the public sector leaders as to where they should prioritise attention and resources.

An interesting illustration of « Balanced Scorecard » in the health care sector is the Northumbria Healthcare Trust Fund (see figure 3). This is one of the largest National Health Service (NHS) in the UK, acknowledged

Figure 3: Example of balanced scorecard in the health sector

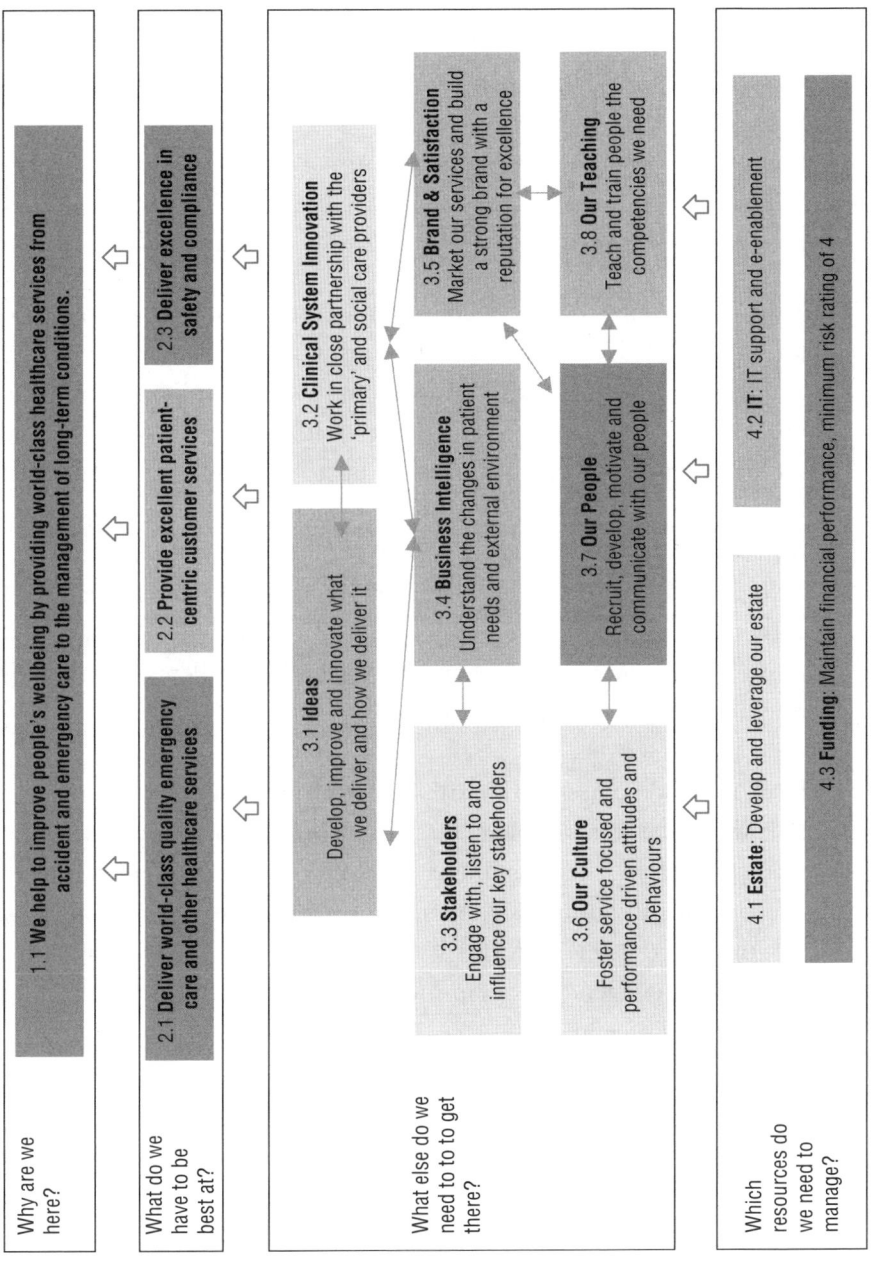

Source: Managing Healthcare Performance, Advanced Performance Institute, 2010

as one of the best NHS. It has received many national awards for its management quality and performance results. For example, in 2008, more than 90 % of its patients reported services quality to be either good or excellent. The Northumbria Healthcare Trust Fund employs 6,000 workers in 10 different hospitals with a budget of £270 million and a target population of about half a million.

4.7 Lean public management

Streamline your process is a collection of methodologies and approaches (of which Six Sigma is perhaps the most popular) that are used systematically to identify and drive waste out of organisational activities and processes. Long-established and proven within the private sector, leaders within the public sector are waking up to the cost-saving potential of Lean within their own setting. Governments have made huge leaps in the last decade using the latest version of "quality" process-improvement tools. The suite of six sigma lean tools, including kaizen events, consistently reduces costs and improves results. Particularly in areas of process-heavy regulation, cycle times and error rates have fallen while freeing up resources for other unmet needs.

Lean methodologies work extremely well when deployed as part of a Balanced Scorecard implementation. When Lean is used as part of a scorecard effort, organisations can ensure that they identify the most effective organisation-wide efficiency opportunities while making sure that the effectiveness performance dimension is not compromised. It also ensures that efficiency programmes are tied to the organisation's longer-term strategic agenda.

4.8 Managing performance

Recently the Advanced Performance Institute (API) conducted the research project, *Strategic Performance Management in Government and Public Sector Organizations – a Global Survey*, which is the largest and most comprehensive global study of Government and public sector Performance

Management to date. This study enabled it to identify best practices and, from this, tested ten principles of good performance management for government and public sector organisations. The impact of these principles on organisational success has been tested using the latest statistical tools, and it was determined how widespread these approaches are, and how effective they are when used. It was found that organisations which have these principles in place are in a position to learn, make better decisions and produce better performance.

Figure 4: Ten principles of performance management

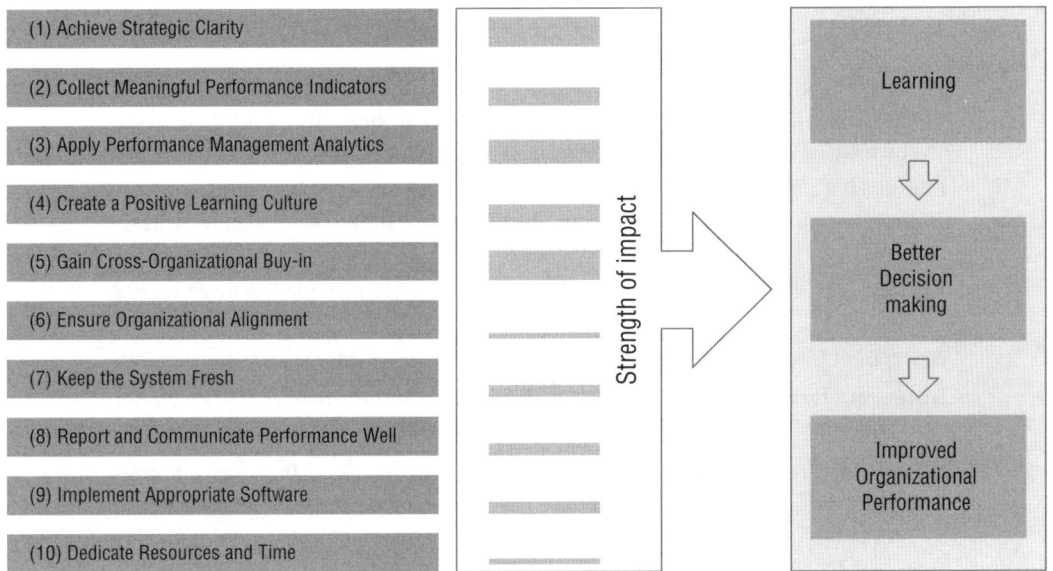

Source : Strategic Performance Management in Government and Public Sector Organizations – a Global Survey, Advanced Performance Institute, 2009

The principles with the strongest individual impact on performance improvement were confirmed to be: (1) creating clarity about the strategy, with agreement on intended outcomes, outputs and necessary enablers, and (4) creating a positive culture of learning and improvement. Both are prerequisites for a meaningful Balanced Scorecard. That said, where all ten principles were found to be in place, the improvement was particularly substantial, confirming that the combined effect is far greater than the sum of the parts.

Further References

Arthuis, J., (2005), « Les objectifs et les indicateurs de performance de la LOLF », *Rapport d'information du Sénat*, n° 220.

Atkinson, T., (2005), *Atkinson Review: Final report, Measurement of Government Output and Productivity for the National Accounts*, Palgrave, McMillan, Londres.

Bousquet, F. et Coulomb, A., (2007), « Mesure de la performance et gestion hospitalière », Complément A in *Performance, incitations et gestion publique*, Rapport du CAE, n° 66, La Documentation française.

Dixit, A.,(1996), *The Making of Economic Policy*, MIT Press, Cambridge, MA.

Hel-Thelier, S., (2007), « La mesure de la production et de la productivité des administrations publiques : la mission Atkinson au Royaume-Uni », Complément C in *Performance, incitations et gestion publique*, Rapport du CAE, n° 66, La Documentation française.

Kravchuk, R. et Schack, R., (1996), "Designing Effective Performance Measurement Systems Under the Government Performance and Results Act of 1993", *Public Administration Review*, n° 56(4), p. 348-358.

Laffont, J.-J., (1999), « Étapes vers un État moderne : une analyse économique », in *État et gestion publique*, Rapport du CAE n° 24, La Documentation française, p. 117-149.

Lambert, A. et Migaud, D., (2005), *Rapport au gouvernement sur la mise en place de la LOLF*.

Marr, B. et Creelman, J., (2011), *More with Less*, Palgrave Macmillan, février 2011.

Milgrom, P. et Roberts, J., (1992), *Economics, Organization and Management*, Prentice Hall

OCDE, (2003), *Revue de l'OCDE sur la gestion budgétaire*, vol. 3 n° 1, Paris, France.

OCDE, (2005), « La modernisation de l'État : la route à suivre », synthèse OCDE, novembre.

Propper, C. et Wilson, D., (2003), "The Use and Usefulness of Performance Measures in the Public Sector", *Oxford Review of Economic Policy*, n° 19(2), p. 250-267.

Wilson, J.Q., (1989), *Bureaucracy: What Government Agencies Do and Why They Do It*, Basic Books, New York.

6.
Social Security

THE ACTIVE WELFARE STATE:
A STYLISED RETROSPECTIVE

Frank Vandenbroucke, with Kim Lievens[1, 2]

INTRODUCTION

Since the mid-1990s, a vast literature has been published on the need for a 'new welfare state', in which three core ideas resonate: new social risks, social investment, and the development of services. Unemployment, old age, ill health, sickness and disability, and the financial burden of raising children were seen as constituting the 'old' risks, which had been increasingly catered for by welfare states since the Second World War. In the category of new social risks one might list the following (Bonoli, 2006): (i) the impossibility of reconciling family responsibility and paid labour; (ii) single parenthood; (iii) long-term care dependency of a family member; (iv) poor or inadequate schooling; (v) insufficient coverage by social security, e.g. because of lack of access to an adequately insured insider position on the labour market. The second core idea, social investment, emphasises that it is better to prevent social risks than to remedy them afterwards, for example through training and activation of jobseekers, through investing in education and lifelong learning. Both goals – addressing new social risks and activation – imply that welfare states need

---

1. Frank Vandenbroucke is Professor at the Faculty of Economics and Business, Katholieke Universiteit Leuven. He was Minister for Social Affairs, Pensions and Employment from 2000 to 2004.
2. We thank Jan Vanthuyne, Bea Cantillon, Kristel Bogaerts, Muriel Dejemeppe, Dirk Moens, Diana De Graeve, Michel Breda, Ri De Ridder, Nicole Fasquelle, Greet De Vil, Guy Van Camp, Koen Vleminckx, Willem Adema, Leen Meeusen, Steven Segaert, Frederic Taveirne, Tuba Bircan and Cis Caes for punctual contributions. The usual disclaimers apply.

to develop services, such as child care or counselling and training, next to benefits. Bismarckian welfare states, to which Belgium historically belongs, are considered to be cash-heavy, giving priority to cash transfers over social services. Scandinavian welfare states are service-heavy. The 'new welfare state' implied the dual ambition of modernising the welfare state, so that it would better address the new risks and needs structure of contemporary societies, and of ensuring its financial sustainability.

In 1999, the Verhofstadt government proposed to turn Belgium into an 'active welfare state'. To some extent, the active welfare state can be associated with the literature on 'the new welfare state'. The active welfare state aimed at a combination of both 'new risk' policies and preventive policies, notably by activation, but it emphasised at the same time the need to maintain adequate social benefits to cater for traditional social risks (Vandenbroucke, 1999; Vandenbroucke and Vleminckx, 2011). Hence, the active welfare state was an attempt to redefine and change the orientation of social policy by developing a complementary strategy: rather than replacing the traditional functions of the welfare state, the idea was to improve them and to add new functions.

As in other Bismarckian welfare states, Belgian employment and social policy is historically characterised by status-preserving distinctions, such as the distinction between blue-collar and white-collar workers and the distinction between the self-employed, employees and statutory civil servants. Would the ambition to improve traditional social programmes entail a radical departure from this legacy? During the past decade the self-employed have obtained quasi the same child benefits[3] and health care reimbursement as employees and civil servants; pensions and incapacity benefits for the self-employed were significantly upgraded. These alignments were a driver of additional social expenditure without matching extra revenue.[4] Specific professional groups, such as artists or *onthaalmoeders/gardiennes d'enfants* in the childcare sector, obtained social security coverage in a pragmatic way. Thus, Belgian social security became pragmatically universal in terms of access. One might say that

---

3. There still is a difference in the basic amount and the age supplement for a child of rank 1, which should be eliminated before the constitutional changes agreed by the Di Rupo government are implemented.
4. However, in health care contribution rates for the self-employed were increased.

social policy thus countered the fifth risk in our list of new risks, that is, the risk of insufficient social coverage. But these *ad hoc* measures did not alter the fundamentally Bismarckian legacy of status-based social security pillars.

Although there was mutual influence, in its conception the active welfare state was not a copy-and-paste of the literature on the new welfare state. Activation became a key issue during Verhofstadt II (2003-2007). Health care policy was inspired by the observation that new social risk profiles had emerged, and policies to reconcile family responsibility and labour market participation were high on the agenda (as they had already been from in the 1990s). But explicit references to 'new' and 'old' risks did not gain prominence in the political discourse. Overcoming status-based differentiation within traditional social programmes was a more salient issue in the political agenda than 'new-versus-old-risks' or 'services-versus-cash'. With hindsight, the policies pursued by Verhofstadt I (1999-2003) may be summarised in the following strategic orientations:

I. maintain and improve where possible the adequacy of social benefits;
II. create employment incentives, not by lowering benefits, but by lowering taxes on earned income and lowering personal social security contributions at the bottom end of the wage scale;
III. bolster competitiveness and labour demand by reducing employers' social security contributions, substituting general revenue for Bismarckian contributions;
IV. guarantee universal access to social security and better protection for the self-employed by pragmatic *ad hoc* measures;
V. accommodate the 'rebound' of health care spending after health care austerity in the 1990s;
VI. locate the fundamental guarantee for future pensioners firmly in the first pillar, but develop a sector-based second pillar with a view to democratising access.

In a similar vein, one might say that the Verhofstadt II government added two orientations:
I. implement a model of activation by 'close monitoring' of the unemployed;
II. tackle early exit from the labour market.

At the same time, the government would aim at budget surpluses to prepare for the cost of ageing; this option was institutionalised with the announcement of the *Silver Fund*.[5] The key challenge was whether it would be possible to reconcile these '8+1' orientations.

Rather than presenting a detailed discussion of policy measures, we propose an assessment on the basis of stylised facts with regard to spending, employment and poverty, which allow both a cross-country comparison and an understanding of the past decade as one chapter in the long-term development of the Belgian welfare state. The question is not only to what extent successive governments delivered on the promise of the active welfare state and the '8+1' orientations listed above. An additional question is whether, before the financial crisis, the Belgian welfare state was gradually achieving a new and sustainable 'equilibrium situation' with lower but stabilised benefit ratios(average benefits divided by average wages for employees or by average earned income for the self-employed) and stable benefit dependency ratios, after the spectacular increase in benefit dependency in the second half of the 1970s and the 1980s.We do not discuss second-pillar pensions and limit the discussion of health care to some summary remarks.

1. SOCIAL SPENDING: STABILITY AND CHANGE

1.1 The long-term evolution of social spending

As a percentage of GDP, Belgian public social spending has displayed stability over the last 25 years, according to the OECD Social Expenditure Database (OECD SOCX). In 1985 public social spending amounted to 26% of GDP; it then declined to 24.6% in 1989, increased again to 26.9% in 1993, declined to 25.4% in 2000, and increased to 26.3% in 2007, the latest year available in OECD SOCX. So, two periods stand out as periods of relative expansion vis-à-vis GDP: 1989-1993 and 2000-2007. Yet, so conceived, Belgian public spending seems the archetype of the

---

5. The Silver Fund was a mechanism for setting aside budget surpluses in a separate account only to be used later, to make it transparent and credible that budgetary surpluses would anticipate (serve as pre-funding for) the future cost of ageing.

'immovable object' described by Pierson in his seminal work on the non-retrenchment of welfare states (Pierson, 2001). The turning points in 1985 and 1993 may partly be explained by the economic environment: unemployment started to diminish from 1985 onwards, until 1992; in the recession year 1993 it increased and remained high until 1998, to decline from 1999 onwards. But policy changes did play an important role: we had years of budgetary austerity until 1988, followed by *le retour du cœur* in 1989-1991; and again budgetary austerity under the Dehaene government in the 1990s, to conform to the Maastricht euro-entry criteria and to prepare for the cost of ageing.

We use OECD SOCX to compare the extent to which the pattern of Belgian social spending accommodated 'new social risks' with evolutions in other welfare states. Therefore, we divide public social spending into five categories, four of which may be seen as reflecting traditional risks, while the fifth category can be construed as reflecting new risks:[6]

I. Health care;
II. Old age (including survivor) programmes;
III. Benefits for families who are 'of working age', including unemployment, work incapacity benefits, housing benefits, social assistance... but excluding child benefits and programmes included in 'new programmes';
IV. Child benefits, including other family allowances in cash;
V. 'New programmes', which include child care, active labour market policies, maternity and parental leave (but not other leave systems), and elderly care not included in health care.

Figure 1 provides the public spending data for these categories for Belgium.

---

6. The exercise serves a cross-country comparison, rather than a precise description of the development of Belgian social spending as such. A more fine-grained analysis of the Belgian data would show that some programmes answering 'new risks', such as care for the frail elderly or part of the expanding 'career break' or 'leave' systems, are classified under 'traditional' programmes (respectively health care, and unemployment benefits). But even in the context of cross-country comparisons one should be cautious; De Deken (forthcoming) lists difficulties one should be aware of when partitioning social spending data on the basis of the 'risk' categories as defined by Bonoli.

Figure 1: Public social spending as a % of GDP, 1985-2007, Belgium

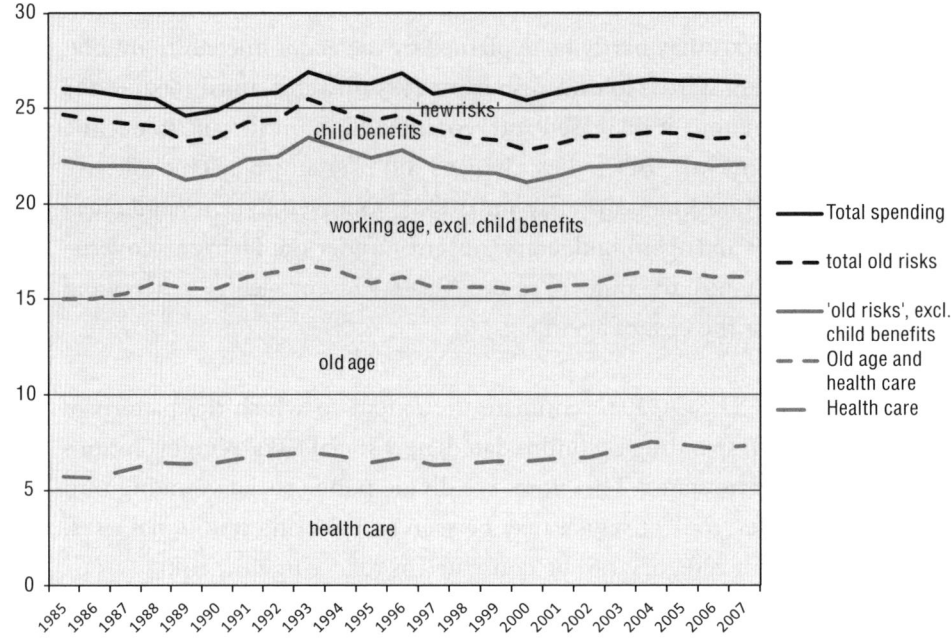

Source: own calculations based on OECD SOCX

In Table 1 we use the 'turning points' in spending(1985, 1989, 1993, 2000) to organise our data, and also add the year 2007.

Table 1: Public spending on 'old' and 'new' welfare programmes in Belgium (% GDP)

	1985	1989	1993	2000	2007
Health care	5,7	6,4	7,0	6,6	7,3
Old age (incl. survivors)	9,3	9,2	9,8	8,9	8,9
Working age benefits, excl. child ben.	9,6	7,7	8,7	7,4	7,3
(of which unemployment)	*3,3*	*2,6*	*3,2*	*2,8*	*3,1*
Child benefits	2,4	2,0	2,0	1,7	1,4
Maternity and parental leave	0,1	0,1	0,2	0,2	0,2
Elderly care, not in health	0,0	0,0	0,0	0,4	0,5
Child care	0,1	0,1	0,2	0,8	0,9
ALMP	1,2	1,1	1,1	1,2	1,2
Total 'old risks'	24,7	23,3	25,5	22,8	23,5
Total 'new risks'	1,4	1,3	1,4	2,6	2,9
Total public spending (old and new)	26,0	24,6	26,9	25,4	26,3

Source: own calculations based on OECD SOCX

'New spending' increased in Belgium during the 1990s, to remain stable thereafter. By 2000, the level of 'new spending' more or less approached the unweighted average of similar spending by our neighbours, Germany, France and the Netherlands. (Below, we refer to this benchmark as 'our neighbours'; obviously, this average conceals different trajectories in the Netherlands, France and pre- and post-unification Germany.) So conceived, Belgium's spending profile was modernised during the 1990s rather than during the 2000s: at first sight, active labour market policy, a hallmark of social investment, was basically flat vis-à-vis GDP over the last 25 years; the main expansion of child care spending happened between 1993 and 2000. At least, that is what the aggregate budgetary figures signal; below we will qualify this conclusion. Simultaneously, this means that spending related to *traditional* social risks decreased more between 1993 and 2000, as a share of GDP, than total spending.

With regard to traditional social spending, the overall Belgian trajectory of the 1980s and 1990s was more or less similar to the average trajectory of our neighbours, but the internal dynamics were somewhat different. Between 1993 and 2000 the sum of health care and old age spending was reduced marginally more in Belgium (vis-à-vis GDP) than in our neighbours. Old age spending decelerated for three reasons: the declining size of survivors' pensions, declining global benefit ratios (discussed below, with some qualifications), and the 1996 pension reform which introduced stricter career requirements for early statutory retirement and increased the statutory pension age of women from 60 to 65 years. The last operation stretched from 1996 to 2009, and induced a remarkable reversal of trends. In the private employee sector, the number of people retiring increased by 16,915 per annum between 1985 and 1991. Between 1991 and 1997 the annual increase accelerated to 22,259 per annum, fuelled by the misguided decision to abolish the reduction coefficients for early retirement in the employee sector in 1991. Between 1997 and 2007 the annual increase decelerated to 7,654, to start accelerating again from 2007 onwards for demographic reasons. Although postponement mainly concerned relatively smaller pensions, the 1996 reform thus contained pension spending (Festjens, 1997, forecasts a reduction of the pension budget by 0.5% of GDP and of the number of those retiring by 168,500, by 2010). But it also created a shift from pension spending to spending on other benefits, such as unemployment benefits and unemployment-based early exit schemes. Herremans (2006) estimates that the main impact of the first phase of the 1996 reform was a shift from retirement to other forms of inactivity; one cannot however rule out that it finally also contributed, in the course of the 2000s, to the increasing employment rates of women in the 60-64 age bracket.

Verhofstadt I considered it necessary to improve minimum pensions and to upgrade older pensioners' pensions to reconnect them, at least to some extent, with the increase in living standards. Relative to GDP, public pension spending remained at the same level between 2000 and 2007.

OECD SOCX registers a spectacular increase, by 43.2%, in the volume of public health care spending between 1986 and 1992 and nearly a standstill over the next six years (+ 4.4% between 1992 and 1998). Between 1998 and 2004 health spending again increased by 33.9%. This S-shaped growth curve can be seen as confirming Cutler's thesis (2002): governments can suppress the growth of health care spending for a number of years below a trend that is to a large extent determined by progress in medical technology, but they always experience a 'rebound' (we return to this issue below). In 2000 health care spending was marginally below the level of that of our neighbours (-0.2 ppt); by 2007 it was marginally higher (+ 0.2 ppt).

In 1993 spending on working age benefits, excluding child benefits, was slightly higher in Belgium than in our neighbours (a difference of 0.5 ppt). In comparison, it was also reduced less during those years of austerity (the difference increased to 1.1 ppt in 2000 and 1.6 ppt in 2007). Hence, the expansion of spending in the 2000s may be seen, at least in part, to be the result of an inevitable rebound or 'return to trend' of both health care and old age spending in Belgium, while spending on working age benefits remained at its comparatively high level, characteristic of our welfare state. Thus, spending on working age benefits amounted to 7.3% of GDP in the relatively prosperous year 2007: surprisingly, this level is comparable to the figures for 1993 and 1985, years characterised by considerable economic stress. Belgium spends more on unemployment benefits than other welfare states; this is partly explained by the fact that Belgian unemployment benefits and related early exit schemes serve social groups which benefit from work incapacity benefits (and/or social assistance or retirement pensions) in other welfare states. This structural policy difference between Belgium and other welfare states emerges clearly when we study the social caseload, below. However, with regard to the level of spending, these caseload differences can only explain a relatively small amount of the Belgian specificity: in 2007 spending on unemployment benefits was 1.8 ppt higher than in our neighbours; public spending on all other 'working age benefits' was only 0.3 ppt lower. In other words, Belgium emerges as a heavy spender on working age benefits *in globo*, notably with regard to working age *cash* benefits. Since general career break or leave systems are counted as unemployment benefits, the expansion of these systems may offer part of the explanation; however, they explain but a relatively small part of spending registered here.[7]

Over the last 30 years, there has been a steady erosion of child benefits: in 1980 2.8% of GDP was spent on child benefits; by 2007 this had fallen to 1.4%.

Obviously, demographic changes are important factors driving spending on pensions and child benefits (just as unemployment has an impact on spending on unemployment benefits and, presumably, on spending on active labour market policies). To assess the impact of needs created by demography (or unemployment) we calculate ratios of 'spending per capita' on GDP per capita:

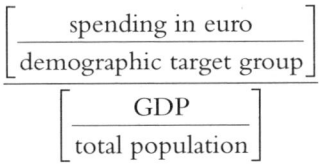

Table 2 provides the indices for each of the spending 'turning points' we selected on the basis of Figure 1, using the ratios for 1985 as the benchmark. We call these indices 'budgetary effort indices'.

---

7. RVA/ONEM figures indicate that leave systems (*loopbaanonderbreking/interruption de carrière* and *tijdskrediet/crédit temps*) amounted to 0.08% of GDP in 1993, 0.09% in 2000, and 0.19% in 2007. For an interesting comparative discussion of the Belgian unemployment system see De Deken (2012).

Table 2: Budgetary effort indices (1985=100), Belgium

	1985	1989	1993	2000	2007
((Old age spending)/(Pop. 65+)) /(GDP/CAP)	100	92	93	78	77
((Child care)/(Pop. <5))/(GDP/CAP)	100	89	134	667	775
(ALMP/unemployed)/(GDP/CAP)	100	129	93	172	163
((Family allowances)/(Pop. < 20))/(GDP/CAP)	100	89	89	77	68

Source: own calculations based on OECD.

The budgetary effort index for old age spending decreased over most of the period under review, but the decline was most marked between 1993 and 2000; between 2000 and 2007 the decline was nearly halted. For the reasons explained earlier, the share of total spending on old age in GDP did not follow the proportion of the elderly in the population in the second half of the 1990s. Improvements in the levels of pensions from 2000 onwards halted this downward development. Does this budgetary effort index inform us about changes in the implicit intergenerational focus of social policy? First of all, a *caveat* should be applied with regard to the denominator in our ratios: GDP per capita reflects all sources of income, i.e. not just earned income by employees and the self-employed, and it is positively influenced by rising employment rates, even if average earnings do not increase. Thus, a decreasing effort index does not presuppose a deterioration in benefit ratios (average benefits divided by average wages for employees or by average earned income for the self-employed), i.e. it does not necessarily imply a deterioration in the quality of the underlying insurance contract from an individual perspective. Second, the intergenerational interpretation depends on the valuation of a pension for an individual pensioner. Today, the elderly live longer on their annual pension income than they used to do in the 1980s; an identical pension (or an identical benefit ratio, for that matter) can be interpreted as an improvement in terms of the pension *capital* a contemporary 65 years old individual may *expect*, compared with what a person of 65 could have expected 20 years ago. Whether the impact of longevity on the pension capital should be considered objective progress in well-being or not is a moot question; yet, we are inclined to say it constitutes an objective source of individual progress in well-being (or at least a policy that accommodates a trend that improves the elderly's well-being; Vandenbroucke, 2012).

The figures for child benefits in Table 2 highlight their steady erosion, due to the fact that child benefits are not indexed to the standard of living and the decline in household size. Budgetary savings introduced by the gradual reduction in 'age allowances' from 1997 were compensated for in the 2000s by the introduction of a premium for children with single parents, a so-called 'yearly allowance', and a new system for disabled children; the overall outcome was that the dispersion of benefit levels increased, making the system more selective (RKW, 2011). Using the population share of individuals below the age of 20 as a benchmark, in 2007 the ratio of 'spending per child' on GDP per capita was only 68% of the corresponding ratio in 1985.[8] In contrast, spending on child care increased spectacularly in the 1990s, using the population share of young children as the benchmark. The expansion of child care was both a precondition and a consequence of the feminisation of the labour market, which we document below for the 2000s.

Similarly, spending on active labour market policies (ALMP) did not match the evolution in the number of unemployed in the first half of the 1990s, but then started to increase relative to the number of unemployed: the ratio of 'ALMP spending per unemployed' on GDP per capita was considerably higher in the 2000s than in the 1990s. This qualifies our earlier observation about spending trends in the 1990s and the 2000s: so conceived, there was a turn to social investment spending in the 2000s, but not at the expense of traditional social spending. Except for family policy, the Belgian policy model was one of 'adding' new functions rather than 'replacing' existing functions. Moreover, the aggregate ALMP figures conceal an important shift from occupational programmes ('direct job creation') in the 1980s to employment assistance in the 2000s. In comparative literature on ALMP, direct job creation is considered less effective than training the unemployed (which did not increase, at least on the basis of OECD SOCX) and activation-oriented employment assistance (which did increase).

---

8. Given the expansion of higher education, one would expect young adults to obtain a larger share of child benefits; however, that appears not to be the case. On the basis of available spending data, we conclude that the indices in Table 2 hardly change if we exclude child benefits for young adults.

Belgian social spending gradually became more service-oriented during the 1990s. The share of 'in kind benefits' increased from 23% in 1985 to 34% in 2000, and subsequently stabilised. The service share remains rather low in comparison with Northern and Anglo-Saxon welfare states. In fact, there never was an explicit policy debate, let alone strategic orientation, with regard to the 'cash/services' balance in Belgian policy. As explained in Vandenbroucke (2010), this regrettable lacuna in strategic thinking is to some extent related to institutional tensions in the Belgian polity.

1.2 The growth norm for health care spending

After the formation of Verhofstadt I, the growth of health care spending became a controversial issue. The government accommodated a rebound after years of spending limits, but it did so in a politically controlled way: the growth rate had to be negotiated in the government year after year. The advantage of that situation was that strong pressure could be brought to bear upon the main actors within the health care system (medical and paramedical professions, hospital managers, sickness funds) to accept a *quid pro quo*, i.e. to accept that high rates of growth would have to be deserved by a steady drive for more internal efficiency and modernisation within the system. This culminated in the *Agenda 2002 for Change in Health Care*, which emphasised the efficiency and individual responsibility of health care professionals and hospitals, made operational via the introduction of non-linear correction mechanisms instead of the linear correction mechanisms often applied in the 1990s. The theme of individual responsibility implied the recognition of unjustified differences in medical practice, sometimes, but not always, on a North–South basis. At the same time the concept signalled that, even if some of these differences could be predicated on a North–South divide, the remedy would not be to 'split the system', but to organise more individual responsibility for choices in health care. Over the years, there have been some successful implementations of increased responsibility and efficiency, informed by evidence-based medicine (such as the lump sum reimbursement system for drugs prescribed in hospitals). With regard to pharmaceuticals, the introduction of 'reference prices' to enhance the prescription of generic drugs, accompanied by various measures to change prescription practice, also had a major cumulative impact.

From 2004 the dynamics of policy making changed, once the Verhofstadt II government introduced a 'health care growth norm' of 4.5% per annum (in volume). This was the unfortunate result of political controversy about health care spending in the run-up to the elections. It was unfortunate, because it diminished the efficiency pressure on health care actors. This is not to say that no efforts were subsequently made to curb spending. But the drive for more responsibility in health care practice on the basis of scientific evidence slowed down rather than increased. Admittedly it is no more than a conjecture, but it seems that an indirect consequence of this is that we still live with the dual financing system in the hospital sector, a cumbersome combination of fees per medical act and direct funding of hospitals which was bound to be challenged if the drive for individual responsibility within the hospital sector had been reinforced.

1.3   Automatic stabilisation during the crisis

For an assessment of the crisis years we have to turn to Eurostat's ESSPROS data on social protection spending. In 2009 social spending was 3.7 ppt higher (vis-à-vis GDP) than in 2007, according to ESSPROS. This considerable increase is comparable to the weighted average for the EU15, and slightly larger than in our three neighbours (+ 3.1 ppt). Most of this increase is explained by the automatic stabilising effect of welfare state transfers, which increase (unemployment benefits) or do not decrease when GDP decreases (child benefits, pensions, ...). Only a minor part can be traced to policy measures such as the changes in levels and leniency with regard to temporary unemployment. Thus, by 2009 public social spending in Belgium was at an unprecedented high level.

2. THE ADEQUACY OF SOCIAL PROTECTION

This section focuses on income replacement. Obviously, assessing the adequacy of social protection also involves health care and family allowances. Relative to public health care spending, patient co-payments declined from 9.3% in 1999 to 6.8% in 2009; the latter figure takes into account the impact of the Maximum Billing system (a cap on the total annual amount of co-payments, in function of the household budget, introduced in 2002). In real terms the average co-payment per inhabitant hardly increased during those ten years.[9] Out-of-pocket payments, other than the official co-payments, did increase, but this development seems to have been checked by measures against supplements in the second half of the decade (De Wolf et al, 2011).[10] Focusing on the income side of the social protection equation should not make us forget the cost compensation side of the equation.

2.1 Benefit ratios: stabilisation and partial repair after two decades of decline

In this section, we first discuss social security and then broaden the scope to social assistance. Figure 2 shows the evolution of global benefit ratios in the social security system for private sector employees for three broad categories of spending: retirement pensions, invalidity (i.e. long-term absence because of illness) and unemployment (including temporary unemployment), drawing on research by the Belgian Federal Planning Bureau (FPB) (De Vil *et al*, 2011; including a forecast until 2020).

---

9. For an evaluation of the Maximum Billing system in health care see Schokkaert *et al* (2008).
10. On the basis of the data provided by *Assuralia*, it seems that out-of-pocket payments grew more or less on a par with total spending on health care. Hence, they grew relative to family budgets, but did not signal a relative shift from public to private funding on a macro level. That does not mean that 'supplements' do not continue to pose serious problems of equity and fairness in parts of the health care system.

Figure 2: Global benefit ratios (average benefit in % of average gross salary), employees

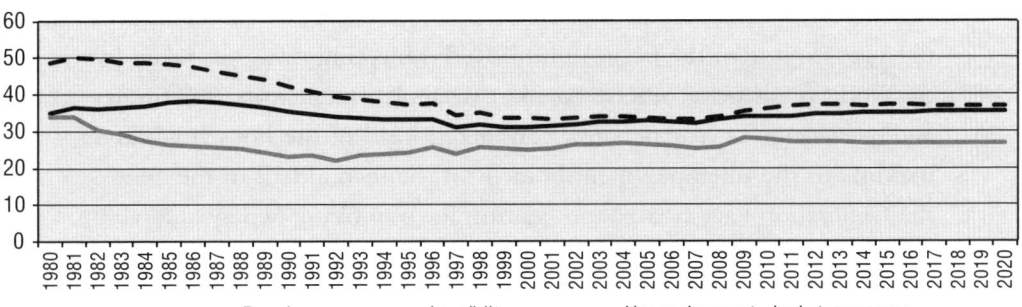

Source: De Vil (2011), Figure 1, p. 29

Benefit ratios are calculated by dividing average spending per beneficiary by gross average wages. Since they do not take into account the taxes and personal social security contributions on wages, their level is less informative than their evolution. For the same reason, the evolution too should be interpreted with due caution: it overlooks changes in taxation or personal social security contributions. The benefit ratios in Figure 2 are global, since they do not take into account changes in specific sub-categories of the social security branches and compositional shifts, such as the increase in the share of retired women. Nevertheless, Figure 2 shows that the decline in benefit ratios which started in the 1980s came to a halt from 2000 onwards, and was even partially reversed.

The observation that a long period of retrenchment with regard to benefit ratios came to an end by the year 2000 is confirmed by the FPB's calculations for specific sub-categories of social security branches. Taken separately, the benefit ratios for male and female pensioners decline somewhat, but not very much, during the 1990s; in the second half of the 2000s they improve. By 2009 they are higher than in 1980 for all sub-categories. The FPB also documents a considerable improvement in the benefit ratio of pensions for male self-employed workers, gradually during the 1990s and spectacularly by 2009: this reflects the considerable increases in minimum pensions for self-employed workers in the 2000s. Similarly, a separate analysis of benefit ratios for different categories of invalidity benefits shows that a considerable decline came to an end, and was reversed. For self-employed workers invalidity benefits were also considerably improved. A more detailed analysis of unemployment benefits shows that the decline in benefit ratios stopped by the end of the 1990s and then the position improved, reflecting measures taken by the Verhofstadt governments to increase replacement rates (for singles and *cohabitants*, i.e. partners not considered head of the household) and maxima in the unemployment branch. In the second half of the 2000s, the Generation Pact created momentum for improving benefits, notably by entrenching the principle of linking benefits to the standard of living.

An often used benchmark for the evolution of social assistance benefits is Net National Income per capita (NNI/cap). Although NNI/cap makes more sense as a benchmark for residual income assistance than average gross wages, one should be aware that it diverges from wages as it is influenced by other sources of income and by changes in the employment/population ratio. Relative to NNI/cap, social assistance benefit levels for the non-elderly were historically high during the 1980s. As a matter of fact, Belgian social security policy increasingly focused on minimum income protection in the 1970s and 1980s, by structuring benefits on the basis of the household status of beneficiaries and by giving priority to minimum benefits, both in social security and social assistance. The drive to improve social security minimum benefits came to a halt early in the 1980s, while social assistance still improved. In the 1990s however, social assistance minima also started to erode relative to NNI (Cantillon et al, 2003). Marx (2009) considers the imperative to maintain a hierarchy between minimum wages and minimum benefits as one of the main reasons why the drive for minimum income protection stalled. The Verhofstadt governments marked a break with measures both to improve social security minima, social assistance minima and benefits in general; as will be shown below, increasing *net* minimum wages was a key factor enabling that change of trend. The agenda was, however, broader than minimum income protection. Next to the aim to re-establish a link between benefits and the standard of living, notably for older beneficiaries, some measures were driven by the aspiration to restore insurance principles rather than to improve minima (however limited the budgetary leeway was to return to insurance principles), for example in the domain of unemployment insurance.

The introduction of the *Inkomensgarantie voor Ouderen* (*Garantie de Revenus aux Personnes âgées*) in 2001 (which replaced the *Gewaarborgd Inkomen voor Bejaarden/Revenu Garanti aux Personnes âgées*) entailed a modernisation of minimum income assistance for the elderly, and signalled the start of a considerable improvement vis-à-vis NNI/cap, notably in 2006. Hence, in the domain of old age and survivors, improving residual minimum income protection re-emerged as an important policy focus *per se*. With regard to the non-elderly population, the picture is more nuanced. Goedemé et al (2012) conclude their synthesis of minimum income protection in the 2000s as follows: important changes and improvements in minimum income protection were implemented, but less for the population deemed fit to work than for the elderly and incapacitated; also, the difference between social security and assistance benefits decreased (as was the case in earlier periods – a trend one might qualify as 'residualisation'), this time notably for the elderly. In the next section we elaborate on income protection for the non-elderly, including for those active at the low end of the labour market.

2.2 The adequacy of minimum wages and benefits for household types, and employment incentives

Benefit ratios provide an indication of the adequacy of benefits from an individual insurance perspective, but to evaluate the adequacy of benefits for households, notably with a view to avoiding poverty, one should assess the impact of benefit packages on the net disposable income of households. Table 3 provides information on the evolution of net disposable incomes of four types of households in working age (singles; single parents; a single earner, i.e. a couple with one income and no children; a single earner with children, i.e. a couple with one income and two children) in six different situations: working full-time for the minimum wage; long-term unemployment on minimum benefit; long-term unemployment on maximum benefit (below we use 'unemployment' as a short-cut for long-term unemployment); invalidity on minimum benefit; invalidity on maximum benefit; social assistance (*leefloon/revenu d'intégration sociale*). The evolution is summarised by the real increase between 1999 and 2010 of net disposable household income, which takes into account all relevant benefits including child benefits, personal social security contributions, taxes, and the cost of child care for the single parent (below, we use 'household income' or 'income' as a short-cut). To evaluate these figures, the real increase in NNI/cap and average gross wages is added (real changes are nominal changes corrected using the general consumption price index). In addition, both for 1999 and 2010 household income is expressed as a ratio of household income when the household lives on a minimum wage. These ratios give a rough indication of the financial incentive for the households under review to find a job at the level of the minimum wage.

Table 3: Adequacy of benefit packages for household types 1999-2010

net disposable household income (incl. child benefit and child care cost for lone parent) real increase 1999-2010 and ratio (% of net disposable household income when minimum wage)		MINIMUM WAGE	UNEMPLOYM. MINIMUM	UNEMPLOYM. MAXIMUM	INVALIDITY MINIMUM	INVALIDITY MAXIMUM	SOCIAL ASSISTANCE
single	increase 1999-2010	14%	24%	36%	16%	23%	11%
	ratio 1999	100%	63%	70%	80%	109%	60%
	ratio 2010	100%	68%	84%	81%	117%	59%
lone parent	increase 1999-2010	20%	4%	4%	11%	6%	13%
	ratio 1999	100%	93%	103%	106%	143%	87%
	ratio 2010	100%	81%	89%	98%	128%	82%
single earner, no children	increase 1999-2010	20%	5%	6%	16%	9%	11%
	ratio 1999	100%	79%	90%	90%	139%	72%
	ratio 2010	100%	69%	79%	87%	127%	67%
single earner, 2 children	increase 1999-2010	16%	9%	9%	16%	9%	13%
	ratio 1999	100%	83%	91%	94%	134%	77%
	ratio 2010	100%	77%	85%	94%	126%	75%
NNI per capita, corrected for CPI		7,57%					
average gross wages, corrected for CPI		1,49%					

Source: simulations provided by *Centrum voor Sociaal Beleid Herman Deleeck* (STASIM model)

Five conclusions can be drawn from Table 3:

1. The income of all household types increases more than NNI/cap, except in three cases for which the income increase is marginally lower than the increase in NNI/cap: unemployed lone parents and

unemployed single earners without children, and lone parents on maximum invalidity benefit. However, all these household types see their purchasing power increase to some extent. Relative to NNI/cap the overall picture is a reversal of erosion trends in the 1990s.

II. The income increase for households living on a minimum wage is significantly higher than the increase in NNI/cap; the gain in purchasing power for this household type is substantial.

III. The incentive to find a job at a minimum wage increases for all household types living on benefits, except for singles. For singles, the incentive decreases, except for singles on minimum invalidity benefits and singles on social assistance, where it remains unchanged. However, compared to other household types, the financial incentive to find a job is still larger for singles. These figures corroborate more detailed studies of the evolution of unemployment traps over the last decade (Bogaerts, 2008; Nevejan,2009, 2011).

IV. The financial incentive to find a job remains weak for lone parents.

V. Social assistance improved more than minimum benefits for the unemployed, except for singles, a fact which may be interpreted as an indication of further creeping residualisation in this specific domain.

In general, this shows that the strategic orientation of successive governments since 1999 to reduce inactivity traps, not by decreasing incomes for households living on benefits (either in absolute terms, or relative to NNI/cap) but by increasing *net* purchasing power for households living on a minimum wage, has been implemented. The reduction in inactivity traps is to a large extent the result of successive cuts in personal social security contributions for low wages from 1999 onwards, and – in Flanders – the reduction in child care costs (and, in second order, tax reform). However, these measures have led to high marginal tax and social contribution rates on wages above the minimum level (Nevejan, 2009, p. 35). Thus, inactivity traps may have been replaced, in part, by wage traps. Moreover, research by Bogaerts shows that the inactivity trap when considering part-time employment has increased (Bogaerts, 2008).

3. THE ACTIVATION TURN: PREVENTIVE AND CLOSE MONITORING RATHER THAN HARSH SANCTIONS

The *Employment Conference* of September 2003, organised by Verhofstadt II, put an end to 15 years of institutional schizophrenia in employment policies. With the decentralisation of training and placement policy in the 1980s, the responsibilities for training and activation of the unemployed on the one hand, and controlling their availability for the labour market on the other, had been decoupled. They would be linked again by an inter-institutional cooperation agreement. The new approach replaced the infamous article 80 of the unemployment code, which organised the systematic suspension of unemployed individuals who were 'abnormally long-term unemployed'. With hindsight, one may say that this mechanism was both rather brutal in its consequences (exclusion from the right to unemployment benefits, often without prior warning that one should look for work), very selective (it concerned only a sub-category of mainly women), and ineffective in terms of activation (since it was not part of an activation trajectory). Article 80 was replaced by a mechanism that was both broader (it concerned all unemployed, yet in a first stage limited to those under 50) and more nuanced (sanctions are gradual), and functions in a preventive way. The essence of the new model is close monitoring rather than harsh sanctions. As a matter of fact, within the activation framework *stricto sensu*, over the years from 2009 to 2011 the number of total and definitive exclusions (5,906 cases) was 30% lower than under the regime of article 80 over the years from 2001 to 2003; apart from total and definitive exclusions, the new system also uses temporary exclusions; over 2009-2011 there were 5,640 cases of only temporary exclusions (RVA/ONEM). This largely preventive model was not unsuccessful, according to research by Cockx *et al* (2011), which is not to say that it cannot be improved. The cooperation agreement also created a new momentum with regard to so-called 'transmissions' by the regional employment services for various contraventions of the unemployment regulation: their number increased significantly, and so did sanctions following from those transmissions. Although these transmissions are not part of the monitoring scheme applied by the RVA/ONEM, they are closely related to the activation drive. Finally, data mining made it possible drastically to improve the fight against benefit fraud, which also resulted in more sanctions, unrelated to the activation drive.

4. THE CASELOAD OF SOCIAL POLICY AND BENEFIT DEPENDENCY

Figure 3 shows the evolution of the social caseload in Belgium as a percentage of the population in the 15-64 age bracket (data from De Deken and Clasen, 2011). The total caseload (the sum of the caseload in unemployment, leave systems, work incapacity, early retirement and social assistance) follows a pattern with more or less the same 'turning points' as we established for spending in Figure 1: after a period of spectacular increase, the caseload reached a first peak in 1985, to stay flat until 1990; it reached a second peak in 1993 and then decreased towards 2000. By 2003 it reached a new peak, to decrease somewhat during the boom years after 2005. In the 2000s, incapacity for work and unemployment start to interact as communicating vessels: the decrease in unemployment is partly offset by an increase in incapacity for work. Despite the small decrease in

Figure 3: Belgian social caseload, % of population 15-64

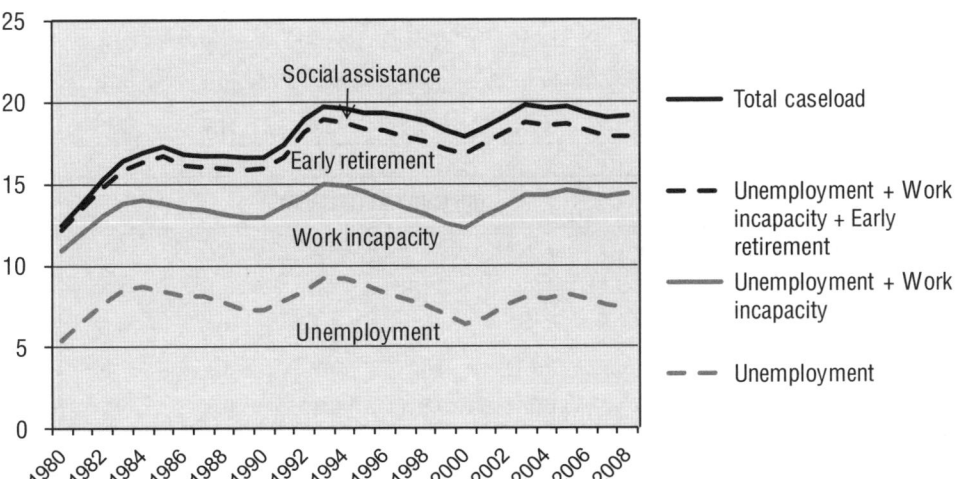

Source: De Deken and Clasen (2011)
Older unemployment beneficiaries exempted from job seeking are included in the category 'Unemployment'.

early retirement in the 2000s, the policies pursued under the banner of the active welfare state were not able to reduce the total caseload during the 2000s.

Table 4 provides a summary comparison of the social caseload in Belgium, Germany, the Netherlands, Denmark and Sweden. In this table, we use the same turning points as in Table 1 (for the OECD SOCX spending data), adding 2008.

Table 4: Caseload in Belgium, Germany, the Netherlands, Denmark and Sweden
(% of population aged 15-64) (! Continued on following page)

	(I) UNEMPLOYMENT					
	1985	1989	1993	2000	2007	2008
Belgium	8,4	7,3	9,2	6,4	7,5	7,4
Germany	3,6	3,3	5,5	5,9	2,0	1,8
Netherlands	6,3	5,3	5,6	3,3	3,6	3,3
Denmark	7,1	7,4	9,7	4,2	2,6	1,4
Sweden	2,0	1,3	6,0	3,8	2,2	1,6

	(II) WORK INCAPACITY					
Belgium	5,4	5,6	5,8	5,9	6,7	7,0
Germany	8,9	8,5	7,6	7,7	6,3	6,4
Netherlands	9,9	11,0	11,7	11,7	9,9	9,6
Denmark	8,8	11,0	9,6	9,9	10,4	10,4
Sweden	9,9	10,9	10,7	13,6	11,9	10,9

	(III) EARLY RETIREMENT					
Belgium	2,9	2,9	3,9	4,5	3,7	3,5
Germany	2,8	3,2	5,1	5,1	3,1	3,5
Netherlands	1,2	1,5	1,9	3,2	4,7	4,5
Denmark	2,8	2,8	3,3	5,1	3,9	3,8
Sweden	0,3	0,3	0,3	0,0	0,0	0,0

(continuation of previous page, Table 4)

	(IV) SOCIAL ASSISTANCE					
	1985	1989	1993	2000	2007	2008
Belgium	0,6	0,8	0,8	1,1	1,1	1,2
Germany	1,7	2,1	2,3	2,7	0,6	0,7
Netherlands	1,9	1,9	1,7	1,1	0,9	0,9
Denmark	3,3	4,0	5,1	3,3	2,5	2,0
Sweden	1,1	1,1	1,9	1,7	1,3	1,3

	(I-IV) TOTAL CASELOAD					
Belgium	17,3	16,6	19,7	17,9	19,0	19,1
Germany	17,0	17,1	20,5	21,4	12,0	12,4
Netherlands	19,3	19,7	20,9	19,3	19,1	18,3
Denmark	22,0	25,2	27,7	22,5	19,4	17,6
Sweden	13,3	13,6	18,9	19,1	15,4	13,8

Source: De Deken and Clasen (2011)

Table 4 first of all emphasises the extent to which differences in the unemployment caseload among those welfare states were compensated for by differences in the incapacity for work caseload. Relatively low unemployment figures in the Netherlands, Sweden and Denmark were accompanied by a relatively high caseload in incapacity for work. Table 4 also shows that only two, Germany and Sweden, of the five welfare states under review were able to reduce the caseload substantially in the 2000s. There is, however, a downside to the German and Swedish performance: in these welfare states poverty increased considerably during the 2000s (Cantillon and Vandenbroucke, forthcoming).

Obviously, the caseload is but one side of a coin. The question of sustainability hinges on the ratio between people who contribute and people who benefit. Figure 4 displays the *benefit dependency ratio* for Belgium for employees and those who are dependent on the employees' social security system, from 1970 to date, with a forecast for 2030. The benefit dependency ratio (black line) is put in context by the *old age dependency ratio*, which measures the population aged 65+ relative to the population 15+ (grey line) and the *adult economic dependency ratio*, which measures the number of individuals aged 15+ who are not in employment, relative to the population (15+) in employment (dashed grey line). The difference between economic dependency and benefit dependency reflects the (changing) role of institutions: unemployed individuals may be economically dependent on their families but not dependent on social security, as was often the case in the heyday of the male breadwinner model.

Figure 4: Old age dependency, adult economic dependency, benefit dependency

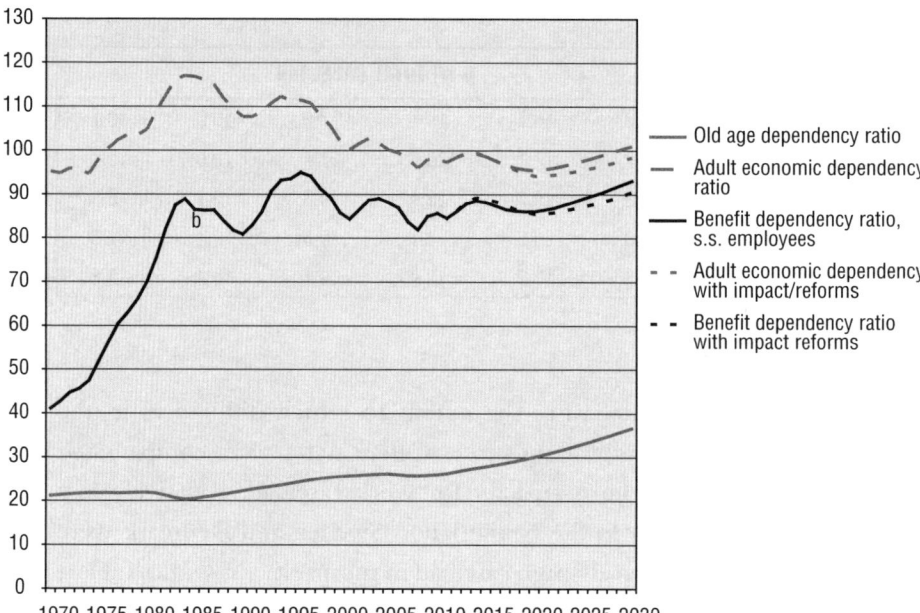

Source: Calculated on the basis of the report 2012 of the *Studiecommissie voor de Vergrijzing* and data supplied by FPB and FPS Social Affairs. With special thanks to Nicole Fasquelle, Christophe Joyeux and Guy Van Camp

In social security for private sector employees, the ratio of the number living on benefits to the number contributing as workers amounted to about 40% in the early 1970s; in increased to nearly 90% in 1984; from then onwards, is has fluctuated between 80% and 90% (with even a peak of 95% in 1996). The explosive growth in benefit dependency in the 1970s did not reflect demographic change: the old-age dependency ratio was constant. It was fuelled first and foremost by economic dependency, reflecting the emergence of mass unemployment and the introduction of early retirement in the second half of the 1970s and the 1980s. Additionally, though, it was driven by the fact that more and more women and young people came to rely on benefits rather than only on familial solidarity, as access to social security became more comprehensive. Notwithstanding demographic ageing from the mid-1980s onwards, adult economic dependency decreased after 1984 (with a lower peak in 1994), reflecting improved employment rates and the feminisation of the labour market; economic dependency had returned (nearly) to its 1975 level by 2008. Benefit dependency also decreased after peaking in 1996, though less so than economic dependency. So conceived, one may say that the 'active welfare state' manifested itself with regard to adult economic dependency (*de facto* earlier than officially promulgated) rather than in respect of benefit dependency *stricto sensu*.

Henceforth, the steep acceleration of demographic ageing will put pressure on both economic and benefit dependency. Figure 4 displays a dependency scenario based on the most recent reference scenario of the *Studiecommissie voor de Vergrijzing*. This scenario assumes that total employment relative to the population in the 15-64 age bracket increases with 4,3 percentage points between 2010 and 2030. The scenario also assumes that, after 2010, benefit dependency increases slightly more than economic dependency. The benefit dependency ratio is positively influenced by an increasing share of individuals over 64 who are entitled to a pension in the employee sector, reflecting the earlier feminisation of the labour market and a declining share of self-employed pensions. But big shocks in the relation between economic dependency and benefit dependency, as in the 1970s and 1980s are not expected. Given these hypotheses, benefit dependency increases gradually but steadily under the impact of demographic ageing.

Two observations follow, at least on the basis of these hypotheses about employment rates. First, after the shocks of the 1970s and 1980s, our welfare state now seems to be moving towards an 'equilibrium configuration' insofar as the *interrelation* of old-age dependency, economic dependency and benefit dependency is concerned. Second, even with a continuation of current trends in employment rates, demographic ageing is becoming so pervasive that it will push economic dependency and benefit dependency steadily upwards. *From the point of view of long-term sustainability, the current 'equilibrium configuration' of dependencies cannot yet be considered satisfactory.*

What will be the impact of the reforms in the pension and early retirement systems, unemployment benefits and career interruption, decided by the Di Rupo government? The dotted lines in Figure 4 are based on the impact assessment by the *Studiecommissie voor de Vergrijzing* (2012). In 2020 the economic dependency rate would be 85,5 (instead of 86,1 in the reference scenario) and the benefit dependency ratio would be 94,2 (instead of 95,5 in the reference scenario); in 2030 the economic dependency ratio would be 98,4 (instead of 101,0) and the benefit dependency ratio would be 90,5 (instead of 93,1). Since these results only concern salaried employees, the impact of the recent reforms on the public sector (which is, in itself, relatively more important) and on the self-employed sector is not taken into account. As such, these reform outcomes are not negligible. Simultaneously, they show that we are only at the beginning of a path of necessary reform: new waves of reform will have to follow. The most worrying aspect with regard to the current wave of reform, seems that the positive 'volume'-impact on dependency ratios is to a large extent neutralized by a 'prize-effect' of increasing average pensions. Average pensions increase as a consequence of the reforms (both because people work longer, but also because of the bonus-systems, notably in the public sector). The net budgetary result is therefore very limited.

5. INDIVIDUAL AND HOUSEHOLD EMPLOYMENT: NOT A FROZEN LANDSCAPE, BUT *HYSTERESIS* IN HOUSEHOLD JOBLESSNESS

5.1 Individual employment rates: feminisation and ageing of the work force

Table 5 provides the percentage point differences between the employment rates in 2000 and 2011, by age, gender and educational attainment, for Belgium and the Flemish and Walloon Regions. In brackets we provide the evolutions for 2000-2008; comparing the 2000-2011 evolutions with those in 2000-2008 highlights the impact of the crisis on employment rates. Table 6 compares employment rates for age-education subgroups in Belgium with the EU15 average in 2011 (in brackets for 2008).[11]

---

11. The next paragraphs mention figures for age sub-groups not shown in the tables, but available on request.

Table 5: Change in employment rates (ppt) by age, gender, educational attainment in Belgium, Flanders, Wallonia, 2000-2011 (changes 2000-2008 between brackets)

BELGIUM	25-34 YEARS		35-44 YEARS		45-54 YEARS		55-64 YEARS		25-64 YEARS		
	M	F	M	F	M	F	M	F	M	F	TOTAL
Low-skilled	-17,2	-11,5	-12,3	-4,5	-2,7	8,9	7,6	9,6	-7,7	0,9	-3,5
	(-12,5)	(-9,5)	(-6,7)	(1,4)	(1,4)	**(11,0)**	(4,9)	(6,1)	(-4,9)	(1,9)	(-1,8)
Medium-skilled	-6,5	-3,2	-3,1	2,3	1,6	**12,1**	8,0	**18,7**	-3,8	2,0	-0,6
	(-2,4)	(-0,4)	(-2,1)	(2,8)	(1,4)	(9,0)	(5,3)	**(14,7)**	(-2,5)	(2,2)	(0,1)
High-skilled	-3,8	-4,3	-3,1	2,6	-2,5	9,4	4,2	**16,5**	-3,6	0,6	-1,6
	(-1,5)	(-2,7)	(-1,0)	(2,4)	(-2,5)	(6,6)	(2,6)	**(10,4)**	(-2,4)	(0,4)	(-1,1)
Total	-6,8	-2,5	-3,3	5,9	1,5	**15,8**	**10,9**	**16,2**	-2,1	6,4	2,1
	(-3,2)	(0,4)	(-1,2)	(6,0)	(2,4)	**(12,9)**	(7,8)	**(10,9)**	(-0,7)	(5,6)	(2,4)

FLANDERS	25-34 YEARS		35-44 YEARS		45-54 YEARS		55-64 YEARS		25-64 YEARS		
	M	F	M	F	M	F	M	F	M	F	TOTAL
Low-skilled	-15,4	-16,3	-5,6	-3,4	-2,9	**13,2**	6,7	**11,8**	-5,9	2,8	-1,5
	(-12,3)	(-12,7)	(-4,0)	(5,8)	(1,8)	**(13,6)**	(5,2)	(7,6)	(-3,4)	(3,3)	(-0,2)
Medium-skilled	-5,8	-2,4	-1,2	7,1	3,2	**15,5**	9,7	**18,7**	-3,1	2,8	0,1
	(-3,0)	(1,1)	(-0,6)	(6,2)	(2,1)	**(12,0)**	(7,4)	**(13,7)**	(-2,7)	(2,8)	(0,3)
High-skilled	-4,4	-3,5	-2,5	3,0	-2,6	8,9	8,1	**14,3**	-3,6	-0,1	-2,0
	(-2,4)	(-0,5)	(-0,9)	(3,0)	(-3,5)	(4,2)	(4,0)	(8,4)	(-2,9)	(0,1)	(-1,6)
Total	-6,3	-2,6	-0,8	7,2	1,8	**19,4**	**12,1**	**17,5**	-0,9	7,8	3,4
	(-3,7)	(1,3)	(0,0)	(7,7)	(2,2)	**(15,0)**	(9,0)	**(11,5)**	(-0,2)	(6,8)	(3,2)

WALLONIA	25-34 YEARS		35-44 YEARS		45-54 YEARS		55-64 YEARS		25-64 YEARS		
	M	F	M	F	M	F	M	F	M	F	TOTAL
Low-skilled	-19,3	-2,6	-16,6	-2,7	1,3	8,9	9,2	6,0	-9,5	0,4	-4,8
	(-14,7)	(-4,9)	(-9,0)	(-0,9)	(3,2)	**(11,3)**	(3,4)	(4,1)	(-7,6)	(1,2)	(-3,6)
Medium-skilled	-9,1	2,2	-4,8	-7,1	-0,2	5,4	9,3	**20,0**	-4,8	0,4	-1,8
	(-3,2)	(5,3)	(-3,6)	(-3,5)	(0,4)	(4,3)	(5,6)	**(18,5)**	(-2,7)	(2,4)	(0,1)
High-skilled	-4,7	-5,1	-1,5	3,4	-3,6	10,0	-2,2	**20,5**	-5,1	1,9	-1,4
	(-1,7)	(-6,0)	(-0,4)	(2,3)	(-2,1)	**(10,5)**	(0,0)	**(14,4)**	(-3,2)	(0,8)	(-1,0)
Total	-8,5	2,2	-4,3	6,0	2,5	**12,3**	10,1	**14,3**	-3,4	5,8	1,2
	(-4,0)	(3,0)	(-2,0)	(4,5)	(3,4)	**(11,9)**	(6,7)	**(11,0)**	(-1,8)	(5,2)	(1,7)

Source: own calculations based on Eurostat and Steunpunt WSE
Bold: x > 10, ☐: -1 ≤ x ≤ 10, ▨: -10 ≤ x < -1, ■: x < -10

Table 6: Comparison of employment rates in Belgium and EU15, by age and educational attainment, 2011 (between brackets 2008) (difference BE-EU15, FL-EU15, WA-EU15, in ppt)

BELGIUM	25-34 YEARS	35-44 YEARS	45-54 YEARS	55-64 YEARS	25-64 YEARS
Low-skilled	-3,7	-3,3	-4,1	-9,4	-7,1
	(-6,1)	(-2,7)	(-4,3)	(-12,1)	(-8,5)
Medium-skilled	3,1	1,5	-1,4	-11,9	-1,1
	(3,3)	(0,2)	(-3,5)	(-12,8)	(-1,9)
High-skilled	5,2	2,4	0,2	-11,0	0,5
	(4,0)	(1,6)	(-1,7)	(-13,5)	(-0,5)
Total	3,8	2,3	-1,4	-10,8	-1,5
	(3,5)	(1,3)	(-3,1)	(-12,9)	(-2,6)

FLANDERS	25-34 YEARS	35-44 YEARS	45-54 YEARS	55-64 YEARS	25-64 YEARS
Low-skilled	6,2	6,6	3,0	-8,6	-2,8
	(3,9)	(6,9)	(2,1)	(-11,2)	(-4,6)
Medium-skilled	**10,1**	6,7	2,5	-11,8	3,2
	(9,9)	(4,5)	(-0,2)	(-12,7)	(1,9)
High-skilled	7,9	4,6	2,5	-11,6	2,6
	(7,3)	(3,6)	(-0,8)	(-15,3)	(1,5)
Total	**10,4**	8,0	3,6	-10,6	2,7
	(10,1)	(6,5)	(0,9)	(-13,1)	(1,1)

WALLONIA	25-34 YEARS	35-44 YEARS	45-54 YEARS	55-64 YEARS	25-64 YEARS
Low-skilled	-8,2	-9,8	-10,1	-10,6	-11,0
	(-12,5)	(-10,6)	(-10,7)	(-13,7)	(-12,9)
Medium-skilled	-3,4	-5,1	-7,0	-13,0	-6,7
	(-2,3)	(-4,7)	(-8,1)	(-13,4)	(-6,3)
High-skilled	3,9	2,6	-2,5	-12,9	-1,2
	(1,6)	(0,8)	(-2,0)	(-13,4)	(-2,4)
Total	-1,0	-2,6	-7,4	-12,5	-6,4
	(-2,0)	(-4,3)	(-7,9)	(-13,8)	(-7,3)

Source: own calculations based on Eurostat and Steunpunt WSE
Bold: x > 10, □: -1 ≤ x ≤ 10, ▨: -10 ≤ x < -1, ■: x < -10

In 2011 the labour market was still recovering from the shock of the crisis. Yet, compared to 2000, the employment rate for women is higher in the 25-64 age bracket, both for all levels of educational attainment (conflating age) and for all age sub-groups (conflating educational attainment), except for the youngest generation (25-29) which suffered the full impact of the crisis. This overall increase in female employment rates at all ages above 29 and all levels of skill reflects complex cohort effects and compositional factors, notably the decrease in the share of low-skilled women in the population and the fact that women who – in increasing numbers – started working at a younger age grow older and continue working – in increasing numbers. Added to this is the substantial impact of the service voucher scheme, which boosted employment rates of low-skilled women, notably in Flanders. Possibly, the 1996 pension reform ultimately also contributed to increasing female employment rates above the age of 60. The outcome is that within nearly all age-education sub-categories the evolution for female employment rates is strikingly more positive than the evolution for men, which is negative except for low- and high-skilled men above 54 and medium-skilled men above 44. In the age cohorts above 44 years of age (for women) and 49 (for men) employment rates increased significantly between 2000 and 2011. So conceived, the impact of the 2008 crisis displays an age profile: employment rates for younger generations decreased; employment rates for older workers continued to increase.

The labour market position of low-skilled people (i.e. with less than upper secondary education) in 2011 was not exactly equal to the position of low-skilled people in 2000. In 2000 41.7% of the Belgian population in the 25-64 age bracket was low skilled; in 2011 that share had decreased to 29.5%. We may assume that the low-skilled of 2011 are in a weaker position on the labour market than the low-skilled of 2000. Given changes in the skill structure of the population, changes in *employment* were more marked than changes in *employment rates*. The proportion of low-skilled individuals in employment decreased from 31.4% to 19.6%. The same observation holds for the impact of age: the proportion of individuals aged 55-64 in employment increased from 5.7% in 2000 to 12.7% in 2011.

Although there was progress between 2000 and 2011, notably for the generation over 50 and for women, the comparison with the average EU15 figures is sobering. Even though the employment level of low-skilled women above 44 years of age has improved, low-skilled people in Belgium are significantly less often in work than in the EU15: in Flanders this is not the case for all age/gender sub-groups of the low-skilled; in Wallonia this is the massive reality for all low skilled sub-groups (just as the employment level of the medium-skilled group in Wallonia lags behind that of the EU15). The same sobering observation applies to older workers: in comparison with the EU15 average, the employment rate of the 50+ is considerably lower in Wallonia; the employment rate of the 55+ is considerably lower everywhere. The difference between Flanders and Wallonia highlights the very different 'problem profile' of the regional labour markets, at least with regard to outcomes. The gaps between the EU15 averages and Flanders mainly have an age profile. The gaps between the EU15 averages and Wallonia mainly have a skill profile.

The figures reported are headcounts; converted into full-time equivalents, the Belgian employment rate decreased (2008: 57.8%; 2011: 56.8%;*Hoge Raad voor Werkgelegenheid*, 2012). Policy actively contributed to the conversion of full-time into part-time jobs, e.g. by the promotion of part-time leave systems. This is not necessarily a negative development, in so far as a sound balance between contributions and later entitlements is safeguarded; an issue which merits attention.

Thus, the Belgian labour market was not a frozen landscape. There have been successes, namely the increase in female employment, which we can associate with long-term policy choices. Service vouchers are an example of a successful reform with a large scale impact on the labour market, shifting our social model more towards service provision (Gerard *et al*, 2011). The originality of this Belgian path is that it did not occur via the collective sector as is the case in the Scandinavian example, but in a subsidised private sector. Obviously, this remains an expensive operation for the public budget.

However, next to those dynamic evolutions there are two big 'buts'. First, two bottlenecks on our labour market remain: the low employment level of the low-skilled in Wallonia and of the elderly everywhere. As the difference between the Flemish labour market and the EU average mainly has an age profile, while the difference between the Walloon labour market and the EU average mainly has an educational profile, it is not easy to point to unambiguous causal factors. Factors that clearly arise are regulatory in nature (the possibilities for early exit have not been fundamentally changed in the Generation Pact) and shortcomings in education (unqualified and wrongly qualified outflow); but the analysis of these bottlenecks should also be economic (does the cost of labour for the low-skilled in Wallonia and Brussels not remain too high in comparison with the possible market yield when they are employed, despite the efforts undertaken in reducing social security contributions?). The activation policy did not fundamentally change these hard facts.

The second 'but' concerns the budgetary cost of employment policy, which was often high. In part, this was probably unavoidable: quality employment policies do not come cheap. However, one may also point to some problems of consistency, a naive belief in the impact of 'bonuses', and/or the wrong-headed design of some policies. Was it consistent to reduce employers' social security contributions (with an impact of 0.8% of GDP by 2006, compared to that in 1999) when this also served to accommodate wage increases? The combination of decreasing contributions and increasing wages should not be considered *a priori* a wrong track. Yet, it might have been better for the Verhofstadt I government first to obtain a commitment by the social partners closely to follow the imperatives of the law on wage cost competitiveness, before launching its ambitious plan to reduce social contributions. This is not to say that we mainly have a problem of labour cost; nuance is indicated here. Yet, reductions in social contributions too often served to facilitate social dialogue.

Launching the service voucher scheme was what economists call a *tâtonnement* process: we were looking for the optimal combination of consumer prices and subsidies to get the scheme off the ground and beat the black market. Initially, the price was deliberately set very low; surprisingly, afterwards this price became a sacred cow in governmental circles; it took too long before it was adjusted. Moreover, the tax deduction linked to the service vouchers was part of a purely political deal, without evidence of real impact. Successive governments also held a naive belief in the impact of 'bonuses' on early exit. We should have known that a pension bonus always has a dual impact on labour supply: like any wage increase, it creates a substitution effect (which is positive: the opportunity cost of leisure – or early exit, for that matter – increases) and an income effect (which is negative: the budget constraint shifts) (Maes, 2008). Apart from possible design flaws, the various bonuses that were launched before the Generation Pact and in the context of that Pact (for statutory civil servants and for private sector employees) were bound to have a mixed effect, at best. In general, the cost-effectiveness of the Generation Pact was weak. One may also say that it took too long before 'non-budgetary' employment policies got off the ground in the 2000s: the new approach to activation which was launched in 2003 was overdue. Other 'non-budgetary' issues in employment policy, such as the distinction between blue- and white-collar workers and the related need to modernise labour market regulation, are waiting to be addressed.

5.2 Jobless households: hysteresis

The traditional focus on *individual* employment rates overlooks the fact that the distribution of jobs across households crucially influences income distribution (which we assess at the household level). European welfare states are characterised by different patterns of individual joblessness and household joblessness (by which we mean: the share of individuals living in a household where no one is employed). In Belgium, in 2010 12.5% of people aged 18-59 lived in a jobless household. This is almost the same figure as in 2000 (12.4%); it was marginally lower only in 2007 and 2008. Similar disquieting figures obtain for children in jobless households. This standstill is not exceptional: it is observed in many welfare states. There are different reasons why an improvement in individual employment rates may not translate into an improvement in household employment. However, nowhere is the gap between household and individual employment rates as large as in Belgium. We measure this gap with a 'polarisation index', defined as the difference between, on the one hand, the hypothetical proportion of individuals living in jobless households assuming that individual employment is distributed randomly across households, and, on the other, the actual share of individuals living in jobless households. Corluy and Vandenbroucke (2012) show that by 2008 Belgium had the highest level of polarisation of jobs over households in the EU. The regional divide explains to some extent (for ca.10%) why the polarisation is so high; evidently, the jobs on the basis of which the *Belgian* individual employment rate is calculated are not randomly distributed over Flemish and Walloon families, given the large difference in regional individual employment rates. However, if we were to consider Wallonia and Flanders as separate countries, *both* regions would be at the top of 'job polarisation' (together with Belgium and the UK) in the EU. Moreover, in contrast to another high polarisation country such as the UK, in which polarisation decreased, polarisation remained high in Belgium. The regional divide did not diminish, and polarisation increased within both Wallonia and Flanders.

6. SOCIAL SPENDING AND POVERTY

Tables 7 and 8 compare poverty in Belgium and the EU15. The at-risk-of-poverty rates are based on a floating national poverty threshold, equal to 60% of the median of equivalent net disposable household income (below, we use 'household income' as a shortcut). In a number of EU Member States this threshold decreased after 2008, as a consequence of the crisis; in some Member States the upshot was improving poverty statistics. This is not the case for Belgium: on the basis of EU SILC, the point estimate of median household income improved considerably in real terms between 2008 and 2010, as may be inferred from Table 7. Unchanged or even decreasing poverty rates between 2008 and 2010 illustrate the fact that the automatic stabilisers that are intrinsic to welfare systems did play their expected role during the early years of the crisis, at least in most EU Member States. With the conventional floating poverty line, the overall picture is one of standstill during the 2000s, both in Belgium and, on average, for the EU15. If we anchor the poverty threshold in time, fixing it at the 2005 level, the poverty rate – so conceived – declined significantly in Belgium, as shown in the bottom row of Table 7.

Table 7: Age profile and dynamics of poverty risks in Belgium and EU15 (%)

		2003	2005	2008	2010
EU15	Total population		15,7	16,2	16,2
Belgium		15,4	14,8	14,7	14,6
EU15	[0-18[		18,1	19,3	19,8
Belgium		16,5	18,1	17,2	18,3
EU15	[18-64]		13,8	14,5	15,1
Belgium		13,2	12,0	12,2	12,1
EU15	[65+		19,8	19,2	16,3
Belgium		22,0	21,4	21,2	19,4
Poverty threshold in Belgium					
Threshold in euros		9.313	9.947	10.791	11.678
Index in euros		100	107	116	125
Corrected for inflation		100	103	105	109
Poverty on the basis of poverty threshold 2005					
EU15	Total population		15,7	13,6	13,9
Belgium			14,8	13,7	11,1

Source: EU SILC, Eurostat
The survey is retrospective: EU SILC T refers to incomes in T-1.
(*Caveat* for impact German SILC figures on EU weighted average: taking into account doubts about the evolution of German SILC and confidence intervals, EU15 figures with floating poverty rates in this table should be interpreted as a standstill)

Table 8: Poverty of population from 18 to 59 by work intensity of the household (%)

	WORK INTENSITY	2003	2005	2008	2010
EU15	Very high]0.85-1]		3,9	4,0	4,2
Belgium		4,7	2,0	2,5	2,4
EU15	Medium [0.45-0.55]		16,0	19,3	18,9
Belgium		13,5	12,7	10,6	13,9
EU15	Very low [0-0.2]		48,2	52,5	53,7
Belgium		41,3	44,1	48,5	48,2

Source: EU SILC, Eurostat

The Belgian at-risk-of-poverty rate is slightly lower than the EU15 average, but the age profile of poverty risks, as summarised in Table 7, differs. Child poverty is relatively high in Belgium, and the tendency is upwards. The poverty risk among non-elderly adults is lower than the EU15 average. The poverty risk among the elderly is higher than the EU15 average, but the tendency at this moment is downwards. With regard to the elderly, this corroborates our description of the evolution of spending patterns and benefit ratios in Belgium: the negative trend in pension indicators stopped in the 2000s. Increasing child poverty is not readily explained; both the decline in the relative value of child benefits and the *hysteresis* of household joblessness may play a role.

In cross-country comparisons, financial poverty tells only part of the story, certainly with regard to the elderly: for instance, the degree of home ownership among the elderly is a crucial parameter for assessing their real standard of living. EU SILC allows an interesting comparison in terms of 'material deprivation'.[12] In most Member States *financial poverty* is higher among the elderly than among the adult non-elderly population; but in Northern and Continental Europe *material deprivation* is typically lower among the elderly than among the adult non-elderly population. In Belgium that pattern is particularly strong: in EU SILC 2010 material deprivation is registered for 12.4% of non-elderly adults, and for only 7.8% of the elderly. The contrasting observation that material deprivation is registered for no less than 15.5% of the Belgian population under the age of 18 highlights a problem that should prompt a shift in the policy focus towards child poverty.

Table 8 shows that individuals in households with very low work intensity are somewhat less poor in Belgium than elsewhere in the EU15, but – taking into account confidence intervals – the difference is not very large; moreover, the poverty risk of individuals in households with very low work intensity did not decrease during the crisis, and is by now clearly higher than in the first half of the decade. The contrast

---

12. The material deprivation rate measures the percentage of the population that cannot afford at least three of the following nine items: 1.to pay their rent, mortgage or utility bills; 2.to keep their home adequately warm; 3.to face unexpected expenses; 4.to eat meat or proteins regularly; 5.to go on holiday; 6.a television set; 7.a washing machine; 8.a car; 9.a telephone.

between this observation and our comparatively high level of spending on working age benefits merits further examination: here is *prima facie* evidence that the efficiency of our social system can be improved. This may be linked to the most striking fact concerning Belgian poverty: the regional divide. The Belgian poverty headcount of 14.6% in EU SILC 2010 conceals a headcount of 10.4% in Flanders and 17.8% in Wallonia. As with the Belgian figures, these regional poverty headcounts did not change much over the 2000s; in so far as change was perceptible, the evolution was downwards in Flanders and upwards in Wallonia.

7. THE QUEST FOR SUSTAINABLE SOCIAL JUSTICE

In the 1990s a *budgetary* strategy was chosen to prepare for the cost of ageing. It would turn vice into virtue. Belgium had a high debt ratio and, associated with it, high levels of taxation and social security contributions. *If* we were to succeed in reducing the debt ratio, then government revenue could be used to pay for increased spending on pensions instead of interest on debt – so the argument went. Research by the FPB indicated that the debt and deficit reductions required by the Maastricht criteria corresponded precisely with the deficit and debt reductions needed to pay for ageing (Festjens, 1995). The consequence of this strategic choice was twofold. It bolstered the motivation of political parties and social partners to make the budget cuts necessary to comply with the Maastricht criteria for entering the Eurozone. On the other hand, it had a paralysing effect on the debate about the welfare state's architecture. We presumed that the challenge of population ageing could be tackled through saving only, without *systemic changes* to the welfare state.

At the beginning of this century the strictly budgetary strategy was explicitly broadened to a double track, consistent with the idea of the active welfare state: on the one hand setting aside budgetary reserves, made pedagogically apparent by the creation of the *Silver Fund*; on the other hand increasing the employment rate. But in practice it was still presumed that no thorough systemic changes in pension provision would be necessary, apart from the generalisation of second-pillar pensions, as a matter of democratic access to a useful top-up of first-pillar pensions. Towards 2007 it became clear that the required budgetary strategy had been insufficiently put into practice, that is, the government had not been able to square the '8+1' orientations listed in the introduction to this chapter. Moreover, in 2008 the budgetary strategy was met head-on by the financial crisis. Vandenbroucke (2010) argues that the budgetary strategy vis-à-vis ageing had to be re-assessed as necessary, but was *intrinsically* insufficient and thus overoptimistic. Simplifying somewhat but not too badly, one may say that the budgetary strategy vis-à-vis ageing implicitly postulated that the budgetary claim by pensions and health care would have priority over any other societal problem coming our way now and in future decades. From a demographic point of view this is disputable: we also face a growing need for child care and education. Many other issues confronting us, such as climate change, will entail budgetary claims. It is naive think that all these claims can be settled in the budgetary straitjacket implied by a purely budgetary strategy to pay for ageing. The societal debate must also focus on parametric and structural reforms within the pension system.[13] In their survey of the Belgian pension system, Berghman and Peeters (2012) rightly stress that the debate should not just be about financial sustainability but also about the social adequacy and fairness of the pension system, including the impact of the second pillar.

8. PREPARING THE NEXT WAVE OF REFORM IS IMPERATIVE

Policies pursued under the banner of the active welfare state were successful in implementing a strategy that aimed at incrementally improving employment incentives, not by lowering benefits but by lowering personal social security contributions at the bottom end of the wage scale and taxes on earned income, linked with an activation model based on close monitoring of the unemployed. With regard to early exit from the labour market the assessment is mixed: employment rates for older workers increased, but the Belgian labour market(s) did not catch

---

13. See the interesting reports on Belgium by Segaert (2009, 2010) for the EU ASISP network, in which this is a recurring theme.

up vis-à-vis labour markets in other EU Member States. More fundamentally, with regard to 'the budgetary strategy to prepare for ageing', the expectations were intrinsically overoptimistic on the one hand and the implementation insufficient on the other hand. Insufficient consistency in some policies and overestimation of the cost-efficiency of certain employment measures may have contributed to this result.

At first sight – disregarding the long-term increase in longevity – one might say that by 2007 the Belgian welfare state had settled into a new equilibrium of lower but stable benefit ratios and higher but relatively stable social dependency ratios. During the financial crisis, it proved its usefulness as a robust shock absorber (with, obviously, important budgetary consequences). At the same time, it became clear that incisive measures would be necessary against early exit and that systemic reform of pensions was on the agenda. The Di Rupo government has embarked upon important reforms with regard to early retirement and early exit, with mid-term effect. As explained in Section 4, the volume-effect is not negligible; but the limited budgetary effect simultaneously emphasises the need for further systemic change in view of the long-term increase in longevity. The overall standstill in poverty, with a tendency for child poverty to increase and very high poverty rates in parts of the country, signals the need to assess the efficiency of our social system in fighting poverty. Achieving sustainable social justice will require the definition and acceptance of a consistent strategy for the next wave of reform.

BIBLIOGRAPHY

Berghman, Jos, and Hans Peeters. "Pension Protection in Belgium. Overview and Challenges." Text prepared for the workshop on the occasion of the honorary degree of John Myles by the KU Leuven, February 2, 2012. http://soc.kuleuven.be/ceso/pensioenbeleid.

Bogaerts, Kristel. "Bestaan er nog financiële vallen in de werkloosheid en in de bijstand in België?" CSB-berichten, Centrum voor Sociaal Beleid Herman Deleeck, 2008.

Bonoli, Giuliano. "New social risks and the politics of post-industrial social policies." In *The Politics of Post-Industrial Welfare States. Adapting post-war social policies to new social risks*, edited by Klaus Armingeon, and Giuliano Bonoli, 3-26. London/New York: Routledge, 2006.

Cantillon, Bea, Ive Marx, and Veerle De Maesschalck. "De bodem van de welvaartsstaat van 1970 tot nu, en daarna." CSB-berichten, Centrum voor Sociaal Beleid Herman Deleeck, 2003.

Cantillon, Bea, and Frank Vandenbroucke, eds. *For Better For Worse, For Richer For Poorer. Labour market participation, social redistribution and income poverty in the EU*. Oxford: Oxford University Press, forthcoming.

Cockx, Bart, Muriel Dejemeppe, and Bruno Van Der Linden. *Evaluation de l'activation du comportement de recherche d'emploi*. Ghent: Academia Press, 2011.

Corluy, Vincent, and Frank Vandenbroucke. "Individual Employment, Household Employment and Risk of Poverty in the EU. A Decomposition Analysis." CSB-Working Paper 12/06, Herman Deleeck Centre for Social Policy, 2012.

Cutler, David M. "Equality, Efficiency, and Market Fundamentals: The Dynamics of International Medical-Care Reform." *Journal of Economic Literature* 40 (2002): 891-906.

De Deken, Johan. "Belgium: a precursor muddling through?" In *Regulating the Risk of Unemployment: National Adaptations to Post-Industrial Labour Markets in Europe*, edited by Jochen Clasen, and Daniel Clegg, 100-120. Oxford: Oxford University Press, 2011.

De Deken, Johan. "Measuring the social investment state." In *For Better For Worse, For Richer For Poorer. Labour market participation, social redistribution and income poverty in the EU*, edited by Bea Cantillon, and Frank Vandenbroucke. Oxford: Oxford University Press, forthcoming.

De Deken, Johan, and Jochen Clasen. "Tracking caseloads: the changing composition of working-age benefit receipt in Europe." In *Regulating the Risk of Unemployment: National Adaptations to Post-Industrial Labour Markets in Europe*, edited by Jochen Clasen, and Daniel Clegg, 297-317. Oxford: Oxford University Press, 2011.

De Deken, Johan. "Belgium: a precursor muddling through?" In *Regulating the Risk of Unemployment: National Adaptations to Post-Industrial Labour Markets in Europe*, edited by Jochen Clasen, and Daniel Clegg, 100-120. Oxford: Oxford University Press, 2011.

De Vil, Greet, Nicole Fasquelle, Marie-Jeanne Festjens, and Christophe Joyeux. "Welvaartsbinding van sociale en bijstandsuitkeringen/Liaison au bien-être des prestations sociales et des allocations d'assistance." Working Paper 4-11, Federal Planning Bureau, 2011.

De Wolf, Françoise, Tonio Di Zinno, Jean-Marc Laasman, Marijke Van Duynslaeger, and Johan Vanoverloop. "Ziekenhuisbarometer. Aard, omvang en evolutie van de kosten ten laste van de patiënt bij een opname in een algemeen ziekenhuis." Brussel: Socialistische Mutualiteiten, 2011.

Festjens, Marie-Jeanne. "Het pensioen. Een lange termijn contract versus het schrikbeeld van de vergrijzing." In *De sociale zekerheid verzekerd? Referaten van het 22ste Vlaams Wetenschappelijk Economisch Congres*, edited by Marc Despontin, and Marc Jegers, 271-331. Brussels: VUBPRESS, 1995.

Festjens, Marie-Jeanne. "De pensioenhervorming. Een nieuwe generatie en een nieuw contract." Planning Paper 82, Federal Planning Bureau, 1997.

Gerard, Maarten, Daphné Valsamis, and Wim Van der Beken. "Evaluatie van het stelsel van de dienstencheques voor buurtdiensten en -banen 2010." IDEA Consult, 2011.

Goedemé, Tim, Greet De Vil, Natascha Van Mechelen, Nicole Fasquelle, and Kristel Bogaerts. "Hoogte en adequaatheid van de Belgische sociale minima in de periode 2000-2011." In *Armoede in België, Jaarboek 2012*, edited by Jan Vranken, Willy Lahaye, Annelinde Gerts, and Catherine Coppée, 215-238. Leuven/The Hague: Acco, 2012.

Herremans, Wim. "Pension reform and pensions paths: the Belgian case." In *De arbeidsmarkt in Vlaanderen. Special Issue. Active Ageing, early retirement and employability*, edited by Nick van den Heuvel, Wim Herremans, Peter van der Hallen, Christine Erhel, and Pierre Courtioux, 141-154. Leuven: Steunpunt Werkgelegenheid, Arbeidsmarkt en Vorming, 2006.

Hoge Raad voor Werkgelegenheid. "Verslag 2012. Actief ouder worden.". Brussel: FOD WASO, 2012.

Maes, Marjan. "Financial and redistributive impact of reforming the old-age pension system in Belgium." Discussion Paper 2008-40, Université Catholique de Louvain, 2008.

Marx, Ive. "The quest for sustainability, legitimacy and a way out of 'welfare without work'." In *The Handbook of European Welfare Systems*, edited by Klaus Schubert, Simon Hegelich, and Ursula Bazant, 49-64. London: Routledge, 2009.

RKW. "De evolutie van de gemiddelde maandelijkse kinderbijslag in het stelsel van de werknemers van 1997 tot 2010." Focus 2011-2, 2011.

Neefs, Boie, Wim Herremans, and Luc Sels. "De doelstelling binnen handbereik? Potentiële tewerkstellingseffecten van een hervorming van de uittredestelsels." *Over.Werk, Tijdschrift van het Steunpunt WSE* 22(2012): 93-101.

Nevejan, Hendrik. "Financiële prikkels tot werkhervatting voor werklozen en leefloontrekkers in België: heden en verleden." Documentatienota No. 2009-1486, Centrale Raad voor het Bedrijfsleven, 2009.

Nevejan, Hendrik. "Financiële werkloosheidsvallen in België in 2010." Documentatienota No. 2011-0189, Centrale Raad voor het Bedrijfsleven, 2011.

Pierson, Paul. *The New Politics of the Welfare State*. Oxford: Oxford University Press, 2001.

Schokkaert, Erik, Joeri Guillaume, Ann Lecluyse, Hervé Avalosse, Koen Cornelis, Diana De Graeve, Stephan Devriese, Johan Vanoverloop, and Carine Van de Voorde. "Evaluatie van de effecten van de maximumfactuur op de consumptie en financiële toegankelijkheid van gezondheidszorg." Report 80A, KCE- Federaal Kenniscentrum voor Gezondheidszorg, 2008.

Segaert, Steven. "ASISIP Annual National Report 2009. Pensions, Health and Long-term Care. Belgium". 2009. http://socialprotection.eu/files_db/208/asisp_ANR09_Belgium.

Segaert, Steven. "ASISIP Annual National Report 2010. Pensions, Health and Long-term Care. Belgium". 2010. http://socialprotection.eu/files_db/884/asisp_ANR10_Belgium.

Vandenbroucke, Frank. "De actieve welvaartsstaat. Een Europees perspectief." Den Uyl lecture, Amsterdam, December 13, 1999. Also in *In het spoor van Den Uyl. Den Uyl-lezingen 1988-2008*, edited by Stichting Dr. J.M. Den Uyl-lezing. Amsterdam: Stichting Dr. J.M. Den Uyl- lezing, 2009.

Vandenbroucke, Frank. *Strategische keuzes voor het sociale beleid*. CSB 'beleid & onderzoek', Centrum voor Sociaal Beleid Herman Deleeck, 2010.

Vandenbroucke, Frank. "Geluk en politiek: een pleidooi voor helder denken." In *Studium Generale 2011-2012*. Gent: Academia Press, forthcoming.

Vandenbroucke, Frank, and Koen Vleminckx. "Disappointing poverty trends: is the social investment state to blame?" *Journal of European Social Policy* 21 (2011): 450-471.

7.
Indebtedness
INTEREST PAYMENT AND PUBLIC DEBT

Natacha Gilson and Jean Deboutte[1]

EXECUTIVE SUMMARY

Belgium's public debt steadily fell from 1993 to 2007. Unfortunately, the financial crisis erupted and led to an increase in the debt-to-GDP ratio from 2008. Nowadays, both academic literature and public debt managers pay attention not only to the public debt level but also to its composition. Actually, a large strand of literature has been devoted to the public debt structure. Nevertheless, as these theoretical models cannot easily be implemented, modern Debt Agencies are mainly based on operational goals aiming at minimising the financing cost of the debt within the framework of appropriate risk management. Moreover, recent trends in the type of public debt instruments issued by several OECD countries, namely the issue of very long-term bonds or of inflation-linked bonds, showed that the need of some investors may also influence the public debt structure. Belgium indeed participated in this trend with the issue of very long-term nominal bonds. Finally, from the point of view of the interest rates paid on the debt instruments which make up Belgium's public debt, it is important to bear in mind that the launch of the euro was a very significant event which took place just before the period under review in this book. Public debt ownership, the implicit interest rate and the spread against the German benchmark were markedly influenced by this major change.

---

1. Natacha Gilson is Professor at the Catholic University of Louvain. Jean Deboutte is Director at the Belgian Debt Agency.

INTRODUCTION

This chapter, entitled "Interest payment and public debt", aims to describe the changes in Belgium's public debt and in its associated interest rates over the 2000-2010 decade. Therefore, this chapter starts with a description of the evolution of Belgium's public debt over the period under review. Next, as the importance of the public debt composition is nowadays widely acknowledged, Belgium's public debt structure will be presented just after a sketched explanation of the differentiation between the theoretical economic development on the optimal public debt structure and the principles guiding the Belgian Debt Agency. Actually, a large strand of literature has been devoted to the public debt structure. Nevertheless, these theoretical models cannot easily be implemented, a fact which explains that current practices in modern Debt Agencies are mainly based on operational goals, aimed at minimising the financing cost of the debt within the framework of appropriate risk management. Moreover, recent trends in the type of public debt instruments issued by several OECD countries, namely the issue of very long-term bonds or of inflation-linked bonds, showed that the need of some investors may also influence the public debt structure. During the 2000s, several countries issued very long term bonds (30 years or more) or inflation-linked bonds. These trends are related to the needs of some investors and the Belgian position in this matter will be explained. Finally, from the point of view of the interest rates paid on the debt instruments which make up Belgium's public debt, it is important to bear in mind that the launch of the euro was a very significant event which took place just before the period under review in this book. The evolutions of Belgium's public debt ownership, of its implicit interest rate and of its spread against the German benchmark will be set out below. The facts presented will show that they were indubitably influenced by this major change.

I. EVOLUTION

Ten years ago, a book on public finance in Belgium over the 1990-2000 decade appeared. The chapter on public debt started with these words[2]: "Belgian public debt, with its huge volume, is the Achilles' heel of Belgian public finance". Ten years later, this assertion can still be considered as true despite the huge efforts made to decrease Belgium's debt-to-GDP ratio. Indeed, above any constraint at the European level, the high public debt-to-GDP ratio in Belgium needed to be reduced in order not only to reduce Belgium's exposure to economic shocks, such as an increase in the interest rate, but also to gain some room for manoeuvre in the event of a slump in economic activity.

The picture below testifies to efforts aiming to reduce the public debt-to-GDP ratio in Belgium. It shows the evolution of the public debt-to-GDP ratio in Belgium from 1993 to 2010.

Figure 1: Evolution of the Debt-to-GDP ratio from 1993 to 2010

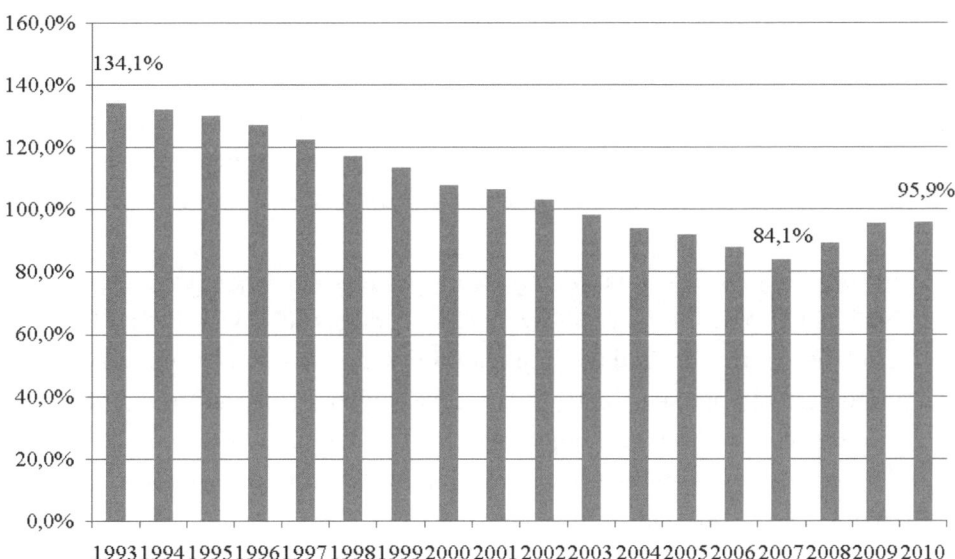

Source: National Bank of Belgium

---

2. Luc Buffel and Jef Vuchelen (2002). Their words were freely translated from Dutch into English for the uniformity of the language used in this paper.

Strikingly, from 1993 to 2007, the debt-to-GDP ratio fell continuously. In total, it decreased by exactly 50% of GDP. Unfortunately, the financial crisis erupted and led to an increase in the debt-to-GDP ratio from 2008.

An IMF country report put the deterioration of the Belgian public debt-to GDP ratio in 2008 down to Belgian politics, saying that "the regionalization of Belgian politics and the absence of a stable federal government since 2007 produced a nontrivial adverse effect on the state of public finances".[3] Nevertheless, it seems very important to underline that huge capital injections into the financial sector amounting to 6.1% of GDP in 2008 led to a debt-to-GDP ratio of 86.9%, while it would otherwise have decreased to 80.8%.[4]

Since 2008, the government debt-to-GDP ratio has continued to increase. If, as explained above, the deterioration in the public debt-to-GDP ratio in 2008 was mainly caused by exogenous factors (public authorities injected liquidities into the financial sector: Dexia, Ethias, Fortis, KBC), the deterioration observed in 2009 was mainly due to endogenous factors: government revenue decreased and primary expenditure (i.e. government expenditure excluding interest spending) increased with the slump in economic activity. Actually, in 2009, Belgian real GDP growth amounted to -2.7%.[5] An economic downturn was also observed in other Euro zone member countries. In the same year, the average real GDP growth in the Euro zone amounted to -4.1%.[6]

In 2010, Belgium's debt ratio increased further. According to the Belgian National Bank[7], this increase was mostly endogenous: even if the GDP growth was stronger and the implicit interest rate lower than in the previous year, the actual primary balance was not large enough to stabilize the public debt ratio. Consequently, the snowball effect, which can be defined as the endogenous increase in public debt fuelled by interest rate charges, was observed in 2010. In fact, the snowball effect reappeared

---

3. Aneja S. et al. (2011)
4. See the Belgian Debt Agency, "2008 Review-2009 Outlook", December 2008
5. Data published by the Belgian National Bank on Belgostat online.
6. Ibidem.
7. National Bank of Belgium, "Report 2010: Economic and Financial Development", p. 97.

in 2009 after a long period of structural decrease in the Belgian public debt which started from 1994 and ended in 2008, as shown on Figure 1 above. The snowball effect was observed both in 2009 and 2010, even if it was less dramatic in 2010 than in the previous year.

For highly indebted countries, supervision of the public debt evolution, in levels, is important. Nevertheless, in the recent past, the management of the public debt structure has become an increasing concern for most Treasuries in OECD countries, while economic theory started to pay attention to the effect of public debt structure and management. Therefore, the section below briefly summarises the economic literature on public debt management and the main goals guiding the Belgian Debt Agency. It also describes the structure of Belgium's public debt.

2. STRUCTURE: MATURITIES, FIXED VS. FLOATING RATES

Section 1 described the evolution of Belgian public debt. However, as already stated above, the composition of the public debt is also important. As Missale (1999) claimed, "Public debt management has important welfare effects".[8] The choice of specific debt instruments (for instance debt denominated in domestic currency, short or long-term debt, debt indexed to the price level, debt denominated in foreign currency,…) leads to a given stock of each debt instrument which determines the public debt structure or composition.

This section will be divided into three parts. Firstly, the economic literature on optimal public debt management will be briefly presented. Secondly, the broad principles guiding the Belgian Debt Agency will be summarised. And, lastly, the evolution of the Belgian public debt structure will be analysed.

---

8. Missale (1999), p. 216.

2.1 In theory

Modern macroeconomics recognises that public debt structure is quite often non-neutral.[9] For instance, Dornbusch and Draghi (1990) wrote, "When debts are large, are there theoretical reasons to favour a particular maturity structure or indexation regime? Should a government favour short rather than long debt, debt denominated in foreign exchange or indexed to the price level to debt that is denominated in home currency? And are there 'equilibrium' debt structures? This latter topic is new in the literature; the recent interest is clearly a reflection of the need to 'manage' debts when they become large ...". Nowadays, a broad economic literature exists on public debt management.

On the theoretical side, this strand of literature showed that a well-chosen debt structure may act as a reputation device when the government in power lacks commitment. It also showed that the 'equilibrium' debt structure hangs very much on aimed targets. In fact, some debt instruments act as shock-absorber devices. These two parts of the literature on public debt management will be presented below.[10]

The economic literature on public debt management states that the optimal public debt structure should aim at minimising the risk of modifying tax rates in the event of economic hazards such as economic downturn caused by negative supply or demand shocks, inflation surge,... Consequently, the optimal debt composition depends on the kinds of shocks hitting the economy. The theoretical literature on debt management identifies many other objectives: the government debt structure may signal the type of government in power when information is asymmetric[11], contribute to the development of national financial markets[12],... Nevertheless, the survey presented here will be limited to the two first goals cited above: the time-consistency device when the government in power lacks commitment and the macroeconomic stabilization device.

---

9. See for instance Pearson and Tabellini (1994).
10. See also N. Gilson (2000).
11. Drudi F. and A. Prati (1997)
12. Wolswijk G. and J. de Haan (2005)

These theoretical developments are based on the seminal paper by Barro (1979), which highlights the optimality of 'tax smoothing'. The 'tax smoothing' result is due to the existence of distortionary taxes, those distortions being more than proportional with increasing tax rates. Consequently, policymakers should minimise the cost of collecting taxes subject to their inter-temporal budget constraint. The solution to this government's optimisation problem amounts to requiring the equalisation of tax rates in all periods. In the economic literature, the result of Barro's paper bears the name of 'tax smoothing'.

Some authors, like Calvo and Guidotti (1992), extended Barro's (1979) model to a context of incomplete policy pre-commitment, which means that the government is unable *ex ante* contractually to commit to some policies. In their model, the government may be tempted to inflate in order to erode the real value of public debt. In fact, *ex ante*, it is always optimal for a government to claim that inflation will be low in order to benefit from a low nominal interest rate on its public debt. But once government bonds have been bought, the government could be tempted to inflate in order to reduce the real value of its debt and of its debt-service costs.[13] These authors showed that the maturity management of government debt may induce 'time-consistent' policies. Other authors, like De Broeck (1997), extended this kind of analysis to the whole public debt structure, i.e. not just in terms of maturity but also in terms of currency denomination, and types of holders (Central Bank, financial institutions and non-financial sector).

Bohn (1990) proposed a stochastic version of the Barro (1979) model. He showed that public liabilities could serve as a hedge against macroeconomic shocks affecting the government budget. The hedging function of the public debt structure is also central in Miller (1997), where foreign denominated debt is presented as an interesting alternative to indexed bonds if foreign inflation realisations co-vary with domestic government expenditures. If foreign inflation reduces the real value of domestic debt denominated in foreign currency when domestic government expenditures are higher than expected, then foreign currency

---

13. Kyndland and Prescott (1997) developed the consequences of this kind of gap between *ex ante* and *ex post* optimal policies. In the economic literature, this kind of gap is called '*time-inconsistency*'.

denominated debt acts as a hedge against shocks affecting the government budget. The hedging function of the public debt structure is also central in Missale (2001). This explored how public debt management may reduce government deficit, considering the Central Bank's preferences regarding inflation stabilisation *versus* output stabilisation. As Missale (2001) wrote, "deficit stabilization calls for using the interest payments on public debt as a hedge against unexpected cyclical downturn. ... Therefore, when choosing debt instruments, the government should consider the stochastic relations between output, inflation and the interest rate which arise from the shocks affecting the economy and the policy response by monetary authority".

Consequently, this literature emphasises that public debt management matters and offers some interesting conclusions for the determination of the composition of public debt. For instance, fixed-rate nominal debt is a good hedging instrument in the event of a bad supply shock because a negative supply shock simultaneously leads to two effects: an unexpected increase in prices and an unexpected decrease in output. The former reduces the real return on nominal debt while the latter lowers government revenue. Thus, this stabilises the government's budget balance as debt-service costs are reduced when government revenues are lower.

Fixed-rate nominal debt is also a good hedging instrument when public spending shocks prevail because public spending shocks simultaneously lead to two effects: an unexpected increase in prices and an unexpected increase in public spending. Thus, the former reduces the real return on nominal debt which offsets the increase in public spending and the government's budget balance is stabilised.

In the event of negative demand shock, floating-rate nominal debt or bonds indexed to the price level are better hedging instruments. In fact, a negative demand shock simultaneously leads to two effects: an unexpected decrease in prices and an unexpected decrease in output. The former depresses debt-service costs of the two pre-cited debt instruments, while the latter reduces government revenue. Thus, the combination of these two effects stabilises the government budget balance.

To sum up the contribution of the papers cited above, the economic literature shows that a well-chosen debt structure may act as a reputation device when the government in power lacks commitment. It also shows that some public debt instruments may be used as a hedge or shelter against macroeconomic shocks.

2.2 In practice

On a more practical note, one needs to acknowledge that 'tax smoothing' is not easy to implement in a direct way. Consequently, public debt managers actually focus on "the impact of the variability in debt-service costs on the variability in the overall budget balance".[14] Although, all other things being equal, low debt-service costs entail lower taxes, debt managers do not consider other parts of the government budget.[15] Therefore, even if, on practical grounds, this objective is understandable, it does not perfectly coincide with the 'tax smoothing objective' supported in the academic literature.[16]

In Belgium, the main goal of public debt management consists of minimising the financing cost of the debt within the framework of appropriate risk management. Public debt management in Belgium also takes into account the general objectives of monetary and budgetary policy.[17]

The main risks considered in Belgium are: refinancing risk, interest-rate re-fixing risk, exchange risk and credit risk. In relation to the first two risks, the Belgian Debt Agency abandoned in 2003 the classic risk parameters such as duration and average life, and it adopted a framework of risk parameters that precisely measure the level of these risks in the portfolio.

---

14. Risbjerg L. and A. Holmlund (2005), p. 43.
15. Nevertheless, Missale (2001) proposed an objective of deficit stabilization (also called '*deficit-smoothing*') which seems closer to practices adopted by national debt agencies than 'tax smoothing' and claims that, in some circumstances, "*the implications for debt management are interestingly similar to those arising from tax-smoothing motivations*". See Missale (2001), pp. 68 and 69.
16. Wolswijk G. and J. de Haan (2005), p.8.
17. See for instance Deboutte J. and B. Debergh (2005)

Refinancing risk, also called rollover risk, refers to the risk that existing debt coming to maturity could not be reimbursed with new borrowings at the then prevailing risk-free market rate. A country's market interest rate may indeed increase due to the addition of risk premia.[18] Moreover, in extreme scenarios, it could even become impossible to borrow to roll the debt over.[19] In order to manage this risk, it is important to smooth the amount of debt coming to maturity on scheduled dates.

Thus, the Belgian Debt Agency limits the proportion of debt coming to maturity in 12 months as well as in 5 years, on an ongoing basis. The respective maxima result in annual borrowing requirements which are believed to be feasible even in stressed scenarios.

Interest-rate re-fixing risk denotes the vulnerability of debt stock and debt service costs to higher interest market rate when part of the debt is rolled over. A government has to manage the structure of the debt in order to be shielded from unexpected increases in interest rates.

Re-fixing risk is closely correlated to refinancing risk, as the maturity profile dictates the pace and volume of new borrowing which will be subject to the unknown future interest rate. Yet in addition to the maturity profile, two other elements are taken into account. First, long-term debt instruments may require payment of a variable coupon: these instruments are generally called 'floaters'. This kind of debt instrument increases the re-fixing risk. Second, derivatives such as interest rate swaps in the portfolio may lead to a re-fixing risk which is higher, or lower, than the one that follows from the maturity schedule.

Consequently, the Belgian Debt Agency also limits the proportion of debt that is subject to a re-fixing of interest rates in 12 months, and in 5 years. These maxima are usually somewhat higher than the corresponding maxima for the refinancing risk.

Exchange risk relates to the risk that a depreciation/devaluation of the domestic currency leads to an increase, in domestic currency, of debt

---

18. As recently experienced by a number of countries in the euro area.
19. No fewer than three countries in the euro area are actually experiencing this extreme situation.

stock and debt service costs. The Belgian Treasury strives to eliminate its exposure to exchange risk in the coming years (see Figure 3 below): indeed, now that Belgium's domestic currency is a reserve currency, the Treasury no longer believes that borrowing in foreign currency could lead to lower interest costs or fewer risks in the long term.

Credit risk, also called default risk, refers to potential losses to the Treasury if at least one of its counterparts fails to pay promised payments as planned. When this type of default occurs, it entails unexpected outlays. Consequently, the Belgian Treasury takes precautions as far as possible to avoid exposure to this risk. So its counterparties are continuously monitored, and quite some credit lines have been suppressed in recent years.

On the whole, Belgium's public debt structure is as such not the optimal outcome of some stochastic macroeconomic model. In the absence of a suitable and reliable long-term model, it was decided to adopt a portfolio structure that remains close to, but never exceeds, the refinancing and re-fixing maxima that are believed to be acceptable. Higher refinancing and re-fixing risks result in portfolios with shorter duration and average life; these portfolios are almost certain to provide for lower borrowing costs over the long term.[20] So the Belgian Debt Agency selected the least expensive portfolio structure that is still compatible with the maximum risk tolerated.

The framework of refinancing and re-fixing risks which was introduced in 2003 proved to be quite useful. For example, in 2007 and 2008, the Belgian Debt Agency diminished the re-fixing risks because of the threat of rising inflation. But on the contrary, in early 2009, when the scenario of a long lasting recession became realistic, the Debt Agency advised increasing the exposure to short-term rates. The Minister of Finance decided to increase the maxima for the re-fixing risk, and the Debt Agency entered into a series of interest rate swaps, which in the course of 2010 were terminated when the risk of a deep recession had receded.

---

20. The theoretical foundation and the empirical evidence underpinning the theory that short-term rates are usually lower than long-term rates are substantial.

According to a well-known adage, good sense recommends avoiding putting all one's eggs in one basket. Analogically, public debt instruments will be diversified in order to avoid large exposure to risks presented above. These risks are quite often exogenous. In other words, they are quite often beyond the control of the government because they depend on macroeconomic developments in the rest of the world and on unanticipated changes in market conditions. Nevertheless, the exposure to these risks can be considered as endogenous because it depends on decisions relating to the public debt composition, which refers to the choice of debt instruments.

The next section presents the evolution of the public debt composition in Belgium, at least during the last decade.

2.3   Evolution of the public debt structure in Belgium

According to the Belgian Debt Agency, during the last ten years the Belgian public debt was mainly made up of long-term euro debt, principally OLOs. Short-term euro debt (especially Treasury Certificates) amounted to less than 20% of the federal government debt outstanding and foreign currency debt was really tiny (see Figure 2 below).

In fact, within the perspective of integration in the Euro zone, the reduction of the debt denominated in foreign currency has been an objective for the Belgian government since the mid-nineties. Actually, as shown in Figure 3, the share of public debt denominated in foreign currency has dropped sharply since this period.

Indebtedness

Figure 2: Public debt outstanding as at 31 December

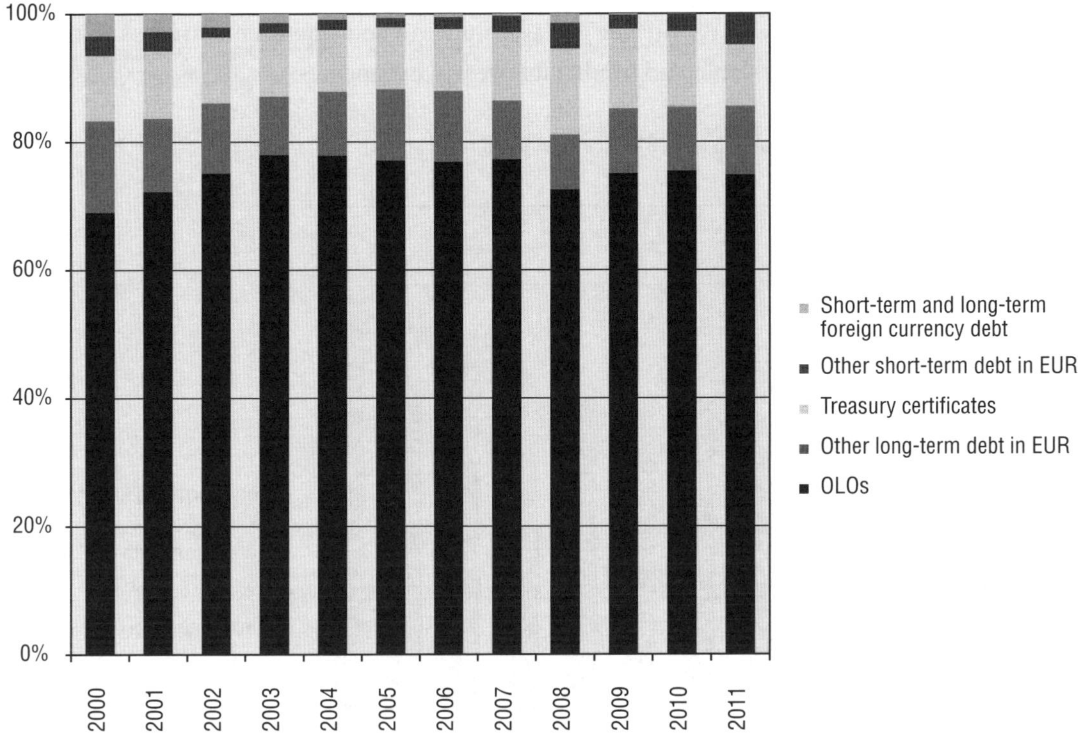

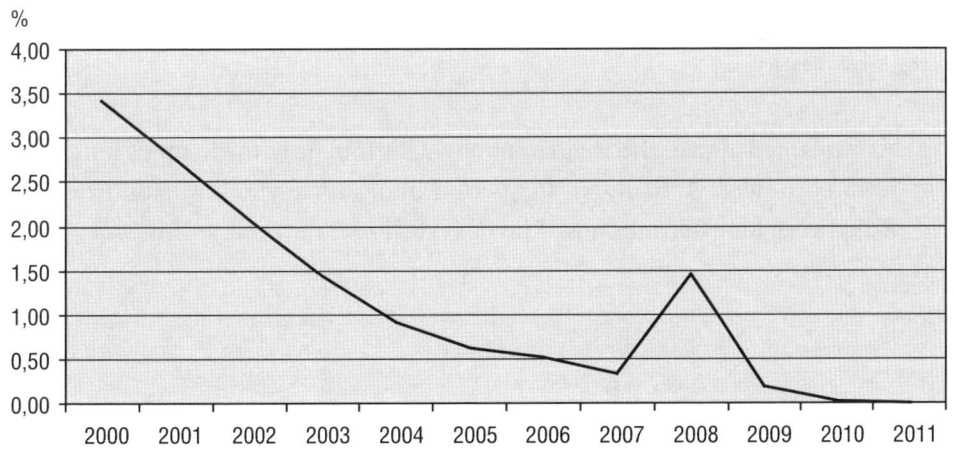

- Short-term and long-term foreign currency debt
- Other short-term debt in EUR
- Treasury certificates
- Other long-term debt in EUR
- OLOs

Source: Belgian Debt Agency

Figure 3: Share of Belgian public debt denominated in foreign currency

Source: Federal Public Service Finance on http://www.docufin.fgov.be/intersalgfr/thema/stat/Stat_financiering_fed.htm

As shown in Figure 2 above and in Figure 4 below, long-term euro debt is mainly made up of OLOs. The maturity schedule has a pattern reflecting the Treasury's strategy of issuing large and liquid benchmarks to benefit from a stable and predictable yearly issuance.

Figure 4: Public debt outstanding as at 31 December (billions of euros)

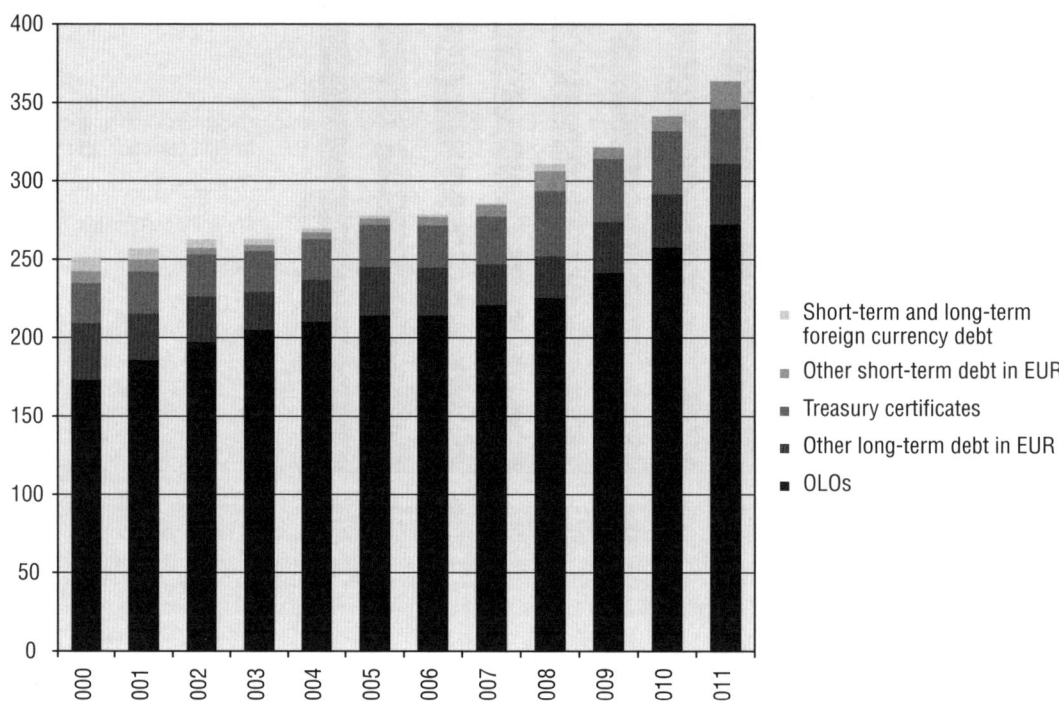

Source: Belgian Debt Agency.

As explained above, the Belgian public debt is mainly made up of long-term euro debt. Actually, in the period under review, several countries issued very long-term bonds. The next section is devoted to this issue.

3. DEBATE ABOUT ISSUING VERY LONG TERM (30 YEARS) AND INFLATION-LINKED BONDS

During the 2000s, several countries issued very long term bonds (30 years or more) or inflation-linked bonds.[21] On the one hand, these issues enable one to benefit from low interest rates. On the other hand, they also meet the investment needs of some investors. In this section, we develop these elements considering the strategies pursued by the debt management agencies in these countries, with a special focus on Belgium.

As explained above, the strategy of public debt management consists in minimising the financing cost of the debt within the framework of appropriate risk management. Consequently, the choice between public debt instruments – including very long-term bonds and inflation-linked bonds – has to be considered in the light of this objective.

The basic economic theory teaches that an increase in bond demand leads to a fall in bond yields. Therefore the maturity and composition of debt issue is also determined according to the needs of investors who are willing to buy government bonds. During the 2000s, a surge in demand for very long term bonds was observed.

This surge in demand for very long term bonds could be explained by the needs of some investors, especially pension funds, who ought rather to invest in long-term assets. Indeed, the goal of pension funds is to collect payments to provide their beneficiaries' retirement income. Therefore, this sector is usually characterised by a balance sheet mismatch: the maturities of its liabilities differ from those of its assets.[22] Its liabilities consist in long-term commitments to provide retirement income and its assets are financial instruments bought with the regular contributions paid to benefit from a pension scheme. Consequently, buying very long term bonds reduces this mismatch. The current trend towards population ageing and its impact on the development of private pension schemes will probably reinforce this demand in very long-term assets preferably

---

21. See Blommestein H. and G. Wehinger (2007)
22. The interested reader can find longer developments in the OECD publication on "Ageing and pension system reform".

indexed for changes in the price level as individuals are willing to protect the real value of their future pension income.

At first glance, the needs of pension funds could seem quite far from the objective of public debt managers. Nonetheless, governments are very well placed to play a central role in this market. Firstly, as explained above, due to the high demand for very long term bonds, the reward for investing longer vanishes. In other words, the extra yield of very long term bonds (30 years or more) is not that much higher by comparison with the yield of 10-year bond issues. Figure 5 illustrates this for Belgium. On average for the period under review, the yield on the Belgian 30-year benchmark loan was 0.48% higher than for the 10-year benchmark. But sometimes the differential was even 0.20% or less.

Figure 5: Yields on Belgian 10-yr and 30-yr benchmarks (2000-2010)

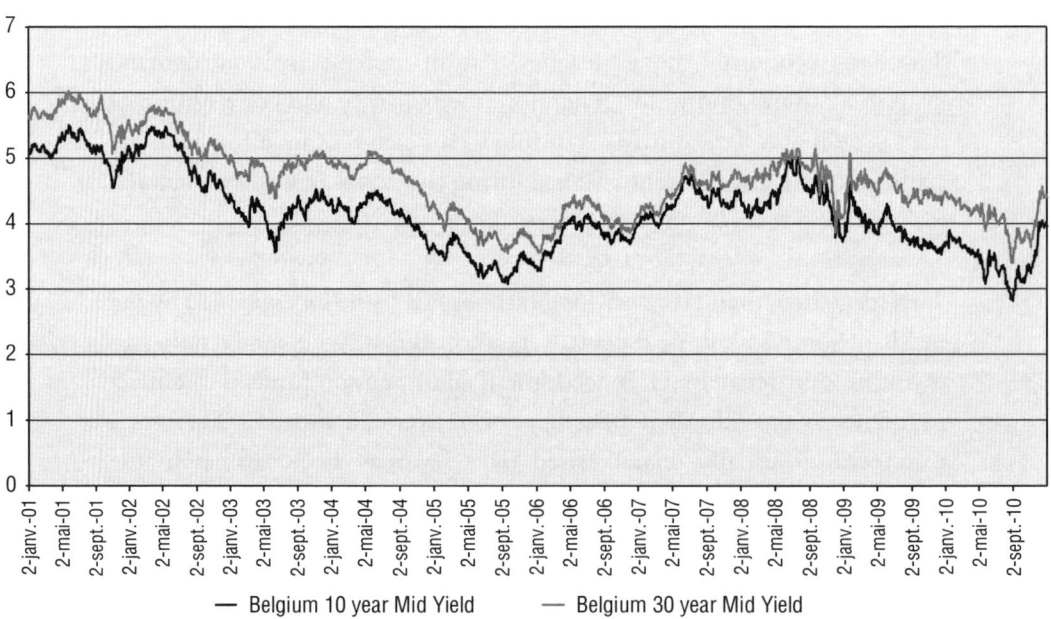

Source: Belgian Debt Agency.

Secondly, the longevity of a sovereign state is *a priori* longer than that of a private firm. Consequently, the risk that governments issuing very long term bonds cease to service them is usually perceived to be lower than in the case of very long term issues made by private firms.

The table below mentions Belgium's very long term reference bonds ('benchmarks') that were launched during the period under review. Please note that, once launched, the issues were tapped on various occasions in the subsequent year(s).

Table

OLO (INITIAL LAUNCH)	YEAR	TERM	AMOUNT
OLO40	2002	15yr	EUR 5.0 billion
OLO44	2004	30yr	EUR 5.0 billion
OLO48	2006	15yr	EUR 4.0 billion
OLO60	2010	30yr	EUR 4.0 billion

Source: Belgian Debt Agency.

Finally, note also that, with regards to index-linked bonds, it is sometimes argued that governments have a natural advantage in terms of issuing index-linked bonds as inflation and government revenue are both pro-cyclical, which means that the cost of these instruments is expected to co-vary with the changes in government revenue. However, most government expenses also increase with inflation, which partly offsets the former relationship. In addition, in small countries like Belgium, it is very important to consider the risk of illiquidity: the size of the bond portfolio was deemed to be insufficient for providing liquidity in both fixed-rate and index-linked issues. As a lack of liquidity would certainly lead to higher borrowing costs, Belgium did not issue index-linked bonds during the period under review.[23]

This section explained that some debt instruments are favoured by some investors. In particular, very long term bonds are favoured by pension funds. The next section will be devoted to the structure of debt ownership. This may convey important information. Indeed, the objective of attracting more foreign investors goes hand in hand with the benefits associated with an increase in competition among sovereign issuers. Actually, this can lead to a decrease in interest charges, which is perfectly

---

23. See the Euroweek Northern European Sovereign Borrowers Roundtable on 15 December 2009 on http://www.euroweek.com

in line with the objective of public debt managers. The main drawback could be that foreign investors may be more sensitive to gregarious behaviour caused for instance by political tensions or contagion from other countries characterised by some similar features. The section below details the ownership structure of Belgium's public debt.

4. DEBT OWNERSHIP

4.1 Foreign ownership versus domestic

By the end of 1999, after the first year of the euro, foreign ownership of OLOs had already gone up from 15.6% to 31.1%. This was mainly attributable to investors in other euro area countries. From 2000 onwards, non-euro investors also gained more interest in holding OLOs, bringing the foreign ownership of OLOs to a peak of 62.3% at the end of 2007 (Figure 6). During the financial and sovereign debt crisis that followed, the proportion of OLOs owned by foreigners decreased somewhat to 55.7% on 31 December 2010.

There were two effects at play. First, the disappearance of foreign exchange risk enabled euro area investors to diversify their domestic bond portfolio into non-domestic euro area issuers. Figure 6 shows that this happened relatively quickly, as much of this diversification was achieved by the end of 1999. Second, the euro became a reserve currency, and the issue of euro debt enabled the Belgian Treasury to sell its debt to non-euro area investors. Internationally active primary dealers, OLO issue through syndication and extensive road shows, all contributed to diversifying OLO ownership throughout the world.

Figure 6: Foreign ownership of Linear Obligations (OLOs) 2000-2010

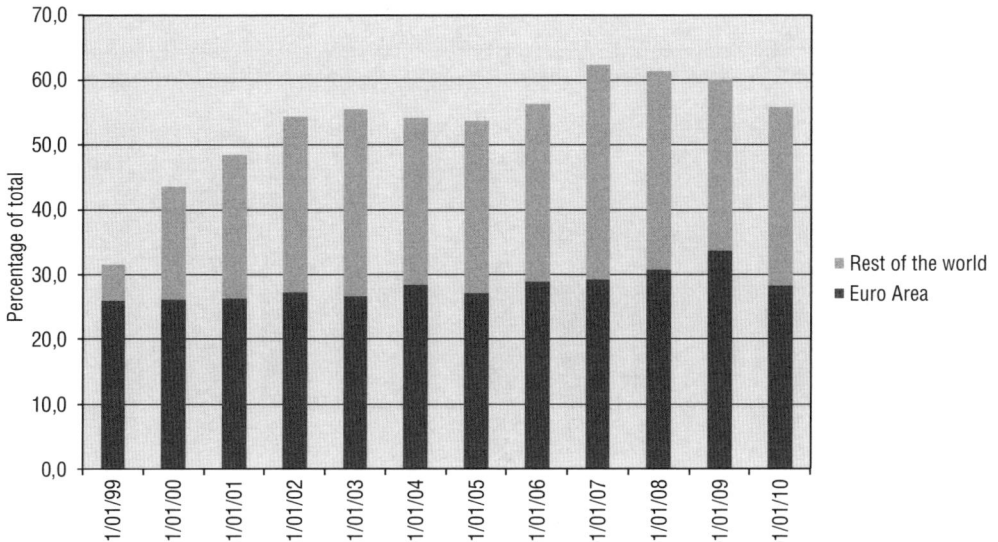

Source: National Bank of Belgium.

The ownership structure of Belgium's prime short-term debt product – Treasury Certificates – evolved in a different way. For a start, foreign investors already owned about half of the amount of the outstanding Treasury Certificates when they were issued in domestic currency. Also, during the early years of the euro, their participation did not increase: on the contrary, by the end of 2002, foreigners owned only 40.6% of these securities. The converging yields in the euro short-term market possibly explain the lack of appetite by foreign investors at that time.

Yet foreign participation in the Treasury Certificate market increased again from 2003 onwards. The Belgian Debt Agency indeed attributed significant weight to short-term paper in its appraisal of the Primary Dealers. Moreover, Belgian Primary Dealers are obliged to organise the market for both long- and short-term paper. By the end of the period under review, the sovereign debt crisis appeared to have given another boost to the foreign ownership of Treasury Certificates. A number of foreign investors probably changed their OLO holdings into Treasury Certificates, enabling them to keep exposure to the euro but to reduce market and credit risk at the same time.

Figure 7: Foreign ownership of Treasury Certificates 2000-2010

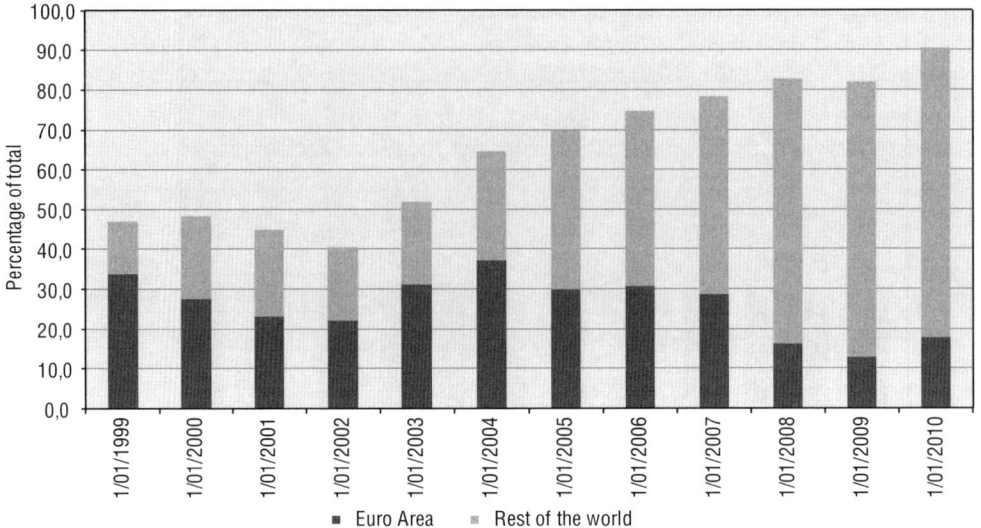

Source: Belgian Debt Agency.

4.2 Institutional owners vs. private

During the years 2000-2010, private investors only played a limited role in the Belgian sovereign debt market. First, despite the European single market, there was never evidence of foreign private investors acquiring significant amounts of Belgian government paper. Second, the OLOs, which had completely replaced former products such as the Philippe loans, were never very popular with the Belgian private investor: at most, one or two per cent of OLOs seemed to be owned by private investors in Belgium. In fact, not only were private investor holdings low at the dawn of the period under review, but they also declined over time. Finally, it was the State Note (Staatsbon/Bon d'Etat), which had been introduced in 1998 as a specifically designed product for the private investor, which actually attracted most of the demand from private investors. In January 2000 a total amount of EUR 4.91 billion of State Notes was outstanding. By the end of 2003, the amount had gone up to EUR 8.51 billion. However, it would never be that high again: by the end of 2010, the amount had fallen back to EUR 3.95 billion.

Thus, the preference of domestic private investors for banking and insurance products was more pronounced in Belgium than in other countries. The extensive distribution channels of the financial institutions as well as the tax advantages that were given to a number of their products partly explain why this was the case. The Treasury however never abandoned the State Note, and the product is relatively well known despite its limited success.

As shown above, the Treasury issues many debt instruments, held by different types of investors and paying different interest rates. Therefore, it could be very convenient to calculate a weighted average interest rate. The section below presents the Belgian implicit interest rate in the period 2000-2010.

5. IMPLICIT INTEREST RATE

The implicit interest rate of a government debt portfolio can be calculated at each point as the weighted average interest rate of all instruments present in the portfolio. However, if the aim is to observe long-term trends, one can also calculate the implicit interest rate by dividing the annual debt servicing cost[24] by the outstanding stock of debt.

The implicit interest rate changes with time as the government reimburses debt that has come to maturity and possibly has to refinance this with new debt issued at interest rates that differ from those on past borrowings. The risk free market interest may indeed change, as well as the spread at which the government has to borrow above this risk free rate. In addition, the government can structurally lengthen or shorten the maturity profile of its debt: the implicit interest rate is then expected to rise, or decrease, all other things being equal.

Figure 8 plots the implicit interest rate on Belgian Government debt over the period under review: it declined substantially from 6.40% in 2000 to 3.51% in 2010. As the average life of the debt portfolio did not materially

---

24. Coupons, measured in accrual terms, to which the amortisation of issue premiums and the possible flows resulting from derivatives such as interest rate swaps are added

change over the period, the decline was caused by the markedly lower interest rates which Belgium had to pay in comparison with those of the 1990s and of the late 1980s. In fact, government bond yields were already declining in the late 1990s, as inflation remained controlled and the euro resulted in a convergence of euro area bond yields.

Figure 8: Implicit interest rate Belgian Government debt portfolio 2000-2010

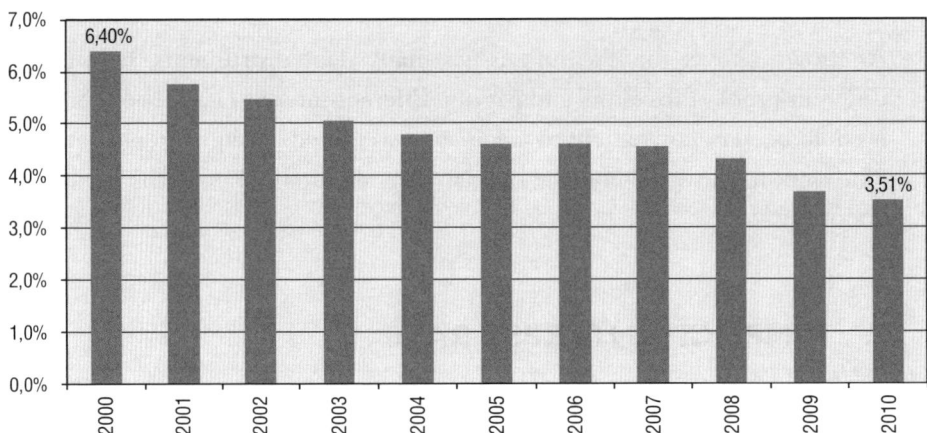

Source: Belgian Debt Agency.

As highlighted above, the implicit interest rate noticeably decreased under the period under review, and this was mainly caused by the decline in interest rates which Belgium had to pay in comparison with those previously paid. The next section will be devoted to the comparison of the interest rate that Belgium pays and that paid by Germany. More broadly, the interest rate spreads of the 11 initial euro area Member States and that of Greece which adopted the euro in 2001 against the German benchmark will also be examined.

6. SPREADS

During the 1990s, interest rate spreads of euro area 10-year government bonds against the German benchmark abruptly dropped. This fall was mainly due to the expected launch of the euro, which removed exchange rate risks. This significant convergence in the bond yields was observed in all the countries participating in the single currency. By the time the euro was introduced, the difference between the highest yielding 10-year euro bond and the lowest yielding one had decreased to less than 50 basis points[25]. Investors were confident that a country which had adopted the euro had only a small chance of going into default. In addition, they were also confident that it had access to a deeper financial market, due to the strong integration of the euro area financial markets. Consequently, both the credit risk premium and the liquidity risk premium decreased at that time.

Figure 9: Long-term (10-year) government bond yield spreads against Germany[26]

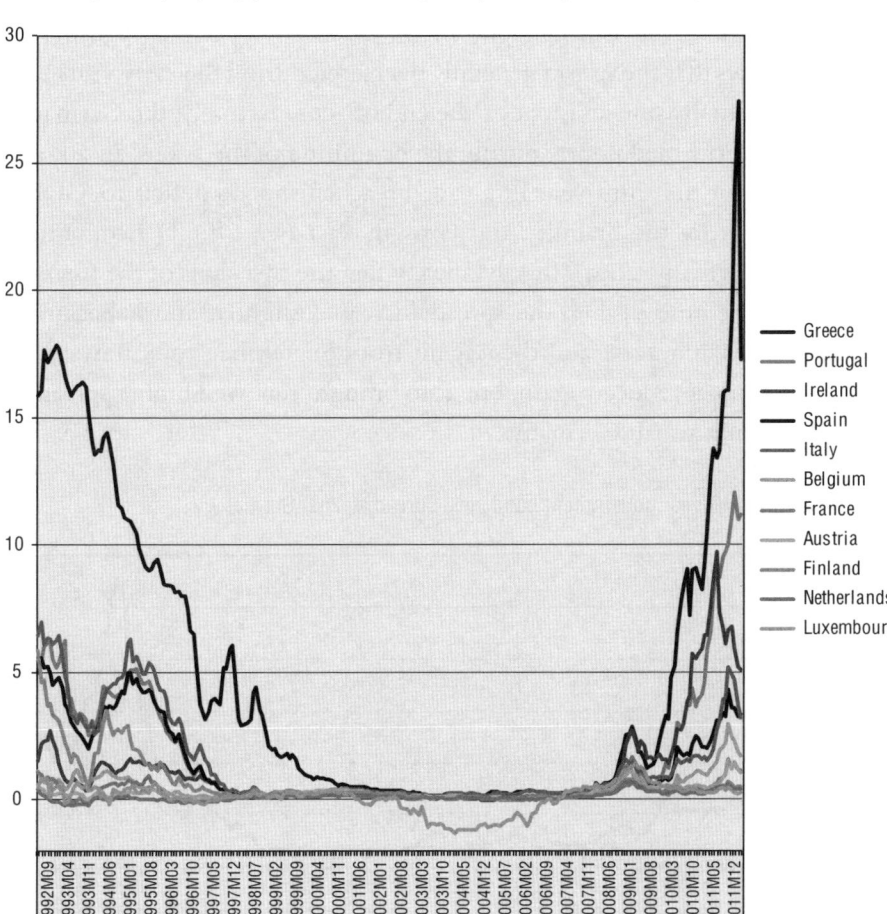

Source of data: Eurostat

25. Greece adopted the euro in January 2001: by then, its bond yields had equally converged vs. the ones of the other euro area countries
26. In Figure 9, the lines representing 10-year government bond yield spreads against Germany are ranked from the highest (for Greece) to the lowest (for Luxembourg) on March 2012.

Figure 9 plots long-term government bond yield spreads against Germany. These spreads are based on central government bond yields with a residual maturity of around 10 years on the secondary market, gross of tax. As shown on Figure 9, during most of the period under review, spreads between different euro area countries remained very low, but the financial crisis and subsequent recession changed the picture, especially after this crisis developed into the sovereign debt crisis in 2010.

Figure 10 focuses on the differential between the Belgian 10-year benchmark yield and the German one in the 2000-2010 period. Figure 10 clearly shows that the spread generally decreased during the early years to become virtually non-existent by the end of 2004. Actually, the German economy performed poorly during the beginning of the 2000s. In 2004, Germany, for the third year in a row, breached the 3% deficit-to-GDP threshold set by the Stability and Growth Pact (see OECD Economic Surveys: Germany, 2004). In July 2007, when the first signs of the financial crisis became visible, the spread increased slightly, and it became higher in March 2008 and then again from September 2008 onwards. During 2009, it reduced again, but 2010 brought renewed higher spreads for Belgium towards Germany.

Figure 10: Belgium's 10-year government bond yield spread against Germany

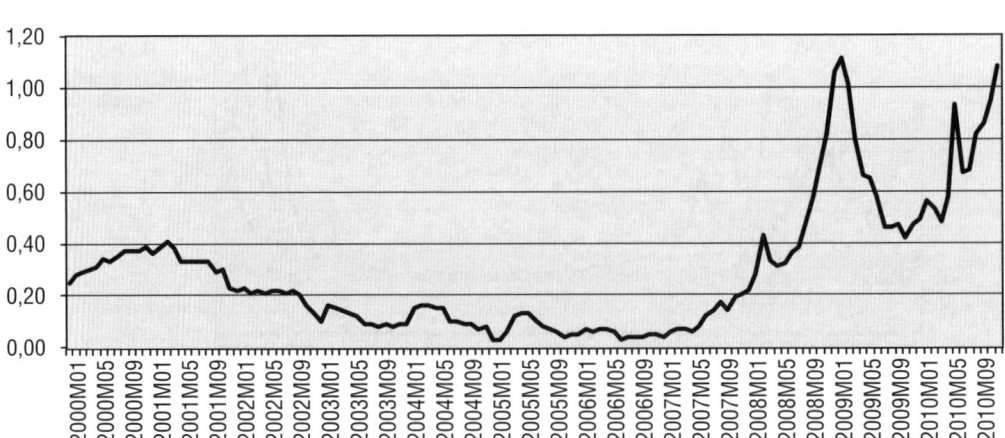

Source of data: Eurostat

CONCLUSION

This chapter was aimed at describing the evolution of Belgium's public debt and of the associated interest rates over the 2000-2010 decade. It was shown above that Belgium's public debt fell steadily from 1993 to 2007. Unfortunately, the financial crisis erupted and led to an increase in the debt-to-GDP ratio from 2008. As the public debt instruments which make up the public debt may strongly influence the risk exposure and interest rates paid, the public debt structure was also depicted. The strand of literature devoted to the public debt structure was also briefly summarised. Moreover, the differentiation between the theoretical economic development on the optimal public debt structure and the principles guiding the Belgian Debt Agency was detailed. Furthermore, recent trends in the type of public debt instruments issued by several OECD countries, namely the issue of very long term bonds or of inflation-linked bonds, showed that the needs of some investors may also influence the public debt structure. Therefore, the Belgian position on this issue was explained. Finally, the importance of the launch of the euro from the point of view of the changes in public debt ownership, the implicit interest rate and the spread against the German benchmark was stressed.

REFERENCES

Sumit Aneja, Kevin Cheng, Yingbin Xiao, and Irina Yakadina, "Belgium: Selected Issues Papers", IMF Country Report No. 11/82, (April, 2011).

Robert J. Barro, « On the Determination of the Public Debt », Journal of Political Economy, vol. 87, n°5, (1979) pp. 940-971.

Belgian Debt Agency, "2008 Review-2009 Outlook", (December, 2008)

Hans J. Blommestein and Gert Wehinger, "Public Debt Management and the Evolving Market for (Ultra-)Long Government Bonds", in Financial Market Trends, n°93, vol. 2007/2.

Henning Bohn, "Tax smoothing with financial instruments", The American Economic Review vol. 80, n°5, December, (1990) pp. 1217-1230.

Luc Buffel and Jef Vuchelen, "De overheidschuld" in "Het einde van het budgettair tekort (1990-2000)", edited by Etienne de Callataÿ, (de boeck, 2002), pp. 135-148.

Guillermo Calvo and Pablo Guidotti, « Optimal Maturity of Nominal Government Debt : an Infinite Horizon Model », International Economic Review, vol. 33, n°4, (November, 1992), pp. 895-919.

Jean Deboutte and Bruno Debergh, "Risk management of Government Debt in Belgium", in Advances in Risk Management of Government Debt", pp. 129-138, (OECD, 2005), pp. 129-138.

Mark De Broeck, « The Financial Structure of Government Debt in OECD Countries: An examination of the time-consistency issue », Journal of Monetary Economics 39, (1997), pp. 279-301.

Rudiger Dornbusch and Mario Draghi, "Introduction" in "Public Debt Management: Theory and History" edited by Rudiger Dornbusch and Mario Draghi, (Cambridge University Press, 1990).

Francesco Drudi and Alessandro Prati,"Differences and analogies between index-linked and foreign currency bonds: a theoretical and empirical analysis" in Managing Public Debt, edited by Marcello De Cecco, Lorenzo Pecchi, and Gustavo Piga, (Edward Elgar, 1997), pp. 195-216.

Natacha Gilson, "La gestion des dettes publiques: l'état actuel des recherches en sciences économiques", Bulletin de documentation du ministère des finances, 60ème année, n°3, (mars – avril 2000), pp. 139-162.

Finn E. Kyndland and Edward C. Prescott, « Rules Rather Than Discretion: the time inconsistency of optimal plans », Journal of Political Economy, vol. 85, n°3, (1997), pp. 473-491. Reprint in « Monetary and Fiscal Policy, volume 1: Credibility », Torsten Persson and Guido Tabellini, (MIT Press, 1994), pp. 35-55.

Victoria Miller, « Why a Government Might Want to Consider Foreign Currency Debt », Economics Letters 55, (1997), pp. 247-250.

Alessandro Missale, "Public debt management", (Oxford University Press, 1999).

Alessandro Missale, "Optimal Debt Management with a Stability and Growth Pact", Public Finance and Management, 1, 1, (2001), pp. 58-91.

National Bank of Belgium, "Report 2010: Economic and Financial Development".

OECD Economic Surveys: Germany (OECD, 2004).

OECD, "Ageing and Pension System Reforms: Implications for financial markets and economic policies" in Financial Market Trends November 2005 – Supplement.

Torsten Persson, and Guido Tabellini, « Introduction », in « Monetary and Fiscal Policy, volume 1 : Credibility », edited by Torsten Persson and Guido Tabellini, (MIT Press, 1994), pp. 1-31.

Lars Risbjerg and Anders Holmlund, "Analytical Framework for Debt and Risk Management" in Advances in Risk Management of Government Debt, (OECD, 2005), 39-58.

Guido Wolswijk and Jakob de Haan, "Government debt management in the Euro Area: recent theoretical development and changes in practice", ECB occasional paper series n°25, (March, 2005)

8.
Fiscal Federalism

THE TRANSITION TO A NEW
MODEL OF FISCAL RELATIONS

Koen Algoed and Frédérique Denil [1]

I.   INTRODUCTION

Federalism in Belgium is an evolving process towards growing decentralisation of responsibilities and revenue. For more than 40 years, various institutional reforms have played an essential role in designing revenue and responsibilities of the Regions and the Communities. The last decade has seen the implementation of the Lambermont agreement and the adoption of the Sixth Reform of the State. While the Lambermont agreement has mainly affected the pattern of funding mechanisms of the sub-national entities, the Sixth Reform of the State seems to organise a major step in the decentralisation of responsibilities as well as their financing. In this way, the reform is expected to increase the role of the Regions and the Communities in the allocation of public goods and services as in the use of taxing power, allowing these entities to better align their policies to their own preferences and priorities. But this reform is also the result of a long bargaining process due to the difficulty of reconciling different principles and the absence of additional funding by the Federal Government given the fiscal outlook of Entity I (Federal Government + Social Security).

---

1. Koen Algoed is Director of Cabinet of the Flemish Minister for Finance, Budget, Work, Town and Country Planning and Sports. Frédérique Denil is Advisor at the Federal Public Service (FPS) Finance (Research Department) and member of the Secretariat of the High Council of Finance. The authors wish to thank Etienne de Callataÿ for his helpful comments.

In this paper, we study therefore the process of the Sixth Reform of the State and its impact as a key issue of fiscal federalism in Belgium. A comparison will be done with the arrangements implemented over the past decade, developing to some extent the challenges involved by the Lambermont Agreement. Much attention is therefore paid to the last institutional agreement in this paper while it is still not implemented. Indeed, the negotiation process started several years ago and has also influenced fiscal federalism in Belgium during the last decade. It seems furthermore rather irrelevant to limit the analysis to a system which is now virtually obsolete.

The first part of this paper studies the reform process that occurred over the past decade from a political economy perspective. In the second part, the impact of the Sixth Reform of the State on the Regions and the Communities will be analysed in more details. To this end, an attempt to estimate the budgetary effects of the Reform on the different governments will be made on the basis of simulations. As these rely on provisional parameters and on various assumptions, they must be interpreted with caution. A third part concludes.

2. POLITICAL ECONOMY OF THE REFORMS OVER THE LAST DECADE

In Belgium as in most of other Federal States, fiscal federalism results from political motivations for decentralisation and organises this decentralisation by designing revenue and responsibilities to the Regions and the Communities, following to some extent arguments of the fiscal federalism theory.

The decentralisation process started in Belgium in 1970 with the creation of the Regions and the Communities. They have been assigned at this time limited expenditure and legislative powers. The Regions have been provided goods and services linked to the territory, while the Communities have been allocated national public goods related to individuals[2]. The overlapping of these two categories of sub-central entities is one of the specific characteristics of the institutional set-up in Belgium and complied with the different political requirements regarding decentralisation across the northern part and the southern part of the country. The Flemish population (northern part) supported indeed the creation of languages Communities on which cultural identity can be build up while the French-speaking population (southern part) had more interest in the decentralisation of economic affairs that are carried out by territorial entities (including a specific entity for Brussels).

This overlapping had significantly influenced the negotiation process of the various institutional reforms as well as their output. The Communities have for instance no taxing power since the Flemish and French-Speaking Communities share the responsibilities in the area of the Brussels-Capital Region. Tax autonomy would indeed involve a difficult trade-off between more accountability and tax competition. Moreover, such taxing power would have otherwise required determining sub-nationalities for the inhabitants of the Brussels-Capital Region or a fixed sharing arrangement (80/20). Since the Flemish Region and the Flemish Community merged, public expenditures related to individuals such as social policy can also be financed by taxes in this Region.

The powers of the Regions and the Communities have been expanded in the **1980** reform but still remained mainly based on earmarked grants. Next, the Reform of **1989** paved really the way to fiscal federalism with a large decentralisation of national public goods and services such as education, transports or housing and the adoption of the Special Law of Finance that designed revenue mechanisms to the Regions and the Communities in order to meet their new spending obligations.

At the beginning of the last decade (2002), the Lambermont Agreement has been concluded. The main output of this Reform was to enlarge taxing power of the Regions and to increase VAT transfers to the Communities with a review of the distribution formula. To the extent

---

2. According to the Constitution (Art. 1, 2 and 3), Belgium is a Federal State made up of three Regions and three Communities: the Flemish Region, the Walloon Region, the Brussels-Capital Region, the Flemish Community, the French-Speaking Community and the German Community.

that the Communities received more transfers from the federal level, this Reform was not budgetary neutral for the Federal Government, although a reduction in the PIT transferred to the Regions compensated the increased regional taxing power (Blöchliger H. and Vammalle C., 2012, p.58).

The Lambermont Agreement occurred under good economic conditions, as the Belgian GDP growth was expected to perform well and the federal Government was in a sound fiscal position due to the fiscal consolidation episode of the nineties. This environment created room for logrolling, which means that the Flemish and the Walloon Regions bundled their interest in the reform, i.e. increase of taxing power and of the transfers to the Communities, even if this bundling was at the expense of the Federal Government (Blöchliger H. and Vammalle C., 2012, pp.55-56). Given that political parties are not only committed to the challenges of the Federal level in the Belgian institutional framework, the Federal Government did not oppose to bundling as it feared in particular the cost of 'non-reform' and hoped to calm down community tensions.

However, as the Federal Government implemented at the same time a reform of the Personal Income Tax (PIT) reducing tax burden and developed alternative financing of the Social Security, a growing pressure has been brought on the federal budget. This raised progressively the question of the fiscal sustainability of the institutional arrangements, especially after the 2009 recession.

As a consequence of the Lambermont Agreement, the Brussels-Capital Region became mainly financed through regional taxes and fees that represented about the half of the regional revenue. Although the Region benefited from this additional taxing power thanks to the sharp increase in the property taxes revenue before the economic crisis, it also became vulnerable to volatility in the tax revenue and to tax competition of the other Regions (OECD, 2009, pp.68-69). Moreover, the Lambermont Agreement did not remedy the structural lack of financial resources of this international and capital city (see below, paragraph 3.1.4) and its internal institutional complexity.

It should also be noticed that the equalisation scheme across the Regions has not been reformed in 2002, while in some other Federal States the increase of taxing power has been combined with fiscal equalisations reforms (Blöchliger H. and Vammalle C., 2012, p.58)[3]. It does not mean however that equalisation left the core of the debate. Conversely, a current flow of academic, scientific and politic literature emerged during the last decade that attempted to assess the size of the financial transfers across the regions[4]. Some of these assessments reported large amounts of interregional transfers from the Flemish population, combining the equalisation mechanisms provided by the Special Finance Law and the transfers through the Social Security System.

These various issues following the Lambermont Agrement, as well as a growing disagreement in the Flemish population against some federal policies (migration, labour market, unemployment benefit etc.), brought more pressure on the institutional framework. As a result, federalist issues have been highlighted in the 2007 election campaign in the northern part of the country. A bargaining process has therefore been launched after the election in view of new institutional set-up but this faced a number of challenges.

At first, the interests of the potential actors of the future reform were rather opposite. Not only political parties in the French-speaking side were not prepared to start a reform process, but they perceived themselves as future losers when considering motivations of the actors in the northern part of the country. Throughout the negotiations, the French-speaking side progressively defined their own interests, such as the refinancing of Brussels-Capital Region or the recognition of equalization mechanisms, while the Flemish side had to soften its initial position to reach a compromise.

3. It was the case in Portugal and Switzerland.
4. See for instance Dury& al (2008), Meunier, Mignolet & Mulquin (2007), Van Gompel & Van Craynest (2004) or Cattoir and de Callataÿ (2007) at the request of the Flemish Community. According to these referred above, the transfers should be just over 8% of GDP to the benefit of the Walloon Region. Concerning the Brussels-Capital Region, the results are substantially different according to whether the assessments measure the revenue on basis of the working place or on basis of the place of residence (from 4% of GDP to the benefit of the Brussels-Capital Region to 2,6% of GDP from the Brussels-Capital Region to the benefit of the Walloon Region).

Such divergences of interests and attitudes towards a new institutional reform have implied strong and very different political mandates in the northern and the southern part of the country, especially in the last federal elections of June 2010. The Flemish political parties promoting the most decentralised federalism framework were largely supported while the dominant French-speaking parties were reluctant towards more devolution and tax autonomy.

Furthermore, the future institutional reform was not only expected to revise fiscal federalism arrangements but had also to find a solution regarding the Brussels-Halle-Vilvoorde electoral district to the extent that these two aspects have been bundled in the reform process by the Flemish parties. The latter claimed for a splitting of the BHV district, while the French-speaking parties aimed to preserve the interest of the French-speaking minorities in this area (as an asymmetric exception to the territoriality principle). The bundling of BHV issue and of the revision of fiscal federalism arrangements obviously made the reform process more complex.

An additional difficulty occurred with the emergence of the economic and sovereign debt crisis, and the related risks for public finance sustainability. Institutional bargaining process was therefore influenced by concerns for intergenerational equity and for fiscal sustainability, in addition to efficiency and interpersonal solidarity.

These various issues delayed the conclusion of the last institutional Reform, although advances have been made during the bargaining process. In December 2010, the National Bank of Belgium and the Federal Planning Bureau have been indeed mandated to achieve various estimates of the potential budgetary impact of the Reform for all governments levels[5]. The negotiators have then relied on these estimates that have been published meanwhile to pursue their discussions.

Finally, following a decision adopted on the BHV district, the institutional agreement has been reached in November 2011, providing significant changes in the revenue mechanisms of the sub-national entities

---

5. These institutions have been mandated by Johan Vande Lanotte who was chosen at that time by the King as mediator ('conciliateur') to drive forward the process of institutional reform.

and the devolution of new responsibilities. This agreement has been endorsed by all political parties across the country with the exception of the Flemish nationalist parties the most important of these having left the negotiations a few months before.

This agreement has been built upon a set of rules that reflects the priorities and interests of the different actors. These rules are expected to be complied to ensure a balanced compromise. Although these rules express for some rather opposite views, they find an implementation in the various provisions of the reform (Institutional Agreement on the Sixth Reform of the State, 2012):
- To avoid unfair competition;
- To maintain the progressive pattern of the Personal Income Tax;
- Not structurally impoverish one or some sub-national governments;
- To ensure sustainability of the Federal State and maintain its tax prerogatives regarding distribution across individuals;
- To strengthen accountability of sub-national governments regarding their responsibilities and their policy, taking into account their starting position and some parameters values;
- To take into account spill-over effects, the sociological reality and the role of the Brussels-Capital Region;
- To take into account the population and number of pupils -criteria;
- To recognise solidarity across levels of governments, without perverse effects;
- To ensure the financial stabilisation of the levels of governments;
- To take into account fiscal effort to be made by all levels of government in view of fiscal consolidation;
- To check whether arrangements are relevant through numerical simulations.

The principle of 'non-impoverishment' of the sub-national entities remains however a rather sensitive issue. Given the magnitude of the current grants, a financing of the Regions based upon tax autonomy could indeed in the long run, depending on the evolution of the tax bases and tax revenues, structurally impoverish some Regions.

In the following paragraphs, we will study in more details the impact of the Sixth Reform of the State on the sub-national entities with a comparison to the current mechanisms coming from the previous reform (i.e. the Lambermont Agreement).

3. THE SIXTH REFORM OF THE STATE

3.1 The Regions

As far as the Regions are concerned, the Reform leads to a further decentralisation of taxing power and of responsibilities. This implies major changes in revenue structure and distribution mechanisms of the Regions. First of all, a proportional surcharge on the Personal Income Tax (PIT) will replace the PIT amount transferred from the Federal Government with the own taxes of the Regions increasing significantly compared to the current system. Secondly, there are additional grants devolved by the Federal Government to finance the new regional responsibilities regarding labour market and tax expenditures.

Table 1: Revenue structure of the Regions under the current system compared to the Sixth Reform of the State

	CURRENT SYSTEM		REFORM
Own tax revenue	Regional taxes and user fees (°)	=	Regional taxes and user fees (°)
	Potential surcharges on PIT	↗	Proportional surcharge on the PIT (°)
Grants	Base Grant (PIT)	≠	
	Grant additional competencies (PIT)	=	Grant additional competencies (PIT)
	Solidarity transfer	→	New Solidarity transfer
	Grants for getting unemployed to work	→	Grants Labour Market responsibilities
	Specific grants for Brussels	→	Refinancing of the Brussels-Capital Region
		+	Grants for devolved tax expenditures
		+	Lump-sum transfer to ensure neutrality

Source: Agreement on the Sixth Reform of the State.
(°) Of which registration duties, some green taxes and circulation taxes.

Attention should also be paid to the reform of the solidarity transfer from the Federal Government to the 'poorer' Regions. The equalisation formula has been significantly changed in the line of one of the basic principle of the reform that promotes 'solidarity without perverse effects'. A lump-sum transfer will be otherwise added to this equalisation mechanism that ensures the budget neutrality of the reform for each level of government the first year of its implementation. Finally, additional funds will be granted to the Brussels-Capital Region to cover spill over effects of the public goods allocated in this area and enabling fair financing of this Region.

These new financing arrangements of the Regions are successively dealt with thereafter on the basis of a discussion on their implications from a political economy perspective. The following part of the text will therefore raise at first the issue of the tax autonomy and the implementation of a proportional surcharge on the PIT, to later develop the new tasks transferred to the Regions. The equalisation mechanisms and the new financing of the Brussels-Capital Region will be analysed in a third and a fourth section respectively.

3.1.1 Increasing the tax autonomy of the Regions: from tax transfer to proportional surcharge

Currently, the Regions receive from the Federal Government an annual grant paid out from the PIT revenue. That grant is indexed to inflation (Prices Consumption Index, PCI) and to real GDP growth. This transfer depends on a lump-sum amount initially granted in 1989[6].

The PIT grant is first divided between the Regions on the basis of their relative shares in the PIT revenue and then corrected by a regional specific negative term. The negative term has been introduced in 2002 for each Region separately. It consists of the average in the period 1999-2001 of the taxes (such as registration duties, circulation taxes) of which the revenue and the tax autonomy have been transferred to the Regions

---

6. For a detailed presentation of the current system, see for example:
    - Bayenet B. & Pagano G., 2011, "Le financement des Entités fédérées: un système en voie de transformation », Crisp.
    - Decoster A. & Sas W., 2011, « De bijzondere financieringswet voor dummies », Flemosi, discussionpaper 4
    - Algoed K. & Van Den Bossche W., 2009, "Bijzondere financieringswet in een notendop", Documentatieblad 2009 n°2, Studie- en Documentatiedienst, FOD Financiën.

from 2002 onwards. As the Regions enjoyed the revenue of the new regionalised taxes, the absence of a negative term would have deteriorated the fiscal position of the Federal level. The negative term was therefore designed to achieve a kind of initial neutrality of the reform for the Federal budget. An alternative would have been to substract immediately an aggregate negative term from the PIT grant[7]. Indeed, given that relative shares of the Regions in the negative term are different from those in the PIT revenue, a negative term, albeit lower (less negative) would have been needed to share the (net) PIT grant according to the regional income tax yield.

The Lambermont Agreement also stated that each Region could increase or reduce the transfer they get by collecting surcharges or allowing relieves on the PIT levied on their area. Some quantitative limits have however been put by the law on this taxing power to the extent that surcharges or relieves cannot exceed 6.75% of the PIT located in the Region area. Since this measure has been implemented, only the Flemish Region has used the taxing power regarding PIT, mainly by allowing a tax cut in 2009 to all the workers living in the Flemish Region ('jobkorting')[8]. The 'jobkorting' has been progressively removed in 2010 and 2011 for budgetary reasons. It should however be noted that all the Regions (including the Walloon Region and the Brussels-Capital Region) have used their taxing power on regionalised taxes by implementing various reforms (Decoster, Valenduc & Verdonck 2009, p.183).

The use of tax autonomy in the Flemish Region and the driving forces for a further decentralisation of taxing power lead us to believe that the PIT is considered in this Region not only as an important source of revenue but also as a key regional policy instrument with the incentive effect of this tax that should be used in particular in relation to regional responsibilities (housing, employment, etc.).

---

7. In formal terms let nt_i be the negative term for region i, y_i the estimated share of region i in PIT revenue, G being the PIT grant, then $G \times y_i - nt_i = \left(G - \dfrac{nt_i}{y_i}\right) \times y_i$

8. The full budgetary cost of 'jobkorting' is estimated to 710 million euro and most of this cost has been imputed on 2009.

It seems that such a consideration, among others, has been taken into account in the Reform as the current PIT grant will be replaced by a system of regional piggy-back personal income tax, i.e. a proportional surcharge on the PIT. The regional surcharges are precisely levied on the federal PIT due after tax cuts have been made (such as zero-rate band, tax credit for replacement income, general reduction factor, etc.).

In practice, the federal PIT resulting from the current computation rules will be reduced by a factor X corresponding to the regional surcharge. The magnitude of this factor is determined, the year the Reform comes into force, by the both following elements to which the regional surcharge will substitute: the PIT grant after deduction of the negative term (art. 33§4 of the Special Law of Finance) and 40% of the tax expenditures which are transferred to the Regions (about 1.897 million euro, 2012 figure[9]).

The Sixth Reform of the State now gets rid of most of the negative term. The aggregate negative term taken into account to determine the amount of regional PIT revenue in the initial year of the Reform is indeed lower (less negative) than the aggregate negative term resulting from the current mechanisms. It has been capped for the Flemish Region and the Brussels-Capital Region to take into account that, contrary to the Walloon Region, their shares in the negative term are higher than their relative shares in the PIT. The current negative term of the Walloon Region and its relative share in PIT revenue[10] will then determine the new negative term.

The remaining residual amount of negative term for the Flemish Region and the Brussels-Capital Region will be included in the equalisation grant. As this computation rule is (ex ante) budgetary neutral for the Walloon Region, there is no effect on the equalisation grant (see further).

---

9. In prices of 2012 the tax expenditures are equal to 1.912 mio euro in the institutional agreement. This figure is fictitious because based upon former previsions of inflation & GDP growth and some reduction factor. The figure here has been derived using the current previsions and the same reduction factor.
10. It should be the relative share of regional PIT revenue after reform in order to have no effect on the equalisation payment for the Walloon Region.

Table 2: Proportional surcharge on the Personal Income Tax (estimates for 2012)

ESTIMATED FIGURES FOR 2012, MILLIONS OF EURO			
CURRENT SYSTEM		**REFORM**	
PIT transferred to the Regions in the *current system*	→ 9.477 ↘	**Proportional surcharge on the PIT,** starting year: 10.593 (= 33%)	↗ The Flemish Region: 6.698
			→ The Brussels-Capital Region: 899
+ Tax expenditure (40%)	→ 759 ↗		↘ The Walloon Region: 2.997

Source: Own calculations based on the Agreement on the Sixth Reform of the State, Decoster A. &Sas W., Federal Planning Bureau (June forecasts).
It should be noticed that the amounts can be different from these of the Institutional agreement as they are here indexed to the most recent parameters (GDP, CPI) for 2012

When related to the total PIT revenue and the tax expenditure estimated for 2012, the surcharge on the PIT represents a share of 33%, which can be considered as a significant proportion. In the future, this rate will be the reference parameter to determine the evolution of the regional tax revenue, knowing that the Regions will be autonomous to change this rate within their available budgetary margins and according to their fiscal targets. The implementation of a proportional surcharge is therefore a step towards further decentralisation of the taxing power and towards increasing **tax autonomy of the Regions**.

In comparison to the current system, there is no quantitative limit anymore on the rate and relieves the Region can apply on the proportion of the PIT they will get. Moreover, the Regions can change the tax rate across the scales of the PIT, to increase or even decrease the progressivity of the PIT paid ultimately by their residents. Nevertheless, in order to prevent harmful tax competition, some limits are set to the reduction of the progressive character:
- If the surcharge rate applied to the PIT differs across the scales, each rate must be at least 90% of the rates in the lower scales;
- When the progressivity of the income tax system is reduced, the average benefit per taxpayer must be less than 1,000 euro;

The Regions as well as the Communities do not have any autonomy to determine the tax base or to differentiate tax rates according to the type of income or the family composition.

As it is a proportion of the PIT, the surcharge on the PIT levied by the Regions will have two major implications on their revenue, which can be called successively 'unchanged policy revenue effect' and 'incentive effect'.

The **'unchanged policy revenue effect'** refers to the fact that the Regions will benefit automatically from the faster increase in the PIT relative to the GDP, due to the progressivity of the individual income taxation[11]. This means an additional benefit compared to the PIT revenue they have been granted up to now. The gain will depend on the elasticity of the PIT to the taxable income in each Region[12] and on the evolution of this taxable income in the regional area, but the tax decisions at the level of the Federal Government will also have an impact. It should indeed be noted that the last PIT tax reform (2002-2006) resulted in a reduction of the global PIT in percentage of GDP in the last decade. The current system, that sets transfers regardless of the evolution of PIT, has therefore prevented the Regions from revenue losses that would have appeared in the case of a proportional surcharge on the PIT and charged to the Federal Government all the budgetary costs of the tax reform it has decided. Indeed, the YOY growth of the regional share in the current PIT grant equals (1 + the inflation rate) times (1 + real GDP YOY growth) multiplied by the change in the regional share in personal income tax revenue.

The **'incentive effect'** comes from the fact that the revenue of the Regions is going to depend directly from the evolution of the regional taxable income, while these regional taxable income variations are just partly taken into account in the current system, since the transfers are adjusted to national economic growth and shared across the Regions according to their tax capacity two years earlier. The new system is therefore expected

---

11. The PIT is indeed a progressive tax of which the inherent elasticity to the taxable income and to the GDP is above one.
12. Some studies have indeed shown that this elasticity is not exactly the same across the Regions (see Frogneux V. & Saintrain M., 2012, "L'élasticité de l'impôt des personnes physiques: approche macroéconomique prospective de l'élasticité nationale et de l'élasticité de l'impôt régionalisé", Working Paper 1-12, Federal Planning Bureau.

to improve efficiency and accountability of the fiscal federalism framework to the extent that Regions will be encouraged to implement effective policies from which they will more directly benefit, or that revenue losses will be incurred in case of poor economic performances.

However, this incentive effect must not be overestimated, mainly for two reasons. First of all, the relation between regional policies and regional taxable income is not so evident, in particular for the Brussels-Capital Region, with a share in national gross domestic product largely in excess of the share in taxable income since more than half of people working in this Region are living in the other Regions. Moreover, the Brussels-Capital Region has also to provide public goods and services with large externalities as it is the Capital Region and an important centre of activity and employment. Next, the incentive effect should be considered together with the equalisation mechanisms that prevent poorer Regions from a strong deterioration of their revenue in case of worsening of their economic situation (see below, paragraph 3.1.3a).

As already mentioned, by substituting a proportional surcharge on the PIT for the current PIT grant to the region, the reform has therefore gone deeper into the decentralisation of taxing power and has followed objectives of increased efficiency and accountability. The reform ensures however simultaneously that significant tax prerogatives remain at the federal level, such as the definition of the tax base (and the deductible expenses), some tax expenditure and the definition of bracket of the tax base which is a very important instrument to influence progressivity and redistribution function of the PIT. Such a distribution in the taxing power is consistent with some 'driving' aspects of the reform, i.e. to ensure the fiscal sustainability of the Federal Government in the long term and to preserve the progressive character of the PIT while avoiding harmful tax competition.

Finally attention should be paid to tax coordination across the levels of government. On the one hand, the decisions of the Federal Government concerning the income tax base will indeed have an impact on the PIT collected by the Regions and can lead to harmful vertical competition as no mechanism even informal is set by the law

Fiscal Federalism

to prevent from this vertical competition (see also 3.1.5). On the other hand, the New Institutional Agreement confirms that the Regions cannot engage in 'unfair competition', but it does not give any criterion to evaluate when competition is unfair[13].

3.1.2 THE NEW RESPONSIBILITIES OF THE REGIONS

As mentioned in the first part, the Sixth Reform of the State does not only change the funding arrangements of the Regions and the Communities, but it also provides an even more significant decentralisation in the provision of public goods and services. The Regions have been assigned new responsibilities regarding labour market policy as well as tax expenditure relating to housing, energy and service vouchers. The Regions will receive specific grants to finance these new responsibilities, but they will autonomously deal with it.

a) Labour market policy

Since 1980, the Regions are in charge of key labour market policies aspects among which job seekers training and placement. The social security system (unemployment and retirement benefit among others) as well as wage determination have remained however at the central level. Without undermining this principle, a direct implication of such a distribution is that the Regions do not deal with the consequences of their placement and training policies on the budgetary cost of unemployment and retirement benefit. Therefore, in order to resolve partially such a difficulty and to give the Regions incentives of getting the unemployed back to work, the law of 1980 provided each year the Regions an additional grant proportional to the creation of job contracts thanks to regional labour market programs. As far as no monitoring of these regional labour market programs has been made on the last years, a lump-sum grant has been transferred to the Region without incentive effect anymore. The poorly functioning of this measure was one of the triggers for a discussion on reforming distribution in labour market responsibilities.

---

13. The Agreement stipulates indeed that the mechanism of the 'conflict of interest' that a sub-central government can use to freeze some decisions from other sub-central government within a period of 60 days in case of conflict of interest will no longer apply in the case of the federal decisions regarding PIT.

Another driving force has come from the political will in some Regions to better align the labour market policies to regional needs and priorities. The level and the evolution of employment rates for various types of workers differ indeed across the Regions, with for instance low performance of youth employment in the Brussels-Capital Region and the Walloon Region, while the employment rate of the older workers is relatively lower in the Flemish Region and the Walloon Region[14].

This last motivation has been taken into account in the reform. Active labour market policies together with reduction in social security contributions for specific groups of workers have been transferred from the Federal Government (and Social Security) to the Regions. The Regions have therefore discretion either to extend, to limit or to reallocate these measures according to their priorities, their financial leeway, and the characteristics of their labour market.

Table 3: Labour market policies transferred to the Regions

LABOUR MARKET POLICY	INSTITUTIONAL AGREEMENT (MILLIONS OF 2011 EURO)	ESTIMATES FOR 2012 (MILLIONS OF EURO) (°)
Expenditure on labour market programmes	2.402	2.461
- Reduced social contributions for some target groups of workers	1.860	1.903
- Activation of unemployment benefits	541	558
Employment subsidy in the service vouchers system	1.444	1.489
Scrutiny of the availability of the unemployed	38	39
Other (allowances for career breaks, training, jobseekers placement, etc)	442	456
Total	**4.326**	**4.446**

Source: Own calculations based on the Agreement on the Sixth Reform of the State, Federal Planning Bureau (June forecasts).
(°) The figures of the Agreement are indexed to the GDP growth and the CPI for 2012 to ensure the consistency with the figures regarding tax expenditure.

Although wage determination and social protection of workers remain at the central level as foundation of the Federal State, it appears that the role of the Regions in the labour market policy has been significantly

---

14. See Conseil supérieur de l'Emploi, rapport 2011, pp.36-39, Hoge Raad voor de Werkgelegenheid: verslag 2011, pp.36-39.

strengthened by the last institutional agreement. This agreement is expected to promote political accountability of the Regions as they will be recognized as essential players in labour market policy in particular for specific groups of job seekers and will be assessed on their performance in this field.

b) Tax expenditure

As it has already been mentioned above, some tax expenditures originally implemented by the Federal Government will be devolved to the Regions in order to broaden their scope in the issues for which they are responsible such as housing and energy, and enable them to use the most relevant tax scheme.

Table 4: Tax expenditure transferred to the Regions by the last Institutional Agreement

TAX EXPENDITURE	ESTIMATES FOR 2012 (MILLIONS OF EURO)
Tax reliefs for the payment of mortgage loans	1.310
Tax reliefs for energy saving investment	447
Tax reliefs for acquisition of service vouchers (domestic services)	130
Others	10
Total	**1.897**

Source: Own calculations based on the Agreement on the Sixth Reform of the State and Federal Planning Bureau (June 2012 forecasts).
Note: as explained in footnote 8, the tax expenditure is estimated to 1.912 million euro in the Institutional Agreement. This figure is fictitious because based upon former forecasts of inflation & GDP growth and some reduction factor. The figure here has been derived using the current forecasts and the same reduction factor.

The most important component brings together all the tax deductions and tax cuts provided to the taxpayers for the payment of their mortgage loans.

c) How are these new responsibilities regarding labour market and tax expenditure financed?

Basically, the Regions will get non-earmarked grants to deal with their new responsibilities. The discretion of the Federal Government on these grants will be weak as far as the distribution formula will be set by the Special Law of Finance, while the Regions will be autonomous to spend the grants according to their priorities.

Table 5: Funding rules of the new regional responsibilities

	LABOUR MARKET POLICY	TAX EXPENDITURES
Budget (millions of euro)	4.446	1.897
What is transferred?	90% (=4,001)	60% (=1,147) - fiscal consolidation measures
-> Compensation?	Equalisation grant (10%)	Surcharge on PIT (40%)
How will the transfer evolve?	70% of Real GDP growth + prices growth	
-> Compensation?	Surcharge on PIT (above unit elasticity)	
Which distribution formula accross the Regions?	(federal) personal income tax yield	

Source: Agreement on the Sixth Reform of the State, Federal Planning Bureau (June 2012 forecasts).

A two-step approach will be implemented to allocate the grants to the Regions.

The vertical transfer: the grants will cover a part, but not the whole, of the expenditure related to the new responsibilities. This part is equivalent to 90% for labour market policy and 60% for tax expenditure, the remaining amount being supposed to be covered respectively by the equalisation grant and by the new surcharge on the PIT. To the extent that they will evolve according to prices evolution and 70% of the real GDP growth, the grants are supposed, as presented in the Institutional Agreement, to cover only partially the future needs of the Regions. It has indeed been decided to ensure fiscal neutrality for the Federal Government, as far as the Regions will benefit from the elasticity of the PIT to the GDP growth that is bigger than one under no policy change scenario.

The rules guiding the vertical transfer mean therefore that new responsibilities are also partly financed by taxing power, which establishes a link between regional tax policy and labour market policy. Moreover, fiscal consolidation is expected to influence the last parameters of the institutional reform since the agreement has provided that grants can be decreased by fiscal consolidation measures. So, until the special law is not formally concluded, the Federal Government has the right to tailor the transfers to the Regions.

The distribution across the Regions: the grants will be shared across the Regions according to their relative shares in the federal personal income tax revenue, following the idea that such a performance indicator is a good criterion to share fairly responsibilities regarding economic and tax policies.

It appears however that the current share of the federal budget designed to finance labour market programs for the benefit of the Walloon Region is higher than its relative income tax yield. The equalisation grant will compensate for this difference the first year of the reform implementation, but as this grant is expected to decrease (see below), this Region will probably no longer receive sufficient amounts to cover its current expenditure in labour market programs. Consideration should therefore be given to labour market policy in the Walloon Region as budgetary decisions are likely to be made (CESW, 2012, pp.41-51).

d) Other responsibilities

The last Institutional Agreement also mentions the devolution of other more limited responsibilities to the Regions (such as tourism, gas and electricity distribution prices, etc.), but without any detailed information, especially on their funding mechanism.

3.1.3 THE EQUALISATION TRANSFERS

The equalisation mechanism may be divided into two components for the Regions: an explicit solidarity transfer to the 'poorer' Regions, and a lump-sum transfer that is expected to ensure budget neutrality of the reform in the year of its implementation.

a) The solidarity transfer

Before 1989 the grant paid out from the proceeds of the federal PIT, was allocated amongst the Regions on the basis of three equally weighted factors: the regional share respectively in population, in the personal income tax revenue and in the surface of the country. Since 1989 the grant is horizontally divided solely on the basis of the regional shares in the personal income tax revenue. As compensation a solidarity mechanism was installed. This mechanism provided the Regions of which personal income tax per inhabitant is below the national average, a Federal transfer proportional to this deviation and adjusted to the regional population and to a lump-sum amount[15].

Figure 1: Regional share in the total Personal Income Tax revenue

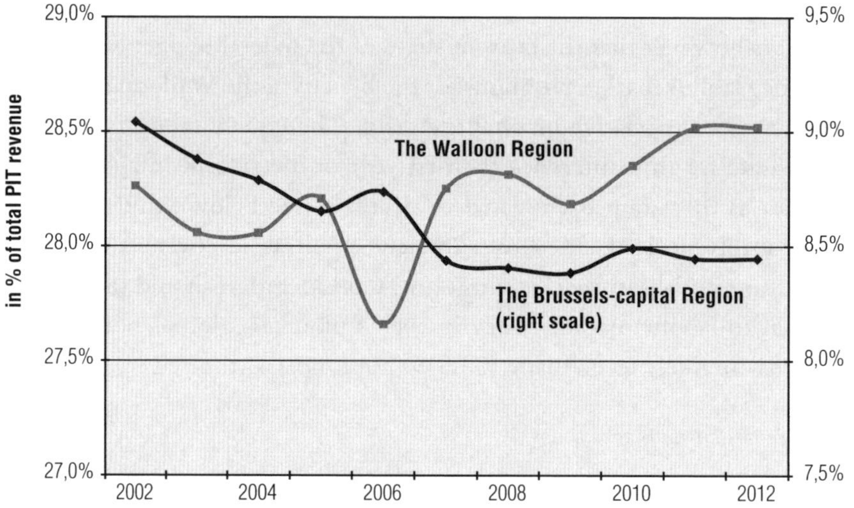

Source: Own calculations

This solidarity transfer was to help the 'poorer' Regions to catch up in economic terms with the other Regions in order to allow a convergence of regional economic performances, and to promote national growth in a country were the Regions are also trading partners. However, this mechanism has been on a regular basis to the core of the institutional debate. The system has therefore been perceived as non-efficient regarding its first objective, to the extent that in the last ten years, the relative income tax yield of the Brussels-Capital Region worsened and this of the Walloon Region did not significantly improve, with the exception of the years 2010 and 2011.

But this perception came from the fact that the solidarity is here defined with reference to the distribution of the personal income tax yield across the Regions, supposed to reflect a 'juste-retour' or 'fair-return' distribution. Such a reference leads to biased information on the relative position

---

15. The initial height of the basic amount has been determined in order to ensure budget neutrality in the initial year (1989) for the Walloon Region.

of the Regions. Indeed, the contribution of the Regions to all the revenue (VAT, excise duties, social security contributions, etc.) should be taken into account to define a 'fair-return' distribution, and not only the PIT contributions. As Decoster (2006,p.5) has shown on the basis of Household Budget Survey of 2001, this can change the relative position of the Regions as the contribution of the Walloon Region and the Brussels-Capital Region to indirect taxes are higher than to the PIT.

As calculated in the Special Finance Law, the solidarity transfer has however been associated to a **poverty trap** for the Walloon Region and the Brussels-Capital Region that would be generated by the solidarity transfer. According to some studies[16], these Regions are not encouraged to improve their economic performances as they receive fewer transfers from the Federal Government when the PIT levied on their area increases. In this case, the loss in the solidarity transfer could exceed indeed the gain they get in terms of PIT transferred.

The solidarity transfer appeared especially problematic when the revenue or the expenditure of the Regions is reported to the regional population. The revenue and the expenditure per capita are indeed lastingly greater in the Brussels-Capital Region and in the Walloon Region than in the Flemish Region[17]. This relationship reverses for the Walloon Region when excluding the solidarity transfer, while it persists for the Brussels-Capital Region but can be justified from other considerations such as the spillover effects, the status of capital, etc. The higher transfers per capita to the 'poorer' Regions can be perceived as fair temporarily and pursuing an efficiency objective, but their persistence suggests that the system overcompensates the economic weaknesses.

In this debate on Regional equalisation, some arguments can also be put forward to mitigate the discouraging effect of the system. First of all, the poverty trap is mitigated when taking into account the effect of GDP growth on own tax revenue (as registration duties, circulation taxes, etc), especially for the Brussels-Capital Region. It is also mitigated when doing the theoretical exercise to integrate revenue of the Walloon

---

16. Among others: Verdonck M., Cattoir Ph., Algoed K. (2009), Heremans D., Peeters Th., Van Hecke (2010).
17. Among others: Heremans D., Peeters Th., Van Hecke A. (2010), Denil F. (2009).

Region and this of the French-Speaking Community[18]. Next, a Region can face significant political difficulties when being financially dependent from another Region (Decoster & Valenduc, 2011, p.259). Finally, equalisation transfers are a main characteristic of the European economies, with relatively larger amounts in some countries such as Spain or the United-Kingdom (Decoster & Valenduc, 2011, p.258).

However, in a context of persistence of these transfers in Belgium and of increased regional transfers towards interpersonal solidarity (Social Security), the detrimental effects of the equalisation mechanism have been progressively highlighted. A greater pressure has therefore been brought on this aspect of the institutional framework, resulting in a reform of the equalisation formula, although the principle of a regional solidarity has remained (and has been extended to community expenditure).

The new solidarity mechanism will be determined as followed.

Table 6: New formula for the solidarity transfer

	FORMULA
Formula for the starting year	80% * ((Population of the Region/total population) - (PIT of the Region/total PIT°))*V
	V: piggyback income tax + grants shared according to tax capacity (regional grants + 50% of communities grants from PIT)
	(°) Regional component of the PIT that finances the Federal Government
Evolution formula	Initial amount adjusted each year to economic growth and prices evolution

Source: Agreement on the Sixth Reform of the State.

To set first the new solidarity mechanism, the Institutional Agreement compares the amount of PIT that will be returned to the Regions and the Communities and the grants that will be allowed to the Regions

---

18. The Communities also receive a grant from the Federal Government which is indexed to GDP growth and shared among them according to their tax capacity. This share is estimated as the regional tax capacity + a proportion of the tax capacity in the Brussels-Capital Region (20% for the Flemish Community, 80% for the French-Speaking Community).

and the Communities according to their tax capacity[19], to an hypothetic amount that they would have received in case of a distribution according to the population criterion (i.e. a need criterion). It has been decided that 80% of the deviation will be compensated. Compared with the current system, the new formula results in a lower solidarity transfer (but the growth rate is expected to be higher than under the actual formula). The first year of the reform implementation, the difference will be provided by means of the equalisation payment to the Walloon Region and the Brussels-Capital Region in order to ensure budgetary neutrality (see below, paragraph b).

In the following years the solidarity transfer is indexed to inflation and to real GDP growth, which has some implications:
− The developments in regional economic disparities will be less taken into account in the evolution of the solidarity transfer. In terms of regional equalisation, this appears therefore more as a lump-sum grant rather than a proportional grant;
− There will be no link anymore with the current grants which have been used to determine the initial basic amount

b) The equalisation grant

An equalisation grant is introduced to ensure overall budgetary neutrality in the initial year of the Sixth Reform of the State. The equalisation grant is constant in nominal terms the first 10 years. Afterwards it will be gradually phased out over the next 10 years. That grant can be positive (to be received) or negative (to be paid), and presents also an horizontal dimension as it will be paid by the Federal level and by the Region(s) benefiting from the 6th Reform of the State.

Each level of government will be provided the same amount compared to the current system, which means that those expected to get a net gain from the new mechanisms of revenue will have to give back this gain the first year.

---

19. More specifically the basic amount (V) is given by the piggy-back income tax revenue, the new grant for the Regions (work, tax expenditures), 50% of the PIT grant for the Communities and 50% of the Lambermont transfers.

The budgetary neutrality in the first year of reform implementation is an important principle to reach a compromise:
- It is politically easier for the levels of government that are reluctant to accept a reform as they perceived them as net losers to joint an agreement if the expected losses occur on the medium and long term and that some policy actions can be undertaken to prevent from such losses;
- The budgetary neutrality ensures a financial stability for the different entities that allows them to pursue their policies on an on-going basis.

In the following table, we illustrate at first the mechanism of the equalisation grant regarding the substitution of a regional piggy-back PIT for the current PIT grant.

Table 7: Gains or losses estimated for the different levels of Governments expected to be involved in the replacement of the PIT grant by a regional surcharge on the PIT (Piggy-back PIT) in the initial year of the Reform

ESTIMATES FOR 2012, EURO	FEDERAL	THE FLEMISH REGION	THE WALLOON REGION	THE BRUSSELS-CAPITAL REGION
The Current PIT grant (negative term deducted)	9.476.666	6.048.954	2.773.338	654.374
Regional shares		63.83%	29.26%	6.91%
Revenue from the new piggyback PIT (°)	9.834.480	6.218.208	2.781.951	834.321
Regional shares		63.23%	28.29%	8.48%
Gains (+)/ losses (-)	-357.814	-169.254	-8.613	-179.947

Source: own calculations based on the Institutional Agreement and on the 2012 adjusted federal budget
(°) After the deduction of the negative term and tax expenditure excluded.

The current PIT grant (art 33§4) is estimated at 14,134,068 euro in 2012, whereas the overall negative term amounts to 4,657,401 euro (of which the Walloon's Region negative term represents 1,216,255 euro). Given that the negative term has been corrected (to 4,299,587 euro), the revenue from the new piggy-back income tax is higher than the current PIT grant.

Fiscal Federalism

The expected share in piggy-back income tax revenue in 2012 is 28.29% for the Walloon Region and 63.23% for the Flemish Region, which is slightly different from the current share in the PIT grant. The piggy-back income tax revenue for the Flemish Region is expected to be 6,218,208 euro, which represent a gain of 169,254 euro compared to the current PIT grant taking into account the negative term. That gain in the initial year will be skimmed off because it belongs to the equalisation grant to be paid by the Flemish Region.

The equalisation grant can indeed be calculated for each component of the future revenue of the Regions when comparing the amounts they will be transferred to and the amounts they currently benefit. The latter can be estimated by the current Special Law of Finance as far as the solidarity transfer and the PIT grant are concerned. When considering the new competencies (labour market and tax expenditure), reference amounts have to be determined. These can be calculated as the estimated regional shares in the Federal budget. In the case of tax expenditure, these regional shares come from the Inventory of tax expenditures that publishes the regional distribution of these expenditures[20]. Regarding labour market, the reference amounts are based on regional share estimated to 52% for the Flemish Region, 35.1% for the Walloon Region and 12.9% for the Brussels-Capital Region[21].

Table 8: Various components of the equalisation grant to be transferred (+) to or to be paid by (-) the Regions in the wake of the Sixth Reform of the State (estimate for 2012)

ESTIMATE FOR 2012, MILLIONS OF EURO (°)	THE FLEMISH REGION	THE WALLOON REGION	THE BRUSSELS-CAPITAL REGION	THE FEDERAL GOVERNMENT
Labour Market	-191,5	412,5	223,6	-444,6
Tax expenditure	81,6	-16,1	-65,4	0,0
Piggy-back PIT	-169,3	-8,6	-179,9	357,8
Solidarity transfer	0	222,6	71,5	-294,1
Total	-279,2	610,3	49,8	-380,9

Source: Own calculations based on the Institutional Agreement and 2012 adjusted federal budget
(°): a positive sign means that an equalisation grant will be transferred, and then that the Region is expected to lose from the new mechanism while a negative sign means that an equalisation grant will be paid.

20. The most recent figure is for the 2009 income.
21. The current labour market grant (drawing rights) excluded.

For instance, the Walloon Region benefits in the initial year from the substitution of the Pit grant/tax expenditure by a piggy-back income tax (gain estimated at 8.6+16.1 million euro). However, the introduction of the new grant related to labour market responsibilities together with the new solidarity mechanism entails a budgetary loss compared with the expenditure received in the unchanged policy scenario. These losses, amounting to respectively 412,5 and 222,6 million euro, dominate the benefits in the initial year and result in a net equalisation grant of 610,3 million euro to be received by the Walloon Region.

Consequently, if the principle of equalisation is relatively easy to understand, it will no longer be evident to ensure its practical application. The lump-sum equalisation transfers are indeed currently assessed on the basis of provisional parameters, and they will need to be updated according to the parameters that will be set finally by the law. Moreover, since the Federal government has cut into some tax expenditures expected to be devolved to the Regions, this raises the question whether this decision must be taken into account in the evaluation of the lump-sum equalisation transfers.

It should also be noticed that the results of the Brussels-Capital Region in the table above need to be analysed in the light of its refinancing.

3.1.4 REFINANCING THE BRUSSELS-CAPITAL REGION

One of the main challenges of the fiscal federalism framework in Belgium is to provide the Brussels-Capital Region a fair proportion of the revenue generated in the country area that allows an efficient provision of public goods and services in this Region. The determination of a "fair proportion" is indeed rather problematic when taking into account following considerations.

An important part of the gross domestic product is generated on the area of the Brussels-Capital Region, as it gathers main head offices of firms and of administrations. In the same time, taxable income in this Region is relatively low, as more than half people working in the Brussels-Capital Region live in the other Regions, and as the revenue of

European Commission civil servants living in Belgium and especially in the Brussels-Capital Region is non- taxable.

Moreover, to the extent that the Brussels-Capital Region is the capital of Belgium and of the European Union, and that it receives everyday many commuters, a major part of its budget is allocated to the provision of public goods with strong spill-over effects, such as public transport, security or cultural infrastructures. The Region gets additional grants to cover these specific responsibilities, but these have often been considered as insufficient (de Callataÿ 2007,van der Stichele 2003).

It has been highlighted however that the financial problems of the Brussels-Capital Region are also somehow endogenous due to inefficiency problems in political structures and especially due to an unemployment rate which is one of the highest amongst capital cities (see notably OECD 2009).

Although the Region also gets the solidarity transfer since 1997 as the income per capita is below the national average, this transfer cannot be considered as a funding of the specific tasks or as compensation for the loss of taxable income that benefit the two other Regions. This solidarity transfer is indeed expected to help this Region to face its own economic difficulties, such as the high unemployment rate, the insufficient knowledge of languages and the average low level of inhabitant's training.

Giving these various elements and in the slipstream of a solution for the BHV electoral district, the Reform has provided the Brussels-Capital Region additional grants that can be divided in two parts according to their implementation date: a first part, composed mainly of earmarked grants has already been implemented in 2012, while a second part which takes into account the impact of commuters flows, will be transferred when the new financing law will be voted.

Table 9: Additional grants to the Brussels-Capital Region (millions of euro)

(MILLIONS OF EURO)	2012	2013	2014	2015
First part	**134**	**175**	**217**	**258**
Earmaked grants (mobility, security,…)	110	151	192	233
Non earmaked grants	24	24	25	25
Second part	**0**	**61**	**129**	**203**
Grant commuters	0	13	28	44
Grant European civil servants	0	48	101	159
Total	**134**	**236**	**346**	**461**

Source: Agreement on the Sixth Reform of the State.

About the half of the additional grants is earmarked and purposed to allow the Region meeting its specific responsibilities of capital and centre of activity. The second part of the grants relates to the loss in revenue faced by the Region due to the taxation of commuters to their place of residence and due to the high proportion of European Commission civil servants on the regional area. The grant supposed to compensate for commuters is a horizontal grant financed by the two other Regions.

This additional funding system calls for some considerations:
- The rather 'weak' spending power of the Brussels-Capital Region for the specific grants (first part) is consistent with the fact that these are purposed to deal with responsibilities of Capital and employment centre that involve all the parts of the country;
- The amount of 461 million euro is close to the results of some previous studies (de Callataÿ 2007 and van der Stichele2003 in OECD 2009);
- This amount is however expected to remain below 0.1% of the GDP after 2015, with the grant commuters and the grant civil servants remaining constant from '2015' onwards to achieve this target. The refinancing system has therefore no dynamic reference criteria after 2015(for instance the numbers of commuters). By this lack of dynamic, a gap between the revenue and the needs of the Brussels-Capital Region could be observed on the middle term with to little resources for the Region, e.g. in the case of growing number of commuters, or a windfall gain in the opposite case;

- A small part of the grant is financed by the two others Regions. This would have been an incentive to limit fiscal competition across the Regions, if it has been expected to evolve in proportion to the number of commuters.

3.1.5 Attempt of empirical assessment over the next few years

In this section we attempt to estimate the budgetary impact of the Reform on the Regions over the next 10 years in terms of gains/losses compared to an unchanged policy scenario. The macroeconomic parameters (GDP growth, inflation) rely on the medium-term outlook of the Federal Planning Bureau (May 2012) and on its inflation forecasts of July 2012.We also make various assumptions, notably in terms of PIT elasticity and tax capacity (see table in annex). We assume in particular that the elasticity of PIT revenue to the real GDP per capita equals 1.5[22].

Furthermore, in the constant policy scenario, the YOY growth of the tax and labour market expenditures are expected to keep ahead with the economic growth rate[23].It should be noticed that neither the refinancing of the Brussels-Capital Region nor the higher contributions for the pensions of the own civil servants are taken into account.

The budgetary impact is calculated taking into account the effect of the equalisation grant. Not only in the initial year but also in the following 10 years the equalisation grant is to be paid or received. Due to this equalisation grant there is no budgetary gain or loss in the initial years but the dynamics of the new financial arrangements will be different. Hence there can be budgetary losses/gains in the future.

A crucial parameter in determining the future budgetary outcome is the GDP elasticity of the personal income tax revenue. The higher this elasticity the greater the gain (loss) for the Regions (Federal Government) as in the constant policy scenario the personal income tax revenue accrue

---

22. This is the implicit elasticity used during the negotiations (see Decoster and Sas (2012)).
23. In the future measures probably will be needed to stabilize these tax expenditures in terms of GDP.

for 100% to the Federal Government (and hence the elasticity gain) whereas the PIT grant evolves with economic growth.

With a GDP elasticity of personal income tax revenue equal to 1.5, the budgetary gains for the Regions increase over time, especially regarding the Flemish Region. Only in the first years of the reform the Walloon Region should suffer budgetary losses. Given the dynamics of the new arrangements, the benefit for this Region and for the Brussels-Capital Region resulting from the PIT surcharge should compensate the (initial) losses on the solidarity transfer and on the devolution of the new responsibilities. The gain for the Flemish Region (estimated at 518 million euro in 2020) should also compensate the budgetary losses for the Flemish Community (see further).

Table 10: Expected gains and losses from the new revenue mechanisms for the various governments over the next years (equalisation grant being deducted), PIT elasticity to the real GDP per capita set at 1,5

MILLION OF EUROS	2012 GROSS	NET	2013	2014	2015	2016	2017	2018	2019	2020
The Flemish Region	-279,2	0.0	36,2	85,4	147,0	218,9	292,2	364,7	437,2	518,0
The Walloon Region	610,3	0.0	-12,0	-20,2	-24,3	-26,3	-7,7	21,1	47,0	77,4
The Brussels-Capital Region	49,8	0.0	12,5	29,6	40,8	53,3	51,1	52,8	68,6	84,7
The Federal Government	-380,9	0.0	-36,7	-94,8	-163,5	-245,8	-335,7	-438,6	-552,7	-680,1
The General Government	0,0	0.0	0.0	0.0	0.0	0.0	0.0	0.0	0.0	0.0

Source: Own calculations based on MT outlook Federal Planning Bureau and on the 2012 adjusted federal budget

The magnitude of the GDP elasticity of PIT revenue has caused a lot of controversy during the negotiations, as the observed elasticity of the PIT to (real) GDP over the last decade has been lower than 1.5 since the Federal Government implemented a tax reform reducing tax burden. If we set a GDP elasticity of personal income tax revenue equal to 1, which reflects the observed elasticity during the previous decades[24], and also results from the assumption that some measures will be implemented

---

24. We can indeed calculate that on the previous period (1990-2007/2009), the PIT kept ahead with the real GDP according to an average elasticity close to 1 (0.97 over 1990-2007, and slightly lower when deducting the exemptions on withholding taxes from the Federal Government).

to offset the inherent increase of PIT compared to taxable income, the budgetary outcomes will be totally different. The Flemish Region should lose revenue, and there would be no further compensation for the losses at the community level. As regards the Walloon Region, the PIT revenue does no longer compensate the budgetary losses incurred with the other aspects of the reform. These results have also been highlighted by Decoster & Sas (2012).

Table 11: Expected gains and losses from the new revenue mechanisms for the various governments over the next years (equalisation grant being deducted), PIT elasticity to the real GDP growth per capita is set at 1

MILLION OF EUROS	2012 GROSS	NET	2013	2014	2015	2016	2017	2018	2019	2020
The Flemish Region	-279,2	0.0	-8,1	-20,4	-32,8	-45,7	-64,7	-92,1	-127,9	-164,0
The Walloon Region	610,3	0.0	-31,7	-67,2	-103,8	-142,7	-164,1	-178,9	-200,2	-221,1
The Brussels-Capital Region	49,8	0.0	6,6	15,1	16,0	16,4	1,3	-11,2	-10,7	-11,3
The Federal Government	-380,9	0.0	33,2	72,4	120,6	172,0	227,4	282,2	338,9	396,4
The General Government	0,0	0.0	0.0	0,0	0,0	0,0	0,0	0,0	0,0	0,0

Source: Own calculations based on MT outlook Federal Planning Bureau and on the 2012 adjusted federal budget

What we observe in such a context is that, conversely to what happened on the last decade, the Regions would be impacted in case of federal reforms reducing tax burden. As we are not anymore in a context of 'unchanged policy', the question to be addressed here is however less the evaluation of gains and losses than the exercise of discretionary power regarding PIT. How this power will be dealt with by the different levels of governments, and which tax coordination is to be provided? This issue is especially sensitive in the context of fiscal consolidation.

3.2 The Communities

The Sixth Reform of the State also changes the financing arrangements of the Communities providing the devolution of new spending obligations in the social policy and significant changes in the revenue mechanisms.

Those measures confirm the special feature of the Belgian fiscal federalism where Communities and Regions exist side by side, with overlap.

The refinancing as decided in 2001 will be scaled back and more weight will be given to the demographic factor in the division of the grants amongst the two main Communities.

Table 12: Revenue structure of the Communities under the current system compared to the Sixth Reform of the State

	CURRENT SYSTEM		**REFORM**
Tax revenue transferred to the Regions and the Communities (VAT & PIT)	Basic grant (PIT)	=	Basic grant (PIT)
	Basic grant (VAT)	=	Basic grant (VAT)
	Grant for radio and television licence fee (PIT)	→	Grant for radio and television licence fee (VAT)
	Refinancing from Lambermont Agreement (LA) (VAT)	↗	Refinancing from LA shared according to number of pupils (VAT)
		↘	Refinancing from LA shared according to tax capacity (PIT)
Grants	Grants for foreign students	=	Grants for foreign students
	Grants for National Lottery	=	Grants for National Lottery
		+	Grants for new responsibilities in social policy (family allowances, health care, elderly care)

Source: Agreement on the Sixth Reform of the State.

Furthermore, some aspects of the social policy will be transferred to the Communities. These are family allowances, elderly care (care homes, hospitals, etc.) and a part of health care. The following part of the text looks first at the consequences of the new revenue distribution across the Communities. Then, the transfer of responsibilities is analysed with an emphasis to the driving forces that lead to this transfer and the issues that arise for the Communities.

3.2.1 EVOLUTION IN THE FINANCING ARRANGEMENTS OF THE CURRENT RESPONSIBILITIES

As they have no taxing power (see part I), Communities are mainly financed by federal grants funded through VAT and PIT revenue. The

Lambermont Agreement (2002) provided the Communities additional amounts of VAT to ensure fiscal sustainability and adequate financing of education especially in the French-Speaking Community. These additional amounts called 'Refinancing' were composed of further lump-sum transfers and of a linkage to the economic growth (according to a coefficient of 91%). At the same time, however, the Lambermont Agreement introduced the personal income tax capacity as criterion of VAT distribution across the Communities while the number of pupils in each Community was traditionally used. In practice, over a 10 years transition period, the 'refinancing' was expected to be shared fully according to tax capacity by 2012.

Consequently, the proportion of VAT transfer distributed following the numbers of pupils decreased on the last decade as well as the implicit solidarity ensured by such a key (see figure 2), the gap between the two lines on the chart reflecting the proportion shared according to tax capacity (i.e. all the refinancing in 2012).

Figure 2: Evolution of the VAT transfers over the last decade

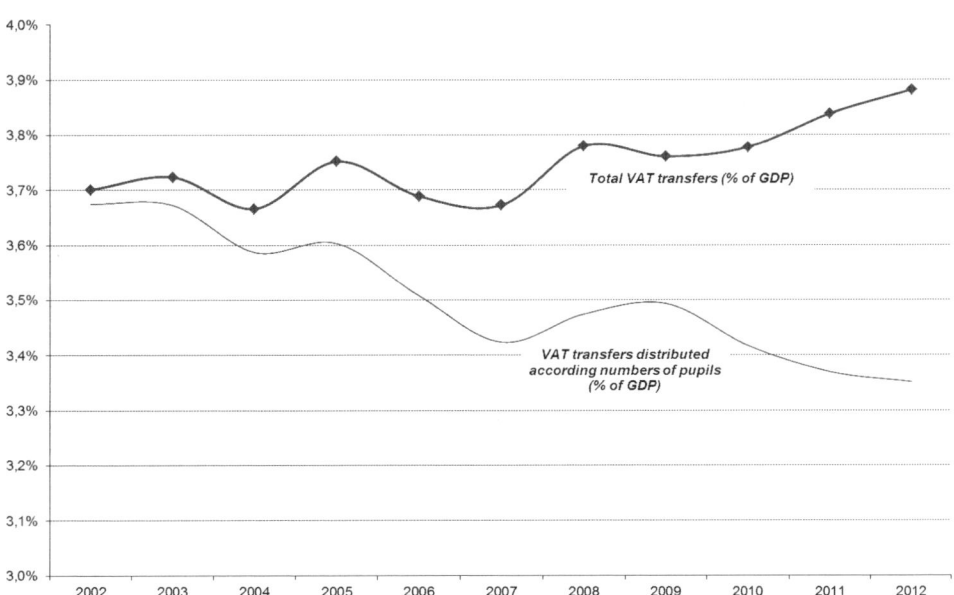

Source: Own calculations based on Federal budget.

As a result, the VAT transferred to the Flemish Community grew clearly faster over the past decade (see figure 3), the income tax yield being a more favourable criterion for this entity than the number of pupils. As far as such a distribution has been considered as a major challenge for the French-Speaking negotiators, a correction of the previous provisions has been made.

In the initial year of the Sixth Reform, the global VAT grant will be calculated according to the present rules, but the Lambermont means (refinancing) will be scaled down as their relative share in the VAT grant is set at its 2010 level (lower than the 2012 level). The other component of the VAT grant, called 'basic grant' will therefore become higher in the initial year and will be indexed to inflation, 0.91% of the economic growth and to the evolution of the number of children aged less than 18 in the Community where it is the more favourable (i.e. the French-speaking Community up to now). This grant will be shared according to the number of pupils in each Community.

The Lambermont means, such as set in the initial year, will be now included in the PIT grant transferred by the Federal Government to the Communities and will be indexed to inflation and 82.5% of real GDP growth. Since these will no longer be linked to the number of children aged less than 18, which is expected to grow further (compared to the '2012' level), there are some additional savings for the Federal Government. Otherwise, the Lambermont means will be distributed, as in the current system, on the basis of the relative shares of the Communities in the federal PIT[25].

The PIT grant transferred to the Communities by the Federal Government will no longer be indexed for 100% to real GDP growth but only for 82.5%.

The R&T licence fee will be allocated among the two Communities on the basis of the relative number of pupils (6-17 years old) and will follow the YOY growth of the VAT (basic) grant. Currently the R&T licence fee is specified for each Community and is indexed to inflation only.

---

25. With the distribution of the PIT in the Brussels-Capital Region remaining based on a key 80%/20% (respectively for the French-Speaking Community and the Flemish Community).

Fiscal Federalism

Figure 3: Evolution of the VAT transfers over the last decade: distribution across the Communities

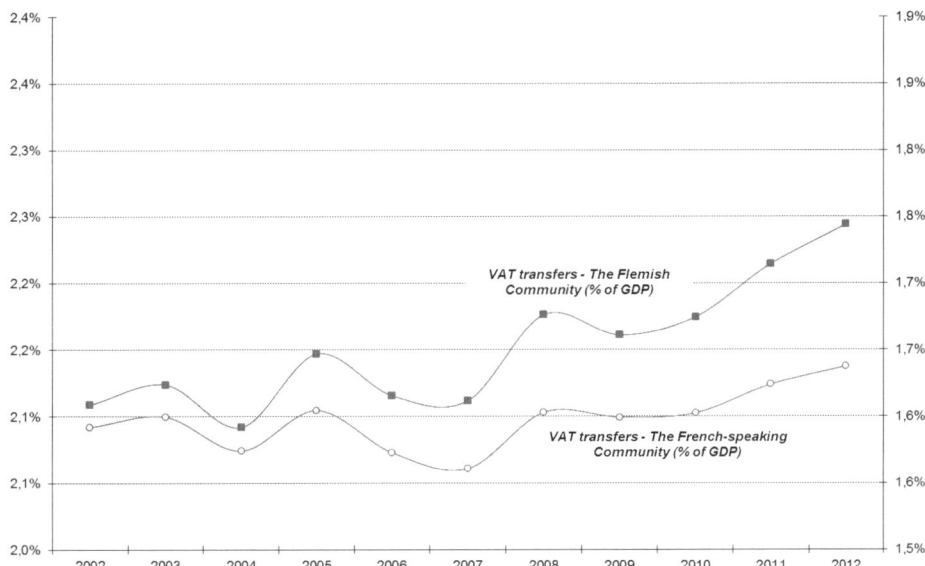

Source: Own calculations based on Federal budget.

3.2.2 EQUALISATION GRANT

Similarly to the Regions, the new financial arrangements for the Communities are made budgetary neutral in the initial year for all the governments involved. For every government an equalisation grant is calculated taking into account the gains and losses of the new arrangements in the initial year vis-à-vis the current arrangements (grants under the unchanged policy scenario).

Table 13: Details of the equalisation grants transferred to (+) and paid by (-) the Communities

ESTIMATE FOR 2012, MILLIONS OF EURO	THE FLEMISH COMMUNITY	THE FRENCH-SPEAKING COMMUNITY	THE FEDERAL GOVERNMENT
Grant for R&T license fee	69,2	-69,2	0,0
PIT grant	-17,6	17,6	0,0
VAT grant	20,3	-20,3	0,0
Total	**71,9**	**-71,9**	**0,0**

Source: Own calculations based on the Institutional Agreement and on 2012 adjusted budget.
(°) Note: a positive sign means that an equalisation grant will be received as the Community is expected to lose from the new mechanism in the initial year whereas a negative sign means that an equalisation grant will have to be paid.

In the initial year there are no losses or gains for the Federal Government. As the new arrangements imply a net transfer from the Flemish community towards the French-speaking community, this will be compensated by an equalisation payment from the French-speaking community towards the Flemish community. This equalisation grant is determined by the gain/loss in the first year of the Reform implementation. In the following ten years this grant is kept constant in nominal terms.

3.2.3 New responsibilities: rationale and financing arrangements

Driving forces towards decentralisation of social protection existed for a long time in the Flemish part of the country, where the regional social policy has always been a sphere of high interest. Various elements reflect this phenomenon, notably the implementation of a care-insurance scheme since 2001, that provides elderly people living in the Flemish Region an allowance to increase welfare in case of high care dependency. The allowance is financed by a mandatory contribution of each inhabitant of the Flemish Region[26]. It also appears that the share of the expenditure designed to social protection is higher in the Flemish Community than in the French-Speaking Community (Deschamps & al., 2011).

There has always been however a strong reluctance to decentralise the social protection in the French-speaking population since such decentralisation is expected to jeopardise the Federal Social Security System that lies at the heart of the Federal State, and to dismantle the national model of insurance and solidarity across people within the country that has been implemented since the end of the Second War.

It should be noted however that Belgium has been characterised up to now by a very low level of decentralisation in health care and social protection in general compared to other Federal Countries as Spain, Austria or

---

26. People living in the Brussels-Capital Region can choose to contribute to the care-dependence scheme.

Switzerland[27]. Political pressure to decentralise some aspects of social protection aligns therefore in the underlying trend of the European countries.

This underlying trend meets some political requirements to reduce solidarity transfers within the countries where socio-economic differences across the sub-central governments are progressively increasing and where policy preferences diverge across regions. In Belgium, as some interregional transfers to the benefit of the French-speaking population can be identified from the Social Security System, the decentralisation of some aspects of social policy also provides an opportunity to set new distribution mechanisms that promote accountability rather than solidarity and decrease the solidarity transfers across the population.

Furthermore, some theoretical approaches promote to some extent the decentralisation of the redistributive function including social action, as the local governments are better informed of the population specific needs and as the richer people should contribute easily for their 'neighbours' (Denil, Mignolet, Mulquin, 2004). Such decentralisation also allows for the implementation of reforms by some sub-national entities on which other entities can draw ('learning from others').

Conversely, there are arguments in favour of the centralisation of the social protection. This prevents harmful competition on social spending across the Communities. Such competition can lead to adverse selection phenomenon with the wealthier people abandoning area where high contribution are collected to finance high level of redistribution, and raises therefore the issue of equity across inhabitants within a country. Moreover, the centralisation of the Social Security System is often combined with the centralisation of the process of wage determination. This latter allows for more equity across working people but also for more efficiency as the firms do not deal with various social partners to negotiate the wages.

---

27. Based on OECD database, it can be calculated that the States governments deal with 2% of total health care in Belgium compared to 30% in Austria, 91% in Spain and 86% in Switzerland. The difference is lower regarding broadly social protection as the proportion of the States governments in total spending is 7% in Belgium compared to 15% in Austria, 10% in Germany, 30% in Spain and 29% in Switzerland.

By decentralising family allowances and some limited aspects of health care and elderly care, the Sixth Reform attempted to strike a compromise between these opposite views. The following table gives some information on how big are these transfers and how it will be distributed.

Table 14: New responsibilities transferred to the Communities

	ESTIMATE FOR 2012 (MILLIONS OF EURO)	DISTRIBUTION ACCROSS THE COMMUNITIES	EVOLUTION FORMULA
Family allowances	5,822	Population 0-18 years in each Community	Evolution of the population 0-18 years in each Community + prices evolution
Elderly care (care homes, hospitals and social allowance)	2,981	Population aged 80 years and over in each Community	Evolution of the population aged 80 years and older in each Community + prices evolution + growth GDP per capita
Other health care and assistance (°)	1,230	Population in each Community	82.5% of GDP growth + prices evolution
Fund to finance specific childcare (°°)	77	to be defined	to be defined

Source: Institutional Agreement on the Reform of the State.
(°) FESC, (°°) Hospitals buildings, psychiatric hospitals

Regarding the devolution of family allowances to the Communities, it should be noted that, to avoid to have two separate regimes in the Brussels-Capital Region, the family allowances will be managed by the joint Commission to the Communities (COCOM) in this area, a body made up for cooperation regarding Community matters in the Brussels-Capital Region.

In contrast to the spending obligations transferred to the Regions, the responsibilities devolved to the Communities will be fully financed through grants and will be shared across the Communities according to needs criteria such as population. This approach reflects the will to observe a more equal distribution of social policy than taxable income given that social policy as well as education is considered as national public goods. In such a case, there is a room for equalisation mechanism as suggested by one of the main rule of the reform that calls for "taking into account population and pupils criteria".

However, despite the maintenance of solidarity through the distribution formula, the Reform involves many issues and challenges regarding the new responsibilities transferred.

One of these challenges comes from the symmetry between the payment of the social benefits that is transferred to the Communities and the collect of the social contributions designed to finance these allocations that remains a prerogative of the Social Security. In such a case, the insurance approach of the Social Security that promotes equal benefits for equivalent taxpayers will probably no longer be strictly implemented as the Communities are expected to make different choices regarding family allowances or elderly care. The interpretation of the insurance principle should then become larger and should refer to the possibility for each inhabitant to choose freely its place to live and therefore its level of allowances (de Borman and de Briey, 2012). Since this possibility is rather theoretical, this raises however the question of horizontal equity.

In the inclusion of the entitlement to family allowances in the Constitution, and the convergence of the family allowances of self-employed with these of employees that is provided in the Institutional Agreement, we can see a preoccupation of the negotiators regarding equity and an attempt to ensure a minimum standard across the country regarding child allowances. This decision is probably based on the fiscal federalism reform of 1989 that has included in the Constitution (art. 24) the principle of equivalent access and equal opportunities in the education system as this system was just devolved to the Communities (de Borman and de Briey, 2012).

It appears otherwise that under the current system the average family allowance is higher in the Walloon and the Brussels area than in the Flemish area as they have more beneficiaries of increased allowances for socio-demographic reasons. The amounts granted to the French-Speaking Community and to the COCOM that will deal with the allowances in the Brussels-Capital Region will therefore just partly cover the current needs regarding family allowances (CESW, 2012).

Moreover, since the grants financing health care responsibilities will evolve according to a part of the GDP growth, this evolution will now depend on the income developments rather than on the needs (de Borman and de Briey, 2012). It should also be noted that the evolution is going to be lower than the growth rule of the health care expenditure (4.5% in real terms).

Finally the Reform will lead the Communities to make policy choices regarding these new responsibilities in social protection, not only in terms of levels and standards of social protection but also in the way to manage these new tasks. It is an open question to see if it will be with a strong implication of social partners as it is the case in the current Federal Social Security or with a prevalent role of the sub-central government and the predominance of an administrative approach (de Borman and de Briey,2012).

3.2.4 ATTEMPT OF EMPIRICAL ASSESSMENT OVER THE NEXT FEW YEARS

As for the Regions, we compare the forecasted budgetary outcomes under the new arrangements with the budgetary forecasts given the current arrangements for the Communities. This comparison also relies on the medium-term outlook of the Federal Planning Bureau (May 2012 + inflation forecasts July 2012) and is based on various assumptions (see table in annex). We do not take into account the budgetary effects of the transfer of the new expenditures to the Communities (contrary to the Regions as few information is available on the evolution of those under no policy change scenario). Hence, budgetary effects to the COCOM are not considered here. As for the Regions, the higher contributions for the pensions of the own civil servants are not taken into account.

The fifth Reform of the State involved a refunding of both communities, albeit at different speed[28]. The Sixth reform will refinance both the Federal Government and the French-speaking community. The addi-

---

28. Expressed in per capita (total population) terms the gap in the per capita grant between the Flemish and the French-Speaking Community has been reduced by the fifth Reform of the State and would become positive at the end of this decade.

tional means for the former are expected to be used to pay the higher pension contributions. The criterion of impoverishment has not been considered at the level of the Flemish Community: depending on the elasticity of the PIT revenue the losses at the Community level will or will not be compensated by the gains of the Flemish Region.

Table 14: Expected gains and losses from the new revenue mechanisms for the various governments over the next years (equalisation grant being deducted)

MILLION OF EUROS	2012 GROSS	NET	2013	2014	2015	2016	2017	2018	2019	2020
The Flemish Community	-71,9	0,0	-2,1	-45,3	-94,6	-146,1	-206,1	-272,0	-342,0	-412,6
The French-Speaking Community	71,9	0,0	28,0	33,4	39,9	47,9	59,4	74,0	90,5	105,2
The Federal Government	0,0	0,0	-25,9	11,9	54,7	98,3	146,7	198,0	251,5	307,4
General Government	0,0	0,0	0,0	0,0	0,0	0,0	0,0	0,0	0,0	0,0

Source: Own calculations based on MT outlook Federal Planning Bureau and on the 2012 adjusted federal budget

3.3 Two accountability mechanisms for the Regions and the Communities

The Sixth Reform finally provides the implementation of two accountability mechanisms regarding respectively the pensions of the civil servants and the investment in renewable energy.

The accountability mechanism regarding the pensions meets one of important issue of the Belgian fiscal federalism that has already been raised, and refers to the fact that the pensions of the civil servants of the Regions and the Communities administration are financed by the Federal Government. The financing of these pensions have indeed never been decentralised during the previous institutional reforms, since this was considered as a share of social protection that remained a core responsibility of the Federal level.

Some attempts have been made to involve the Regions and the Communities in the financing of the pension expenditure of their civil servants but they led to a rather limited contribution. In particular, a

Special Law of 2003 brought a new mechanism called 'accountability contribution' but has never been effectively applied.

However, given that the ageing costs mainly come under the Federal Government (Social Security) as well as the public debt service, and that the latter financial position strongly deteriorated notably with the emergence of the economic crisis (but also due to a lack of prefunding of the ageing costs via a greater debt reduction), a broad consensus has been reached in view of a greater involvement of the sub-national entities in the funding of ageing cost. One solution is suggested by transferring to the sub-national entities a share of the cost of their civil servant pension scheme, as it was even recommended among others by the OECD (OECD, 2009, p.63).

The Sixth Reform of the State materialised this consensus by providing the effective implementation by 2012 of the Special Law of 2003. Hence the Regions and the Communities should pay to the Federal Government an additional amount of about 90 million euro in 2012 through accountability contribution (FPB, 2012, p.119). From 2016, a new mechanism that measures the contribution as a growing share of the regional and community civil servant payroll[29] can be applied as soon as the amount exceeds this resulting from the Special Law of 2003. According to some estimates, the contribution of the sub-national entities should reach in total 0.21% of GDP by 2030 (Bisciari and Van Hensel, 2012, p.84).

The Reform also provides an accountability mechanism to encourage the Regions to invest in energy efficiency. In practice, the Regions will be assigned multi-annual targets in reducing greenhouse gas emissions in the building sector. They will get a bonus from the Federal Government if they surpass their objective while they will have to pay the Federal Government a fine if they miss their target. In this case, the amount transferred will be proportional to the gap and the Federal Government will in turn use it to invest in reducing greenhouse gas

---

29. Actually, this contribution will reach a maximum of 8.86% of the gross payroll that is comparable to the rate applied on the payroll of the contract staff.

emissions. The operational details of such a mechanism are expected to be detailed in a following law.

It should be noticed that the accountability mechanisms are not taken into account in the equalisation transfers as these mechanisms will lead to net transfers across level of governments.

4. CONCLUSION AND OUTLOOK

The Sixth Reform of the State provides a significant devolution of new responsibilities to the Regions and to the Communities, and implies major changes in the revenue mechanisms (designed to these entities).

The Communities receive new responsibilities regarding childcare (family allowances) and health care (elderly care among others). Such decentralisation allows for 'learning from others', with the implementation of specific reforms in one Community providing room for improvement in the other Communities. On the revenue side, the decisions regarding the Communities are characterised by the prevalence of solidarity across the entities, in compliance with the principle that national public goods (education, health and childcare) of which the Communities are in charge must be more equally distributed than the income. This solidarity has been materialised by using demographic keys to share spending power regarding new responsibilities, but also by switching to growing importance of the pupil's criterion in the distribution of the Lambermont transfers (refinancing).

Moreover, a part of the transfers financing current responsibilities are now evolving according to less generous parameters, as the PIT grant becomes only partially linked to the economic growth (82.5%). As a result of the new vertical and horizontal distribution of the *current transfers* the Federal Government, as well as the French Community, should benefit from the reform while the Flemish Community should receive less revenue compared to an unchanged policy scenario. Considering the *new responsibilities of the Communities,* we have too little information available to make a global empirical evaluation over the next years. However, relying on some elements, it appears that policy choices will probably have to be done regarding social protection standards and social governance, especially in the French-Speaking Community where the current use of Federal Budget regarding family allowances remains higher than the share expected to be transferred on the basis of demographic keys.

Taxing power of the Regions has been extended by the Sixth Reform of the State, as a significant part of their revenue will rely on a piggyback income tax (surcharge on the Personal Income Tax) and as they will get the competence for tax expenditure related to their responsibilities (housing, energy saving). The Regions will be autonomous to increase or decrease the surcharge rate and the tax expenditure, within some limits to preserve the progressive character of the Personal Income Tax and to avoid unfair tax competition (while the latter is not defined). Furthermore, the Regions will receive additional responsibilities regarding labour market, and in particular active labour market policies.

The increase of taxing power and the devolution of new responsibilities to the Regions are expected to allow these entities to better align their policies to their preferences and their priorities. From the budgetary perspective, the impact of the Sixth Reform of the State on the Regions depends on some mechanisms. At first, the Regions will benefit from the faster growth than GDP of the Personal Income Tax, as part of their revenue becomes a proportion of the PIT. This benefit depends however on the elasticity of the PIT. It is estimated to 1.58 (to the real income per capita) by the Federal Planning Bureau under a no policy change scenario. In practice, it could be however lower if the inherent increase of the PIT revenue was (partly) offset by federal tax reforms reducing tax burden (which corresponds usually to the general assumption regarding long-term elasticity of the PIT). Next, the grants designed to finance additional labour market and tax expenditure should just partly cover the current expenditure, as they are linked partially to the real economic growth (70%). This provision is supposed to compensate the benefit for the Regions resulting from the proportional surcharge and ensure a kind of neutrality for the Federal level. Finally, the solidarity transfer from the Federal Government to the Regions of which PIT per capita is lower than the national average is reformed. The equalisation will now more refer to the needs of the entities than to the regional differences between income tax yields, which is supposed to eliminate the so-called 'poverty trap'.

Within various assumptions regarding macroeconomic context but also regarding the value of some key parameters (among which PIT elasticity to GDP supposed to be 1.5), it appears that the Regions should get more revenue from the Reform over the next 10 years, especially the Flemish Region, while the Federal Government should face a loss in revenue (on the 'regional side' of the Reform). In a sensitivity analysis relying on a lower elasticity of PIT to GDP growth (close to 1), we observe rather different evolutions, i.e. that the Walloon Region should lose revenue and that the benefit of the Flemish Region should not suffice anymore to compensate for the estimated losses at the Community level. It means that the Regions would be impacted in case of federal reforms reducing tax burden, conversely to what happened on the last decade. The use of taxing power by the different levels of government and tax coordination arise therefore as rather sensitive issues, especially in a context of fiscal consolidation.

Beyond the devolution of new responsibilities and the changes in the current revenue mechanisms, the Sixth Reform of the State also provides a refinancing for the Brussels-Capital Region and two accountability mechanisms, regarding respectively the pensions of civil servants and the investment in energy efficiency. The Refinancing of the Brussels-Capital Region is aimed to allow this Region a fair funding, regarding its specific spending obligations and its contribution to the GDP. This refinancing is first tailored to various needs criteria such as the number of commuters, civil servants, etc., but has a more lump-sum character after 2015. The two accountability mechanisms have been included in the Reform in order to enforce the Regions and the Communities to deal with the fiscal consequences of their decisions regarding their civil servants and regarding the investment in energy efficiency.

The net budgetary impact of the Sixth Reform of the State on the Communities and the Regions is therefore difficult to assess in the middle and long run. For the Regions, this impact is in particular highly sensitive to the value of the elasticity regarding GDP growth (see above). For all the entities, it will furthermore depend on the assumptions regarding unchanged policy scenario, especially regarding the evolution of the expenditure devolved to the Communities and the Regions. How to know how childcare, elderly care, labour market policies should have evolved when remaining at the Federal level? The Federal Government could for instance benefit from the devolution of new responsibilities if the growth of these tax expenditure or social expenditure was expected to be higher than the planned evolution of the grants.

While there is uncertainty on the budgetary impact over the next 10 years, the fiscal neutrality in the first year of implementation is a key rule of the Reform, with an equalisation grant being transferred from the entities supposed to benefit from the Reform to the entities supposed to lose revenue (in the first year). As set out in the institutional Agreement, any consolidation measure from the Federal Government, the refinancing of the Brussels-Capital Region and the transfers resulting from accountability mechanisms are not taken into consideration in the equalisation grant. This equalisation grant remains constant over the next 10 years and decreases progressively afterwards.

However, if they must be taken into account in terms of political economy, these considerations on the potential gains or losses across the levels of government have also to be replaced in an even larger framework of national welfare. As highlighted in Decoster and Sas (2012, p.33), the welfare of the Flemish, Walloon and Brussels citizens also results from national policies (e.g. social protection and justice).

This issue of national welfare should in particular be addressed with regard to the consolidation path. The Sixth Reform of the State reduces indeed the fiscal leeway of the Federal Government which transfers new spending power and taxing power to the Regions and the Communities while it remains responsible for most of ageing costs and for the major part of the debt (and debt service). Such a situation makes the Federal Government vulnerable to sovereign debt risks. As recommended by the High Council of Finance (HCF), the finalisation of the Sixth Reform of the State should allow for the contribution of the Regions and the Communities to the fiscal consolidation efforts in view of a fair-burden sharing of these efforts and the fiscal sustainability of each level of Government.

5. BIBLIOGRAPHY

Accord institutionnel pour la Sixième Réforme de l'Etat/Institutioneel Akkoord voor de Zesde Staatshervorming, http://www.lachambre.be/kvvcr/pdf_sections/home/NLdirupo.pdf

Algoed K. and Van Den Bossche W., (2009), Bijzondere financieringswet in een notendop, Documentatieblad 2009, n°2, Studie- en Documentatiedienst, FOD Financiën.

Algoed K., Cattoir Ph., Verdonck. M. (2009), *Assessment of the belgian fiscal equalisationmechanism and proposals for reform*, 18ème congrès des économistes de langue française.

Bayenet B., Pagano G., (2011), *Le financement des Entités fédérées : un système en voie de transformation*, Crisp.

Bisciari P., Van Meensel L. (2012), *La réforme de la loi de financement des communautés et régions*, National Bank of Belgium, Economic Review, June 2012.

Blöchliger, H. and C. Vammalle (2012), *Reforming Fiscal Federalism and Local Government: beyond the Zero-Sum Game*, OECD Fiscal Federalism Studies, OECD Publishing.

Cattoir Ph., de Callataÿ E. (2007), « Les transferts interrégionaux en Belgique : de quoi parlons-nous ? », *17ème Congrès des Economistes belges de Langue française*, Centre interuniversitaire de formation permanente (CIFOP).

Conseil Economique et Social de la Région Wallonne (CESW), *Regards sur la Wallonie : edition 2012*.

Conseil Supérieur de l'Emploi, *rapport 2011* / Hoge Raad voor de Werkgelegenheid, *verslag 2011*.

de Callataÿ, E. (2007), *Finances publiques et réformes institutionnelles: le rôle central de la Région de Bruxelles-Capitale*, in Regards économiques, IRES-UCL, No.52.

de Streel A., Deschamps R., Hermans E., Schmitz V., Scorneau B., (2011), *Comparaisons interrégionale et intercommunautaire des budgets de dépenses 2011 des Entités fédérées*, Cahiers de recherche n°60-2011/09.

Decoster A., (2006), *Regionale variatie in the indirecte belastingen?*, Center for Economic Studies, KU Leuven.

Decoster A., Sas W., 2011, *De bijzondere financieringswet voor dummies*, Flemosi, discussionpaper 4.

Decoster A. and Sas W. (2012), *De nieuwe financieringswet: anders, maar ook beter?*, Centrum voor Economische Studiën, KU Leuven, Januari 2012.

Decoster A., and Valenduc Ch. (2011), *L'impôt et la politique fiscale en Belgique*, Editions de l'Université Libre de Bruxelles.

Decoster A., Valenduc Ch., and Verdonck M. (2009), *L'autonomie fiscale des Régions en Belgique: évaluation et perspectives*, Bulletin de Documentation du SPF Finances, n°4, IV 2009.

Denil F. (2009), « Les dépenses communautaires et régionales : instrument de développement économique et social? », *Wallonie-Bruxelles : analyses et enjeux*, Reflets et Perspectives de la vie économique, n°1-2.

de Borman A. and de Briey L. (2012), *Mode de gouvernance des compétences de Sécurité sociale transférées : Modèle Fépros*, Rapport final, Collection 'CEPESS'.

Denil F., Mignolet M., Mulquin M-E., (2004), *La théorie du fédéralisme fiscal et ses enseignements*, in Le Fédéralisme fiscal : leçons de la théorie économique et expérience de 4 Etats fédéraux, De Boeck.

Dury D., Eugene B., Langenus G., Van Cauter K., Van Meensel L. (2008), *Transferts et mécanismes de solidarité interrégionaux via le budget des administrations publiques*, Revue économique de la BNB, septembre 2008.

Federal Planning Bureau (2012), *Economic Outlook 2012-2017*, Forecasts and Outlook, May 2012.

Frogneux V. and Saintrain M., (2012), *L'élasticité de l'impôt des personnes physiques: approche macroéconomique prospective de l'élasticité nationale et de l'élasticité de l'impôt régionalisé*, Working Paper 1-12, Federal Planning Bureau.

Heremans D., Peeters T., Van Hecke A. (2010), *Towards a more efficient and responsible financing mechanism for the Belgian federation*, Vives Beleidspaper.

Meunier O., Mignolet M., Mulquin M-E (2007), *Les transferts interrégionaux en Belgique*, Cahiers de recherche, Série Politique Economique n°19 (2007/9), Centre de recherches en Economie Régionale et Politique Economique, FUNDP.

OECD (2009), *OECD Economic Survey: Belgium*, OECD Publishing.

van der Stichele, G. (2003), *Les modes alternatifs de financement de Bruxelles*, update of the study of 1999 by Cattoir, Ph., J-P Lambert, M. Taymans, H. Tulkens, M. Tulkens, G. van der Stichele and M. Verdonck, Saint-Louis University, Brussels.

Van Gompel J., Van Craynest B. (2004), *Financiële transfers tussen de Belgische Gewesten: actualisering*, studie in opdracht van het Ministerie van de Vlaamse Gemeenschap (ABAFIM), in Cattoir Ph., de Callataÿ E.

6. ANNEX

Table 15: Main assumptions regarding parameters of the Regions and the Communities to develop a reform as a no policy change scenario

	2012	2013	2014	2015	2016	2017	2018	2019	2020
GDP growth	0,50%	1,30%	1,70%	1,90%	2,00%	2,00%	2,00%	2,00%	2,00%
inflation	2,60%	1,50%	1,80%	1,80%	2,00%	2,00%	2,00%	2,00%	2,00%
Evolution of aged less 18 (denatality)	1,041504	1,049	1,058	1,066	1,072299	1,079399	1,086204	1,092276	1,097711
Share in number of pupils									
The Flemish-Community	56,6%	56,5%	56,5%	56,5%	56,5%	56,6%	56,7%	56,8%	56,9%
The French-Community	43,4%	43,5%	43,5%	43,5%	43,5%	43,4%	43,3%	43,2%	43,1%
Share in regional PIT (after reform):									
The Flemish Region	63,23%	63,25%	63,25%	63,29%	63,33%	63,38%	63,39%	63,38%	63,35%
The Walloon Region	28,29%	28,19%	28,09%	27,97%	27,84%	27,78%	27,74%	27,72%	27,73%
The Brussels-Capital Region	8,48%	8,56%	8,66%	8,74%	8,83%	8,84%	8,87%	8,89%	8,92%
Share in federal PIT (after reform):									
The Flemish Region	63,48%	63,51%	63,51%	63,57%	63,61%	63,66%	63,68%	63,68%	63,66%
The Walloon Region	28,01%	27,91%	27,80%	27,68%	27,55%	27,48%	27,44%	27,42%	27,41%
The Brussels-Capital Region	8,51%	8,58%	8,68%	8,76%	8,84%	8,85%	8,88%	8,90%	8,93%
Share in PIT (before reform):									
The Flemish Region	63,19%	63,21%	63,21%	63,24%	63,25%	63,31%	63,35%	63,41%	63,43%
The Walloon Region	28,23%	28,18%	28,12%	28,01%	27,90%	27,77%	27,64%	27,57%	27,53%
The Brussels-Capital Region	8,59%	8,61%	8,67%	8,74%	8,85%	8,92%	9,01%	9,02%	9,05%

Conclusion

Françoise Thys-Clément [1]

One of I.B.F.P.'s (Belgian Institute of Public Finance) main missions is to provide precise analyses of the evolution of public finances. It is on this basis that, since after WWII, it has regularly published books on the decennial evolution of budgetary and fiscal policies. We must thank Etienne de Callataÿ to have conducted this monograph, as he had ten years ago, that describes the evolution of public finances from 2000 to 2010. The title clearly emphasizes the difficulties regarding the efforts carried out during the previous 20 years to bring the Belgian economy back on track. The book also presents an essential questioning of the future since the economic and politic paradigm has changed during the last ten years.

How indeed can one not consider the future?

Economists try to propose correcting measures of budgetary policies to face the damages caused to the real economy by the turmoil and turbulences induced by the world's financial sector and the increasing public debt inflated by large budget deficits. Furthermore, they have to take into account that our country faces a double institutional transformation of both its internal federal structure as well as its international integration into a Euro zone that is struggling to prove its capacity to retain its current structure.

---

1. Françoise Thys-Clément is Professor at the Université libre de Bruxelles and member of the Académie Royale de Belgique – Classe des Lettres et des Sciences morales et politiques. She particularly wishes to thank Etienne de Callataÿ for the lively discussions that followed their meetings during the preparation of this book.

What economists advocate is a change in the behavior of both citizens and politicians. Indeed, most of them highlight the mistakes in the macroeconomic governance and propose necessary actions to curb the current pessimism.

It is clear that we have to improve the efficiency and equity of public interventions and, obviously, of the taxes and other levies needed to finance them.

The problem of efficiency and effectiveness of the public sector is not studied sufficiently and even though this monograph raises this question, it does not provide concrete answers.

The question of equity and in particular intergenerational equity is also insufficiently discussed even though it is well-known that younger generations will have to carry the burden of the reconstruction of the economic and financial systems in addition to moving towards a more sustainable development that has become essential given the energy crisis.

The authors of the chapters of this book are all high level professionals and some of them have very important political and monetary responsibilities. They clearly point out that it is not possible to compare the decade studied in the book with the previous years.

Belgium has changed its paradigm: as a small open economy in the Euro zone, it has lost control over many of its economic instruments, in particular the exchange rate. Furthermore, being in an institutional federal transformation, it faces the setbacks of world financial shocks and of the lack of governance of banking institutions. It is inexorably dragged in the existential difficulties of the Euro zone.

According to Herman Van Rompuy, Belgium has become "too small", especially to be able to host large financial institutions.

Too small to act on economic policy instruments, the difficulty of its action rests mainly on preserving its competitiveness on the real economy which means monitoring the evolution of wages and prices which leads to lively debates. A modification of the taxation system, a fiscal "devaluation" limiting the burden on labor compensated by VAT and capital income taxes have to be thoroughly studied.

The increases of health expenditures and spending related to the needs of the elderly induced by major demographic changes and the lengthening of the life-span is often put forward to justify a reduction of other public expenditures.

The problems faced by the international financial sector and the lack of a satisfactory governance of the Euro has also pointed out that the assumption of rationality of markets, the keystone of the European construction, is questionable. Indeed markets cannot handle targeted programs; economies cannot rely on autopilot.

The criticisms raised by the economists of the National Bank of Belgium highlight to what extent "sound fiscal rules to reduce budgetary imbalances that existed at the start of the Euro area were not adequately enforced and neither the soft EU coordination approach nor the market forces fostered the required macroeconomic convergence".

The global analysis of the period 2000-2010 in Belgium is provided by economists of the Research Department of the National Bank of Belgium and "the comeback of the public budget deficit" is examined closely by Reginald Savage who states that the institutional complexity of Belgium imposes a detailed reading of expenditures and revenues in each of Belgian public entities.

A recent book (2011)[2], also published by the I.B.F.P. and edited by André Decoster and Christian Valenduc, sheds light on Belgian public finances. The authors cited above jointly with Marcel Gérard state in their contribution that "the fiscal environment changed radically at the turn of the century with reforms that produced a tax to GDP ratio which exhibits a downward trend". Therefore, it is clear that if the

---

2. Decoster A. et Valenduc C. (2011), L'impôt et la politique fiscale en Belgique, Editions de l'Université de Bruxelles ; Decoster A. et Valenduc C. (2011), Belastingen en fiscaalbeleid in België, Acco, Leuven.

debt and deficit have indeed exploded, this is partly due to a reduction in revenues. In a long chapter related to public expenditures, several authors, among which Robert Deschamps, show that the study of regional Belgian policies is extremely interesting and would deserve a monograph on its own. Several specific aspects are tackled in this chapter such as the evolution of public employment and its contracting practices, for instance. The central question of the efficiency of our public expenditures is however not directly tackled, as stated by Jean Hindriks, in particular due to some estimation problems related inter alia to the lack of data on prices.

Frank Vandenbroucke, jointly with Kim Lievens, provide "a stylized retrospective of the active welfare state in particular with regard to spending for employment and poverty". They consider that "the system proved its usefulness as a robust shock absorber but with important budgetary consequences". They furthermore state that "the Di Rupo government has embarked with important reforms for early retirement and exit" but underline "that the need for further systemic change and consistent strategy is still imperative".

Natacha Gilson and Jean Deboutte confirm that the intergenerational question is always implicitly underlying in the analysis. They indeed find that if Belgium "has made huge efforts to decrease debt-to-GDP ratio in the decade 2000-2010, the assertion that the public debt is still Achilles' heel of Belgian public finance is always true".

Facing the impossibility of forecasting international financial ups and downs, we have to admit that the evolution of public expenditures related to the interest on the public debt are, again, disturbing. Will the levels of interest rates remain low in the future? Is a new "snowball"[3] effect possible?

Can the "crowding-out" effect of expenditures due to the evolution the public debt be constrained? Who owns Belgium's public debt? We are naturally brought back to the question: are the active generations paying

---

3. Bogaert H. (1984), « Déficit des finances publiques : l'effet boule de neige, 6ème Congrès des Economistes belges de langue française, Commission 2, Rapport préparatoire, CIFOP, Charleroi.

too many taxes because of past expenditures and for whom? What will the burden be for future generations?

Because one of our main challenges is to reform Belgian institutions, Koen Algoed and Frédérique Denil analyzed "in detail the impact of the Sixth Reform of the State on the sub-national entities with a comparison of the previous Lambermont agreement, Their attempt to estimate the budgetary effects of the Reform is made on the basis of simulations and the authors note that as their estimates rely on provisional parameters and assumptions they are thus to be interpreted with caution.". The contribution of these researchers must be read with caution as it calls on the federal future of the country.

Going back to the introduction of this book, Etienne de Callataÿ recalls that "economic history allows for better policy action" but also states that past experience has shown "that ideas take time to become realities" and hopes that "by the way, the ongoing crisis may shorten the time lag between academic proposals and political decisions."

To the points discussed by the authors of the monograph, I would like to add that each major crisis offers unique opportunities for recovery. The choice of the path to follow is most certainly risky, but going towards a more optimistic vision of the future and concentrating on the possibility of young generations to improve the economic efficiency has to be an absolute priority. Twenty years ago, I had already highlighted the need for the new generations to benefit from a strong education and professional training![4] This conclusion assumes cooperation between (Belgian and European) public entities that manage expenditures in research and innovation.

A targeted macroeconomic framework must compensate the negative effects of burdens of the past; it should include an increased coordination of fiscal and social security contributions' systems to compensate the negative effects of fiscal competition and social dumping. This cooperation

---

4. Thys-Clément F. (1990), « Recherche et enseignement-Efficacité, équité et volonté collective », Discours prononcé à l'occasion de la séance de rentrée de l'ULB le 1er octobre.

would allow to reach a higher efficiency with an improvement of equity and henceforth social progress.

Keeping Europe and Belgium harmoniously in the future world calls for coordinated institutional efforts both for political and, more importantly, economic policies.

Annex 1
PRESENTATION OF THE BELGIAN INSTITUTE OF PUBLIC FINANCE

Aloïs Van de Voorde [1]

The Belgian Institute of Public Finance, commonly referred to in Dutch as BIOF, i.e. "Belgisch Instituut voor Openbare Financïen" and in French as IBFP for "Institut belge de finances publiques", was founded in January 1939 by Max-Léo Gérard (1879-1950) (1). During the first Van Zeeland government (March 1935-May 1936) he played an important part in the implementation of Prime Minister Van Zeeland's recovery plan. He was appointed Minister of Finance for a second but short term in the first Paul-Henri Spaak government in May 1938. It was at his instigation that the department of Inspection of Finance was set up in order to strengthen the internal supervision of budgetary transactions.

Between 1939 and 1951, M.-L. Gérard was the authoritative Chairman of the "Bank van Brussel/Banque de Bruxelles". In 1946 he was also the creator of the International Institute of Finance, which he chaired until 1955.

The aim of the BIOF/IBFP was to stimulate research performed by civil servants, personalities from the academic world and representatives from the private sector in the domain of public finance. They were to make the results of their research available in the form of solidly documented and argued evidence given to the decision makers.

---

1. Aloïs Van de Voorde is Honorary General Secretary of the Belgian Ministry of Finance.

The BIOF/IBFP is an independent scientific institution with the juridical status of a (Belgian) VZW/ASBL (non-profit organisation). According to its statutes the mission of the BIOF/IBFP is "the study and research of Belgian and foreign public finance in all its dimensions, and particularly in its interaction with other scientific disciplines". The Institute is permitted to undertake any activity which could promote this aim, such as the organisation of workshops, conferences and lectures, the awarding of prizes and the publication of books and periodicals. Since its foundation the BIOF/IBFP has always had the privilege of enjoying the moral and logistic support of the Ministry of Finance. In this context, it should be pointed out that a number of higher civil servants have regularly been members of the Institute's board of directors.

Until 1980 the BIOF/IBFP was traditionally presided over by a former Minister of Finance. So the chairmanship was held by the following former ministers: Max-Léo Gérard (1939-1946), Georges Theunis (1946-1954), Jean Van Houtte (1954-1971), Robert Henrion (1972-1974) and André Vlerick (1974-1980). They were followed by university professors, notably: Max Frank (ULB) (1980-1986), Vic Van Rompuy (KUL) (1986-1995), Henri Tulkens (UCL) (1995-1998), Paul Van Rompuy (KUL) (1999-2006), and Françoise Thys-Clément (ULB) (2006-2012). Last February (2012) Thys-Clément was succeeded by Christian Valenduc, general adviser at the Study and Documentation Centre of the Federal Department of Public Finance.

In 1991 the BIOF/IBFP Board decided to award an annual prize with a view to the encouragement of research in the area of public finance and economy. This prize is meant to reward a valuable dissertation written by students of the 2nd (master's) or 3rd grade (doctorate) – however not including doctoral dissertations proper – or a report on a period of practical training of level one of the administration, which deals with a subject relating to the public economy. Any student of a Belgian university or a college of higher education (polytechnic) can qualify for it. Hitherto some ten laureates have already have been awarded this prestigious prize. They can briefly present their study at a workshop or a lunch talk.

The BIOF/IBFP also makes itself useful by editing the "Geschiedenis van de openbare financïen van Belgïe / Histoire des finances publiques en Belgique", started just before the second World War, again at the initiative of M.-L. Gérard. Up till now six volumes have appeared, respectively relating to the periods 1830 – 1950 (vol. I, II. and III), 1950 – 1980 (vol. IV, 1 & and 2), 1980 – 1990 (vol. V), and 1990 – 2000 (vol.VI). This book is volume VII, dealing with the history of some major aspects of Belgian public finance and covers the 2000-2010 period.

It should also be mentioned that in 2011 BIOF/IBFP published a didactic work on the Belgian tax system and policy, which was badly needed. This work came to fruition under the editorship of Professor André Decoster and Professor Christian Valenduc (2).

Besides the traditional workshops dealing with the federal budget, organised annually since 1983, the BIOF/IBFP also holds a number of workshops, half-day workshops, conferences and lunch talks every year about topics that are broadly related to the public economy. During the 1985-2010 period there were no fewer than 102 activities. As appears from the examples cited hereafter of subjects that are covered during these activities, they closely tie in with present-day problems, such as: Privatization of public enterprises, Reform of the state's accountability, Municipal finance, Future sustainability of our pensions, External costs and the eco tax system, The national debt of Belgium, Fiscal problems of the multinational enterprises, Public expenses and the federalisation of the Belgian state, Budgetary policies in the European Monetary Union, Performance measuring in the public sector, Taxation of enterprises in Europe, The selling of issue rights in Great Britain. The BIOF/IBFP also succeeds in engaging eminent people, both from Belgium and abroad, either as speakers or consultants and discussants. Ministers, European Commissioners, governors of the National Bank of Belgium, high-ranking functionaries of the "Plan", principal private secretaries, as well as numerous university professors regularly contributed to the BIOF/IBFP activities.

In 1996 the BIOF/IBFP started a new type of activity in addition to the traditional workshops, namely the organisation of lunch discussions concerning one topical subject broadly connected with public finance.

The BIOF/IBFP has a website which can be consulted either in Dutch or in French; these are the addresses: http://www. ibfp.be – http://www.biof.be.

1. G. KURGAN-VANHENTENRYK, Max-Léo Gérard. *Un ingénieur dans la cité (1879-1955)* 2010, pp. 188, 189, 192, 231, 249, 253, 289. Editions de l'Université de Bruxelles.
2. A. DECOSTER, C. VALENDUC, *L'impôt et la politique fiscale en Belgique – Belastingen en fiscaal beleid in België*, 2011, Bruxelles : Editions de l'Université de Bruxelles (French version) / Leuven/Den Haag : Acco (Dutch version).

Annex 1

COMPOSITION OF THE BOARD OF THE INSTITUTE OVER THE PERIOD 2000-2010

	Start date	End date
Remi Boelaert	2002	2011
Alfons Boon	2002	2008
Frans De Braekeleer	1997	2008
Etienne de Callataÿ	1997	n.a.
Marc De Pauw	1997	2005
Peter De Roeck	2002	2005
Laurent De Ryck	1997	2005
Gert De Smet	2005	n.a.
André Decoster	2005	n.a.
Jean-Marc Delporte	1997	2002
Niko Demeester	2001	2005
Stéphane Depret	2002	n.a.
Michel Englert	2002	n.a.
Marcel Gérard	1997	n.a.
Pierre Pestieau	1997	2002
Jeannine Roland-Bayet	2002	2005
Reginald Savage	2005	2010
Erik Schokkaert	1997	2001
Jan Smets	2005	n.a.
Isabelle Standaert	2005	2008
Françoise Thys-Clément	1997	2001
	2006	n.a.
Pieter Timmermans	1997	2001
Christian Valenduc	1997	n.a.
Aloïs Van de Voorde	1997	2008
Hedwig Van der Borght	2002	n.a.
Paul Van Rompuy	1997	2008
Tanguy van Ypersele	2002	2004
Magali Verdonck	2008	n.a.
Luc Voets	2009	n.a.

Annex 2
STATISTICAL OVERVIEW[1]

Maud Nautet and Luc Van Meensel *

Belgium
TABLE 1: General government budget balance and debt
TABLE 2: Cyclically-adjusted and structural budget balances
TABLE 3: Revenue, expenditure and overall balance of general government
TABLE 4: Revenue of general government
TABLE 5: Primary expenditure of general government
TABLE 6: Social benefits of general government
TABLE 7: Revenue, expenditure and overall balance of federal government
TABLE 8: Revenue, expenditure and overall balance of social security
TABLE 9: Revenue, expenditure and overall balance of communities and regions
TABLE 10: Revenue, expenditure and overall balance of local government
TABLE 11: Debt of general government
TABLE 12: Consolidated gross debt by sub-sector
TABLE 13: Consolidated gross debt of general government per original and residual maturities
TABLE 14: Determinants of the change in the consolidated gross debt of general government
TABLE 15: Consolidated gross debt of general government per holders
TABLE 16: Consolidated gross debt of general government per instrument
TABLE 17: Employment in the general governement sector

International comparison
TABLE 18: General government primary expenditure
TABLE 19: General government total expenditure
TABLE 20: General government revenue
TABLE 21: General government primary balance
TABLE 22: General government overall balance
TABLE 23: General government consolidated gross debt

* Maud Nautet is a member of the Public Finance Division of the Research Departement at the National Bank of Belgium.
Luc Van Meensel is Head of the Public Finance Division of the Research Department at the National Bank of Belgium.
1. Data up to date at the end of June 2012.

TABLE 1: General government budget balance and debt

	IN € MILLION			PERCENTAGES OF GDP	
	OVERALL BALANCE[1]	CONSOLIDATED GROSS DEBT	GDP	OVERALL BALANCE	CONSOLIDATED GROSS DEBT
1970	-696	0	33.417	-2,1	
1975	-3.175	0	59.379	-5,3	
1980	-8.563	67.230	90.799	-9,4	74,0
1985	-12.626	144.347	125.404	-10,1	115,1
1990	-11.290	211.050	167.989	-6,7	125,6
1995	-9.407	270.679	207.927	-4,5	130,2
2000	-92	272.186	252.542	-0,0	107,8
2001	1.056	276.647	259.803	0,4	106,5
2002	-232	277.716	268.620	-0,1	103,4
2003	-291	271.637	276.156	-0,1	98,4
2004	-379	273.881	291.287	-0,1	94,0
2005	-7.550	279.014	303.435	-2,5	92,0
2006	1.214	280.413	318.829	0,4	88,0
2007	-173	282.106	335.814	-0,1	84,0
2008	-3.409	309.198	346.385	-1,0	89,3
2009	-19.008	326.186	340.788	-5,6	95,7
2010	-13.492	340.302	354.688	-3,8	95,9

Sources: NAI, NBB.
[1] As in the other tables in this annex, including -in accordance with the rules laid down for the excessive deficit procedure (EDP)- net interest on financial transactions such as swaps.

TABLE 2: Cyclically-adjusted and structural budget balances
Percentages of GDP

	OVERALL BALANCE	OBSERVED CHANGE					STRUCTURAL CHANGE OVERALL BALANCE[1]	INTEREST CHARGES CHANGE	STRUCTURAL CHANGE PRIMARY BALANCE
		TOTAL	CYCLICAL CHANGE			IMPACT OF NON-RECURRING ELEMENTS CHANGE			
			TOTAL	GDP GROWTH	COMPOSITION EFFECTS				
		(1)	(2)			(3)	(4)=(1)-(2)-(3)	(5)	(6)=(4)+(5)
1993	-7,5								
1994	-5,1	2,3	-0,1	0,6	-0,7	0,1	2,3	-1,6	0,7
1995	-4,5	0,6	0,1	0,1	-0,0	0,1	0,4	-0,3	0,1
1996	-4,0	0,5	-0,3	-0,5	0,2	-0,0	0,9	-0,5	0,4
1997	-2,2	1,7	0,3	0,7	-0,4	-0,2	1,7	-0,7	0,9
1998	-0,9	1,3	-0,1	-0,3	0,2	-0,0	1,4	-0,4	1,1
1999	-0,6	0,3	0,8	0,6	0,2	0,1	-0,6	-0,5	-1,1
2000	-0,0	0,6	0,2	0,7	-0,6	-0,1	0,6	-0,3	0,3
2001	0,4	0,4	-0,2	-0,8	0,6	0,5	0,1	-0,1	-0,0
2002	-0,1	-0,5	-0,4	-0,4	0,0	-0,2	0,1	-0,7	-0,7
2003	-0,1	-0,0	-0,2	-0,7	0,5	1,3	-1,1	-0,4	-1,5
2004	-0,1	-0,0	0,1	0,7	-0,6	-0,5	0,4	-0,6	-0,2
2005	-2,5	-2,4	-0,2	-0,0	-0,2	-3,0	0,8	-0,5	0,4
2006	0,4	2,9	0,3	0,6	-0,3	2,8	-0,3	-0,2	-0,5
2007	-0,1	-0,4	0,5	0,8	-0,4	-0,9	-0,0	-0,1	-0,1
2008	-1,0	-0,9	-0,1	-0,2	0,1	0,0	-0,9	-0,0	-0,9
2009	-5,6	-4,6	-0,8	-2,3	1,5	-0,9	-3,0	-0,2	-3,2
2010	-3,8	1,8	0,5	0,6	-0,2	1,0	0,3	-0,3	0,1

Sources: NAI, NBB.
1 According to the methodology described in Bouthevillain C., Ph. Cour-Thimann, G. van den Dool, P. Hernández de Cos, G. Langenus, M. Mohr, S. Momigliano and M. Tujula (2001), Cyclically adjusted budget balances: an alternative approach, ECB Working Paper Series, n° 77 (September).

TABLE 3: Revenue, expenditure and overall balance of general government
In € million

	REVENUE	PRIMARY EXPENDITURE	PRIMARY BALANCE	INTEREST CHARGES	OVERALL BALANCE
1970	12.733	12.294	439	1.135	-696
1975	25.795	26.597	-802	2.373	-3.175
1980	41.289	44.053	-2.764	5.799	-8.563
1985	60.608	60.191	417	13.043	-12.626
1990	76.486	68.269	8.216	19.506	-11.290
1995	98.926	89.895	9.030	18.438	-9.407
2000	123.746	107.235	16.512	16.603	-92
2001	128.518	110.754	17.763	16.707	1.056
2002	133.295	118.250	15.045	15.277	-232
2003	140.452	126.240	14.212	14.503	-291
2004	142.527	129.312	13.214	13.593	-379
2005	149.445	144.316	5.130	12.680	-7.550
2006	155.545	141.732	13.813	12.599	1.214
2007	161.676	148.883	12.794	12.967	-173
2008	168.804	158.979	9.825	13.234	-3.409
2009	163.763	170.409	-6.647	12.362	-19.008
2010	173.194	174.764	-1.571	11.921	-13.492
PERCENTAGES OF GDP					
1970	38,1	36,8	1,3	3,4	-2,1
1975	43,4	44,8	-1,4	4,0	-5,3
1980	45,5	48,5	-3,0	6,4	-9,4
1985	48,3	48,0	0,3	10,4	-10,1
1990	45,5	40,6	4,9	11,6	-6,7
1995	47,6	43,2	4,3	8,9	-4,5
2000	49,0	42,5	6,5	6,6	-0,0
2001	49,5	42,6	6,8	6,4	0,4
2002	49,6	44,0	5,6	5,7	-0,1
2003	50,9	45,7	5,1	5,3	-0,1
2004	48,9	44,4	4,5	4,7	-0,1
2005	49,3	47,6	1,7	4,2	-2,5
2006	48,8	44,5	4,3	4,0	0,4
2007	48,1	44,3	3,8	3,9	-0,1
2008	48,7	45,9	2,8	3,8	-1,0
2009	48,1	50,0	-2,0	3,6	-5,6
2010	48,8	49,3	-0,4	3,4	-3,8

Sources: NAI, NBB.

Annex 2

TABLE 4: Revenue of general government
In € million

	DIRECT TAXES	of which		INDIRECT TAXES	ACTUAL SOCIAL SECURITY CONTRIBUTIONS	CAPITAL TAXES	FISCAL AND PARAFISCAL REVENUE	OTHER REVENUE	TOTAL
		Individuals	Companies						
1970	3.355	2.625	721	4.425	3.193	117	11.090	1.643	12.733
1975	8.975	7.350	1.608	6.826	7.055	178	23.033	2.761	25.795
1980	15.112	13.342	1.756	10.293	10.838	309	36.553	4.736	41.289
1985	22.038	19.218	2.793	14.383	17.599	326	54.346	6.262	60.608
1990	25.607	22.050	3.525	19.399	23.438	504	68.948	7.537	76.486
1995	33.766	28.622	5.029	24.675	29.768	761	88.970	9.956	98.926
2000	42.969	34.322	8.363	32.515	35.017	1.175	111.675	12.071	123.746
2001	44.733	36.126	8.371	32.404	36.645	1.206	114.988	13.529	128.518
2002	45.818	37.091	8.449	33.872	38.438	1.256	119.384	13.911	133.295
2003	45.798	37.238	8.215	34.888	39.249	1.390	121.325	19.127	140.452
2004	48.421	38.822	9.373	37.507	40.433	2.177	128.539	13.988	142.527
2005	51.248	40.595	10.447	39.330	41.367	1.873	133.818	15.627	149.445
2006	52.637	40.675	11.786	41.622	42.984	2.153	139.396	16.149	155.545
2007	54.595	42.186	12.194	42.666	45.534	2.216	145.011	16.665	161.676
2008	56.977	44.744	12.093	43.206	48.077	2.370	150.630	18.174	168.804
2009	51.691	42.514	9.008	42.542	49.082	2.235	145.549	18.213	163.763
2010	55.259	44.961	10.131	45.498	50.199	2.490	153.445	19.748	173.194
PERCENTAGES OF GDP									
1970	10,0	7,9	2,2	13,2	9,6	0,4	33,2	4,9	38,1
1975	15,1	12,4	2,7	11,5	11,9	0,3	38,8	4,6	43,4
1980	16,6	14,7	1,9	11,3	11,9	0,3	40,3	5,2	45,5
1985	17,6	15,3	2,2	11,5	14,0	0,3	43,3	5,0	48,3
1990	15,2	13,1	2,1	11,5	14,0	0,3	41,0	4,5	45,5
1995	16,2	13,8	2,4	11,9	14,3	0,4	42,8	4,8	47,6
2000	17,0	13,6	3,3	12,9	13,9	0,5	44,2	4,8	49,0
2001	17,2	13,9	3,2	12,5	14,1	0,5	44,3	5,2	49,5
2002	17,1	13,8	3,1	12,6	14,3	0,5	44,4	5,2	49,6
2003	16,6	13,5	3,0	12,6	14,2	0,5	43,9	6,9	50,9
2004	16,6	13,3	3,2	12,9	13,9	0,7	44,1	4,8	48,9
2005	16,9	13,4	3,4	13,0	13,6	0,6	44,1	5,2	49,3
2006	16,5	12,8	3,7	13,1	13,5	0,7	43,7	5,1	48,8
2007	16,3	12,6	3,6	12,7	13,6	0,7	43,2	5,0	48,1
2008	16,4	12,9	3,5	12,5	13,9	0,7	43,5	5,2	48,7
2009	15,2	12,5	2,6	12,5	14,4	0,7	42,7	5,3	48,1
2010	15,6	12,7	2,9	12,8	14,2	0,7	43,3	5,6	48,8

Sources: NAI, NBB.

TABLE 5: Primary expenditure of general government
In € million

	COMPEN-SATION OF EM-PLOYEES	INTER-MEDIATE CON-SUMP-TION	TAXES PAID	SOCIAL BENEFITS	SUBSI-DIES TO ENTER-PRISES	CURRENT TRANSFERS TO THE REST OF THE WORLD	OTHER CURRENT TRANS-FERS	CAPITAL EXPENDI-TURE	TOTAL
1970	3.081	1.091	6	4.729	725	401	380	1.882	12.294
1975	7.002	2.234	10	11.522	1.485	434	670	3.241	26.597
1980	11.747	3.546	9	19.578	2.458	337	1.163	5.215	44.053
1985	15.477	5.327	9	28.725	3.041	494	1.853	5.265	60.191
1990	18.235	4.913	11	35.343	2.846	551	2.075	4.296	68.269
1995	24.722	6.518	20	46.063	2.542	953	2.933	6.145	89.895
2000	29.039	8.270	49	53.896	3.073	2.006	2.871	8.031	107.235
2001	30.326	8.767	55	56.652	3.200	2.167	3.044	6.543	110.754
2002	32.532	10.185	50	59.791	3.209	2.427	3.177	6.880	118.250
2003	33.833	10.325	105	63.276	3.680	2.787	3.484	8.750	126.240
2004	34.664	10.640	26	66.344	3.397	3.099	3.771	7.374	129.312
2005	36.422	10.931	28	69.007	4.826	3.249	4.025	15.828	144.316
2006	38.093	11.377	42	71.097	5.524	3.307	4.267	8.027	141.732
2007	39.624	11.691	53	74.559	6.487	3.303	3.940	9.226	148.883
2008	41.837	12.504	-5	80.217	7.197	3.610	4.382	9.237	158.979
2009	43.483	13.105	10	86.055	7.399	4.065	4.867	11.426	170.409
2010	44.768	13.410	9	88.673	8.759	4.057	5.287	9.801	174.764
PERCENTAGES OF GDP									
1970	9,2	3,3	0,0	14,1	2,2	1,2	1,1	5,6	36,8
1975	11,8	3,8	0,0	19,4	2,5	0,7	1,1	5,5	44,8
1980	12,9	3,9	0,0	21,6	2,7	0,4	1,3	5,7	48,5
1985	12,3	4,2	0,0	22,9	2,4	0,4	1,5	4,2	48,0
1990	10,9	2,9	0,0	21,0	1,7	0,3	1,2	2,6	40,6
1995	11,9	3,1	0,0	22,2	1,2	0,5	1,4	3,0	43,2
2000	11,5	3,3	0,0	21,3	1,2	0,8	1,1	3,2	42,5
2001	11,7	3,4	0,0	21,8	1,2	0,8	1,2	2,5	42,6
2002	12,1	3,8	0,0	22,3	1,2	0,9	1,2	2,6	44,0
2003	12,3	3,7	0,0	22,9	1,3	1,0	1,3	3,2	45,7
2004	11,9	3,7	0,0	22,8	1,2	1,1	1,3	2,5	44,4
2005	12,0	3,6	0,0	22,7	1,6	1,1	1,3	5,2	47,6
2006	11,9	3,6	0,0	22,3	1,7	1,0	1,3	2,5	44,5
2007	11,8	3,5	0,0	22,2	1,9	1,0	1,2	2,7	44,3
2008	12,1	3,6	-0,0	23,2	2,1	1,0	1,3	2,7	45,9
2009	12,8	3,8	0,0	25,3	2,2	1,2	1,4	3,4	50,0
2010	12,6	3,8	0,0	25,0	2,5	1,1	1,5	2,8	49,3

Sources: NAI, NBB.

TABLE 6: Social benefits of general government
In € million

	PENSIONS	HEALTH CARE	UNEMPLOYMENT BENEFITS	EARLY RETIREMENT PENSIONS, CAREER BREAKS AND TIME CREDIT	FAMILY ALLOWANCES	OTHER	TOTAL
1970	1.759	879	136	0	984	969	4.729
1975	4.302	2.209	868	0	1.821	2.323	11.522
1980	7.395	3.745	1.768	459	2.501	3.711	19.578
1985	10.720	5.535	3.043	1.024	3.068	5.336	28.725
1990	13.340	7.821	3.101	1.327	3.405	6.349	35.343
1995	17.674	11.222	4.219	1.425	3.961	7.562	46.063
2000	20.968	14.025	4.381	1.399	4.324	8.801	53.896
2001	21.866	15.052	4.637	1.427	4.433	9.237	56.652
2002	22.942	15.372	5.356	1.496	4.564	10.061	59.791
2003	23.812	16.745	5.747	1.616	4.637	10.721	63.276
2004	24.779	18.053	6.024	1.727	4.731	11.030	66.344
2005	25.921	18.896	6.121	1.813	4.850	11.407	69.007
2006	27.021	19.256	6.097	1.890	5.023	11.810	71.097
2007	28.895	20.286	5.746	2.006	5.154	12.472	74.559
2008	30.960	22.262	5.774	2.143	5.421	13.656	80.217
2009	32.768	23.778	6.903	2.251	5.663	14.692	86.055
2010	33.965	24.491	6.879	2.347	5.761	15.230	88.673
PERCENTAGES OF GDP							
1970	5,3	2,6	0,4	0,0	2,9	2,9	14,1
1975	7,2	3,7	1,5	0,0	3,1	3,9	19,4
1980	8,1	4,1	1,9	0,5	2,8	4,1	21,6
1985	8,5	4,4	2,4	0,8	2,4	4,3	22,9
1990	7,9	4,7	1,8	0,8	2,0	3,8	21,0
1995	8,5	5,4	2,0	0,7	1,9	3,6	22,2
2000	8,3	5,6	1,7	0,6	1,7	3,5	21,3
2001	8,4	5,8	1,8	0,5	1,7	3,6	21,8
2002	8,5	5,7	2,0	0,6	1,7	3,7	22,3
2003	8,6	6,1	2,1	0,6	1,7	3,9	22,9
2004	8,5	6,2	2,1	0,6	1,6	3,8	22,8
2005	8,5	6,2	2,0	0,6	1,6	3,8	22,7
2006	8,5	6,0	1,9	0,6	1,6	3,7	22,3
2007	8,6	6,0	1,7	0,6	1,5	3,7	22,2
2008	8,9	6,4	1,7	0,6	1,6	3,9	23,2
2009	9,6	7,0	2,0	0,7	1,7	4,3	25,3
2010	9,6	6,9	1,9	0,7	1,6	4,3	25,0

Sources: NAI, NBB.

TABLE 7: Revenue, expenditure and overall balance of federal government
In € million

	REVENUE*	FINAL PRIMARY EXPENDITURE**	TRANSFERS TO OTHER GENERAL GOVERNMENT SUB-SECTORS	PRIMARY BALANCE	INTEREST CHARGES	OVERALL BALANCE
1970	8.606	6.686	1.837	83	961	-878
1975	16.966	13.105	4.884	-1.023	1.914	-2.937
1980	28.039	20.565	9.257	-1.783	4.748	-6.530
1985	39.085	27.764	12.769	-1.448	11.662	-13.111
1990	45.265	15.220	22.875	7.171	18.240	-11.069
1995	56.930	17.491	30.263	9.176	16.926	-7.749
2000	72.865	21.007	37.388	14.470	15.529	-1.059
2001	74.827	20.511	40.956	13.360	15.606	-2.246
2002	73.944	21.489	38.504	13.951	14.465	-514
2003	79.391	24.028	40.859	14.504	13.527	977
2004	79.198	21.417	45.415	12.365	12.718	-352
2005	84.042	31.417	48.170	4.455	12.036	-7.581
2006	86.848	24.089	50.591	12.168	12.109	59
2007	89.163	27.265	53.341	8.557	12.243	-3.686
2008	93.593	29.129	57.766	6.699	12.326	-5.627
2009	87.246	32.183	57.726	-2.663	11.568	-14.231
2010	94.022	31.858	61.811	353	11.134	-10.782
PERCENTAGES OF GDP						
1970	25,8	20,0	5,5	0,2	2,9	-2,6
1975	28,6	22,1	8,2	-1,7	3,2	-4,9
1980	30,9	22,6	10,2	-2,0	5,2	-7,2
1985	31,2	22,1	10,2	-1,2	9,3	-10,5
1990	26,9	9,1	13,6	4,3	10,9	-6,6
1995	27,4	8,4	14,6	4,4	8,1	-3,7
2000	28,9	8,3	14,8	5,7	6,1	-0,4
2001	28,8	7,9	15,8	5,1	6,0	-0,9
2002	27,5	8,0	14,3	5,2	5,4	-0,2
2003	28,7	8,7	14,8	5,3	4,9	0,4
2004	27,2	7,4	15,6	4,2	4,4	-0,1
2005	27,7	10,4	15,9	1,5	4,0	-2,5
2006	27,2	7,6	15,9	3,8	3,8	0,0
2007	26,6	8,1	15,9	2,5	3,6	-1,1
2008	27,0	8,4	16,7	1,9	3,6	-1,6
2009	25,6	9,4	16,9	-0,8	3,4	-4,2
2010	26,5	9,0	17,4	0,1	3,1	-3,0

Sources: NAI, NBB.
* Including fiscal and parafiscal revenue transfered to other genral government sub-sectors.
**Transfers to other general government sub-sectors not included.

Annex 2

TABLE 8: Revenue, expenditure and overall balance of social security
In € million

	REVENUE	FINAL PRIMARY EXPENDITURE	TRANSFERS TO OTHER GENERAL GOVERNMENT SUB-SECTORS	PRIMARY BALANCE	INTEREST CHARGES	OVERALL BALANCE
1970	4.162	3.897	8	257	9	248
1975	9.995	9.679	36	280	20	260
1980	16.679	16.765	334	-420	123	-542
1985	25.634	24.604	433	598	164	434
1990	30.025	29.524	57	445	145	299
1995	38.116	38.235	51	-169	151	-320
2000	45.833	44.358	168	1.307	94	1.213
2001	48.865	46.839	329	1.696	18	1.678
2002	50.512	49.078	168	1.266	8	1.258
2003	51.402	52.120	146	-864	6	-870
2004	56.234	55.984	206	44	8	37
2005	58.328	58.413	211	-296	1	-297
2006	61.281	60.205	230	846	1	845
2007	64.445	62.572	181	1.692	1	1.691
2008	69.307	67.536	184	1.587	1	1.586
2009	70.239	72.432	212	-2.405	3	-2.408
2010	75.214	75.269	212	-266	6	-273
PERCENTAGES OF GDP						
1970	12,5	11,7	0,0	0,8	0,0	0,7
1975	16,8	16,3	0,1	0,5	0,0	0,4
1980	18,4	18,5	0,4	-0,5	0,1	-0,6
1985	20,4	19,6	0,3	0,5	0,1	0,3
1990	17,9	17,6	0,0	0,3	0,1	0,2
1995	18,3	18,4	0,0	-0,1	0,1	-0,2
2000	18,1	17,6	0,1	0,5	0,0	0,5
2001	18,8	18,0	0,1	0,7	0,0	0,6
2002	18,8	18,3	0,1	0,5	0,0	0,5
2003	18,6	18,9	0,1	-0,3	0,0	-0,3
2004	19,3	19,2	0,1	0,0	0,0	0,0
2005	19,2	19,3	0,1	-0,1	0,0	-0,1
2006	19,2	18,9	0,1	0,3	0,0	0,3
2007	19,2	18,6	0,1	0,5	0,0	0,5
2008	20,0	19,5	0,1	0,5	0,0	0,5
2009	20,6	21,3	0,1	-0,7	0,0	-0,7
2010	21,2	21,2	0,1	-0,1	0,0	-0,1

Sources: NAI, NBB.

TABLE 9: Revenue, expenditure and overall balance of communities and regions
In € million

	REVENUE	FINAL PRIMARY EXPENDITURE	TRANSFERS TO OTHER GENERAL GOVERNMENT SUB-SECTORS	PRIMARY BALANCE	INTEREST CHARGES	OVERALL BALANCE
1990	18.581	14.139	4.938	-496	191	-687
1995	26.164	21.447	5.626	-909	756	-1.664
2000	33.291	25.995	5.962	1.334	724	610
2001	36.341	27.407	6.211	2.723	769	1.953
2002	36.817	30.175	6.363	278	660	-382
2003	39.054	31.425	6.938	692	666	26
2004	40.922	33.425	6.913	584	594	-9
2005	43.137	34.823	7.481	834	457	377
2006	45.058	36.349	7.805	904	365	539
2007	47.456	37.759	7.981	1.716	461	1.254
2008	50.025	40.212	9.385	428	521	-94
2009	49.136	42.397	8.659	-1.921	601	-2.521
2010	50.767	43.581	8.898	-1.712	638	-2.350
PERCENTAGES OF GDP						
1990	11,1	8,4	2,9	-0,3	0,1	-0,4
1995	12,6	10,3	2,7	-0,4	0,4	-0,8
2000	13,2	10,3	2,4	0,5	0,3	0,2
2001	14,0	10,5	2,4	1,0	0,3	0,8
2002	13,7	11,2	2,4	0,1	0,2	-0,1
2003	14,1	11,4	2,5	0,3	0,2	0,0
2004	14,0	11,5	2,4	0,2	0,2	-0,0
2005	14,2	11,5	2,5	0,3	0,2	0,1
2006	14,1	11,4	2,4	0,3	0,1	0,2
2007	14,1	11,2	2,4	0,5	0,1	0,4
2008	14,4	11,6	2,7	0,1	0,2	-0,0
2009	14,4	12,4	2,5	-0,6	0,2	-0,7
2010	14,3	12,3	2,5	-0,5	0,2	-0,7

Sources: NAI, NBB.

Annex 2

TABLE 10: Revenue, expenditure and overall balance of local government
In € million

	REVENUE	FINAL PRIMARY EXPENDITURE	TRANSFERS TO OTHER GENERAL GOVERNMENT SUB-SECTORS	PRIMARY BALANCE	INTEREST CHARGES	OVERALL BALANCE
1970	1.874	1.711	7	156	222	-66
1975	3.862	3.813	12	37	534	-498
1980	6.287	6.723	14	-450	1.040	-1.490
1985	9.217	7.824	10	1.383	1.332	51
1990	10.634	9.387	8	1.239	1.072	167
1995	13.933	12.723	109	1.102	775	326
2000	15.666	15.874	120	-328	527	-855
2001	16.462	15.997	141	324	653	-329
2002	17.664	17.508	164	-9	585	-594
2003	19.029	18.668	140	221	646	-424
2004	19.273	18.486	192	595	649	-54
2005	20.340	19.663	178	499	549	-50
2006	21.533	21.089	174	269	498	-229
2007	22.742	21.287	243	1.212	645	566
2008	23.748	22.103	184	1.461	737	725
2009	24.361	23.397	247	717	565	152
2010	24.675	24.057	219	400	487	-88
PERCENTAGES OF GDP						
1970	5,6	5,1	0,0	0,5	0,7	-0,2
1975	6,5	6,4	0,0	0,1	0,9	-0,8
1980	6,9	7,4	0,0	-0,5	1,1	-1,6
1985	7,3	6,2	0,0	1,1	1,1	0,0
1990	6,3	5,6	0,0	0,7	0,6	0,1
1995	6,7	6,1	0,1	0,5	0,4	0,2
2000	6,2	6,3	0,0	-0,1	0,2	-0,3
2001	6,3	6,2	0,1	0,1	0,3	-0,1
2002	6,6	6,5	0,1	-0,0	0,2	-0,2
2003	6,9	6,8	0,1	0,1	0,2	-0,2
2004	6,6	6,3	0,1	0,2	0,2	-0,0
2005	6,7	6,5	0,1	0,2	0,2	-0,0
2006	6,8	6,6	0,1	0,1	0,2	-0,1
2007	6,8	6,3	0,1	0,4	0,2	0,2
2008	6,9	6,4	0,1	0,4	0,2	0,2
2009	7,1	6,9	0,1	0,2	0,2	0,0
2010	7,0	6,8	0,1	0,1	0,1	-0,0

Sources: NAI, NBB.

TABLE 11: Debt of general government
In € billion

	GROSS DEBT	OF WHICH FINANCIAL INSTRUMENTS NOT INCLUDED IN THE CONSOLIDATED GROSS DEBT	FINANCIAL ASSETS PLACED WITH GENERAL GOVERNMENT	CONSOLIDATED GROSS DEBT (MAASTRICHT DEFINITION)	FINANCIAL ASSETS OTHER THAN THOSE PLACED WITH GENERAL GOVERNMENT	TOTAL FINANCIAL ASSETS	NET DEBT
	(a)	(b)	(c)	(d=a-b-c)	(e)	(f=c+e)	(g=a-c-e)
1980	69,7	0,7	1,9	67,2	21,6	23,5	46,3
1985	146,9	0,7	1,8	144,3	23,8	25,5	121,3
1990	220,8	0,9	8,8	211,1	31,6	40,4	180,4
1995	294,1	12,2	11,2	270,7	42,2	53,4	240,7
2000	305,3	15,4	17,6	272,2	41,6	59,2	246,0
2001	313,9	15,2	22,1	276,6	45,3	67,4	246,5
2002	319,9	14,5	27,7	277,7	42,1	69,7	250,2
2003	314,0	14,6	27,7	271,6	37,3	65,0	248,9
2004	318,2	13,0	31,3	273,9	43,4	74,7	243,5
2005	325,0	12,9	33,1	279,0	43,2	76,3	248,7
2006	325,8	12,8	32,6	280,4	47,6	80,2	245,6
2007	339,5	14,2	43,2	282,1	50,9	94,1	245,4
2008	365,7	14,7	41,7	309,2	69,6	111,3	254,3
2009	380,7	15,5	38,9	326,2	70,5	109,4	271,2
2010	404,4	15,7	48,3	340,3	71,9	120,3	284,1
PERCENTAGES OF GDP							
1980	76,8	0,7	2,0	74,0	23,8	25,8	51,0
1985	117,1	0,6	1,4	115,1	18,9	20,4	96,7
1990	131,4	0,5	5,2	125,6	18,8	24,0	107,4
1995	141,4	5,9	5,4	130,2	20,3	25,7	115,8
2000	120,9	6,1	7,0	107,8	16,5	23,5	97,4
2001	120,8	5,8	8,5	106,5	17,4	25,9	94,9
2002	119,1	5,4	10,3	103,4	15,7	26,0	93,1
2003	113,7	5,3	10,0	98,4	13,5	23,6	90,1
2004	109,2	4,5	10,7	94,0	14,9	25,6	83,6
2005	107,1	4,2	10,9	92,0	14,2	25,1	82,0
2006	102,2	4,0	10,2	88,0	14,9	25,2	77,0
2007	101,1	4,2	12,9	84,0	15,2	28,0	73,1
2008	105,6	4,3	12,0	89,3	20,1	32,1	73,4
2009	111,7	4,6	11,4	95,7	20,7	32,1	79,6
2010	114,0	4,4	13,6	95,9	20,3	33,9	80,1

Sources: NAI, NBB.

Annex 2

TABLE 12: Consolidated gross debt by sub-sector
In € billion

	FEDERAL GOVERNMENT	COMMUNITIES AND REGIONS	LOCAL GOVERNMENT	SOCIAL SECURITY	CONSOLIDATED GROSS DEBT[1]
1990	192,2	5,3	14,1	-0,4	211,1
1995	243,4	14,8	12,3	0,2	270,7
2000	251,5	13,9	11,8	-5,0	272,2
2001	257,5	12,7	13,0	-6,5	276,6
2002	258,4	13,5	13,4	-7,6	277,7
2003	250,6	14,7	13,2	-6,9	271,6
2004	252,0	14,9	14,1	-7,1	273,9
2005	258,6	12,9	13,7	-6,2	279,0
2006	261,2	12,3	14,4	-7,5	280,4
2007	264,2	11,3	15,7	-9,1	282,1
2008	289,8	13,6	15,7	-9,9	309,2
2009	297,0	20,8	16,0	-7,6	326,2
2010	307,6	22,8	17,4	-7,5	340,3
PERCENTAGES OF GDP					
1990	114,4	3,1	8,4	-0,3	125,6
1995	117,0	7,1	5,9	0,1	130,2
2000	99,6	5,5	4,7	-2,0	107,8
2001	99,1	4,9	5,0	-2,5	106,5
2002	96,2	5,0	5,0	-2,8	103,4
2003	90,8	5,3	4,8	-2,5	98,4
2004	86,5	5,1	4,8	-2,4	94,0
2005	85,2	4,3	4,5	-2,0	92,0
2006	81,9	3,9	4,5	-2,4	88,0
2007	78,7	3,4	4,7	-2,7	84,0
2008	83,7	3,9	4,5	-2,9	89,3
2009	87,1	6,1	4,7	-2,2	95,7
2010	86,7	6,4	4,9	-2,1	95,9

Sources: NAI, NBB.
1 The consolidated gross debt is the debt as defined in European Regulation EC 479/2009 concerning the implementation of the Protocol on the excessive deficit procedure annexed to the Treaty on European Union (Treaty of Maastricht) of 7th February 1992.

TABLE 13: Consolidated gross debt of general government per original and residual maturities
In € billion

	SHORT-TERM DEBT	LONG-TERM DEBT	TOTAL	DEBT WITH RESIDUAL MATURITY UP TO 1 YEAR	DEBT WITH RESIDUAL MATURITY OVER 1 YEAR AND UP TO 5 YEARS	DEBT WITH RESIDUAL MATURITY OVER 5 YEARS	TOTAL
1990	62,1	148,9	211,1	77,5	70,0	63,6	211,1
1995	50,5	220,2	270,7	65,2	90,6	114,9	270,7
2000	28,8	243,4	272,2	54,0	102,0	116,2	272,2
2001	28,8	247,9	276,6	46,4	103,1	127,1	276,6
2002	26,7	251,0	277,7	46,3	105,2	126,3	277,7
2003	23,3	248,4	271,6	46,2	108,6	116,8	271,6
2004	27,5	246,4	273,9	48,6	100,6	124,8	273,9
2005	28,0	251,0	279,0	48,8	107,9	122,3	279,0
2006	30,5	249,9	280,4	52,6	98,2	129,6	280,4
2007	31,9	250,3	282,1	61,9	91,3	129,0	282,1
2008	55,1	254,1	309,2	75,8	106,7	126,7	309,2
2009	48,6	277,6	326,2	77,8	118,8	129,6	326,2
2010	50,6	289,7	340,3	81,3	120,9	138,1	340,3
PERCENTAGES OF CONSOLIDATED GROSS DEBT							
1990	29,4	70,6	100,0	36,7	33,1	30,1	100,0
1995	18,7	81,3	100,0	24,1	33,5	42,4	100,0
2000	10,6	89,4	100,0	19,9	37,5	42,7	100,0
2001	10,4	89,6	100,0	16,8	37,3	45,9	100,0
2002	9,6	90,4	100,0	16,7	37,9	45,5	100,0
2003	8,6	91,4	100,0	17,0	40,0	43,0	100,0
2004	10,0	90,0	100,0	17,7	36,7	45,6	100,0
2005	10,0	90,0	100,0	17,5	38,7	43,8	100,0
2006	10,9	89,1	100,0	18,7	35,0	46,2	100,0
2007	11,3	88,7	100,0	21,9	32,4	45,7	100,0
2008	17,8	82,2	100,0	24,5	34,5	41,0	100,0
2009	14,9	85,1	100,0	23,9	36,4	39,7	100,0
2010	14,9	85,1	100,0	23,9	35,5	40,6	100,0

Sources: NAI, NBB.

TABLE 14: Determinants of the change in the consolidated gross debt of general government
Percentages of GDP, unless otherwise stated

	DEBT LEVEL (END OF PERIOD)	CHANGE IN THE DEBT	ENDOGENOUS CHANGE[1]	PRIMARY BALANCE REQUIRED TO STABILISE THE DEBT	IMPLICIT INTEREST RATE ON THE DEBT	CHANGE IN NOMINAL GDP[2]	ACTUAL PRIMARY BALANCE	CHANGE RESULTING FROM OTHER FACTORS	EQUITY INVESTMENT[3]	LOANS[4]	DEPOSITS AND CASH[5]	FINANCIAL DERIVATIVES[6]	OTHER[7]
1990	125,6	3,8	-0,2	4,7	10,1	6,0	4,9	4,0	0,0	0,0	0,0	0,0	4,0
1995	130,2	-2,0	-0,1	4,2	7,0	3,7	4,3	-1,8	0,0	0,0	-1,7	0,0	-0,2
2000	107,8	-5,8	-6,1	0,4	6,1	5,7	6,5	0,3	-0,1	-0,1	0,2	-0,0	0,4
2001	106,5	-1,3	-3,4	3,4	6,1	2,9	6,8	2,1	0,1	-0,1	-0,4	-0,1	2,6
2002	103,4	-3,1	-3,4	2,2	5,5	3,4	5,6	0,3	-0,0	0,0	-0,2	-0,1	0,6
2003	98,4	-5,0	-2,7	2,4	5,2	2,8	5,1	-2,3	0,1	-2,2	0,2	-0,0	-0,3
2004	94,0	-4,3	-5,0	-0,4	5,0	5,5	4,5	0,6	-0,3	-0,1	0,1	-0,1	1,0
2005	92,0	-2,1	-1,3	0,4	4,6	4,2	1,7	-0,8	-0,1	-0,1	0,1	-0,1	-0,6
2006	88,0	-4,0	-4,8	-0,5	4,5	5,1	4,3	0,8	0,1	-0,0	-0,0	-0,1	0,9
2007	84,0	-3,9	-4,4	-0,6	4,6	5,3	3,8	0,5	0,3	-0,0	0,4	-0,0	-0,1
2008	89,3	5,3	-1,6	1,3	4,7	3,1	2,8	6,8	4,5	0,0	1,9	-0,0	0,5
2009	95,7	6,5	7,0	5,1	4,0	-1,6	-2,0	-0,6	1,1	0,1	-1,0	-0,1	-0,7
2010	95,9	0,2	0,1	-0,4	3,7	4,1	-0,4	0,2	-0,0	0,2	0,3	-0,7	0,4

Sources: NAI, NBB.

1 The endogenous change in the public debt is indicated by the difference between the primary balance required to stabilise the debt – i.e. the balance equal to the difference between the implicit interest rate on the debt and the nominal GDP growth rate, multiplied by the ratio between the debt at the end of the previous year and the GDP of the period considered – and the actual primary balance.
2 Percentage changes compared to the previous year.
3 Net equity investment, excluding transactions with the NBB.
4 In 2010, this item essentially comprises the loan to the Greek State.
5 The exceptional changes in this item in 2008 and in 2009 are due to a deposit placed on a bank account between the end of 2008 and the spring of 2009 by the FPIC, which is part of the general government sector.
6 In 2010, this item corresponds mainly to two exceptional transactions concerning the unwinding of swap positions.
7 Principally changes in sector classification, transactions with the NBB (particularly capital gains on gold), the net formation of other financial assets, the impact of foreign exchange differences and issue and buy-back premiums, the impact of accounts payable and receivable, and statistical discrepancies.

TABLE 15: Consolidated gross debt of general government per holders
In € billion

	DEBT HELD BY RESIDENTS					DEBT HELD BY NON-RESIDENTS			
	TOTAL	CENTRAL BANK	OTHER MONETARY FINANCIAL INSTITUTIONS	OTHER FINANCIAL INSTITUTIONS	OTHER RESIDENTS	TOTAL	EURO AREA	NON-EURO AREA	TOTAL
1990	169,5	2,5	125,1	20,0	21,9	41,5	19,5	22,0	211,1
1995	207,9	1,7	155,7	32,8	17,7	62,7	31,9	30,8	270,7
2000	169,7	2,5	118,6	30,8	17,8	102,5	59,3	43,1	272,2
2001	159,6	2,6	109,3	29,8	17,9	117,1	64,3	52,8	276,6
2002	147,4	2,3	98,9	28,7	17,5	130,4	67,8	62,6	277,7
2003	135,7	2,2	90,4	26,9	16,1	135,9	68,9	67,0	271,6
2004	134,9	2,1	87,3	28,5	17,0	139,0	77,5	61,5	273,9
2005	134,0	2,3	85,8	29,3	16,5	145,1	75,0	70,0	279,0
2006	128,7	2,5	82,0	29,2	15,0	151,8	79,5	72,2	280,4
2007	111,7	3,5	65,6	28,4	14,2	170,4	81,1	89,3	282,1
2008	118,9	3,7	69,7	29,9	15,6	190,3	91,0	99,3	309,2
2009	133,7	3,9	72,8	40,8	16,2	192,4	104,1	88,4	326,2
2010	141,6	4,9	78,8	43,7	14,2	198,7	102,6	96,1	340,3
PERCENTAGES OF CONSOLIDATED GROSS DEBT									
1990	80,3	1,2	59,3	9,5	10,4	19,7	9,3	10,4	100,0
1995	76,8	0,6	57,5	12,1	6,5	23,2	11,8	11,4	100,0
2000	62,4	0,9	43,6	11,3	6,6	37,6	21,8	15,9	100,0
2001	57,7	0,9	39,5	10,8	6,5	42,3	23,2	19,1	100,0
2002	53,1	0,8	35,6	10,3	6,3	46,9	24,4	22,5	100,0
2003	50,0	0,8	33,3	9,9	5,9	50,0	25,4	24,7	100,0
2004	49,3	0,8	31,9	10,4	6,2	50,7	28,3	22,4	100,0
2005	48,0	0,8	30,7	10,5	5,9	52,0	26,9	25,1	100,0
2006	45,9	0,9	29,3	10,4	5,3	54,1	28,4	25,8	100,0
2007	39,6	1,2	23,2	10,1	5,0	60,4	28,7	31,7	100,0
2008	38,5	1,2	22,6	9,7	5,0	61,5	29,4	32,1	100,0
2009	41,0	1,2	22,3	12,5	5,0	59,0	31,9	27,1	100,0
2010	41,6	1,5	23,2	12,8	4,2	58,4	30,2	28,2	100,0

Sources: NAI, NBB.

TABLE 16: Consolidated gross debt of general government per instrument
In € billion

	TOTAL	CURRENCY AND DEPOSITS	SECURITIES OTHER THAN SHARES, EXCLUDING FINANCIAL DERIVATIVES			LOANS		
			TOTAL	SHORT-TERM	LONG-TERM	TOTAL	SHORT-TERM	LONG-TERM
2000	272,2	0,6	241,4	25,8	215,6	30,1	2,4	27,8
2001	276,6	0,5	246,3	26,6	219,7	29,9	1,7	28,2
2002	277,7	0,5	247,2	24,5	222,6	30,0	1,6	28,4
2003	271,6	0,7	240,7	20,7	219,9	30,3	1,8	28,4
2004	273,9	0,8	242,8	24,8	218,0	30,3	1,9	28,4
2005	279,0	0,9	245,8	24,9	221,0	32,3	2,2	30,1
2006	280,4	1,0	247,0	27,0	220,0	32,4	2,5	29,9
2007	282,1	1,1	249,3	28,8	220,5	31,7	1,9	29,8
2008	309,2	1,2	275,0	50,0	225,0	33,0	3,9	29,2
2009	326,2	1,3	290,9	42,0	248,9	34,0	5,4	28,7
2010	340,3	1,4	302,8	43,0	259,7	36,1	6,1	30,0

PERCENTAGES OF CONSOLIDATED GROSS DEBT

	TOTAL	CURRENCY AND DEPOSITS	TOTAL	SHORT-TERM	LONG-TERM	TOTAL	SHORT-TERM	LONG-TERM
2000	100,0	0,2	88,7	9,5	79,2	11,1	0,9	10,2
2001	100,0	0,2	89,0	9,6	79,4	10,8	0,6	10,2
2002	100,0	0,2	89,0	8,8	80,2	10,8	0,6	10,2
2003	100,0	0,3	88,6	7,6	81,0	11,1	0,7	10,5
2004	100,0	0,3	88,6	9,1	79,6	11,1	0,7	10,4
2005	100,0	0,3	88,1	8,9	79,2	11,6	0,8	10,8
2006	100,0	0,4	88,1	9,6	78,4	11,6	0,9	10,7
2007	100,0	0,4	88,4	10,2	78,2	11,2	0,7	10,5
2008	100,0	0,4	88,9	16,2	72,8	10,7	1,2	9,4
2009	100,0	0,4	89,2	12,9	76,3	10,4	1,6	8,8
2010	100,0	0,4	89,0	12,6	76,3	10,6	1,8	8,8

Sources: NAI, NBB.

TABLE 17: Employment in the general government sector
Number of persons, data adjusted for breaks in the series[1]

	FEDERAL GOVERNMENT AND SOCIAL SECURITY			COMMUNITIES AND REGIONS					LOCAL AUTHORITIES				GENERAL GOVERNMENT SECTOR
	Total	Administration[2]	Defense	Total	Education	Administration	Transport[3]	Total	Administration	Education	Transport[3]		
1995	174,425	125,128	49,297	320,499	256,661	43,043	20,795	227,443	155,338	52,861	19,244		722,367
1996	169,684	122,128	47,556	314,297	248,813	44,161	21,323	234,942	157,684	57,346	19,912		718,923
1997	171,016	124,557	46,459	312,881	245,240	45,760	21,881	230,636	153,977	57,391	19,268		714,533
1998	174,504	127,858	46,646	315,437	246,459	46,041	22,937	232,100	155,075	58,023	19,002		722,041
1999	177,325	131,046	46,279	319,900	248,913	47,602	23,385	236,688	159,924	57,797	18,967		733,913
2000	178,598	132,114	46,484	318,370	247,769	47,243	23,358	241,310	164,034	57,710	19,566		738,278
2001	179,802	134,314	45,488	319,133	247,886	47,742	23,505	246,209	166,631	59,819	19,759		745,144
2002	181,462	136,841	44,621	323,347	250,051	48,352	24,944	250,187	171,519	60,608	18,060		754,996
2003	177,910	133,266	44,644	331,466	254,891	51,012	25,563	254,128	175,793	59,002	19,333		763,504
2004	178,415	134,239	44,176	336,933	259,640	54,675	22,618	261,323	179,805	61,666	19,852		776,671
2005	180,292	136,083	44,209	343,119	264,426	56,000	22,693	267,054	183,709	63,840	19,505		790,465
2006	178,974	136,084	42,890	345,522	266,623	55,351	23,548	272,983	188,041	65,034	19,908		797,479
2007	179,655	137,583	42,072	348,230	267,543	56,094	24,593	276,896	191,198	66,014	19,684		804,781
2008	178,763	137,717	41,046	355,094	272,860	56,970	25,264	281,888	194,383	67,588	19,917		815,745
2009	178,516	138,586	39,930	364,294	280,514	57,696	26,084	285,936	194,708	71,086	20,142		828,746
2010	177,410	138,076	39,334	368,211	283,966	57,970	26,275	290,403	197,664	72,276	20,463		836,024

Sources: NAI, NBB for the breakdown by sub-sector and by branch of activity.
1 In order to avoid breaks in the series due to statistical reclassification, the public broadcasting corporations and Aquafin were dropped from the data. They were also adjusted to neutralise the impact of the transfer, in 2002, of 8,500 former gendarmes from the federal government to the local authorities.
2 At federal level, jobs which come under education and publishing were reclassified in the administration branch.
3 Scheduled passenger transport (only for Regions) and other supporting transport activities.

Annex 2

TABLE 18: General government primary expenditure
Percentages of GDP

	1995	1999	2000	2001	2002	2003	2004	2005	2006	2007	2008	2009	2010
Euro area	47,6	44,0	42,3	43,4	44,0	44,7	44,3	44,3	43,7	43,0	44,1	48,4	48,1
Belgium	43,2	43,3	42,5	42,6	44,0	45,7	44,4	47,6	44,5	44,4	45,9	50,1	49,3
Germany	51,4	45,1	41,9	44,5	45,0	45,4	44,2	44,1	42,5	40,7	41,3	45,4	45,4
Estonia	40,7	39,9	35,9	34,7	35,6	34,6	33,8	33,4	33,4	33,8	39,3	45,0	40,5
Ireland	35,7	31,5	29,2	31,6	32,0	31,9	32,4	32,7	33,2	35,6	41,4	46,8	63,6
Greece	34,8	37,3	39,7	39,2	39,9	40,1	41,0	39,9	40,5	42,8	45,5	48,7	44,4
Spain	39,3	36,4	36,0	35,6	36,2	36,0	36,8	36,6	36,7	37,6	39,9	44,5	43,7
France	51,0	49,6	48,8	48,6	49,9	50,6	50,5	50,9	50,4	49,9	50,4	54,3	54,1
Italy	40,7	41,2	39,5	41,4	41,5	42,9	42,8	43,2	43,8	42,7	43,5	47,3	46,1
Cyprus	31,4	33,6	33,7	34,6	36,8	41,0	39,1	39,6	39,3	38,3	39,3	43,7	44,1
Luxembourg	39,3	38,9	37,3	37,8	41,3	41,6	42,4	41,4	38,4	36,0	36,8	42,6	42,0
Malta	37,6	39,3	36,7	39,1	39,1	43,4	41,6	41,0	40,9	39,5	40,9	40,4	40,2
Netherlands	50,8	41,7	40,5	42,2	43,4	44,5	43,6	42,4	43,3	43,1	44,0	49,4	49,3
Austria	52,2	49,9	48,3	47,8	47,3	48,2	50,8	47,0	46,3	45,7	46,7	50,1	50,0
Portugal	36,3	38,6	38,6	40,2	40,2	42,0	42,8	44,0	42,4	41,4	41,7	46,9	48,4
Slovenia	50,2	43,8	44,1	45,0	44,0	44,3	44,0	43,7	43,2	41,2	43,1	47,9	48,6
Slovakia	46,2	44,7	48,1	40,5	41,5	37,6	35,5	36,3	35,1	32,8	33,7	40,1	38,7
Finland	57,6	48,8	45,6	45,3	46,9	48,4	48,5	48,7	47,7	46,0	47,9	54,7	54,2
European Union	47,0	43,0	41,1	42,7	43,4	44,2	43,9	44,0	43,6	42,9	44,3	48,4	47,9
United Kingdom	40,3	36,0	34,0	37,8	39,1	40,1	41,0	42,0	42,1	41,6	45,6	49,6	47,4
United States	32,6	30,4	30,3	31,8	33,1	33,7	33,6	33,7	33,3	34,0	36,4	40,2	39,8
Japan	32,1	34,6	35,2	35,4	35,9	35,8	34,8	34,7	34,2	33,9	35,0	39,9	38,8

Source: EC.

TABLE 19: General government total expenditure
Percentages of GDP

	1995	1999	2000	2001	2002	2003	2004	2005	2006	2007	2008	2009	2010
Euro area	53,0	48,0	46,2	47,2	47,5	48,0	47,5	47,3	46,7	46,0	47,1	51,2	51,0
Belgium	52,1	50,1	49,1	49,1	49,8	51,0	49,2	51,9	48,5	48,3	49,8	53,8	52,8
Germany	54,9	48,2	45,1	47,6	47,9	48,5	47,1	46,9	45,3	43,5	44,0	48,1	47,9
Estonia	41,3	40,1	36,1	34,8	35,8	34,8	34,0	33,6	33,6	34,0	39,5	45,2	40,6
Ireland	40,9	33,9	31,2	33,0	33,4	33,1	33,5	33,8	34,3	36,6	42,8	48,8	66,8
Greece	46,2	44,8	47,1	45,7	45,5	45,1	45,9	44,6	45,2	47,6	50,6	53,8	50,2
Spain	44,5	39,9	39,2	38,7	38,9	38,4	38,9	38,4	38,4	39,2	41,5	46,3	45,6
France	54,4	52,6	51,7	51,7	52,9	53,4	53,3	53,6	53,0	52,6	53,3	56,8	56,6
Italy	52,2	47,9	45,9	47,7	47,1	48,1	47,5	47,9	48,5	47,6	48,6	51,9	50,5
Cyprus	33,4	36,7	37,1	38,0	40,0	44,6	42,4	43,1	42,6	41,3	42,1	46,2	46,4
Luxembourg	39,7	39,2	37,6	38,1	41,5	41,8	42,6	41,5	38,6	36,3	37,1	43,0	42,4
Malta	39,7	43,1	40,3	42,4	42,6	46,7	45,2	44,6	44,4	42,8	44,1	43,5	43,3
Netherlands	56,4	46,0	44,2	45,4	46,2	47,1	46,1	44,8	45,5	45,3	46,2	51,5	51,2
Austria	56,3	53,4	51,9	51,3	50,7	51,3	53,8	50,0	49,1	48,6	49,3	52,9	52,6
Portugal	41,9	41,5	41,6	43,2	43,1	44,7	45,4	46,6	45,2	44,4	44,8	49,8	51,3
Slovenia	52,3	46,2	46,5	47,3	46,2	46,2	45,7	45,3	44,6	42,5	44,2	49,3	50,3
Slovakia	48,6	48,1	52,1	44,5	45,1	40,1	37,7	38,0	36,5	34,2	34,9	41,5	40,0
Finland	61,5	51,8	48,4	48,0	49,0	50,3	50,2	50,4	49,2	47,4	49,3	56,1	55,5
European Union	52,2	46,8	44,8	46,1	46,6	47,2	46,8	46,8	46,3	45,6	47,1	51,1	50,6
United Kingdom	43,9	38,9	36,8	40,2	41,1	42,1	43,0	44,1	44,2	43,9	47,9	51,5	50,3
United States	37,2	34,2	33,9	35,0	35,9	36,3	36,1	36,3	36,0	36,8	39,1	42,7	42,5
Japan	35,5	38,0	38,5	38,0	38,2	37,8	36,6	36,5	36,0	35,8	37,0	41,9	40,8

Source: EC.

TABLE 20: General government revenue
Percentages of GDP

	1995	1999	2000	2001	2002	2003	2004	2005	2006	2007	2008	2009	2010
Euro area	45,5	46,5	46,1	45,2	44,8	44,8	44,5	44,8	45,3	45,3	45,0	44,8	44,7
Belgium	47,6	49,5	49,0	49,5	49,6	50,9	48,9	49,3	48,8	48,2	48,8	48,1	48,9
Germany	45,4	46,6	46,2	44,5	44,1	44,3	43,3	43,6	43,7	43,7	44,0	44,9	43,6
Estonia	42,4	36,7	35,9	34,7	36,0	36,5	35,6	35,2	36,1	36,4	36,5	43,2	40,9
Ireland	38,9	36,5	35,9	34,0	33,1	33,6	34,9	35,4	37,2	36,7	35,5	34,8	35,6
Greece	37,0	41,7	43,3	41,2	40,6	39,4	38,4	39,0	39,2	40,8	40,7	38,2	39,7
Spain	37,3	38,7	38,2	38,1	38,7	38,0	38,8	39,7	40,7	41,1	37,0	35,1	36,3
France	48,9	50,8	50,2	50,0	49,6	49,3	49,6	50,6	50,6	49,9	49,9	49,2	49,5
Italy	44,8	45,9	45,0	44,5	44,0	44,4	44,0	43,4	45,0	46,0	45,9	46,5	46,0
Cyprus	32,5	32,3	34,7	35,7	35,6	38,0	38,3	40,7	41,4	44,8	43,1	40,1	41,1
Luxembourg	42,1	42,6	43,6	44,2	43,6	42,2	41,5	41,5	39,9	39,9	40,1	42,2	41,6
Malta	35,5	35,3	34,4	36,0	36,7	37,5	40,5	41,7	41,6	40,5	39,5	39,7	39,5
Netherlands	47,2	46,4	46,1	45,1	44,1	43,9	44,3	44,5	46,1	45,4	46,7	46,0	46,2
Austria	50,4	51,0	50,1	51,1	49,8	49,7	49,2	48,2	47,5	47,6	48,3	48,7	48,1
Portugal	36,5	38,4	38,3	38,3	39,6	40,9	41,4	40,1	40,6	41,1	41,1	39,6	41,4
Slovenia	44,0	43,1	42,8	43,4	43,8	43,6	43,5	43,8	43,2	42,4	42,4	43,2	44,2
Slovakia	45,2	40,7	39,9	38,0	36,8	37,4	35,3	35,2	33,3	32,4	32,8	33,5	32,4
Finland	55,4	53,4	55,4	53,1	53,1	52,8	52,5	53,0	53,3	52,7	53,6	53,4	52,7
European Union	45,0	45,7	45,3	44,6	44,0	44,0	43,9	44,3	44,8	44,7	44,7	44,2	44,1
United Kingdom	38,0	39,8	40,4	40,7	39,0	38,7	39,5	40,7	41,5	41,1	42,9	40,1	40,2
United States	34,0	34,9	35,4	34,4	32,0	31,4	31,6	33,1	34,0	34,1	32,7	31,1	31,8
Japan	30,8	30,7	31,0	32,0	30,5	30,2	30,7	31,7	34,7	33,7	35,1	33,1	32,5

Source: EC.

TABLE 21: General government primary balance
Percentages of GDP

	1995	1999	2000	2001	2002	2003	2004	2005	2006	2007	2008	2009	2010
Euro area	-1,8	2,5	3,8	1,8	0,8	0,2	0,2	0,5	1,5	2,3	0,9	-3,5	-3,4
Belgium	4,3	6,2	6,5	6,8	5,6	5,1	4,5	1,7	4,3	3,8	2,8	-2,0	-0,4
Germany	-6,0	1,6	4,3	0,0	-0,9	-1,1	-0,9	-0,5	1,2	3,0	2,7	-0,5	-1,8
Estonia	1,6	-3,2	-0,0	0,1	0,5	1,9	1,9	1,8	2,6	2,6	-2,7	-1,8	0,4
Ireland	3,2	5,0	6,7	2,4	1,0	1,7	2,5	2,7	3,9	1,1	-6,0	-12,0	-28,0
Greece	2,2	4,3	3,7	2,0	0,8	-0,7	-2,6	-1,0	-1,3	-2,0	-4,8	-10,4	-4,7
Spain	-2,1	2,3	2,3	2,5	2,5	2,0	1,9	3,1	4,0	3,5	-2,9	-9,4	-7,4
France	-2,0	1,2	1,4	1,4	-0,3	-1,3	-0,8	-0,3	0,2	-0,0	-0,4	-5,1	-4,7
Italy	4,1	4,6	5,4	3,1	2,5	1,5	1,2	0,2	1,2	3,4	2,5	-0,8	-0,0
Cyprus	1,2	-1,3	1,1	1,1	-1,2	-3,0	-0,8	1,1	2,1	6,5	3,8	-3,6	-3,1
Luxembourg	2,8	3,7	6,3	6,4	2,4	0,7	-0,9	0,2	1,5	3,9	3,3	-0,4	-0,4
Malta	-2,2	-4,0	-2,3	-3,1	-2,3	-5,9	-1,1	0,7	0,8	1,0	-1,4	-0,6	-0,7
Netherlands	1,3	4,7	5,6	2,9	0,7	-0,6	0,7	2,1	2,7	2,4	2,7	-3,4	-3,1
Austria	-1,8	1,1	1,8	3,3	2,4	1,4	-1,6	1,2	1,2	1,9	1,7	-1,3	-1,8
Portugal	0,2	-0,2	-0,3	-1,8	-0,6	-1,0	-1,4	-4,0	-1,8	-0,2	-0,6	-7,3	-7,0
Slovenia	-6,2	-0,7	-1,3	-1,6	-0,3	-0,7	-0,6	0,1	0,0	1,2	-0,7	-4,7	-4,4
Slovakia	-1,0	-4,0	-8,2	-2,5	-4,7	-0,3	-0,2	-1,1	-1,7	-0,4	-0,8	-6,6	-6,3
Finland	-2,2	4,7	9,7	7,7	6,2	4,3	4,0	4,3	5,6	6,8	5,7	-1,3	-1,5
European Union	-1,8	2,8	4,2	2,0	0,6	-0,2	-0,0	0,3	1,2	1,8	0,4	-4,2	-3,8
United Kingdom	-2,3	3,8	6,3	2,8	-0,1	-1,4	-1,5	-1,3	-0,7	-0,5	-2,7	-9,5	-7,3
United States	1,4	4,5	5,1	2,7	-1,1	-2,3	-1,9	-0,6	0,7	0,1	-3,7	-9,0	-8,0
Japan	-1,2	-3,9	-4,2	-3,3	-5,4	-5,6	-4,1	-3,1	0,5	-0,2	0,1	-6,8	-6,4

Source: EC.

TABLE 22: General government overall balance
Percentages of GDP

	1995	1999	2000	2001	2002	2003	2004	2005	2006	2007	2008	2009	2010
Euro area	-7,2	-1,5	-0,1	-2,0	-2,7	-3,1	-2,9	-2,5	-1,4	-0,7	-2,1	-6,4	-6,2
Belgium	-4,5	-0,6	-0,0	0,4	-0,1	-0,1	-0,1	-2,5	0,4	-0,1	-1,0	-5,6	-3,8
Germany	-9,5	-1,6	1,1	-3,1	-3,8	-4,2	-3,8	-3,3	-1,6	0,2	-0,1	-3,2	-4,3
Estonia	1,1	-3,5	-0,2	-0,1	0,3	1,7	1,6	1,6	2,5	2,4	-2,9	-2,0	0,2
Ireland	-2,0	2,7	4,7	0,9	-0,4	0,4	1,4	1,7	2,9	0,1	-7,3	-14,0	-31,2
Greece	-9,1	-3,1	-3,7	-4,5	-4,8	-5,7	-7,6	-5,5	-5,7	-6,5	-9,8	-15,6	-10,3
Spain	-7,2	-1,2	-0,9	-0,5	-0,2	-0,3	-0,1	1,3	2,4	1,9	-4,5	-11,2	-9,3
France	-5,5	-1,8	-1,5	-1,6	-3,3	-4,1	-3,6	-2,9	-2,3	-2,7	-3,3	-7,5	-7,1
Italy	-7,4	-1,9	-0,8	-3,1	-3,1	-3,6	-3,5	-4,4	-3,4	-1,6	-2,7	-5,4	-4,6
Cyprus	-0,9	-4,3	-2,3	-2,2	-4,4	-6,6	-4,1	-2,4	-1,2	3,5	0,9	-6,1	-5,3
Luxembourg	2,4	3,4	6,0	6,1	2,1	0,5	-1,1	0,0	1,4	3,7	3,0	-0,8	-0,9
Malta	-4,2	-7,7	-5,8	-6,4	-5,8	-9,2	-4,7	-2,9	-2,8	-2,4	-4,6	-3,8	-3,7
Netherlands	-4,3	0,4	2,0	-0,2	-2,1	-3,1	-1,7	-0,3	0,5	0,2	0,5	-5,6	-5,1
Austria	-5,8	-2,3	-1,7	-0,0	-0,7	-1,5	-4,4	-1,7	-1,5	-0,9	-0,9	-4,1	-4,5
Portugal	-5,4	-3,1	-3,3	-4,8	-3,4	-3,7	-4,0	-6,5	-4,6	-3,1	-3,6	-10,2	-9,8
Slovenia	-8,3	-3,0	-3,7	-4,0	-2,4	-2,7	-2,3	-1,5	-1,4	-0,0	-1,9	-6,1	-6,0
Slovakia	-3,4	-7,4	-12,3	-6,5	-8,2	-2,8	-2,4	-2,8	-3,2	-1,8	-2,1	-8,0	-7,7
Finland	-6,1	1,7	6,9	5,1	4,1	2,6	2,5	2,8	4,1	5,3	4,3	-2,5	-2,5
European Union	-7,0	-1,0	0,6	-1,5	-2,6	-3,2	-2,9	-2,5	-1,5	-0,9	-2,4	-6,9	-6,5
United Kingdom	-5,9	0,9	3,6	0,5	-2,1	-3,4	-3,5	-3,4	-2,7	-2,7	-5,0	-11,5	-10,2
United States	-3,2	0,8	1,5	-0,5	-3,9	-4,9	-4,4	-3,2	-2,0	-2,8	-6,4	-11,5	-10,6
Japan	-4,7	-7,3	-7,5	-6,0	-7,7	-7,7	-5,9	-4,8	-1,3	-2,1	-1,9	-8,8	-8,4

Source: EC.

TABLE 23: General government consolidated gross debt
Percentages of GDP

	1995	1999	2000	2001	2002	2003	2004	2005	2006	2007	2008	2009	2010
Euro area	72,0	71,6	69,2	68,2	68,0	69,2	69,6	70,2	68,6	66,3	70,1	79,9	85,6
Belgium	130,2	113,6	107,8	106,5	103,4	98,4	94,0	92,0	88,0	84,1	89,3	95,8	96,0
Germany	55,6	61,3	60,2	59,1	60,7	64,4	66,3	68,6	68,1	65,2	66,7	74,4	83,0
Estonia	8,2	6,5	5,1	4,8	5,7	5,6	5,0	4,6	4,4	3,7	4,5	7,2	6,7
Ireland	81,2	48,0	37,5	35,2	31,9	30,7	29,4	27,2	24,7	24,8	44,2	65,1	92,5
Greece	97,9	94,9	104,4	104,7	102,6	98,3	99,8	101,2	107,3	107,4	113,0	129,4	145,0
Spain	63,3	62,4	59,4	55,6	52,6	48,8	46,3	43,1	39,6	36,2	40,2	53,9	61,2
France	55,4	58,9	57,4	56,9	59,0	63,2	65,0	66,7	64,0	64,2	68,2	79,2	82,3
Italy	120,9	113,0	108,5	108,2	105,1	103,9	103,4	105,4	106,1	103,1	105,7	116,0	118,6
Cyprus	51,8	59,3	59,6	61,2	65,1	69,7	70,9	69,4	64,7	58,8	48,9	58,5	61,5
Luxembourg	7,4	6,4	6,2	6,3	6,3	6,1	6,3	6,1	6,7	6,7	13,7	14,8	19,1
Malta	35,3	57,1	54,9	60,9	59,1	67,6	71,7	69,7	64,4	62,3	62,3	68,1	69,4
Netherlands	76,1	61,1	53,8	50,7	50,5	52,0	52,4	51,8	47,4	45,3	58,5	60,8	62,9
Austria	68,2	66,8	66,2	66,8	66,2	65,3	64,7	64,2	62,3	60,2	63,8	69,5	71,9
Portugal	59,2	49,4	48,4	51,1	53,7	55,7	57,5	62,5	63,7	68,3	71,6	83,1	93,3
Slovenia	18,6	24,1	26,3	26,5	27,8	27,2	27,3	26,7	26,4	23,1	21,9	35,3	38,8
Slovakia	22,1	47,8	50,3	48,9	43,4	42,4	41,5	34,2	30,5	29,6	27,9	35,6	41,1
Finland	56,6	45,7	43,8	42,5	41,5	44,5	44,4	41,7	39,6	35,2	33,9	43,5	48,4
European Union	NA	65,7	61,9	61,0	60,4	61,9	62,3	62,9	61,6	59,0	62,5	74,8	80,2
United Kingdom	51,2	43,7	41,0	37,7	37,5	39,0	40,9	42,5	43,4	44,4	54,8	69,6	79,6
United States	71,9	61,2	55,1	55,0	57,4	60,7	68,6	68,2	66,9	67,5	76,5	90,4	99,1
Japan	85,1	125,2	133,6	141,5	149,9	155,3	163,8	174,5	172,4	167,9	175,2	194,0	197,6

Source: EC.

Annex 3
LIST OF CONTRIBUTORS

KOEN ALGOED is Director of Cabinet of the Flemish Minister for Finance, Budget, Work, Town and Country Planning and Sports.

JEAN DEBOUTTE is Director at the Belgian Debt Agency.

ETIENNE DE CALLATAŸ is chief economist at Bank Degroof, senior fellow at the Itinera Institute, and guest lecturer at the University of Namur and at the Catholic University of Louvain (UCL).

ANDRÉ DECOSTER is Professor at the Catholic University of Leuven (KU Leuven) and Deputy Director of the Belgian Institute of Public Finance.

FRÉDÉRIQUE DENIL is Advisor at the Federal Public Service (FPS) Finance (Research Department) and member of the Secretariat of the High Council of Finance.

ROBERT DESCHAMPS is professor at CERPE, Faculty of Economics, University of Namur.

MARCEL GÉRARD is Professor at the Catholic University of Louvain (UCL).

NATACHA GILSON is Professor at the Catholic University of Louvain.

JEAN HINDRIKS is Professor in the Economics Department, Co-director of the Centre for Operations Research and Econometrics (CORE) at the Université catholique de Louvain, and Senior Fellow at the Itinera Institute.

GEERT LANGENUS is a member of the Research Department of the National Bank of Belgium.

MAUD NAUTET is a member of the Public Finance Division of the Research Department at the National Bank of Belgium.

GUY QUADEN is Honorary Governor of the National Bank of Belgium.

REGINALD SAVAGE is General Advisor at the Federal Public Service (FPS) Finance (Research Department) and Professor at the UCL. He is member of the Secretariat of the High Council of Finance.

VALÉRIE SCHMITZ is researcher at CERPE, Faculty of Economics, University of Namur.

BASTIEN SCORNEAU is researcher at CERPE, Faculty of Economics, University of Namur.

JAN SMETS is Board Member of the National Bank of Belgium.

FRANÇOISE THYS-CLÉMENT is Professor at the Université libre de Bruxelles and member of the Académie Royale de Belgique – Classe des Lettres et des Sciences morales et politiques.

CHRISTIAN VALENDUC is General Advisor at the Belgian Ministry of Finance, guest lecturer at the University of Namur and at the Catholic University of Louvain (UCL), and Director of the Belgian Institute of Public Finance.

FRANK VANDENBROUCKE is Professor at the Faculty of Economics and Business, Katholieke Universiteit Leuven. He was Minister for Social Affairs, Pensions and Employment from 2000 to 2004.

MARTIJN VAN DEN HURK is PhD candidate at Research group Public Administration & Management, University of Antwerp.

ALOÏS VAN DE VOORDE is Honorary General Secretary of the Belgian Ministry of Finance.

STEVEN VAN GARSSE is Professor at the University of Antwerp.

LUC VAN MEENSEL is Head of the Public Finance Division of the Research Department at the National Bank of Belgium.

STEFAN VAN PARYS is a member of the Public Finance Division at the Research Department at the National Bank of Belgium.

HERMAN VAN ROMPUY is President of the European Council.

KOEN VERHOEST is assoc. Research Professor at the Research Unit of Public Administration and Management, Department of Political Sciences (University of Antwerp), affiliated to the Public Management Institute (University of Leuven).